JENSEN'S SURVEY
OF THE
OLD TESTAMENT

Moody Press, a ministry of the Moody Bible Institute, is designed for education, evangelization and edification. If we may assist you in knowing more about Christ and the Christian life, please write us without obligation to: Moody Press, c/o MLM, Chicago, Illinois 60610.

JENSEN'S SURVEY OF THE OLD TESTAMENT

Search and Discover

by

IRVING L. JENSEN

MOODY PRESS
CHICAGO

ACKNOWLEDGMENTS

Grateful acknowledgment is made to The Lockman Foundation for permission to quote from *The New American Standard Bible,* © 1960, 1962, 1963, 1968, 1971, 1972, 1973 and 1975.

Most of the charts and maps in this volume were drawn by artist Henry Franz.

© 1978, by
THE MOODY BIBLE INSTITUTE
OF CHICAGO

Library of Congress Cataloging in Publication Data

Jensen, Irving Lester.
  Jensen's Survey of the Old Testament.

  Bibliography: p. 475.
  Includes index.
  1. Bible. O. T.—Study—Text-books. I. Title.
II. Title: Survey of the Old Testament.
BS1194.J46   221   77-16582
ISBN 0-8024-4307-9

8 9 10 11 12 Printing/BB/Year 87 86 85 84 83

Printed in the United States of America

Contents

Part 3

Reflections and Worship
During the Monarchial Years

Part 4

Ministries of the Prophets

Publisher's Note

Enlarged charts related to the lessons of this study guide are available in *Jensen Bible Study Charts* (Vol. I, General Survey; Vol. II, Old Testament; Vol. III, New Testament). The charts are especially valuable for Bible study groups.

The 8½×11″ charts can be reproduced as Xerox copies or as transparencies for overhead projectors. Selected transparencies are included in each volume.

Charts

*Available in larger format in *Jensen's Bible Study Charts* (Chicago: Moody, 1981).

Maps

*Available in larger format in *Jensen's Bible Study Charts* (Chicago: Moody, 1981).

Foreword

This survey provides practical guidance for reading the Old Testament. The overall perspective and the relationship to the New Testament delineated here stimulates the reader's interest in the biblical text itself.

To many people the Old Testament consists of thirty-nine fragmented literary units. Irving Jensen, in this volume, repeatedly provides the overview that is unfolded in the Old Testament as a whole, from the creation of man to the coming of Jesus Christ. Helpful insight is offered in presenting this development in its geographical and historical context. For the student who wants a deeper involvement, the author provides an extended bibliography for further study.

Helpful suggestions in various methods of Bible study offered in this volume will undoubtedly lead the reader into a comprehensive use of the Old Testament. Consequently, those who read the Old Testament individually or study it in Bible classes will find intellectual and devotional enrichment in this survey.

May the author's purpose to involve the reader in a firsthand survey of the Bible text itself be realized by everyone who reads the following pages.

SAMUEL J. SCHULTZ

Preface

The main purpose of this Old Testament survey guide is to involve the reader in a firsthand survey of the Bible text itself. All too often students of Bible survey read what others say is contained in a certain book of the Bible and fail to spend time reading the Bible text for themselves. This book has been written to start the reader on paths of study in each Old Testament book, to *search and discover* for himself the great themes of those books. Throughout the chapters, much help is supplied (e.g., outlines) on what the Bible books teach, but these suggestions are intended to confirm and amplify the reader's personal study and to maintain a momentum of study in the more difficult Old Testament portions. The reader is always encouraged to do his own independent study before dwelling long on help from others.

Another aim of this book is to guide the reader in seeing *how* the message of each Old Testament book is organized structurally, because, for a full understanding of the Bible text, one needs to know not only *what* God said, but *how* He said it. This partly accounts for the appearance of many charts throughout the book, since charts show structural organization clearly and vividly.

Students of Bible survey often overlook the application stage of their study, because in survey they do not analyze the Bible text in detail. But survey study should not rule out practical application. One of this book's purposes is to lead the reader into a time of personal reflection as he considers practical spiritual applications of the Bible book that he has just surveyed. Here the slogan is: *reflect and apply*. This is how all Bible study should conclude.

This survey guide also includes other important helps for study, as seen in the following descriptions of the parts of each chapter.

I. Preparation for Study

The opening pages of each chapter prepare the reader for his survey of the Bible book assigned to that chapter. This is a crucial

9

part of one's study, because here is where motivation and momentum are gained.

II. Background

Every book of the Bible was originally written in a particular local setting. This section of the chapter discusses that background, much information of which is not always supplied by the text of the Bible book itself. Some important items are intentionally repeated from time to time to help impress them on the reader's mind.

III. Survey

The actual survey process is the main part of each chapter and should occupy most of the reader's time. The basic Bible version used throughout the studies is the *New American Standard Bible*. Chapter 2 is devoted entirely to a discussion of the survey method of study. Here the reader will learn what procedures are recommended in the stage of surveying a book of the Old Testament.

IV. Prominent Subjects

Immediately following the survey section is a discussion of prominent subjects of the Bible book. Technical subjects or problems of the Bible text are not included, since these are not part of survey study. The comments which are shared are intended to round out the student's survey and to give suggestions for further study at a later time.

V. Key Words and Verses

Certain words and verses can usually be identified with the particular theme of each Bible book. Suggestions are made here, but the reader is urged to look for more.

VI. Applications

The questions asked here will help the reader apply the teachings of the Old Testament book to his own life and times.

VII. Further Study

Suggestions for further study are intended for those who want to pursue various themes of the book in greater detail. This study is not a part of the survey process.

VIII. Selected Reading

Three types of books are cited here: general introduction, commentary, and special subjects. For the most part, the lists are of books in print, written from a conservative, evangelical viewpoint. (Exceptions are not identified as such.)

IX. SURVEY CHART

At the end of each chapter is a complete survey chart for the Old Testament book. Many of the charts in this book appear in *Jensen Bible Study Charts,* Volume 2 (Moody Press). They are 8½ x 11" and may be made into overhead transparencies for group Bible study.

I hope that this survey guide will introduce the reader to many fascinating and inspiring journeys through this wonderful book of God, the Old Testament. Priceless are the promises to him who delights in the Scriptures. In the words of the psalmist, such a believer "will be like a tree firmly planted by streams of water, which yields its fruit in its season, and its leaf does not wither; and in whatever he does, he prospers" (Psalm 1:3).

Introduction to the Old Testament

The Survey Method of Study

1

Introduction to the Old Testament

Many pleasant surprises are in store for the one who embarks on a study of the Old Testament. Not the least of these is the discovery of its contemporary application to everyday life. The purpose of this introductory chapter is to offer some motivation and direction for the reader's survey study of this part of God's wonderful Book. Regular studies in the Bible text begin with the next chapter.

I. WHY STUDY THE OLD TESTAMENT?

There are many compelling reasons why every Christian should study the Old Testament. Consider the following:

A. THE BIBLE IS INCOMPLETE WITHOUT THE OLD TESTAMENT

Both Old and New Testaments make up the inspired Scriptures The New Testament was never intended to replace the Old Testament. Instead, the New was given to complement the Old, to complete its story. For example, the Old prophesies the coming of the Redeemer; the New reports the fulfillment of that prophecy in Jesus. The New Testament is the sequel to the Old Testament's origins, heir of its promises. fruit of its seed, the peak of its mountain. The diagram on page 16 illustrates various relationships of the two Testaments.

What associations between the Old and New Testaments do you see suggested by the illustration?

B. THE MINISTRY OF CHRIST WOULD BE AN ENIGMA WITHOUT THE OLD TESTAMENT

For example, why did Jesus say, "I was sent only to the lost sheep of the house of Israel" (Matt 15:24)? In what sense was Jesus the

15

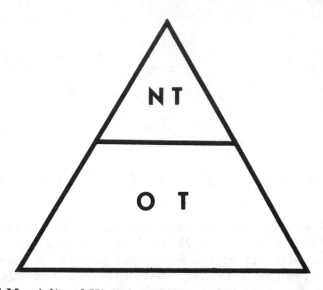

promised Messiah and King, long awaited by the Jews?[1] And why did He have to die? Are His cross and crown irreconcilable? Read Isaiah 53:10-12 for an example of how the Old Testament answers such questions.

C. THE HISTORICAL SETTING OF CHRISTIANITY IS FURNISHED BY THE OLD TESTAMENT

Christianity did not emerge mysteriously out of a vacuum. God had been moving among the peoples of the world, especially Israel, for many centuries before Christ. Then, "when the fulness of the time came, God sent forth His Son, born of a woman, born under the Law, in order that He might redeem those who were under the Law, that we might receive the adoption as sons" (Gal 4:4-5). Erich Sauer connects the Old Testament with the New in these words:

> The Old Testament is promise and expectation, the New is fulfilment and completion. The Old is the marshalling of the hosts to the battle of God, the new is the Triumph of the Crucified One. The Old is the twilight and dawn of morning, the New is the rising sun and the height of eternal day.[2]

Even though the last book of the Old Testament was written about four hundred years before Christ's birth, our knowing the Old

---

1. See John F. Walvoord, *Jesus Christ Our Lord,* pp. 79-95, for an excellent discussion of the subject, "Christ in Old Testament Prophecy."
2. Erich Sauer, *The Dawn of World Redemption,* p. 186.

Testament is to know the religious, social, geographical, and, in part, the political setting of the New. Besides, the Old Testament was the Bible of Jesus, the apostles, and New Testament writers. When they spoke or wrote, they often quoted or referred to the Old Testament's history and teaching. This in itself is reason enough for every Christian to be acquainted with the Old Testament.

D. KEY REVELATIONS OF GOD ARE TO BE FOUND IN THE OLD TESTAMENT

The Old Testament is mainly history, but it is *sacred* history. That is, it reveals especially how God moves in and through the lives of people and the courses of nations. We might also say that the Old Testament is *redemptive* history, for "God actively directs human history for the purpose of redeeming men to Himself."[3] The Holy Spirit inspired the writers of the Old Testament to record what would adequately reveal that redemptive purpose. Thus, the writers have much to say about such crucial facts as these:

1. God is the sovereign Creator.
2. Man is a sinner in need of salvation.
3. God is holy, and He judges sin.
4. God is love, and He offers salvation to sinful man.
5. A Saviour would be born to die for the sins of man.
6. Man is saved by faith, not by works.
7. Israel was sovereignly chosen to be God's channel of the redemptive message to the world.
8. All history will culminate at the throne of the sovereign Lord.

The Old Testament is especially valuable for its inspired record about origins. Consider, for example, the historical record of the first man and woman; the first sin committed by a human; the first communications of God with man; and the first revelation of the way of restored fellowship to God.

Miracles are also a key part of the Old Testament, preparing the reader for the climactic event of the Great Miracle, the resurrection of Jesus Christ. John Raven rightly concludes that "Christ and the Old Testament are so united by mutual testimony that a low view of the credibility of the latter must result in a low view of the credibility of the former."[4] The factuality of miracles rests solidly on the person of the miracle-worker. This is one of many reasons why so much is revealed in the Old Testament about *who* God is.

---

3. J. Barton Payne, *The Theology of the Older Testament,* p. 3.
4. John H. Raven, *Old Testament Introduction,* p. 6.

E. THE OLD TESTAMENT IS SPIRITUAL FOOD FOR THE CHRISTIAN

Paul was referring directly to the Old Testament when he wrote, "All Scripture is inspired by God and profitable for teaching, for reproof, for correction, for training in righteousness; that the man of God may be adequate, equipped for every good work" (2 Tim 3:16-17). The different parts of the Old Testament reach the reader in various ways:

1. Its indictments bring conviction of sin (Jer 2).
2. Its laws and counsel show the way to please God (Exod 20).
3. Its psalms encourage praise and prayer (Psalm 107).
4. Its testimonies inspire the reader to walk in paths of righteousness (Deut 31:24—32:47).
5. Its historical facts give perspective and direct the reader to learn from the God of all history (Psalm 78).
6. Its prophecies warn of danger and plant hope in the hearts of all believers (Zech 14).
7. Its story of Israel's kingdom gives background for our understanding of the millennial reign of Christ and His kingship (2 Sam 7:4-17; Zech 14:9).

Read the passages cited above to see the relevancy of the Old Testament to the twentieth century.

II. THE OLD TESTAMENT FROM GOD TO US

The plan of writing Scriptures originated with God (2 Tim 3:16-17; 2 Pet 1:21). So, from its very source, the Bible is a supernatural book. It is the revelation of God, written by divinely inspired human authors. Through the subsequent stages of transmission, canonization, and translation, God has preserved His Word so that today, as we hold a copy of the Bible in our hands, we may be fully confident of its trustworthiness. Let us look briefly at the overall history of the Old Testament. The starting point of such a history is divine revelation.

A. REVELATION

Revelation is God's communication of truth to man, without which man cannot know God. Before the first Old Testament book was written,[5] God revealed Himself to man through such media as conscience and nature (*general* revelation) and direct conversation with people (*special* revelation). (Read Rom 1:18-21 for an application of general revelation, and Gen 3:8-19 for an example of special

---

5. It is not known which was the first Old Testament book to be written. If Moses was the earliest Bible author, then there was no Scripture before around 1500 B.C.

revelation.) But God also wanted to reveal Himself in the form of permanent writing, so that there would be a clear and fixed record of this revelation for all the succeeding generations. So He commissioned chosen men to write on various subjects. In the words of Gleason Archer,

> If there be a God, and if He is concerned for our salvation, this is the only way (apart from direct revelation from God to each individual of each successive generation) He could reliably impart this knowledge to us. It must be through a reliable written record such as the Bible purports to be.[6]

B. INSPIRATION

Two crucial questions at this point are: How did the human authors know what God wanted them to write? and Were their writings without error? We cannot explain the supernatural process of inspiration, which brought about the original writings of the Bible. Paul refers to the process as *God-breathing*. (Read 2 Tim 3:16, where the phrase "inspired by God" translates the Greek *theopneustia*, which literally means "God-breathed.") Peter says the Bible authors were undergirded, or carried along, by the Holy Spirit. ("Men spoke from God as they were carried along by the Holy Spirit," 2 Pet 1:21, Berkeley.) These verses, along with many others, assure us that when the Bible authors wrote, their words expressed perfectly and infallibly the truths which God wanted to convey to mankind. In the original autographs, all the words were infallible as to truth, and final as to authority. Such accuracy applies to every part of the originals—to matters of history and science as well as to spiritual truths. If the Bible student does not believe this, his study of the biblical text will be haunted by confusing and destructive doubts.

C. THE ORIGINAL AUTOGRAPHS

The thirty-nine books of the Old Testament were written over a period of about a thousand years (c. 1500-400 B.C.), by about twenty-five to thirty different authors. All but a few portions were written in Hebrew.[7] The writing material of most of the autographs was paperlike papyrus. (Some autographs may have been written on animal skins.) Sheets of papyrus about ten inches high were attached together to make a long, rolled-up scroll, easy for reading. (The page-

---

6. Gleason L. Archer, *A Survey of Old Testament Introduction,* p. 15. Read this same source for a good discussion of the inadequacies of oral tradition as a sole transmitter of God's special revelation to man.

7. These were the exceptions, written in Aramaic: Genesis 31:47; Jeremiah 10:11; Daniel 2:4*b*—7:28; Ezra 4:8—6:18; 7:12-26.

type codex, or book, did not supplant the roll until the second or third century A.D.) The Bible text was written with pen and ink in vertical columns, with no space between words, sentences, or paragraphs. Only the consonants of the words were recorded.[8] Read Jeremiah 36 for an example of how a portion of Scripture originated. How did Jeremiah receive the message from God? How did the scribe receive it from Jeremiah?

Practically nothing is known about the history of each individual autograph of the Old Testament. During the years of Solomon's Temple, it is likely that some autographs were among the Scriptures deposited there (cf 2 Kings 22). Probably all of the original papyrus scrolls perished within a century or two after they were written, due to such causes as fire and rotting.

D. TRANSMISSION

Transmission is the process by which the biblical manuscripts have been copied and recopied down through the ages. God allowed each of the original Old Testament autographs to disappear from the scene, but not before copies were already in the hands of His people.[9] Handwritten scribal copyings of the Hebrew text were made up to the time of the printing press (fifteenth century A.D.).

No ancient writing has been so carefully preserved in the process of scribal copying as have the Old Testament Scriptures. This was due in part to the Jews' almost superstitious veneration of their written Scriptures. During the fifth to sixth centuries of our era, a group of Jewish scholars, now referred to as Masoretes, produced a standard edition of the Old Testament by comparing the existing manuscripts available to them. Minor scribal errors had crept into the manuscripts along the way,[10] and the Masoretes wanted to put into circulation one standard text which would be as close to the originals as possible. When they completed their work to their own satisfaction, this text (later known as the Masoretic text) was the basis of all future scribal copyings, and the existing, not so accurate manuscripts were withdrawn from circulation. Various checkpoints were recorded in the margins of the new manuscripts, to insure that no letter or word would be deleted or added in future manuscripts. The Hebrew Old Testament was so meticulously preserved through the remaining centuries that when the Dead Sea Scrolls (c. 150 B.C.) were discovered

8. Vowels were added to copies of the Old Testament around A.D. 600-800, to help preserve the pronunciation of the Hebrew words.
9. One of God's reasons for not preserving the original autographs may have been man's proneness to worship material objects. Also, even if a genuine biblical autograph existed today, many people would still doubt any proofs offered of its genuineness.
10. Even Bibles printed in the modern twentieth century have printers' errors!

in 1948 and subsequently compared with extant (existing) Hebrew manuscripts of A.D. 900-1000, they were almost identical. Thus was confirmed the dependability of our English Old Testament, which had been based mainly on the Masoretic manuscripts of that tenth century.[11] Also, this preservation of the text accounts for the fact that there are relatively few differences between modern versions of the Old Testament, if they are exact translations (not paraphrases).

So although some scribal errors were committed from time to time in the copying process, God has preserved the Old Testament text so that no doctrinal truth is jeopardized by such errors. Archer writes:

> Do we have any objective evidence that errors of transmission have not been permitted by God to corrupt and pervert His revelation? Yes, we have, for a careful study of the variants . . . of the various earliest manuscripts reveals that none of them affects a single doctrine of Scripture.[12]

As divine Author, God wrote an infallible Book (inspiration); as divine Protector, He has preserved the text down through the ages from doctrinal error (transmission).

E. CANONIZATION

Canonization is the identification of a writing as being one of the divinely inspired Scriptures. It was not enough that God inspired the *writing* of each book of the Bible. He also gave to His people, in a collective sense, the spiritual perception to *recognize* in each of those books the genuine marks of divine inspiration and authority. With the Holy Spirit's guidance, they knew what spurious writings to reject, as well as what genuine writings to accept. Thus, over the centuries as the Old Testament books were being written, the Old Testament canon (list or group of inspired books) kept growing until it reached its completed form. It was God who foreknew and determined what books would comprise the complete Old Testament. The details of the long human process are veiled in obscurity. But it is clear that God's supernatural hand, working through humans, brought His inspired writings into the canon, while He excluded other writings.

By the time of Christ and the apostles, the Old Testament was a complete set of books that were usually referred to as Scripture(s).

---

11. Among the major extant Hebrew manuscripts of this period are: Cairo Codex (A.D. 895); Leningrad Codex of the Prophets (916); Aleppo Codex (930); Leningrad Old Testament (entire Old Testament) (1008).
12. Archer, pp. 18-19.

(Refer to an exhaustive concordance to see the many New Testament references to this name.)

The total number of books in the *Hebrew* Old Testament is twenty-four. Actually, those twenty-four books are the equivalent of the *English* Bible's thirty-nine, due to various combinations. For example, the Jews regard the twelve books of the minor prophets as one book, which they call "The Twelve." Also, Samuel, Kings, and Chronicles are each one book, and Ezra is combined with Nehemiah.

By the time of Christ, the Jews had grouped the Old Testament books into three major sections: Law, Prophets, and Writings. This threefold division is probably what Jesus had in mind when He said that "all things which are written about Me in the Law of Moses and the Prophets and the Psalms must be fulfilled" (Luke 24:44).[13] Study the groupings shown on Chart 1.[14]

CHART 1

THE HEBREW OLD TESTAMENT ARRANGEMENT		
LAW (Torah)	PROPHETS (Nebhiim)	WRITINGS (Kethubhim)
1. Genesis[15]	A. *Former Prophets*	A. *Poetical Books*
2. Exodus	6. Joshua	14. Psalms
3. Leviticus	7. Judges	15. Proverbs
4. Numbers	8. Samuel	16. Job
5. Deuteronomy	9. Kings	
		B. *Five Rolls (Megilloth)*
	B. *Latter Prophets*	17. Song of Songs
	10. Isaiah	18. Ruth
	11. Jeremiah	19. Lamentations
	12. Ezekiel	20. Ecclesiastes
	13. The Twelve	21. Esther
		C. *Historical Books*
		22. Daniel
		23. Ezra-Nehemiah
		24. Chronicles

Note the following concerning the books listed on Chart 1:

---

13. Psalms was the first and longest book of the Writings, and so the name may have been used to represent the entire section.

14. At times Hebrew Bibles have appeared with minor variations from this arrangement.

15. These book titles originated with the Greek Septuagint translation of the Old Testament. In the Hebrew Bible, however, the books were named by the first few significant words appearing in the text. For example, Genesis is called *Bereshith* ("In the Beginning"); Exodus is *Shemoth* ("Names"); Numbers is *Bedmidhbar* ("In the Desert").

1. The books of "Former Prophets" are historical in content, and yet are classified under "Prophets." The reason for this may be that their authors had the official status of a prophet, or, as F. F. Bruce holds, they reported events "to illustrate the great principles on which the prophets insisted."[16]

2. Each of the five "rolls" was read at an annual Jewish feast or commemoration, in this chronological order: Song of Songs at Passover (first month); Ruth at Feast of Weeks (Harvest) (third month); Lamentations at the anniversary of the destruction of Jerusalem (fifth month); Ecclesiastes at Tabernacles (seventh month); and Esther at Purim (twelfth month).[17]

3. Chronicles appears last in the Hebrew Bible. This is why Jesus used the expression "from the blood of Abel to the blood of Zechariah" (Luke 11:51) to sum up all the martyrs whose blood had been shed in Old Testament times. Abel was the first and Zechariah was the last martyr appearing in this order of the Hebrew Bible. Read

CHART 2

THE PROTESTANT OLD TESTAMENT ARRANGEMENT[18]		
LAW (Pentateuch) 1. Genesis 2. Exodus 3. Leviticus 4. Numbers 5. Deuteronomy	**POETRY** 18. Job 19. Psalms 20. Proverbs 21. Ecclesiastes 22. Song of Solomon	
HISTORY 6. Joshua 7. Judges 8. Ruth 9. 1 Samuel 10. 2 Samuel 11. 1 Kings 12. 2 Kings 13. 1 Chronicles 14. 2 Chronicles 15. Ezra 16. Nehemiah 17. Esther	**PROPHECY** A. *Major* 23. Isaiah 24. Jeremiah 25. Lamentations 26. Ezekiel 27. Daniel	B. *Minor* 28. Hosea 29. Joel 30. Amos 31. Obadiah 32. Jonah 33. Micah 34. Nahum 35. Habakkuk 36. Zephaniah 37. Haggai 38. Zechariah 39. Malachi

16. F. F. Bruce, *The Books and the Parchments,* p. 92.
17. Consult a Bible dictionary for descriptions of these feasts.
18. The Catholic Old Testament includes all of these books plus seven apocryphal (noncanonical) writings, as well as apocryphal additions to some of the inspired books.

the account of Zechariah's martyrdom in the last book of the Hebrew Bible: 2 Chronicles 24:20-21.

The books of our Protestant English Old Testament are grouped in a fourfold arrangement, different from the Hebrew threefold format. This fourfold arrangement is traceable back to the Latin Vulgate version (c. A.D. 383-405), which derived its format from the Greek Septuagint (c. 280-150 B.C.). Chart 2 shows this familiar breakdown of the list of thirty-nine books.

The following facts apply to the books listed on Chart 2:

1. The first seventeen books chronologically record selected highlights of man's history from creation to the marriage of Abraham (Gen 1-11), and from the birth of the nation of Israel to its return to Canaan after the Babylonian Captivity (Gen 12—Nehemiah).[19] The section called History may be subdivided into these three groups:

a) Period of confederacy among the tribes: Joshua, Judges, Ruth
b) Rise and fall of the monarchy: 1 Samuel through 2 Chronicles
c) Captivity and return: Ezra, Nehemiah, Esther

2. The books of Law are so designated because of the prominence of God's Law in the experience of Israel during those centuries. (The name *Pentateuch* comes from the Greek, meaning "fivefold vessel." The name *Torah* is the Hebrew word for "Law.")

3. The five books of Poetry are mainly reflections, hymns, dialogues, and maxims, directed to the reader's inner life. They are classified as poetry because this is the prominent literary style of the books.

4. The distinction between major and minor books of prophecy is based only on length. Although Lamentations is not long, it is in the major group because it could be considered as an appendix to Jeremiah.

5. All of the prophets ministered in the period of about 900 to 400 B.C. Most of their messages were directed to either Israel (Northern Kingdom) or Judah (Southern Kingdom), or to both. More is said about this later in the chapter. Chronologically, Malachi is the last Old Testament voice to speak.

F. TRANSLATIONS

If the Old Testament had never been translated, it could only be read and understood by students of Hebrew. But God intended the

---

19. The chronological pattern is not always followed in this order. For example, the account of Esther is between Ezra and Nehemiah, and the books of Chronicles parallel much of the books of Kings.

Scriptures to be everyman's Book; hence, the many translations (versions) made over the centuries.

The first translation of any portion of the Old Testament was the Greek Septuagint (LXX).[20] It was made for the benefit of Greek-speaking Jews of Alexandria, who could not read Hebrew. The Pentateuch was translated around 280 B.C. Before the coming of Christ, the entire Testament was translated, and it became the Scriptures of many people throughout the Mediterranean world. Such timing was according to divine schedule. Greek was the universal language at that time, and because the New Testament was soon to be written in Greek, God was using this Greek Old Testament version to prepare the way for the New Testament. It must have been a very dependable translation, for out of thirty-seven Old Testament quotations credited to Jesus in the gospels, thirty-three are from this Septuagint version.

During the early centuries of the Christian Church, many translations of the Bible appeared as the natural outcome of Christianity's expansion to foreign lands. The Latin Vulgate (A.D. 383-405), the most prominent, was the official Bible of Christendom on the Continent for a thousand years.

The Reformation brought a revival of translation activity, spurred on by renewed interest in Hebrew and Greek Bible manuscripts, and by the recent invention of the printing press. These were the years when the famous early English versions were appearing, such as Wycliffe, Tyndale, Coverdale, Great Bible, Bishops, King James.

Then came the modern missions era of translation activity, beginning around 1800. It is aptly called *modern* because the era has not yet ended. In fact, one of the brightest aspects of the Christian witness today is the unprecedented production of new Bible translations. Portions of Scripture are reaching people of many languages and cultures in the remotest parts of the world. And in America, new English versions and paraphrases, written in contemporary style, are geared to such needy mission fields as homes without a church, and campuses with drifting youth. For the serious Bible student today who wants to analyze a Bible text which is virtually the same as the originals minus the translation factor, various excellent versions are available, such as the *American Standard Version* (ASV of 1901), the

---

20. The Roman numeral LXX (seventy) and the Latin word *septuaginta* (seventy) were assigned to this version because of a story which said that seventy-two translators were engaged in the original work. Actually, the name *Septuagint* was not assigned to the whole Greek Old Testament until the time of the Church scholar Origen (early third century A.D.).

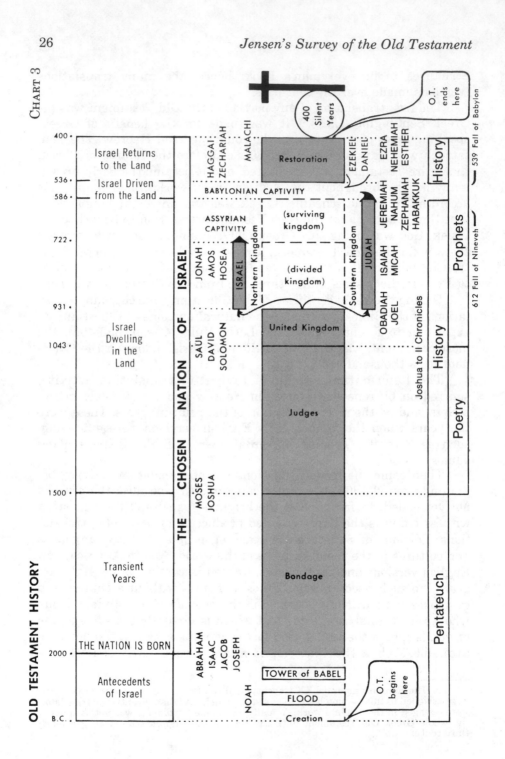

CHART 3

OLD TESTAMENT HISTORY

400	Israel Returns to the Land	
536	Israel Driven from the Land	
586		BABYLONIAN CAPTIVITY
722		ASSYRIAN CAPTIVITY
931	Israel Dwelling in the Land	
1043		
1500		
2000	Transient Years	
	THE NATION IS BORN	
	Antecedents of Israel	
B.C.		Creation

THE CHOSEN NATION OF ISRAEL

HAGGAI ZECHARIAH
MALACHI

JONAH AMOS HOSEA

SAUL DAVID SOLOMON

MOSES JOSHUA

ABRAHAM ISAAC JACOB JOSEPH

NOAH

400 Silent Years

O.T. ends here

Restoration

EZEKIEL DANIEL
EZRA NEHEMIAH ESTHER

(surviving kingdom)

Northern Kingdom ISRAEL
Southern Kingdom JUDAH

(divided kingdom)

JEREMIAH NAHUM ZEPHANIAH HABAKKUK

ISAIAH MICAH

OBADIAH JOEL

United Kingdom

Judges

Bondage

TOWER of BABEL

FLOOD

O.T. begins here

Joshua to II Chronicles

History
Prophets
History
Poetry
Pentateuch

539 Fall of Babylon
612 Fall of Nineveh

New American Standard Bible (NASB of 1971), and the *New International Version* (NIV of 1978).

Thus, the Bible, with its Old Testament, has come a long way—*from God to us.* And the most thrilling part of it is that, not counting the translation difference, "we hold in our hands to-day a Bible which differs in no substantial particular from the originals of the various books as they came from the hands of their authors."[21]

III. The Setting of the Old Testament

A. HISTORICAL SETTING

All the books of the Old Testament are intimately involved in a historical strand that begins with the creation in Genesis 1 and ends with the last prophecy of Malachi (c. 430 B.C.). The first eleven chapters of Genesis report highlights of the beginnings of man and the world. At Genesis 12, the nation of Israel is divinely born at the call of Abraham; and for the remainder of the Old Testament, the nation or individual Israelites are in view.

Chart 3 shows how the different books of the Old Testament are related to this historical strand. Study the chart carefully. You will want to refer to it often as you proceed in your survey study from book to book.

Use Chart 3 to answer the following questions:

1. About when was Israel founded? What four patriarchs are identified with its earliest years?

2. The word *bondage* identifies the first crucial experience of Israel, which took place in Egypt. What words describe the next two periods? 1500-1043 B.C.; 1043-931 B.C.

3. What two men did God use to lead Israel from bondage in Egypt to their homeland of Canaan?

4. The Jews were ruled by judges during the first few centuries in Canaan. Then the Jews demanded to have kings to be like their idolatrous neighbors, wholly independent of God. God let them have their own way, but He warned them of future troubles because of such inroads of idolatry. Read 1 Samuel 8. Who were the first three kings of the united kingdom?

5. What are the names of the two kingdoms that resulted from the split of the united kingdom in 931 B.C.?[22]

---

21. G. T. Manley, *The New Bible Handbook*, p. 19.
22. In the Old Testament, the name Israel usually refers to all of God's chosen people. During the years of the divided kingdom, however, it more often refers only to the Northern Kingdom. The context will usually indicate which meaning is intended.

6. At what dates did each of the two kingdoms go into captivity?

7. When did the captive Jews begin returning to their homeland of Canaan?

8. Without looking at the chart, see how much you can recall of the highlights of Israel's history in Old Testament times. As memory aid, visualize the four shaded blocks of the following chart.

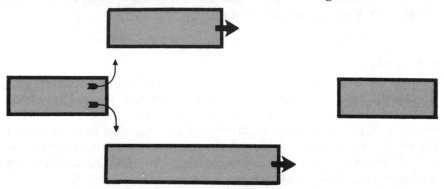

It is not an overstatement to say that the above diagram of four blocks represents the heart of Old Testament history. This is why it is so important to thoroughly learn the outlines shown on Chart 3.

9. Now you are ready to see how the books of the Old Testament contribute to this setting. Review the list of books that was discussed earlier, in this fourfold arrangement: Law (or Pentateuch), history, poetry, prophecy. Note at the bottom of Chart 3 where these four groups appear. What is the time span of the five books of the Pentateuch? Read Genesis 50:26 and Deuteronomy 34:5. What deaths are recorded here? Locate the two names on the chart.

10. The history books from Joshua to 2 Chronicles cover what periods of Israel's history? The last three history books (Ezra, Nehemiah, Esther) are of what time?

11. Over what span of years were the books of poetry written? Note that David and Solomon, who wrote most of the biblical poems, lived during the middle of this period.

12. The names of the prophets appear on the chart approximately when and where they ministered. Who were prophets mainly to the Northern Kingdom? Who prophesied to Judah? Who was the first writing prophet? Who were the two prophets of the captivity period? What three prophets ministered during the closing years of the Old Testament?

13. Account for the designation "400 Silent Years" on the chart. Did God forget about Israel after He inspired Malachi to write the last book? Read the last chapter of the Old Testament for the answer.

Whenever you are studying in an Old Testament book, get in the habit of mentally locating it in this historical scheme of Chart 3.

B. GEOGRAPHICAL SETTING

Most of the Old Testament is action, and action involves places. This is why geography is a key ingredient of Old Testament setting.

Someone has said, "To visualize is to empathize." If you want to help yourself *feel* the action of ancient Bible history, visualize where it is taking place as you read the Bible text. This should be one of the strongest motivations for you to learn the geography of the Old Testament.

One basic Old Testament map and two related maps will be studied in this chapter. These maps show the large areas of setting. Other more detailed maps appear at appropriate places throughout the book. It is important to have a good grasp of the large, overall geographical setting before zeroing in on the details of the smaller areas.

1. Three major regions of Old Testament geography. The accompanying Map A shows where virtually all Old Testament history took place.

Observe the following on the map:

1. There are three major regions (encircled). The middle region is Canaan, the homeland of Israel. It is strategically located at the crossroads of international traffic. For example, the land route from Egypt in the west to Babylon in the east followed the Fertile Crescent through Canaan because the desert lands of Arabia were impassable.[23]

2. To the north and east of Canaan are the lands of Syria, Assyria, and Babylonia. All three nations were Israel's strongest and bitterest enemies at some time or other.

3. The ancient kingdom of Egypt was Israel's foe in the southwest. A quick glance at an exhaustive concordance shows that the name Egypt appears hundreds of times throughout the Bible. This indicates the important part the nation played in Bible history.

4. A number of small kingdoms (e.g., Edom, south of the Dead Sea), which were a constant threat to Israel's peace, were located around the southern and eastern borders of Canaan. These are not shown on this map.

5. There were six major journeys of the people of Israel in Old

---

23. The semicircular strip of habitable land from Canaan to Babylonia has been appropriately called the Fertile Crescent. It was the center of civilization from man's beginning to the golden age of Greece in the fifth century B.C. The two key waterways of the long Mesopotamian Valley are the Tigris and Euphrates rivers.

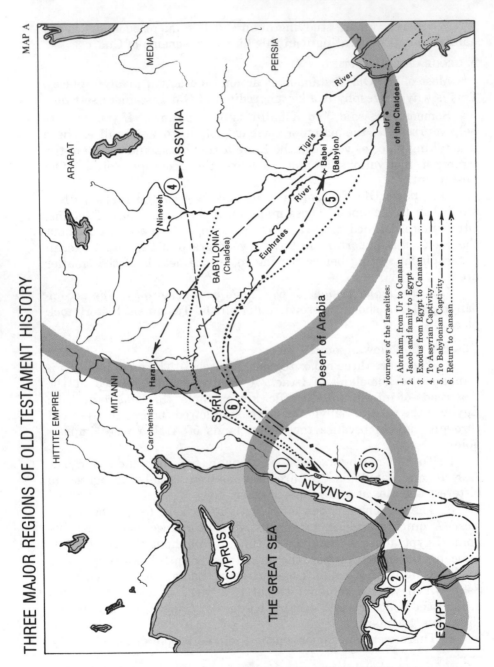

THREE MAJOR REGIONS OF OLD TESTAMENT HISTORY

MAP A

MEDIA

PERSIA

ARARAT

ASSYRIA

Nineveh

BABYLONIA
(Chaldea)

Tigris River

Euphrates River

Babel
(Babylon)

Ur
of the Chaldees

HITTITE EMPIRE

MITANNI

Carchemish

Haran

SYRIA

Desert of Arabia

CYPRUS

THE GREAT SEA

CANAAN

EGYPT

Journeys of the Israelites:
1. Abraham, from Ur to Canaan
2. Jacob and family to Egypt
3. Exodus from Egypt to Canaan
4. To Assyrian Captivity
5. To Babylonian Captivity
6. Return to Canaan

Testament history. They marked turning points in the experience of God's chosen nation. Follow the journeys on the map, using the encircled numbers:

① The first journey of the first Israelite family, Abraham's. From Ur of Chaldea to Canaan (c. 2000 B.C.). Read Genesis 11:27—12:9.

② Migration of Jacob and his relatives from Canaan to Egypt, to join Joseph (1875 B.C.). Read Genesis 37:28; 46:1-34.

③ Exodus of over two million Israelites from the bondage of Egypt to the promised land of Canaan (1445 B.C.). Read Exodus 12:40-41; Joshua 1:1-9; Galatians 3:17.

④ The Northern Kingdom of Israel carried away into exile to Assyria (722 B.C.). Read 2 Kings 18:9-12.

⑤ The Southern Kingdom of Judah taken captive to Babylon (586 B.C.). Read 2 Kings 25:1-12.

⑥ Two separate, large groups of Israelites return from Babylon to their homeland, led by Zerubbabel (536 B.C.) and Ezra (458 B.C.). Read Ezra 1-2; 7:1-10; 8:1-21.

    2. Physical features of Palestine.[24] The best way to recall the locations of Old Testament cities is to picture the physical features of the land where they were started. Other values of learning this physical geography are understanding the strategy of battles and recognizing why journeys followed certain routes.

Study the general features of Palestine as shown on Map B. The natural contours of the land run north-south. As you move from west to east on the map, you will observe six major types of contour.

Observe the following about each of these:

① *Coastal Plain.* This follows the coast up to the promontory of Mount Carmel. Relatively few cities were located here during Old Testament times, partly because of the absence of navigable harbors.

② *Shefelah (also called Lowlands).* Here the terrain begins to ascend from the low coastal plain. Many cities sprang up here, due in part to the semifertile soil.

③ *Hill Country (also called Cis-Jordan Hills).* Follow on the map the prominent north-south ridge which bisects these hills, especially in the southern half of the country. Many cities were built along this ridge, especially because of the natural fortifications.

---

24. The name *Palestine* is derived from the Hebrew *eres Pelistim*, meaning "land of the Philistines." Philistia was a small region in the southwest, but by the fifth century B.C. the name was applied to the entire land of Canaan.

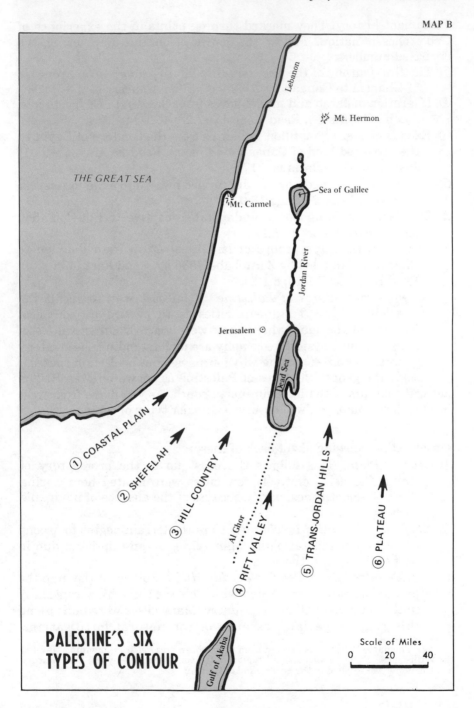

THE GREAT SEA

Lebanon

☼ Mt. Hermon

Sea of Galilee

Mt. Carmel

Jordan River

Jerusalem ☉

Dead Sea

① COASTAL PLAIN

② SHEFELAH

③ HILL COUNTRY

Al Ghor

④ RIFT VALLEY

⑤ TRANS-JORDAN HILLS

⑥ PLATEAU

**PALESTINE'S SIX
TYPES OF CONTOUR**

Gulf of Akaba

Scale of Miles

0   20   40

Jerusalem is on the ridge, just west of the northern tip of the Dead Sea. The one major break in this ridge is at the Plain of Esdraelon, just southwest of the Sea of Galilee.

④ *Rift Valley.* This is the most consistent feature of the north-south contour. Its average width is about ten miles. For the entire length of Palestine, the depression is below the level of the Great Sea (Mediterranean). Follow this depression from north to south on Map B as you read the descriptions given below.

Valley west of Mount Hermon. The Jordan River originates here, north of the Sea of Galilee. Between the Lebanon and Hermon ranges, the rift valley is very prominent.

Lake Chinnereth (New Testament name: Sea of Galilee). The sea is 685 feet below the level of the Great Sea. This beautiful area was not inhabited as heavily as in New Testament times.

Jordan River. The river is entirely below sea level, from the Sea of Galilee to the Dead Sea. The hot and humid climate of this valley discouraged the building of cities. Jericho was an exception.

Salt Sea (Dead Sea). This is 1,286 feet below sea level. What main river flows into it? The sea has no outlet, hence its dense mineral content. A few cities were located on its shores. See Maps E and K.

Al Ghor (Araba). A hot, dry valley. No cities here.

Gulf of Aqaba. Solomon built a fleet of ships at the north end of this gulf (1 Kings 9:26).

⑤ *Trans-Jordan Hills.* The rugged hills rise sharply from the low rift valley to the high plateau. Few cities located here.

⑥ *Plateau.* From the fertile tableland of the north to the semidesert south, this plateau was the scene of no little Old Testament history. Its rolling land was used mostly for grazing livestock. See Maps E and G for the location of cities, such as Ramoth-gilead and Damascus.

As you proceed with your survey of the Old Testament, visualize the topography which you have just studied.

3. Climate of Palestine. Palestine is of the same latitudes as southern United States. Its climate is controlled generally by the prevailing westerly winds from the Mediterranean Sea. However, because of the diversity of topography, the climate varies considerably from place to place. Overall, there are two seasons: warm, dry summers, and cool, wet winters. The rainy season lasts from

November to March. Average temperature ranges for Jerusalem, representing recent records, are forty-one to fifty-four degrees (Fahrenheit) in January and sixty-five to eighty-five degrees in August. The moderating effect is caused by the more constant temperatures of the Mediterranean Sea.

In the regions around the Sea of Galilee, the climate is more moderate and pleasant than around Jerusalem. In Old Testament times, however, more people inhabited the warmer regions. Hot desert winds (*sirocco*) plague the plateau lands east of the Jordan. This is one of the main reasons for sparse population there in biblical times.[25]

WEATHER MAP OF THE BIBLE LANDS   MAP C

Climate is distinguished from weather in that the former is the prevailing atmospheric condition over a period of time, whereas weather is the condition at a particular time. The accompanying

25. The above observations are based on the reasonable assumption that Palestine's climate has not changed much since Old Testament times.

weather map (Map C) of the Bible lands shows the weather pattern prognosticated for noon of April 18, 1970. The cold front over Cyprus is moving from west to east, and is about two hundred miles west of the coast of Palestine. When it has passed through Palestine, the sixty-four-degree temperature (Fahrenheit) at the Gaza Strip will not lower too much, because the front is not very strong, as shown by the Cyprus reading behind the front. Much of the rainfall of Palestine during the winter season is induced by oncoming fronts similar to the one shown here.

C. LEADING POWERS IN THE OLD TESTAMENT WORLD

Throughout their career in Old Testament times, the Israelites were well aware of the universal truth that man does not live in isolation. We saw in earlier geographical studies that Palestine was located at the hub of the world powers: Egypt to the southwest; and Syria, Assyria, Babylonia, and Persia to the north and east. For the most part, this central location meant conflict, for each foreign nation coveted the strategic military position which Palestine offered, not to mention the economic booty. But such conflict was not outside divine providence, for God was sovereignly guiding even the foreign nations to fulfill His purposes with His chosen people. For example, when Israel persisted in rejecting God as Lord, He sent the Babylonian invaders into the land to take the people into captivity. It was a military encounter, but basically it was divine judgment.

Because the Old Testament has so much to say about Israel's relations with foreign powers, it is important at the outset of your studies to get an overview of each nation's history during Old Testament times, for whatever bearing this had on Israel's experience. The discussion which follows stresses highlights rather than details of those histories. At a later time you should refer to comprehensive outside sources to fill in the details. Our present purpose is of a panoramic scope, so that we do not overlook the forest when viewing the individual trees.

First, review Map A "Three Major Regions of Old Testament History." Note especially the locations of Egypt, Syria, Assyria, Babylonia, and Persia. These were the five most powerful nations which played such vital roles in Israel's history.[26] When you study history, always visualize the geography involved.

26. Although Syria's domain was not geographically extensive, that nation is studied here with the other four because of its direct relation to the Northern Kingdom of Israel for two centuries.

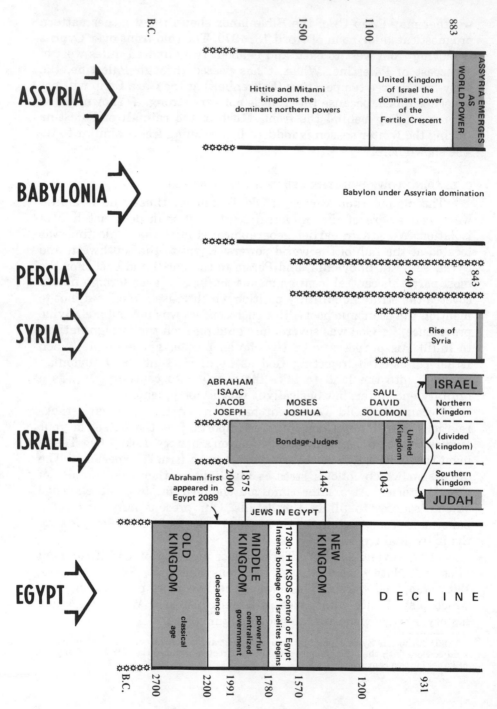

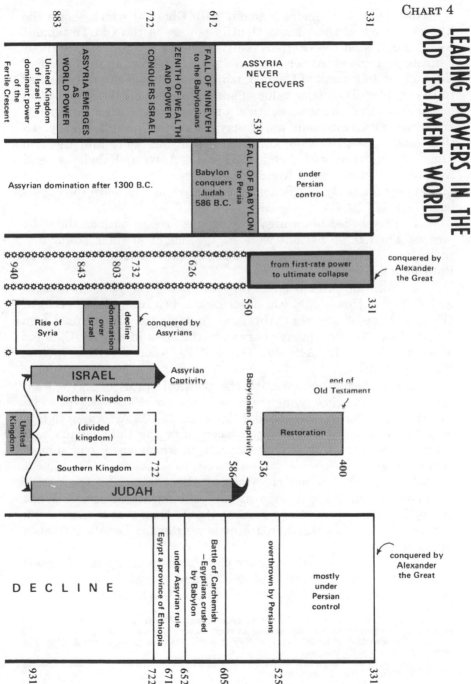

CHART 4

LEADING POWERS IN THE OLD TESTAMENT WORLD

ASSYRIA EMERGES AS WORLD POWER

ZENITH OF WEALTH AND POWER
CONQUERS ISRAEL

FALL OF NINEVEH to the Babylonians

United Kingdom of Israel the dominant power of the Fertile Crescent

ASSYRIA NEVER RECOVERS

Assyrian domination after 1300 B.C.

Babylon conquers Judah 586 B.C.

FALL OF BABYLON to Persia

under Persian control

883   722   612   539   331

from first-rate power to ultimate collapse

conquered by Alexander the Great

940   843   803   732   626   550   331

Rise of Syria

domination over Israel

decline

conquered by Assyrians

ISRAEL   Assyrian Captivity

Northern Kingdom

(divided kingdom)

United Kingdom

Southern Kingdom

JUDAH

Babylonian Captivity

end of Old Testament

Restoration

536   400

722   586

DECLINE

Egypt a province of Ethiopia

under Assyrian rule

Battle of Carchemish —Egyptians crushed by Babylon

overthrown by Persians

mostly under Persian control

conquered by Alexander the Great

931   722   671   652   605   525   331

Now begin to acquaint yourself with Chart 4, which shows the history of each of the leading Gentile powers in the Old Testament world. First, scan the chart to see its general organization, without pausing over any of the details. Israel's history shown in the middle of the chart is an excerpt of Chart 3, which you studied carefully earlier in the chapter. The major value of superimposing all the histories on one chart is that the total political picture of any particular year or era of the Old Testament world may be viewed simultaneously. To illustrate, note that when the united kingdom split into the two kingdoms of Israel and Judah (931 B.C.), Assyria, Babylonia, and Egypt were not dominant world powers.

Follow the study suggestions given below as you learn the significant facts of Chart 4.

1. The shaded block areas of the five foreign nations show the periods when those nations were at the height of their power and influence.[27] Note how the ascendancy moved from Assyria to Babylonia to Persia.

2. Note the three bright kingdom eras of Egypt between 2700 and 1200 B.C. How would you describe the two intervening periods? Observe when it was that Abraham first visited Egypt (read Gen 12:10—13:4). For how many years were the Jews in Egypt? (Cf. Exod 12:40-41; Gen 15:13; Acts 7:6; Gal 3:17.)[28] When did their intense bondage begin?

3. How would you describe the political status of Egypt from 1200 to 331 B.C.? How many times does the chart show Egypt to be subject to another nation? (Read 2 Kings 25:22-26.) According to this passage, some Jews fled to Egypt soon after the Babylonians conquered Jerusalem. According to Chart 4, to whom was Egypt subject at this time?

4. Study the section on Assyria. About when did the nation originate? When did it emerge as the reigning world power? What nearby kingdoms were strong prior to that?[29] Note that it was during Solomon's reign that the united kingdom extended Israel's influence the farthest.

5. When did Assyria conquer the Northern Kingdom of Israel? When did it reach its zenith of wealth and power? How long after Israel was conquered did Assyria fall to the Babylonians?

---

27. The blocks show *general* eras of ascendancy. Within an era, a nation could experience temporary decline, depending on such factors as who was king.

28. The duration of Israel's stay in Egypt is discussed in Leon Wood, *A Survey of Israel's History*, pp. 83-109.

29. See Map A, "Three Major Regions of Old Testament History" for the locations of the Hittite and Mitanni empires.

6. Did Babylon arise as an independent nation about the time of Assyria? What was the relationship between the two from 1300 to 626 B.C.? The Chaldean (Babylonian) dynasty began in 626 B.C. with King Nabopolassar. The empire at this time is usually referred to as the Neo-Babylonian Empire, to distinguish it from the Old Babylonian Empire of about a thousand years earlier. What key Bible event happened in 586 B.C.? How soon after that was Babylon conquered by the Persians?

7. Around 1000 B.C., immigrants from various lands were beginning to merge with the local inhabitants of the land of Persia to form what was to be a first-rate empire. Cyrus the Great began his reign in 550 B.C. How long after that was Persia conquered by Alexander the Great?[30]

8. The Jews in Babylonian captivity were granted permission to return to Canaan during the ascendancy of what empire? In this connection, read Ezra 1:1-4.

9. What were the three periods of Syria's history, as shown on the chart? When were the Syrians conquered by the Assyrians? How soon after that did the Assyrians take Israel captive?

10. One of the important things to observe on the chart is that during the years when Israel was ruled by kings (1043-586 B.C.), the worst troubles for the Jews came by the hands of foreign powers: Syria, Assyria, and Babylonia. Recall from your earlier reading of 1 Samuel 8 that the Israelites, in demanding kingly rule against God's will, wanted to be like their neighbors: "No, but there shall be a king over us, that we also may be like all the nations, that our king may judge us and go out before us and fight our battles" (1 Sam 8:19-20). Little did they know then what devastating battles would ultimately be fought when their God, whose lordship they rejected, would grant victory to their enemies!

D. EVERYDAY LIFE IN CANAAN DURING OLD TESTAMENT TIMES

The Old Testament was written by Orientals about Orientals. People of Western cultures need to keep this in mind to better appreciate the Bible stories and testimonies coming out of those ancient times. Fortunately the foundational doctrines which are taught in that Oriental setting are timeless and universal, such as man's sinfulness and God's holiness. So the Bible is not a closed book

---

30. Alexander the Great was king of Macedonia from 336 to 323 B.C. He conquered the Greek city-states and the whole Persian Empire from the coasts of Asia Minor and Egypt to India. Palestine was under Persian control at the time, so it also fell into Alexander's hands.

to those not acquainted with the everyday life of the people of Israel. But it can be sharper and clearer if that setting is at least mentally visualized and felt.

Bible dictionaries and commentaries are among the best sources for learning the local settings of the Old Testament text. Also, there are books which specifically discuss this subject, such as E. W. Heaton, *Everyday Life in Old Testament Times;* H. F. Saggs, *Everyday Life in Babylonia and Assyria;* and Fred H. Wight, *Manners and Customs of Bible Lands.*[31] It is beyond the scope of this introductory chapter to describe in detail the typical everyday life in Canaan during Old Testament times. The following list is included, however, to suggest a thumbnail sketch of such a setting.[32] As you read the list, use a little imagination and let a picture gradually emerge which will be etched upon your memory for later studies in the Old Testament. The most fruitful outcome of this short exercise may not be so much the learning of new facts as becoming alert to the Oriental flavor of the Old Testament.

An Oriental town or city—walls, gates, towers, narrow streets, and busy marketplaces—location of a city preferably on an elevated site, such as Jerusalem on Mount Zion—fields and grazing plots outside the city limits

Water supply—wells, cisterns, streams, and reservoirs

Houses[33]—average size of houses of the common people: one room[34]— roofs constructed of beams overlayed with reeds, bushes, and grass—earthen floors; mud-brick walls—few windows on the street side—fireplace on the floor in the middle of the room— furnishings: mats and cushions, storage chest, lampstand, handmill for grinding grain, cooking utensils, goatskin bottles, broom

Domestic animals—dogs, donkeys, mules, horses, camels, sheep, goats

Foods—barley and wheat bread, oil, buttermilk, cheese, fruits (olives, figs, grapes, raisins, pomegranates), vegetables, grain, honey; eggs, meat, poultry, and fish were eaten, but not regularly; fish was a major food in the cities around the Sea of Galilee; gener-

31. An interesting chapter on this subject, written in narrative style, is "Israel at Home," by John B. Taylor, in his book *A Christian's Guide to the Old Testament,* pp. 12-20. This is highly recommended reading.

32. All of these items are described, at least briefly, in Fred H. Wight's *Manners and Customs of Bible Lands,* from which this list is constructed. It should be understood that all of the items are not necessarily part of every setting. Also, the descriptions are of life *after* the nomadic years of the earliest patriarchs, like Abraham.

33. Before settling down in Canaan, the Israelites dwelt in tents. The main purpose of tents and houses was that of shelter. The average Israelite spent less time in his abode than does the average person of Western culture.

34. Houses with more than one room were built around an open courtyard.

ally, the people ate two meals a day: breakfast, and late dinner (about 5 p.m.)

Dress—both men and women: inner garment (tunic); girdle for the tunic; outer garment (mantle) used as shelter from wind, rain, cold, heat, and as a blanket at night; turban (head); sandals— women only: longer tunics and larger mantles, veil (entirely covering the head in public), elaborate ornamentations (ear- rings, bracelets)

Education—children educated mainly by their parents: Hebrew reli- gion and Scripture, reading and writing, practical skills— advanced training for leaders: such as in schools of the prophets, and by tutors

Worship—worship by the family in each home—called worship meet- ings in public areas[35]—temple worship in Jerusalem: regular participation by residents of the vicinity; participation at the annual religious feasts by Israelites from far and near

Trades and professions—agriculture (grain, grapes, olives, figs), sheep-raising, fishing, hunting, pottery, carpentry, masonry, metal work, tentmaking, merchants, physicians

Women's tasks—grinding grain, weaving, making clothes, washing, care of flocks, carrying water, cooking, housecleaning, rearing and educating the children—children of the home, especially girls, helped in these daily chores

Travel—usually in groups, for the sake of safety—mode: most often by animals, sometimes by foot—meals: lunch brought along, as the main source—overnight lodging: at homes, sometimes inns

The following two paragraphs illustrate how one writer has used his imagination, based on known facts, to describe the everyday life of the average Israelite. Do the same in your own thinking as you study the stories of the Old Testament.

> Tucked away along the winding streets of the town of Ramah, five miles north of Jerusalem, you will find the tiny one-roomed dwelling where Benaiah lives with his family. He lives much the same sort of life as the people round about him, never far from starvation level, cooped up in the city through the cold rainy months of winter and longing for the springtime when he can get out into the fields and work his ground.
> . . . .
> For beds the family shared two straw mats which were laid on the bare,

35. During the Babylonian Captivity the Jews began worshiping regularly in meeting places, later called "synagogues" (from the Greek *synagoge*, "place of assem- bly"). They probably continued this tradition upon returning to their homeland, though there is no specific reference to it in the postexilic books of the Old Testament. By New Testament times the synagogue was a well-established institution.

earthen floor; for blankets they used the cloaks which were their normal outdoor garb. The little oil lamp burned dimly on a ledge in the corner. It was never allowed to go out except when the fire was alight in the daytime. It was the only box of matches they had! However, it gave very little light and so once you had settled down for the night it was impossible to get up without waking the whole household (farmyard and all!) and a caller late at night was never welcome.[36]

E. THE HEAVEN-EARTH SETTING

As much as the Old Testament concerns people and nations, with all of their frailties and sins, it is unique along with the New Testament in that the dimension of miracle controls its story. In its pages, heaven touches earth, God comes down and works through man. This heaven-earth setting pervades the entire book. He who wants to know what God is communicating in the temporal, local setting must accept and believe the supernatural dimension, for the message is meaningless without it. More will be said about this below, as we think about how to approach the Old Testament and what to look for in our study of its pages.

IV. How to Approach the Old Testament

Without the right approach and clear guideposts, it is easy to get lost when studying the myriads of historical facts of the Old Testament. Also, it is easy to become discouraged and confused over difficult or obscure portions of the text. But these pitfalls can be avoided in various ways. One way is to keep in mind *the key revealed truths* which underlie all the details of the whole Old Testament story. You are on firm ground when you recognize these truths as you study a Bible passage. Some of the main ones are discussed below.[37]

A. GOD ALWAYS ACTS IN CONFORMITY TO HIS NATURE

One of the main purposes of the Old Testament is to reveal *who* God is. He is eternal Spirit, alive and personal, "the first cause, Himself uncaused."[38] He is holy, righteous, just, loving, merciful, gracious, true, omnipresent (Psalm 139:7-12); omniscient (Psalm 147:5); omnipotent (Job 42:2; Jer 32:17); and immutable (unchangeable, Mal 3:6). All of these divine attributes are absolutely perfect and eternally concurrent. When He sends awful judgment for sin, because He is a holy God, He does not thereby nullify His grace. For

---

36. Taylor, pp. 12, 17.
37. The Bible itself is the revelatory source of these key truths. This will become more apparent to you as you survey the various books of the Old Testament.
38. Compare this quote by the theologian Thomas Aquinas with the truth suggested by Exodus 3:14.

God never acts contrary to His *manifold* nature. In our human limitations we may not always understand His workings, and may even ask such questions as Why did a loving God permit the ravages of war in Old Testament times? By faith we must see God as the never changing One, who is holy but always acts in love, and who is loving but never violates His holiness. There is absolutely no alternative to this approach.

B. ALL HISTORY IS IN GOD'S SOVEREIGN CONTROL

There are no accidents in world history. God directs or permits the course of events in a person's or nation's career according to His sovereign and perfect will. For example, He granted Israel's evil demand for kingly rule, and in righteous judgment He sent the Babylonian conqueror. In both diverse actions He was sovereign, and in both He revealed His own nature as well as man's.

Whenever you have unanswered questions about Old Testament history (such as Why?), rest confidently in the truth that God is Lord of all history, in whose will every event fulfills His perfect purposes.

C. ISRAEL WAS GOD'S DIVINELY CALLED AND FAVORED NATION

God called Abraham to be the father of the nation of Israel, and then God made the nation (Gen 12:1-2). Humanly speaking, it was not an act of favoritism in the sense that out of many existing nations God picked one of intrinsic superiority to be His exclusive favorite (read Deut 10:14-17). And yet it is true that He sovereignly chose from the world's population one man, Abraham, to be the nation's father. If you are disturbed about why God would elect one nation to be the object of special blessing (Gen 12:2), keep in mind that sovereign election also applies to His saving of individuals (Eph 1:4-5). Even though you cannot fully comprehend it, be assured that God, in the exercise of His rightful sovereignty over the entire universe, never violates His attribute of justice in the expression of His love.[39]

D. GOD WANTED TO USE ISRAEL AS HIS CHANNEL OF COMMUNICATION TO THE REST OF THE WORLD

God has always used people to communicate to others the message of salvation. In New Testament times, He started with a nucleus of believers in Jerusalem, to whom Christ gave the commission, "You shall be My witnesses both in Jerusalem, and in all Judea and Samaria, and even to the remotest part of the earth" (Acts 1:8). The

---

39. Read Sauer, pp. 90-92, for an extended treatment of God's sovereign calling of Israel.

same principle of believer reaching out to unbelievers applies today. Back in Old Testament times, God wanted Israel to enjoy the fullest blessings of fellowship with Him in this life, and thus be a living witness of this to the nations around them. Israel, for the most part, failed God's purposes during the fifteen hundred years of its Old Testament career, and that is one reason why relatively few stories of evangelistic outreach to foreign nations appear in the Bible text. God did not overlook these foreign nations, but neither was He able to use His chosen nation, Israel, to the extent that He had desired.[40]

E. REDEMPTION IS THE KEY SUBJECT OF THE OLD TESTAMENT REVELATION

There are other vital ingredients in the story of the Old Testament, such as the creation account (cosmogony). But from the time of Genesis 3, when Adam and Eve sinned and broke fellowship with God, to the last words of Malachi, the message centered on how sinful man can be redeemed and reconciled to God.[41] Erich Sauer says this about the Old Testament: "Thus the whole pre-Christian history of salvation is a guiding of mankind to the Redeemer of the world. The people of Israel were prepared in advance by historical revelation; the peoples of the world by the happenings of politics and civilization."[42]

The Old Testament makes it very clear that God seeks to save all lost sinners, not only Israelites. Also, because their spiritual deliverance is infinitely more important than any physical help, He uses even the severest of measures, such as war and captivity, to bring them to conviction of sin, repentance, and faith.

Another clear redemptive truth in the Old Testament is that man is saved by faith, not works. Abraham was an example (read Gen 15:6; Rom 4:1-3). If we find that a large portion of the Old Testament text is about the Israelites' attempts to appear religious, we may conclude that God wants us to see the futility of depending on works for salvation.

Because redemption is the key subject of the Old Testament, we may expect that each of the thirty-nine books contributes measurably to this theme. And we may also expect that at times the biblical

---

40. The book of Jonah is the story of such a mission to foreign nations. Sauer writes that the Old Testament from end to end is "full of promises of salvation for the whole human race." Read ibid., pp. 92-95, for a discussion of God's dealings with the Gentile world during Old Testament times.

41. The doctrine of salvation in the Old Testament is not confined to theological terms such as "redemption." More often it is designated by descriptive language, such as "delivered" (Joel 2:32); "life" (Deut 30:20); "walk in the light" (Isa 2:5); "his God" (Isa 50:10); "return to the LORD" (Isa 55:7); "heal" (Isa 57:18). Read Psalm 19:14 and Job 19:25 for two appearances of the word "redeemer."

42. Sauer, p. 186. This book is highly recommended for its analysis of the Old Testament's redemptive theme.

writers omitted details which had no direct relation to that theme. The Holy Spirit was responsible for such selectivity in inspiration.

F. THE OLD TESTAMENT CONSTANTLY POINTS FORWARD TO THE COMING SAVIOUR AND KING, WHO IS JESUS CHRIST

If redemption is the key subject of the Old Testament, and if Christ (the "anointed One," the Messiah) is the Redeemer of the world, then we may expect to find many Old Testament passages pointing to Christ. These may prophesy solely of a glorious future for Israel as a nation under Christ's rule, or they may point to the blessings of salvation to all who believe in the coming Saviour. Read Isaiah 53, which is a classic Messianic prophecy of Christ's substitutionary death for sinners. It should be pointed out that Old Testament references to the person and work of Christ often appear in the form of type and symbol (e.g., the Levitical offerings), not necessarily in direct predictive language.

Christ was literally, according to the flesh, the Son of David, the Son of Abraham, the promised seed, the Heir to David's throne (Matt 1:1; Luke 1:32; Gal 3:16; Isa 9:7; Jer 23:5). G. T. Manley writes of Jesus:

> He is the second Adam, and there is not a name in the long line of His genealogy, nor any event in the Old Testament story of redemption which does not illuminate in greater or lesser degree His wonderful Person and work.[43]

Norman Geisler has written very effectively about Christ as the theme of the Old Testament. He says:

> Viewing the Old Testament Christocentrically is not an interpretive (hermeneutical) option; for the Christian it is a divine imperative. On five different occasions Jesus claimed to be the theme of the entire Old Testament: (1) Matthew 5:17; (2) Luke 24:27; (3) Luke 24:44; (4) John 5:39; (5) Hebrews 10:7.[44]

Geisler sees in these verses four different Christocentric ways to view the Old Testament. These are shown on Chart 5, adapted from his book.[45]

Read the five New Testament passages as you study this chart, and you will see why the Old Testament must be studied with this Christocentric perspective.

---

43. G. T. Manley, *The New Bible Handbook,* p. 14.
44. Norman L. Geisler, *Christ: The Theme of the Bible,* p. 31.
45. Ibid., p. 32.

CHART 5

FOUR CHRISTOCENTRIC VIEWS OF THE OLD TESTAMENT		
Christ's own words	Christ the Fulfiller of	Christ Viewed as
Luke 24:27,44	Messianic Prophecy	Messiah and King
Hebrews 10:7	Levitical Priesthood	Priest and Sacrifice
Matthew 5:17	Moral Precepts	Prophet and Teacher
John 5:39	Salvation Promises	Saviour and Lord

G. MIRACLES IN OLD TESTAMENT TIMES WERE ONE OF GOD'S WAYS TO REVEAL HIMSELF

Jesus performed miracles during His earthly ministry to vindicate His claim to being the Christ, the Son of God, with the ultimate purpose that people might be saved through faith in Him (read John 20:30-31). In pre-Christian times also, the Lord revealed Himself through miracles, that men might turn their hearts to Him. Since the creation of man, a common purpose of all biblical miracles has been to manifest the nature of the Lord of heaven as He has been moving among people on earth. Any reader of the Bible who disbelieves miracles is refusing to listen to God's voice. This is where most Old Testament critics commit intellectual and spiritual suicide.

H. THERE IS A PROGRESSION OF REVELATION IN THE BIBLE

The most obvious test of progression in the Bible is to compare the first book (Genesis) and the last (Revelation). Genesis records origins and God's first words to man. Revelation prophesies end times, and shows Christ enthroned forever as King of kings and Lord of lords. What happened in the intervening years, particularly up to the close of the first century A.D., is the progressing story of how God was revealing more and more of Himself and His redemptive work to men.

One progression of this revelation may be cited.[46] In the Garden of Eden, God first showed His authority over Satan and announced the coming of Christ, as the seed of the woman Eve, who would ultimately deal Satan the deathblow ("He shall bruise you on the

---

46. Only selected highlights of the progression are cited here. You may want to pursue this further by citing other parts of the progression.

head," Gen 3:15); with Noah, He established a covenant guaranteeing protection of the earth from any future universal flood (Gen 9:9-17); to Abraham, He promised blessing for the new nation (Israel) which He would make (Gen 12:2-3); through Moses, He instructed His people how to live pleasing to Him (Exod 20:1-17); through the prophets, He foretold in detail Christ's birth and ministry (e.g., Isa 9:6); through John the Baptist, He announced the inauguration of Christ's public ministry (John 1:6-36); to the apostles and New Testament writers, He revealed the full and deep truths of the new life in Christ (e.g., Eph 1-3); and final visions, which He gave to John at Patmos, were of Satan cast into the lake of fire and brimstone forever (Rev 20:10), and of Christ on the throne in the New Jerusalem, saying, "It is done" (Rev 21:6).

Earlier in this chapter we studied the progression of history unfolded in the drama of the Old Testament (e.g., Chart 3). Intimately involved in this historical progression were the ever enlarging and deepening revelations which God gave to man (doctrinal progression). When we study the Old Testament we must keep this in mind, otherwise we might force upon an early book a doctrine which is not there, or fail to see in a later book a truth that is really there. This does not mean, however, that in studying the Old Testament we should not interpret it in the light of events which took place hundreds of years later, during New Testament times. We who have been enlightened with the truth of the New Testament should always be looking for the anticipation of it in the Old.[47] This is how Jesus and the New Testament writers applied the Old.

I. THE OLD TESTAMENT IS GOD'S VOICE TO US TODAY, ANCIENT AS THE BOOK IS

If we discard a message only because it is ancient, we would reject the New Testament as well. But God's Book—both Old and New Testaments—is timeless in its application. That is why the apostle Paul, writing to his friend Timothy about their ancient Bible, asserted dogmatically that "all Scripture is inspired by God and profitable for teaching, for reproof, for correction, for training in righteousness; that the man of God may be adequate, equipped for every good work" (2 Tim 3:16-17). In the same context, Paul had

---

47. An example of this was cited earlier, where Christ is interpreted in Genesis 3:15 as being the seed of the woman Eve. An Old Testament Messianic passage is not always clear and specific in its reference to the story of Christ. For example, who would have seen Jeremiah 31:15 as a prophecy of the weeping mothers of Bethlehem, were it not for Matthew's interpretation in Matthew 2:17-18?

reminded Timothy that it was the sacred writings which had given Timothy "the wisdom that leads to salvation through faith which is in Christ Jesus" (2 Tim 3:15). So it is correct to say that all spiritual lessons derived from passages in the Old Testament have something to say, directly or indirectly, about these two timeless, vital life truths: *way to* God, or *walk with* God. The Old Testament is that contemporary. And so we must open our hearts to its message. In the words of Edward Young,

> In approaching the Bible . . . we need to remember that it is sacred ground. We must approach it with humble hearts, ready to hear what the Lord God says. The kaleidoscopic history of negative criticism is but further evidence that unless we do approach the Bible in a receptive attitude, we shall fail to understand it. Nor need we be ashamed to acknowledge that the words of Scripture are of God. . . . The attempt to explain them as anything less than Divine is one of the greatest failures that has ever appeared in the history of human thought.[48]

Some Review Questions

1. What are some of the important reasons for studying the Old Testament?

2. In what ways is the Old Testament related to the New?

3. In your own words, describe the history of the Bible's coming from God to man.

4. What is revelation, as referring to God? What is the difference between general revelation and special revelation?

5. How were the original Scriptures inspired by God? Were the original autographs inerrant?

6. Do we have any portion of the original autographs? Are the existing ancient copies of the Bible inerrant in every letter and word? If not, how confident can we be that they accurately represent what the authors originally wrote?

7. What did the discoveries of the Dead Sea Scrolls confirm?

8. How can we be sure that God intended the Old Testament canon to be no larger or smaller than the present existing group of books?

9. How does our arrangement of thirty-nine books differ from the Hebrew arrangement of twenty-four books? Is the text of one list longer than the text of the other?

10. What has been the history of the Old Testament as far as translation is involved?

11. What highlights of Israel's history formed the setting of the

---

48. Edward J. Young, *Introduction to the Old Testament,* pp. 10-11.

writing of the Old Testament books? How much of Chart 3, "Old Testament History," can you recall? (Try putting this down on paper.)

12. When did the writing prophets first appear in Israel's life?

13. What were the three major regions of the world in Old Testament geography?

14. What do you recall about the topography of Canaan? In what regions did many towns and cities appear?

15. Describe the general climate of Palestine. What are the annual seasons?

16. What five foreign powers did Israel have contact with in Old Testament times? How did each one affect Israel's history?

17. Describe the setting of a typical house and family in a small town of Canaan during the days of King David.

18. How a person approaches the Old Testament is crucial in the study process. This chapter discussed nine recommended approaches. Recall as many as you can, and explain why each approach is so vital.

V. SELECTED READING FOR FURTHER STUDY

A. DIVINE REVELATION

Chafer, L. S. *Systematic Theology,* 1:48-60.

Henry, Carl H. *Revelation and the Bible.*

Kelso, James L. *Archaeology and the Ancient Testament,* pp. 13-19.

Manley, G. T. *The New Bible Handbook,* pp. 6-8.

Packer, J. I. "Revelation and Inspiration." In *The New Bible Commentary,* pp 24-30.

Pinnock, Clark H. *Biblical Revelation.*

Warfield, B.B. "Revelation." In *The International Standard Bible Encyclopedia,* 3:2573-82; and *The Inspiration and Authority of the Bible,* pp. 71-102.

B. INSPIRATION

Allis, Oswald T. *The Old Testament: Its Claims and Its Critics,* pp. 1-171. These pages are on the facts, doctrines, and literary form of the Old Testament.

Archer, Gleason L. *A Survey of Old Testament Introduction,* pp. 13-27.

Clark, Gordon H. "How May I Know the Bible Is Inspired?" In *Can I Trust My Bible?,* edited by Howard F. Vos, pp. 9-34.

Gaussen, L. *Theopneustia: The Plenary Inspiration of the Holy Scriptures.*

Geisler, Norman L., and Nix, William E. *A General Introduction to the Bible,* pp. 26-124.

Hodge, C. *Systematic Theology,* pp. 151-86.

Manley, G. T. *The New Bible Handbook,* pp. 8-18.

Pache, René. *Inspiration and Authority.*

Payne, J. Barton. *The Theology of the Older Testament,* pp. 505-19.

Unger, Merrill F. *Introductory Guide to the Old Testament,* pp. 22-45.
Walvoord, John F. ed., *Inspiration and Interpretation.*

C. TRANSMISSION

Archer, Gleason L. *A Survey of Old Testament Introduction,* pp. 31-38; 47-58.
Bruce, F. F. *The Books and the Parchments,* pp. 114-24.
Geisler, Norman L., and Nix, William E. *A General Introduction to the Bible,*
    pp. 235-66.
Laird, R. "How Reliable Is the Old Testament Text?" In *Can I Trust My
    Bible?,* edited by Howard F. Vos, pp. 119-34.
Skilton, John H. "The Transmission of the Scriptures." In *The Infallible
    Word,* edited by N. B. Stonehouse and Paul Woolley.
Unger, Merrill F. *Introductory Guide to the Old Testament,* pp. 115-47.

D. CANONIZATION

Archer, Gleason L. *A Survey of Old Testament Introduction,* pp. 59-62.
Bruce, F. F. *The Books and the Parchments,* pp. 95-104; 163-75.
Geisler, Norman L., and Nix, William E. *A General Introduction to the Bible,*
    pp. 127-78.
Harris, R. Laird. "What Books Belong in the Canon of Scripture?" In *Can I
    Trust My Bible?,* edited by Howard F. Vos, pp. 67-87.
Manley, G. T. *The New Bible Handbook,* pp. 26-32; 38-39.
Robinson, G. L. "Canon of the Old Testament." In *The International Standard
    Bible Encyclopedia,* 1:554-63.
Unger, Merrill F. *Introductory Guide to the Old Testament,* pp. 46-114.

E. TRANSLATION

Archer, Gleason L. *A Survey of Old Testament Introduction,* pp. 38-46.
Bruce, F. F. *The Books and the Parchments,* pp. 125-62; 191-94; 201-11;
    219-38.
Geisler, Norman L., and Nix, William E. *A General Introduction to the Bible,*
    pp. 297-343.
Purkiser, W. T. *Exploring the Old Testament,* pp. 27-37.
Unger, Merrill F. *Introductory Guide to the Old Testament,* pp. 148-79.

F. HISTORICAL SETTING OF THE OLD TESTAMENT

Bright, John. *A History of Israel,* pp. 23-66.
Harrison, R. K. *Introduction to the Old Testament,* pp. 147-63. Technical
    discussion.
Kline, Meredith G. "Is the History of the Old Testament Accurate?" In *Can I
    Trust My Bible?,* edited by Howard F. Vos, pp. 135-54.
Manley, G. T. *The New Bible Handbook,* pp. 77-106. Concise treatment of the
    historical background of all parts of the Old Testament.
Payne, J. Barton. *An Outline of Hebrew History,* pp. 13-15. Condensed
    summary.
Schultz, Samuel J. *The Old Testament Speaks.* Historical setting is in-
    terspersed throughout this excellent work.

Unger, Merrill F. *Unger's Bible Handbook,* pp. 8-17. Tabulation of dates and
    events.

G. GEOGRAPHICAL SETTING

Adams, J. McKee. *Biblical Backgrounds,* pp. 52-85.
Aharoni, Yohanan. *The Land of the Bible.*
Baly, Dennis. *The Geography of the Bible,* pp. 125-266.
Orni, Efraim, and Efrat, Elisha. *Geography of Israel.* An excellent, large map
    of Palestine appears in a flap under the back cover.
Payne, J. Barton. *An Outline of Hebrew History,* pp. 15-19; 23-32.
Pfeiffer, Charles F. *Baker's Bible Atlas.*
Pfeiffer, Charles F., and Vos, Howard F. *The Wycliffe Historical Geography of
    Bible Lands.*
The Sacred Land. Excellent topographical maps.
Smith, George Adam. *The Historical Geography of the Holy Land.*
Wilson, Clifford A. *Exploring Bible Backgrounds,* pp. 39-47.
Wood, Leon. *A Survey of Israel's History,* pp. 19-26.

H. EVERYDAY LIFE IN OLD TESTAMENT TIMES

Bailey, A. E. *Daily Life in Bible Times.*
Corswant, W. A. *A Dictionary of Life in Bible Times.*
Freeman, James M. *Manners and Customs of the Bible.*
Gordon, Cyrus. "Biblical Customs and the Nuzu Tablets." *Biblical Ar-
    chaeologist* 3: (February 1940).
Grosvenor, Gilbert, ed. *Everyday Life in Ancient Times.*
Harrison, R. K. *Old Testament Times.*
Heaton, E. W. *Everyday Life in Old Testament Times.*
La Sor, William Sanford. *Daily Life in Bible Times.*
Manley, G. T. *The New Bible Handbook,* pp. 428-38.
Miller, M. S., and Miller, J. L. *Encyclopedia of Bible Life.*
Pritchard, James B. *The Ancient Near East in Pictures.*
Saggs, H. F. *Everyday Life in Babylonia and Assyria.*
Taylor, John B. *A Christian's Guide to the Old Testament,* pp. 12-20.
Wight, Fred H. *Manners and Customs of Bible Lands.*

I. ISRAEL, GOD'S CHOSEN NATION

Douglas, J. D. ed. *The New Bible Dictionary,* pp. 578-83.
Sauer, Erich. *The Dawn of World Redemption,* pp. 89-120.
Unger, Merrill F. *Unger's Bible Dictionary,* pp. 541-43.

J. CHRIST IN THE OLD TESTAMENT

Baron, David. *Rays of Messiah's Glory.*
Baxter, J. Sidlow. *The Strategic Grasp of the Bible,* pp. 141-56.
Cooper, David L. *Messiah: His First Coming Scheduled,* pp. 136-56.
Geisler, Norman L. *Christ: The Theme of the Bible,* pp. 9-101.
Hengstenberg, E. W. *Christology of the Old Testament,* pp. 1-12.
Sauer, Erich. *The Dawn of World Redemption,* pp. 141-64.
Walvoord, John F. *Jesus Christ Our Lord,* pp. 36-95.

2

The Survey Method of Study

The method of study called *survey* is more than just reading a book. It is important to know what is involved in this method so we can use it to fullest advantage in our study of the Old Testament books. The next few pages discuss especially the purposes and procedures of survey study. More detailed directions and suggestions are given throughout the manual in connection with each Old Testament book. In the latter half of this chapter we will see how to use this book as a guide to our survey studies.

I. Purposes and Procedures of Survey Study

A. THE FULL SCOPE OF BIBLE STUDY

Bible study is of three phases, in the following order:[1]
Observation—seeing what the text says
Interpretation—determining what the text means
Application—applying the Bible to life
In survey study we are especially engaged in the observation phase, though the other two phases are also involved.

Survey, as applied to the study of a book of the Bible, is an overall view of the book, made from various perspectives. Other names given to this method are synthesis, overview, panoramic study, skyscraper view.

Survey should always precede analysis. This follows the standard rule, "Image the whole, then execute the parts." That is, first survey the whole book to see the overall picture; then analyze each of the small parts in detail. This study manual does not involve analysis;

---

1. The order is very important. For example, one is not prepared to interpret a Bible text until he has first seen what the text really says.

hence, we will always be in the survey process for all thirty-nine books of the Old Testament. At times we will tarry over details, but only in connection with the survey at hand.

B. PURPOSES AND AIMS OF SURVEY STUDY

The fact that survey should be made before analysis reflects two main purposes of survey study.

1. To see each part in its intended emphasis. Making a survey of the highlights of a book before analyzing the details is a guard against the two extremes of overemphasizing *or* minimizing the point of any one part of Scripture.

2. To see each part in its relation to the other parts. Knowing one's bearing in the forest of many facts is a tremendous help in Bible study. This is illustrated by an experience of Charles Lindbergh. On one of his early flights, he lost a valuable instrument overboard. He watched it fall and land in the dense fields below. Later he landed a smaller plane in the general vicinity, and scoured the area by foot in search of the instrument, but to no avail. He resorted to a simple expedient. Taking off his coat, he spread it on a bush, and returned to the air. From the air he saw both the coat and the instrument. So he moved the coat to another bush, and repeated the sighting from the air. With this additional bearing he finally was able to locate the instrument.

Many questions on the interpretation of a verse in the Bible are answered when the location of the verse in the book, with reference to its context, is recognized. Survey study brings out this overall context.

Related to the above purposes are some other important things that survey study aims to accomplish.

1. Observing the total structure of the book. A book of the Bible is not just a mass of words. The words are meaningful because their

THE BOOK OF 2 SAMUEL

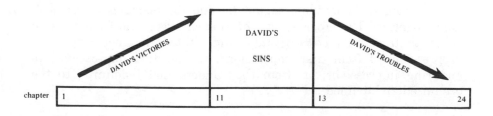

writer organized them around themes in such a way as to express the intended truths and impress the inquiring reader. For example, what impresses you about the overall structure of 2 Samuel shown in the accompanying diagram?

The apostle Paul was aware of structure in the text of his Scriptures, as evidenced by such comments as Ephesians 6:2. Read this verse. What was Paul observing about the structure of the Ten Commandments (Exod 20:1-17) when he said, "which is the first commandment with a promise"?

2. Observing the content of the book. In survey study we are interested in *what* the Bible says (content) as well as *how* the Bible says it (structure). But in surveying the content we do not tarry over details, as we would do later in analyzing the text. Here we keep our eyes open to highlights, such as key events, prominent persons, emphasized truths. These are the best clues for us in determining the book's main theme.

3. Getting the feel of the book's atmosphere. Your personal involvement in the Bible text will greatly help to make your study effective. Survey study helps you catch the tone of the book you are studying, as though "you were there."

4. Relating each book to the others and to the Old Testament as a whole. This is best and most easily done after a survey of the books has been made.

5. Deriving spiritual lessons from the book's overall thrust. In survey study we especially see what the *important* issues of life are, because we are constantly observing *emphasized* truths. We should never lose sight of this practical goal as we proceed with our survey studies.

C. PROCEDURES OF SURVEY STUDY

After you have studied the background of the writing of a particular book of the Old Testament (e.g., date and authorship), you are ready to survey the Bible text itself. There are various possible procedures to follow in survey study. Basically, however, three main stages are involved: (1) making the initial acquaintance of the book; (2) scanning the individual segments; and (3) seeing how the book holds together. The progression within each stage, and from stage to stage, is this: *from obscurity to sight.* Stated in other ways, the progression is: from first impressions, to repeated impressions, to enduring impressions; or, from the random and indefinite, to the organized and defined.

Some of the things which you will be doing in these stages are described below.[2]

1. Stage One: Making the Initial Acquaintance.

a) Scan the book in one sitting if possible. It is not necessary to read every word or line at this time. If your Bible has paragraph divisions, reading the first sentence of each paragraph will suffice. If your Bible has chapter or paragraph headings, note these as you scan the book.

b) Write down your first impressions of the book.

c) Try to identify the atmosphere of the book as a whole. This is not always detectable at this early stage.

d) List any key words and phrases that stand out as of this first reading.

2. Stage Two: Scanning the Individual Segments.

a) Using the set of segment divisions supplied by this manual, scan each of the segments and determine the main subject of each. (A segment is a group of paragraphs which represent a unit of thought. A segment may be longer or shorter than a chapter.)[3]

b) Assign a segment title to each unit, and record these on paper. (A segment title is a strong word or short phrase, preferably taken from the text, intended to serve as a clue to at least one main part of the segment.) The value of this step of survey is not in the segment title itself, but in the mental process of beginning to identify parts and movements of the book.

c) Record any new observations and impressions of the book, now that you have begun to look at smaller parts.

3. Stage Three: Seeing How the Book Holds Together.

Up to this point most of your observations have been about individual items. In this last stage you should be especially interested to observe how those individual items blend together in a pattern. This will help you see the theme more clearly and in more depth in its full scope. Again, remember that it is important to learn not only *what* God said (content) but *how* He said it (structure).

a) Look for groups of material. Such groupings might be about places, people, things, doctrines, speeches, events, and so forth. For example, Exodus 25-31 is a group of chapters giving specifications for the tabernacle.

---

2. The stages, as such, will not be identified in the survey studies of the succeeding chapters. Basically, however, the procedures will be followed as described here.

3. The nomenclature used in this book is as follows: a segment is a group of paragraphs; a section is a group of segments; and a division is a group of sections.

b) Compare the beginning and end of the book. This will tell you much about the book, especially if it is narrative.

c) Look for a key turning point in the narrative. Not every book has such a pivotal point. The example of 2 Samuel cited earlier illustrates the principle of pivot.

d) Look for a climax. If the book has a climax, try to observe a progression in the story leading up to that point.

e) Read your list of segment titles a few times, and see if you can detect any movement in the action, if the book is historical; or in the discourse, if the book is nonhistorical. Keep working on this until you can formulate an outline of the book. Use paper and pencil freely. The observations you made earlier in this stage will be of great help here.

f) Try to state the book's theme in your own words.

II. Using This Manual as a Guide for Survey Study

The main purpose of this study guide is to help you see for yourself what each book of the Old Testament says. This independent-type study is aptly represented by the word *discovery*. When your personal experience is discovery, the Old Testament will come alive to you in many ways. Dr. James M. Gray, who mastered in the developing and teaching of the book survey method of study, rightly maintained that one's own original and independent study of the broad pattern of a Bible book, imperfect as the conclusions may be, is of far more value to the student than the most perfect outline obtained from someone else. This is not to minimize the work of others, but to emphasize that recourse to outside aids should be made only *after* the student has taken his own skyscraper view.

In serving as a guide, however, this book also includes instructive material to support and supplement your own independent study. The book is neither a commentary nor a so-called introduction to the Old Testament; yet it includes a little of the kind of material found in both of these types of writings.

The various guides and supporting materials of this book are described below.

A. GUIDES

The suggestions for survey study vary throughout the book, depending on which Old Testament book is being studied. The kinds of guides remain constant, however, from book to book.

1. Directions. Specific directions about such things as what to look for, and where, constitute the major part of your survey. You will be constantly urged to record your observations, of whatever kind they are, on paper. Your faithfulness in doing this may make the difference between mediocre and excellent study. As someone has well said, "The pencil is one of the best eyes."

2. Questions. Answering questions is an effective learning experience. Whenever possible, write out your answers. If you faithfully answer the questions and follow all the directions, you will be subconsciously establishing habits and methods of effective Bible study.

3. Uncompleted charts. Occasionally you will have opportunity to record observations on an uncompleted chart which appears in the manual. If you prefer to record these on paper instead, be sure to refer to the chart as you record. Charts as visual aids are effective in representing a panoramic view of Scripture, which is what survey is all about.

4. Applications. Ways to apply the messages of the Old Testament books are suggested at the end of each survey. For example, biblical laws will be seen as defining God's timeless standards; history as furnishing "examples . . . written for our instruction" (1 Cor 10:11); testimonies and prayers (like those of Psalms) as inspiring and challenging; and prophecy as warning and comforting the reader. Also, it is highly recommended that you spend time meditating over key words and phrases, which you will underline in your Bible during the course of your survey. This is one of the best fruits of marking your Bible.

5. Further study. Some readers using this study guide will want to look further into the subjects suggested at the end of each chapter. The continuity of the study guide will not be jeopardized, however, if these optional studies are passed over.

B. SUPPORTING MATERIALS

Along with suggestions for your own survey of the Old Testament books, various kinds of instructive material are given to support your study.

1. Background. The background and setting of each Old Testament book is given at the beginning of each study unit. Much of this information (e.g., date written, authorship) is not always provided in the Bible text; hence, its inclusion here. The treatment can only be brief, due to limitations of space. You may want to refer to supplementary sources for more extensive research.

2. Comments. Much of each study unit includes comments and descriptive notes to furnish substantive positions from which you may launch your surveys.

3. Maps. Much of the Old Testament is history, so it is important to visualize the locations of action. Maps will appear from time to time to help you in the mental focusing.

4. Historical charts. Historical charts similar to Chart 3 show the settings of Bible passages and books. You will find this visual aid valuable for survey study.

5. Completed survey charts. At the end of the survey of each Old Testament book, a completed survey chart appears. It is recommended that you postpone looking at each chart until after you have completed your own survey of the particular book. This will keep the door open for you personally to experience the joys of discovery. Actually, the survey charts which are shown are not exhaustive. You may want to add your own observations and outlines to them.

6. Bibliography. For each book of the Old Testament a few selected works, such as commentaries, are cited as recommended reading.

C. TOOLS FOR SURVEY STUDY

Here is a basic list of recommended study tools:

1. A good study version of the Bible. This should have easy-to-read print, and include cross-references. An edition without commentaries and outlines is best for independent study. This will encourage you to focus on the Bible text itself. Unless otherwise cited, all quotations in this book are from the *New American Standard Bible.* It would help you to have access to a modern speech paraphrase, such as *The Living Bible,* for quick help in obscure passages.

2. An exhaustive concordance.[4] Often you will want to see how many times (and where) a particular word appears in an Old Testament book. Such a concordance shows the pattern with one glance.

3. A one-volume commentary.[5] You will use this mainly in connection with difficult passages or such things as customs, geography, and history.

4. Pencil and paper. Always keep a pencil in your hand while studying, either to mark your Bible or to jot down observations on paper. This advice cannot be overemphasized. Some students like to use a notebook in addition to separate sheets of paper. Recording not

---

4. James Strong's *An Exhaustive Concordance* is recommended especially for survey study.

5. *The Wycliffe Bible Commentary* and *The New Bible Commentary,* rev. ed., are two excellent sources.

only provides a permanent record of what has been observed in Bible study; it also initiates other lines of inquiry.

5. *Colored pencils.* Here is an illustration of how valuable a colored pencil can be: As you survey a book, you might underline in blue every reference to the mercy of God. You would do the same for a few other subjects, using other colors.[6] A comparative study of these underlined references can then be very revealing.

A CONCLUDING THOUGHT

The challenge of studying the Old Testament is a thrilling one indeed. This is because of who its Author is, and what He has written. If you would gain much from the survey study which you are about to embark upon, determine now to spend *time* with much *patience*. The great naturalist Fabre always referred to his two best instruments as "time" and "patience." Patience on the part of young Clyde Tombaugh is what led him finally to discover the planet Pluto. After astronomers calculated a probable orbit for this "suspected" heavenly body that they had never seen, Tombaugh took up the search in March 1929. *Time* magazine records the investigation:

> He examined scores of telescopic photographs, each showing tens of thousands of star images, in pairs under the blink comparator, or dual microscope. It often took three days to scan a single pair. It was exhausting, eye-cracking work—in his own words, "brutal tediousness." And it went on for months. Star by star, he examined 20 million images. Then on February 18, 1930, as he was blinking a pair of photographs in the constellation Gemini, "I suddenly came upon the image of Pluto!" It was the most dramatic astronomic discovery in nearly 100 years, and it was made possible by the patience of an American.[7]

Full Bible study, whether survey or analysis, calls for reflection and meditation. Reflection requires time and concentration, and the good Bible student will give both. For his patience he will be rewarded, as was the astronomer Tombaugh, with the pleasure and excitement of discovering stars of divine truth that he had never seen before.

------

6. The use of color loses its effectiveness whenever it is overdone. Hence, the advice here is to use this particular method of underlining for only a *few* major subjects.

7. *Time* magazine, April 1, 1966, p. 10.

Some Review Questions

1. What are the three phases of Bible study, in the correct order? Justify the order.

2. What basically is survey study? How does it differ from analysis?

3. Why should survey be made before analysis?

4. What are the three general stages of survey study discussed in this chapter? Can you recall some of the things which are done in each stage?

5. What are the values of firsthand, independent Bible study?

6. In what ways does this book serve as a guide to your firsthand study of the Bible? What supporting materials does it furnish to supplement your own personal study?

7. What basic study tools are recommended for your survey studies?

8. Why is the habit of recording observations so important?

Part 1

Origins of the Human Race

and

The Early Centuries of Israel's Life

The first five books of the Bible, known as the Pentateuch, record the origins of the human race, of the chosen Hebrew nation, and of other related institutions and things. He who shrugs off these books as myths or obsolete stories is rejecting the foundations of God's written revelation about Himself and mankind. Every Christian should master these books, and unbelievers must come face to face with their miracle story.

Genesis
Exodus
Leviticus
Numbers
Deuteronomy

3

Genesis: Book of Beginnings

The first five words of the Bible are a very appropriate introduction: "In the beginning God created." This was the first moment of time as we know it, and the coming into being of the universe. God had no beginning, for He existed from eternity, but this was the first work He did *outside of Himself*.[1] The opening subject of origin in Genesis is a clue as to what we may expect to read in the remainder of the book. Genesis is a book of beginnings, a revelation written by the only One qualified to write it—God.

I. Preparation for Study

1. Your approach to Genesis and study of its text will set patterns for your study of the other books of the Old Testament. Depend on the Holy Spirit to open your eyes and heart to the sublime truths of this great first book of the Bible. Genesis is rightly "the foundation on which the whole superstructure of Divine revelation rests."[2]

2. Read John 1:1-5, and compare the opening words with those of Genesis 1:1. Also, read Colossians 1:13-20. According to these two New Testament passages, what part did Christ play in creation and redemption?

II. Background

A. THE PENTATEUCH

Genesis is one of the group of five books called the Pentateuch. Let us look at the group as a whole before we concentrate our attention on Genesis.

---

1. Theologians refer to this as creation *ad extra*.
2. W. Graham Scroggie, *Know Your Bible*, 1:22.

1. Titles. The Jews have always referred to the first five books of
Scripture as the *Torah* ("Law"). Another title frequently assigned to
the books is *Pentateuch* (literally, "fivefold vessel"). The theologian
Origen (A.D. 185-254) may have been the first person to use this
name.

In the Bible itself there are many references to this group of
books. Read the following selected references, and make a list of the
titles: *Old Testament:* Joshua 8:34; 24:26; 2 Kings 22:8; 1 Chronicles
16:40; 2 Chronicles 17:9; Ezra 6:18; Nehemiah 8:1; 9:3; 10:28; Daniel
9:11. *New Testament:* Matthew 12:5; Mark 12:26; Luke 2:23; John
7:23; Galatians 3:10. What do these titles indicate as to the main
subject of the books; the form of communication; and authorship?

2. Unity. Both internal and external evidence support the view
that the first five books of the Old Testament were written by one
author, with one unifying theme. In his book *The Five Books of Moses,*
Oswald T. Allis has ably answered the denials of this view by liberal
critics. At the close of his work he writes,

> Despite the most confident denials of a rationalistically controlled
> literary and historical criticism, the majority of Christians throughout
> the world continue and will continue to believe and maintain that the
> Pentateuch is not a late, anonymous, untrustworthy composite, but is
> correctly described as "The Five Books of Moses," the man of God.[3]

Writing on the internal evidence, Unger says,

> The genuineness and unbroken continuity of its history, the consistency
> of its plan, the sublimity of its purpose, the universality of its appeal,
> the omnitemporality of its message, the coherence of its subject matter,
> the naturalness and beauty of its literary quality and the spirituality of
> its meaning bind it together and demonstrate it to be the work of one
> great mind in vital contact with God.[4]

3. Author. Except for a few parts, such as the reporting of his
own death (Deut 34), Moses wrote the five books of the Law.[5] Such
Mosaic authorship does not rule out the employment of preexisting
documents for writing certain parts of the books.[6] This is normal
procedure for historians, and in the case of biblical authors, it did not
rule out divine inspiration. (Read Deut 31:24-26 for an interesting
reference to Moses' writing. Also, read Exod 17:14; 24:4-8; 34:27; Num
33:1-2; Deut 31:9.)

---

3. Oswald T. Allis, *The Five Books of Moses,* p. 288.
4. Merrill F. Unger, *Introductory Guide to the Old Testament,* p. 274.
5. This is the traditional view, strongly supported by both internal and external
evidence.
6. There is archaeological evidence of the art of writing in the ancient Near East
dated as early as the fourth millennium B.C., which was long before Moses' time.

Moses does not appear in the Bible until the book of Exodus, where specific mention is made of his writing "the words of the LORD" (e.g., Exod 24:4). But although there is no reference in Genesis to writing by Moses, the unity of the Pentateuch points to Mosaic authorship of this first book. Manley says, "No one has yet maintained that Genesis does not form a unity with the other four books. Hence, if Moses is accepted as the author of the legal sections, he may safely be accepted as the author of Genesis."[7] It may be observed here also that the narrative of Exodus is a natural continuation of that of Genesis (read Gen 50:22—Exod 1:7.)

4. Theme. The Pentateuch's theme is historical, legislative, and spiritual. Historically, it records the origins of the human race and the origins and early fortunes of the Hebrew race. Legislatively, it records the laws that God gave to the Hebrew nation, under which they should live. D. A. Hubbard identifies key points of its spiritual thrust:

> It is the record of God's revelation in history and His Lordship over history. It testifies both to Israel's response and to her failure to respond. It witnesses to God's holiness, which separates Him from men, and His gracious love, which binds Him to them on His terms.[8]

A thumbnail sketch of Israel's history as reported in the Pentateuch could be represented thus:

Genesis	Israel's origin and early years	Beginnings
Exodus	Their deliverance from bondage in Egypt	Deliverance
Leviticus	Their worship, directed by the Levites	Legislation
Numbers	Wilderness wanderings in the Sinai Peninsula	Testing
Deuteronomy	Second giving of the Law, awaiting entrance into Canaan	Preparation

B. DATE AND PLACE OF THE WRITING OF GENESIS

There is no specific evidence about this setting. Moses wrote Genesis either during his stay in Egypt or Midian (before 1445 B.C.), or soon after the Exodus, during his wilderness journeys (after 1445 B.C.).[9] The latter view seems more likely.

---

7. G. T. Manley, *The New Bible Handbook*, p. 116.
8. D. A. Hubbard, "Pentateuch," in *The New Bible Commentary*, p. 964.
9. The first forty years (1525-1485 B.C.) of Moses' life were spent in Pharaoh's court. The next forty years (1485-1445 B.C.) saw him in exile in Midian (see Map F).

C. GEOGRAPHY OF GENESIS

Look at Map A, "Three Major Regions of Old Testament History." Note the three key journeys: (1) from Ur to Canaan; (2) from Canaan to Egypt; (3) from Egypt to Canaan. This is the geography involved in most of the Pentateuch, namely, from Genesis 11:28 to the end of Deuteronomy.

The location of the Garden of Eden (Gen 2:8), which was the first dwelling place of man, is unknown. Some think it was north of Babel, where the Euphrates and Tigris rivers are closest to each other.

Note on the map where the region of Ararat is located. According to Genesis 8:4, Noah's ark "rested upon the mountains of Ararat."

Note the location of the city of Babel. This is where the descendants of Noah were building "a tower whose top will reach into heaven" (Gen 11:4). It is in this eleventh chapter that the story of Abraham begins, at the city of Ur.

D. MAIN DATES OF GENESIS 12-50

Chart 6 shows the main dates of the story of Israel as recorded in Genesis 12-50.[10] Study the chart and answer the following:

1. Who lived the longest of the four patriarchs (Abraham, Isaac, Jacob, Joseph)?

2. Was Abraham still living when Jacob was born? How many years passed between Abraham's arrival at Canaan and the moving of Jacob and his family to Egypt?

III. SURVEY

We come now to the heart of our survey study, involving the Bible text. Keep in mind throughout the survey process that you are aiming to see mainly the overall general patterns, and also highlights. To detect patterns you must observe individual items, but only as they are related to the other parts.

1. Note how many chapters there are in Genesis. Scan the whole book by reading the first verse of each chapter. Also, as you move from chapter to chapter, read the headings at the top of your Bible, identifying subject matter. What are your first impressions of the book? What persons and events are among the key parts of Genesis?

2. Next you will want to scan each chapter, not slowly, to observe its main content.[11] Record on paper a segment title for each of

---

10. Dates are from John C. Whitcomb's chart, *Old Testament Patriarchs and Judges*.

11. Each full chapter of Genesis is a study segment, with these exceptions: chapter 25 has two segments, 25:1-18 and 25:19-34. Also, the segment of chapter 37 begins at 37:2*b*. Mark these in your Bible now.

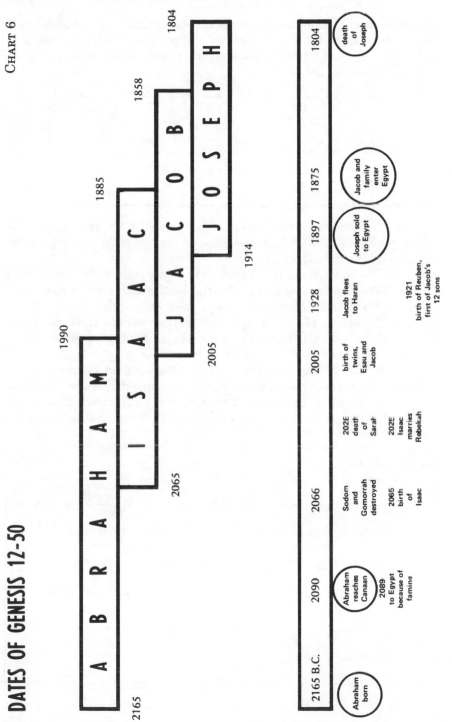

CHART 6

DATES OF GENESIS 12-50

ABRAHAM
2165 1990

ISAAC
2065 1885

JACOB
2005 1858

JOSEPH
1914 1804

2165 B.C. 2090 2066 2005 1928 1897 1875 1804

Abraham born

Abraham reaches Canaan
2089 to Egypt because of famine

Sodom and Gomorrah destroyed
2065 birth of Isaac

2028 death of Sarah
2026 Isaac marries Rebekah

birth of twins, Esau and Jacob

Jacob flees to Haran

1921 birth of Reuben, first of Jacob's 12 sons

Joseph sold to Egypt

Jacob and family enter Egypt

death of Joseph

the segments. (Examples are shown below.) One suggested way to record these titles is on the following oblique chart. What are some of your new impressions of the book after doing this? Do any key words or phrases stand out?

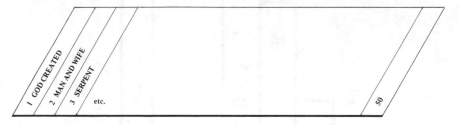

3. Compare the first chapter of Genesis with the last paragraph of the book (50:22-26). What are some of your conclusions, especially concerning the human race?

4. The story of Israel begins with Abraham, when God called him to leave his country and go "to the land which I will show you." Read 12:1-3. (Note: Abraham's name was originally Abram. Read 17:5 for the origin of the change.) From your survey thus far, what names of Abraham's descendants are prominent in Genesis from chapter 12 to the end of the book?

5. What are the prominent events recorded in chapters 1-11? Compare your observations thus far with the outlines of Chart 7. How was sin involved in the three stories of the Fall, Flood, and Babel tower? How does such a setting introduce the story that begins with Abraham's call?

GENESIS 1-50   CHART 7

1		12	50
EVENTS PREDOMINANT		PERSONS PREDOMINANT	
CREATION–FALL–FLOOD–BABEL TOWER		ABRAHAM–ISAAC–JACOB–JOSEPH	
The race as a whole		*The family of Abraham*	

6. Scan the book of Genesis again and note generally what chapters are about the above four events and four persons.

7. Think more about the contents of chapters 1-11. In these chapters are recorded many *firsts,* — for example, the first man and woman. List on paper other prominent firsts or origins of these chapters. Compare your list with that shown on the survey Chart 11.

8. A key phrase of Genesis is "these are the generations of."[12] The phrase is always the heading of the section which follows. For example, "the generations of Shem" (11:10) introduces the section dealing with the offspring of Shem (11:10-12). Read each of the following references where the phrase (or a similar one) appears, and record on paper the names involved: 2:4; 5:1; 6:9; 10:1; 11:10; 11:27; 25:12; 25:19; 36:1; 37:2. The continuous chain of genealogical listings from Adam to the descendants of Jacob (37:2-4) shows the line in which the Saviour, Jesus, was to be born (cf. Luke 3:23-38). One of the main purposes of the formal genealogies of the Old Testament is to teach spiritual lessons, such as God's faithfulness to the *heirs* of promise.[13]

At times in Genesis a parallel line is recorded, but the narrative returns quickly to that of the chosen people. (Examples of such related lines are those of Cain, 4:16-24; and of Ishmael, 25:12-18.)

9. The interval of time from Adam to Abraham (chaps. 1-11) was over two thousand years,[14] whereas it was only about three hundred years from Abraham to Joseph's death (chaps. 12-50). Stated another way, only one-fifth of the book of Genesis is devoted to such vital subjects as creation and the Fall, as compared with four-fifths devoted to the four patriarchs Abraham, Isaac, Jacob, and Joseph. What does this quantitative distribution reveal, if anything, about the purpose and message of Genesis?

10. Relate the narrative of Genesis to the regions of Map A. Where did most of chapters 1-11, involving the human race, take place? Where was the remainder of the action?

11. Study the survey Chart 11. Observe how various outlines have been recorded on the chart, involving survey studies made up to this point. Note that Abraham, Isaac, Jacob, and Joseph are the main characters, respectively, beginning at these references: 12:1; 25:19; 27:1; and 37:2*b.* A quick look at a concordance shows the births of

---

12. The word "generations" in this phrase signifies "that which is begotten."
13. Manley, p. 126.
14. There is no way of knowing how long this interval was, even though the genealogical listings include time data.

these patriarchs at 11:26; 21:3; 25:26; 30:24. Hence, the overlappings on the chart.

In the next study unit, you may want to try recording your studies of Exodus by this chart method. What are some of the values of such a chart?

IV. PROMINENT SUBJECTS

The purpose of these studies is to focus on each of the prominent subjects of Genesis, without making any detailed analysis. Again, our interest is mainly in the highlights of the passages involved, in keeping with the survey method.

The order of subjects to be studied is the order in which they appear in the Bible text.

A. CREATION OF THE HEAVENS AND THE EARTH (1:1—2:3)

1. First, read the passage, observing key repeated words and phrases. Then scan the contents of 2:4-25. How are the following structural laws evidenced in the total passage?

Law of Particularization (moving from the general
    to the particular):
             universe (1:1-5)
             earth (1:6-31)
             man (1:26-30; 2:7-25)

Law of Progression: What is the climactic creative work
    of the six days?

Law of Centrality: Who is the principal person of the account?

2. Observe fiat[15] and fulfillment repeated throughout the account.

3. Do you observe any pattern in the creations of the six days:

(1) light	(4) light bearers
(2) firmament, divisions of waters	(5) birds, fishes
(3) dry land, vegetation	(6) animals, man

(7) day of rest

B. GENERATIONS OF THE HEAVENS AND THE EARTH (2:4-15)

The statement of 2:4 introduces the account, not of the creation of the heavens and the earth, but, rather, of man for whom they had been created as the stage.[16]

1. How was the first man created? How was the first woman created?

2. How do chapters 1 and 2 distinguish man from animal life? Consider his distinctives (cf. 1:27), his dominion, and his destiny.

---

15. Latin for "let it be done."
16. See Edward J. Young, *Introduction to the Old Testament*, p. 54.

3. The Bible text does not date the creation of man. It has been correctly observed that the *unity* of the human race is of far greater theological import than its *antiquity*. Does Genesis teach the unity of the human race?

4. What is revealed about God by chapters 1 and 2?

C. THE FALL OF MAN (3:1—4:26)

First, read the passage. Without telling where the serpent originated, the opening verse of chapter 4 narrates his spiritual attack upon Eve. Read 2 Corinthians 11:3,[17] which confirms that this story is historical fact. Also read Revelation 12:9 and 20:2, where the serpent is identified as Satan.

1. Who are the main characters of chapter 3? Of chapter 4? How are the two stories related to each other?

2. What parts of the account teach the following:
a) the deceitful activity of Satan against man
b) the righteous indictment of God against sinful man
c) the gracious provisions of God
d) the bright promise of God to slay man's enemy (3:15; cf. John 12:31; Rev 12:9-11)
e) the ongoing propagation of the human race

3. Compare the relations of man to God at the time of these three verses: 3:8; 3:24; 4:26.

4. What do the two chapters teach about God? What do they teach about man's sin and guilt, and about how he may be restored to communion with God?

D. THE FLOOD (6:1—9:29)

1. What was the spiritual condition of mankind which brought on the judgment of the Flood?

2. Noah was spared because he "found favor in the eyes of the LORD" (6:8). What was the basis for that favor? (Cf. 6:22; 7:1,5; 8:20; Heb 11:7.)

3. How cataclysmic was the Flood? (7:11, 21-23; cf. 2 Pet 3:4-7). Does this suggest a universal flood?

4. The sequel to judgment is always significant. Evaluate these sequels:
Noah's altar (8:20; the first altar of the Bible)
God's benediction (9:1-7)
Covenant with Noah and his descendants (9:9-17)

---

17. Cf. John 8:44.

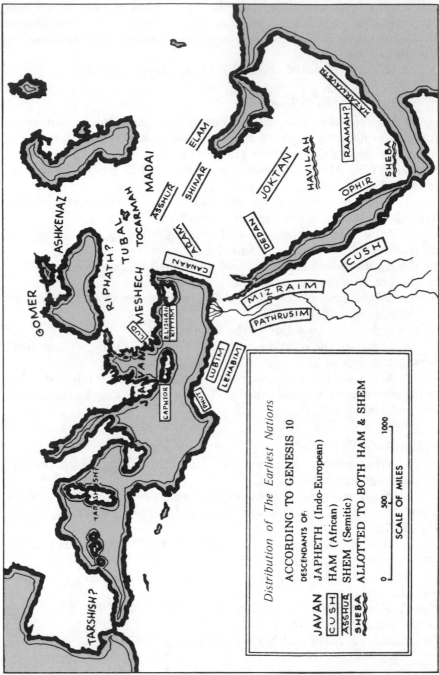

Distribution of The Earliest Nations

ACCORDING TO GENESIS 10

DESCENDANTS OF:

JAVAN JAPHETH (Indo-European)
CUSH HAM (African)
ASSHUR SHEM (Semitic)
SHEBA ALLOTTED TO BOTH HAM & SHEM

SCALE OF MILES

0   500   1000

E. THE BIRTH OF NATIONS (10:1—11:32)

These two chapters form a link between Noah and Abraham through the line of Shem. Shem was the second son of Noah, and the progenitor of the Semitic race.[18] First read 10:1, followed by 11:10-27. The chronological order of events was: (1) Flood (2) new start of the human race in the family of Noah (3) migration to Shinar and the building projects (city and tower) at Babel (4) confusion of languages and geographical scattering. Now read 10:2-32. (Note the opening phrases of verses 2,6,22.) The geographical distribution cited in chapter 10 (e.g., 10:19) was subsequent to the dispersion of 11:9. Refer to Map D and observe where the descendants of Noah were scattered. In what general direction were the sons of Japheth scattered? The sons of Ham? The sons of Shem?

1. What important spiritual lessons are taught by the Babel story (11:1-9)? Was this judgment irreparable? (See Acts 17:26-27.)

2. The name "Abram" (Abraham) appears first in the Bible at 11:26. Abraham was the father of the nation Israel. In what ways do chapters 10 and 11 introduce the story of this great patriarch?

F. ABRAHAM, FATHER OF ISRAEL (12:1—25:18)

Up to this point the narrative of Genesis is about the human race as a whole. Beginning at chapter 12, and continuing to the end of the Old Testament, the story focuses on the family of Abraham, that is, the nation of Israel. This supports the conclusion that the Bible is not so much the history of man as it is *the history of the redemption of man.* Merrill Unger comments, "Heretofore the divine healing had been with the whole Adamic race, now sunk into universal idolatry. God purges off a tiny rill through which he will eventually purify the great river itself."[19]

We should observe here that the world of Genesis 11 was in spiritual darkness, without hope. God's call to Abraham thus began a new chapter in world history.

1. Review your survey of chapters 12-25. You may want to scan the chapters once more to see their highlights. Follow Abraham's journeys with the help of Map A and Map E.

2. God's call and promise to Abraham are milestones in Bible history. First read Acts 7:2-4 and note where Abraham was when God called him (cf. Gen 11:31). Then compare the promises which God gave to Abraham at these places:

---

18. The word *Semitic* is derived from the name *Shem.* Some think the word *Hebrew* can be traced to Eber, great-grandson of Shem (Gen 11:14).
19. Merrill F. Unger, *Unger's Bible Handbook,* p. 63.

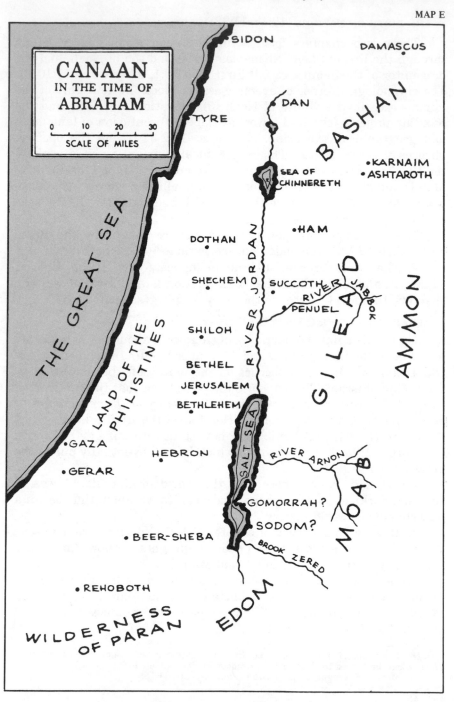

CANAAN
IN THE TIME OF
ABRAHAM

0   10   20   30
SCALE OF MILES

THE GREAT SEA

SIDON

DAMASCUS

TYRE

DAN

BASHAN

SEA OF
CHINNERETH

KARNAIM
ASHTAROTH

DOTHAN

HAM

RIVER JORDAN

SHECHEM

SUCCOTH

RIVER
JABBOK

PENUEL

GILEAD

AMMON

LAND OF THE PHILISTINES

SHILOH

BETHEL

JERUSALEM

BETHLEHEM

SALT SEA

GAZA

HEBRON

RIVER ARNON

GERAR

GOMORRAH?

SODOM?

MOAB

BEER-SHEBA

BROOK ZERED

REHOBOTH

EDOM

WILDERNESS
OF PARAN

Haran: 12:1-3
Shechem: 12:7
Bethel: 13:14-17
Hebron: 15:5,18; 17:1-8

3. One thing which is prominent in this story of Abraham is the many times God tested his character. These were purifying and strengthening experiences, designed by God to build solid foundations for the family of Israel. Below is an outline of these chapters related to the topic, *Abraham's Tests*. Read each passage in the Bible text, observing the different kinds, purposes, and outcomes of the tests.

Test of Obedience   (12:1)
Test of Values   (13:5-18)
Test of Love and Loyalty   (14:1-24)
Tests of Faith   (15:1—21:34)
The Most Severe Test   (22:1-19)
Final Years   (22:20—25:18)

4. Read again God's call to Abraham (12:1-3). What does the last line of that call reveal about the ultimate purpose of Israel's calling? Then read the verses cited below, which reveal some of the ways Israel was to perform its mission.

As custodian of divine revelation   (Deut 4:5-8; Rom 3:1-2)
As witness to heathen in darkness   (Isa 43:9-12)
As witness of the security of serving God   (Deut 33:16-29)
As blood location (i.e., physical line) for the birth of the Messiah   (Gen 49:10)

G. ISAAC, CHILD OF PROMISE (25:19—26:35)

Steven Barabas describes Isaac thus:

> Of the three patriarchs [Abraham, Isaac, Jacob], Isaac was the least conspicuous, traveled the least, had the fewest extraordinary adventures, and lived the longest. He was free from violent passions; quiet, gentle, dutiful; less a man of action than of thought and suffering.[20]

1. First read 21:2-3 and 35:29, which record Isaac's birth and death. The span of Isaac's life thus covers fifteen chapters of Genesis. But he is the main character only in the short section 25:19—26:35, as shown on Chart 11. Read this passage.

2. Isaac was a strong spiritual link in the chain of the earliest patriarchs. When Abraham died, God's blessing of Israel continued through Isaac. Read 26:24-25 for God's renewal of the promise given earlier to Abraham.

---

20. Steven Barabas, "Isaac," in *The Zondervan Pictorial Bible Dictionary*, p. 383.

H. JACOB, THE TRANSFORMED BROTHER (27:1—37:2a)

The story of Jacob shows how God can lay hold of a selfish, willful, deceitful man striving by his own efforts to gain material blessing, and so transform his life that in the end his character is noble and beautiful, with a new outlook on what is true blessing.

1. Review Chart 11 and note that Jacob is the main character of ten chapters of Genesis (27:1—37:2a). Chart 8 shows a general breakdown of these chapters. Record the outlines and divisions in your Bible. The geographical outline shows Jacob in three places, with a journey in between each.[21] What does the two-part outline on *blessing* suggest about Jacob's career?

JACOB THE SUPPLANTER   CHART 8

27:1	28:5	29:1	31:1	33:18	37:2a
IN CANAAN	JOURNEY	IN PADDAN—ARAM	RETURN	IN CANAAN	
~~	TO	~~~~~~~~~~	TO	~~~~~~~~~~	
deceitful Jacob	*Paddan-Aram*	*marriages of Jacob*	*Canaan*	*transformed Jacob*	
STRIVING FOR BLESSING			LEARNING TRUE BLESSING		

2. Read 25:19-34 for the story of the birth of Jacob.

3. Read 27:1—30:43 with a view to seeing how Jacob strove to gain blessing. On paper, record the experiences of these passages: 27:1—28:9; 28:10-22; 29:1-30; 29:31—30:24; 30:25-43. How was the experience of 28:10-22 different from the others? Why was it crucial?

4. Jacob's four wives—Leah, Zilpah, Bilhah, and Rachel—bore twelve sons to Jacob. Most of these names later became the names of the twelve tribes of Israel.[22] Read 29:32—30:24 and 35:18 for the names of the sons. Check the names with those shown on Chart 9.

5. For how Jacob learned true blessing, read 31:1—37:2a. Briefly stated, this is a story of Jacob's immediate problems; of their solutions; and of his finally seeing who he really was and then surrendering completely to God. The highlights of the chapters are the three times when Jacob had an experience with God.

---

21. Paddan-Aram is either the region where Haran is located, or another name for Haran itself. See Map A for the location of Haran.

22. In the land allotments to the tribes, the sons of Levi (Levites) were given no land inheritance. Also, Joseph was represented in two shares of territory by his sons, Ephraim and Manasseh.

These were at Haran (31:1-16); at Peniel (32:22-32); and at Bethel (35:1-15).

6. Read 32:22-32. In what ways was this Peniel experience a spiritual turning point in Jacob's career?

7. Jacob's experiences at Bethel (35:1-15) were the brightest of his life. Compare these with the earlier crisis experience at Bethel, as recorded in 28:10-17 (over twenty years earlier).

I. JOSEPH, BELOVED SON OF JACOB (37:2*b*—50:26)

Even though Joseph was not of the Messianic line (Chart 9), of the twelve sons of Jacob, God sovereignly chose him to be the benefactor of Israel during the next crucial years of dwelling in Egypt. While in Egypt, the descendants of Joseph and his brothers

PATRIARCHAL FAMILY TREE   CHART 9

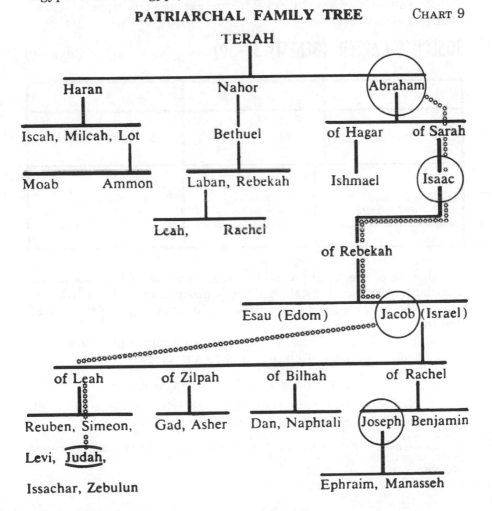

multiplied rapidly, and soon became a large nation. (See Exod 1:7, *The Living Bible.*)

1. Chart 10 shows a broad survey of Joseph's career. Read Genesis 37-50 with this overview in mind. What kind of a man was Joseph? Consider how some of his experiences were *types* of Christ's ministry. (An Old Testament *type* is a figure or representation of something to come.) A type's fulfillment (antitype) usually is seen in the New Testament. About half of the Old Testament types foreshadow the person and ministry of Christ. The patriarch Joseph is considered by some to be the most complete type of Christ. For example, he was acknowledged to be the saviour and ruler of Egypt (Gen 47:25); and Christ shall be acknowledged as Saviour and Ruler of the world (Phil 2:10-11).[23]

2. You may want to develop an extended outline of these chapters about Joseph.

JOSEPH'S CAREER (GENESIS 37-50)   CHART 10

37	41	46 50
PRISONER	BENEFACTOR	SON AND BROTHER
separated from his family	42 *reunited with his family*	*dwelling with his family*

3. One of the bright verses toward the end of Genesis is the Messianic promise of 49:10. This is a promise of Judah's inheritance, to be fully realized in the person of Jesus Christ, of the line of Judah.

4. Read Genesis 50:24. How is this an appropriate conclusion to the book of Genesis? Relate it to 3:19 and 12:1-3.

V. KEY WORDS AND VERSES OF GENESIS

1. Now that you have seen the highlights of Genesis, what verses would you consider as key verses in the book?

---

23. See John F. Walvoord, *Jesus Christ Our Lord,* pp. 62-78, for a good discussion of this subject.

2. Write a list of key words and phrases.

3. In your own words, what is the theme of Genesis?

VI. APPLICATIONS

Applications of the text of Genesis have been suggested from time to time in the previous studies. Here are a few more of the prominent ones:

1. If you are a Christian, why would you appreciate the message of Genesis more than one who is not a believer? How is this book related to the ministry of Christ? In what ways is Genesis an important message for unbelievers?

2. God referred to Himself as "the God of Abraham, the God of Isaac, and the God of Jacob" (Exod 3:6,15). Why would He use such a title?

3. In what ways is man distinct from animals? What are the implications of this, as related to man's present life and his future destiny?

4. What does Genesis teach about the sins of man? What kinds of sins stand out in the Genesis account? What are the practical applications of these teachings?

5. How do Romans 5:12 and 1 Corinthians 15:21-22 interpret the account of man's first sin?

6. What have you learned from Genesis about the following (cite specific examples):
the omnipotence and omniscience of God
the holiness of God
the grace of God
the sovereignty of God

7. What traits of godly living are manifested in the stories of Genesis?

8. Why do you think Abraham was called the "friend" of God (2 Chron 20:7; Isa 41:8; James 2:23)?

9. Why has God chosen frail and sinful men to be His channels of communication?

10. How was a person saved during the patriarchal era? (Cf. Gen 15:6 and Rom 4:1-5.)

11. What sacrifices and altars do you recall studying in Genesis? Are sacrifices and altars part of Christian living? If so, what kind? (E.g., Rom 12:1.)

12. Divine electing grace, one of the Bible's great mysteries, is prominent in Genesis. Read Ephesians 1:4-6. Then consider these examples:

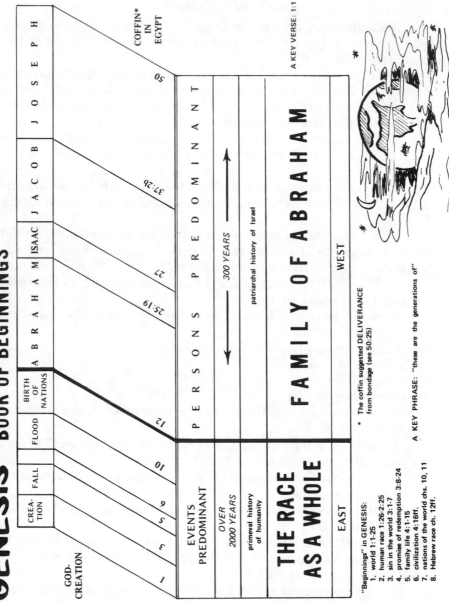

GENESIS BOOK OF BEGINNINGS

A KEY VERSE: 1:1

| GOD-CREATION | CREA-TION | FALL | FLOOD | BIRTH OF NATIONS | A B R A H A M | ISAAC | J A C O B | J O S E P H | COFFIN* IN EGYPT |

| 1 | 3 | 5 | 6 | 10 | 12 | 25:19 | 27 | 37:2b | 50 |

EVENTS PREDOMINANT

OVER 2000 YEARS

primeval history of humanity

THE RACE AS A WHOLE

EAST

P E R S O N S   P R E D O M I N A N T

← *300 YEARS* →

patriarchal history of Israel

FAMILY OF ABRAHAM

WEST

"Beginnings" in GENESIS:
1. world 1:1-25
2. human race 1:26-2:25
3. sin in the world 3:1-7
4. promise of redemption 3:8-24
5. family life 4:1-15
6. civilization 4:16ff.
7. nations of the world chs. 10, 11
8. Hebrew race ch. 12ff.

*   The coffin suggested DELIVERANCE from bondage (see 50:25)

A KEY PHRASE: "these are the generations of"

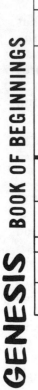

Of Adam's sons, Cain drops out, and Seth is taken; of Noah's sons, Ham and Japheth drop out, and Shem is taken; of Terah's sons, Nahor and Haran drop out, and Abram is taken; of Abraham's sons, Ishmael drops out, and Isaac is taken; of Isaac's sons, Esau drops out, and Jacob is taken; and of Jacob's sons, Judah is elected to be the line of the Messiah (chapter xlix. 10). *Beneath and behind the historic redemption is the eternal election* (italics added).[24]

VII. FURTHER STUDY

Subjects suggested for extended study are:
1. The length of the days of Genesis 1.
2. The antiquity of the earth and man.
3. The origin of Satan.
4. Extent of the Noahic Flood: universal or local.
5. Messianic passages of Genesis.
6. Types of Christ in Genesis.
7. Names of God in these chapters: 1, 2, 14, 17, 31, 48, 49.
8. Character studies of the key persons of Genesis (a Bible dictionary is a good source book for this).

VIII. SELECTED READING

GENESIS AND SCIENCE

American Scientific Affiliation Symposium. *Modern Science and Christian Faith*, pp. 1-195.
Frair, Wayne, and Davis, P. William. *The Case for Creation*
Harris, R. Laird. *Man: God's Eternal Creation.*
Kelso, James L. *Archaeology and the Ancient Testament,* pp. 20-32.
Lammerts, Walter E., ed. *Scientific Studies in Special Creation.*
Marsh, Frank Lewis. *Life, Man and Time.*
Whitcomb, John C. *The Early Earth.*
Whitcomb, John C., and Morris, Henry M. *The Genesis Flood.*

HISTORICAL SURVEYS AND BACKGROUNDS

Archer, Gleason L. *A Survey of Old Testament Introduction,* pp. 169-208.
Baumann, Hans. *In the Land of Ur.*
Edersheim, Alfred. *The Bible History,* 1: 17-190.
Kelso, James L. *Archaeology and the Ancient Testament,* pp. 28-76.
Kitchen, K. A. *Ancient Orient and Old Testament,* pp. 35-111.
Livingston, G. Herbert. *The Pentateuch in Its Cultural Environment.*
Payne, J. Barton. *An Outline of Hebrew History,* pp. 33-48.
Pfeiffer, Charles F. *Patriarchal Age.*

---

24. Scroggie, 1:22.

Sampey, J. R. *The Heart of the Old Testament,* pp. 15-41.
Unger, Merrill F. *Unger's Bible Handbook,* pp. 36-82.
Walvoord, John F. *Jesus Christ Our Lord,* pp. 36-95. Three chapters are
    about Christ in Old Testament history, typology, and prophecy.
Wood, Leon J. *A Survey of Israel's History,* pp. 27-82.
Young, Edward J. *An Introduction to the Old Testament,* pp. 47-66.

COMMENTARIES

Carroll, B. H. *Genesis.*
Davis, John J. *Paradise to Prison.*
DeHaan, M. R. *Portraits of Christ in Genesis.*
Driver, S. R. *The Book of Genesis.* Westminster Commentary.
Erdman, Charles R. *The Book of Genesis.*
Pfeiffer, Charles F. *The Book of Genesis.*
Pieters, Albertus. *Notes on Genesis.*
Ryle, H. E. *The Book of Genesis.*
Yates, Kyle M. "Genesis." In *The Wycliffe Bible Commentary.*

4

Exodus: Book of Redemption

The book of Exodus reports the first of God's deliverances of Israel, as He had promised Abraham. This second book of the Pentateuch picks up the story where Genesis left it, and so it is its sequel. In Genesis the divine purpose is revealed, and in Exodus the divine performance is exhibited.[1]

This deliverance from bondage was a crucial event in the experience of the Israelites. Centuries later, many authors of the prophetic books and Psalms acclaimed it as the most significant miracle in their history. The deliverance is a beautiful type of the sinner's redemption from the bondage of sin. Thus Exodus is rightly called the "Book of Redemption."

I. PREPARATORY FOR STUDY

1. Recall the highlights of Genesis, as you surveyed that "Book of Beginnings." Review especially the survey Chart 11 and the chronology of Chart 6.

2. Various comparisons may be made of Genesis and Exodus. Study the following comparisons, which will give you a general idea as to what to anticipate in the book you are about to study.[2]

GENESIS	EXODUS
human effort and failure	divine power and triumph
word of promise	work of fulfillment
a people chosen	a people called
God's electing mercy	God's electing manner
revelation of nationality	realization of nationality

---

1. See W. Graham Scroggie, *Know Your Bible,* 1:26.
2. The comparisons are from Scroggie, ibid.

CHART 12

THE ISRAELITES IN EGYPT

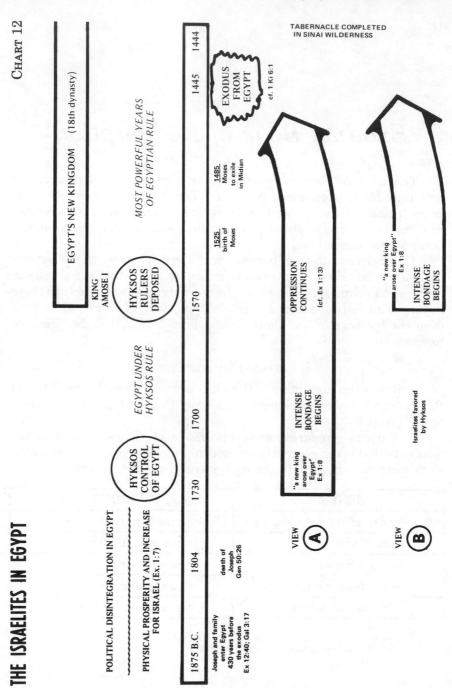

II. Background

A. TITLE

The English title *Exodus* originated with the Greek Septuagint's *Exodos* ("departure," or "exit"). The title appropriately represents the key event of the book, the Israelites' miraculous flight from bondage in Egypt.

B. WRITING

Moses probably wrote this book soon after the completion of the tabernacle, described in Exodus 35-40. The date is in the last half of the fifteenth century B.C. (The tabernacle was completed in 1444 B.C. Cf. 40:17.)

C. HISTORICAL SETTING

Chart 12 shows the highlights of the historical setting of Exodus. Study it carefully to gain a clear historical perspective of this second book of the Bible.

Note the following on this chart:

1. A general survey of Egypt's political status is shown above the dateline. The two key events are the Hyksos invasion of Egypt (1730 B.C.), and the overthrow of this foreign group (1570 B.C.)[3]

2. References to Israel are shown below the dateline.

3. Read Exodus 1:7. Where on Chart 12 is this verse dated?

4. Read Exodus 1:8. There are two different views as to the identity of this "new king." View Ⓐ identifies him as one of the Hyksos rulers[4] According to View Ⓑ, the "new king" was Amose I, the first of the eighteenth dynasty.[5] The main practical difference between the two views is the *duration* of Israel's oppression

5. The date of the Exodus is shown as 1445 B.C.[6] This is derived from two sets of facts:

Arrival of Jacob and his family in Egypt	1875 B.C.
Duration of stay in Egypt (Exod 12:40; Gal 3:17)	− 430 years
	= 1445 B.C.

Beginning of Solomon's Temple	965 B.C.
Interval since the Exodus (1 Kings 6:1)	+ 480 years
	= 1445 B.C.

---

3. The Hyksos were Asiatic seminomads of Semitic origin. Very little is known about them. Their use of a new weapon, the horse-drawn chariot, was the key to their conquest of Egypt.

4. This view is held by Gleason Archer and John Whitcomb.

5. Among the writers who hold to View B. are Samuel Schultz, J. Barton Payne, and W. T. Purkiser.

6. A later date of 1270 B.C. is held by some. Read Leon Wood, *A Survey of Israel's History,* pp. 83-109, for a thorough discussion of the date of the Exodus.

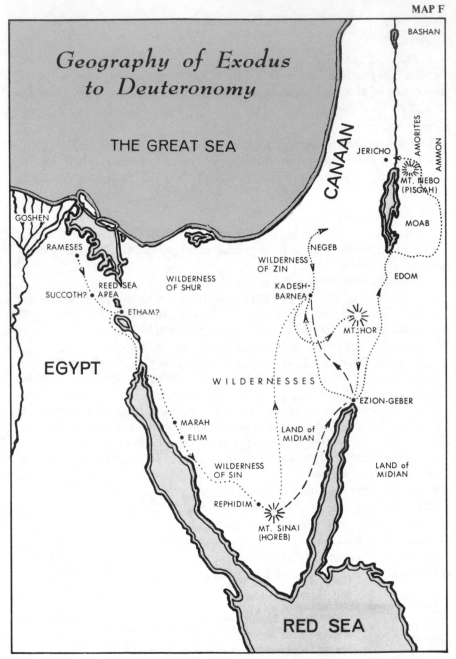

Geography of Exodus
to Deuteronomy

THE GREAT SEA

GOSHEN

BASHAN

CANAAN

JERICHO

AMORITES

AMMON

MT. NEBO
(PISGAH)

MOAB

NEGEB

EDOM

RAMESES

WILDERNESS
OF ZIN

WILDERNESS
OF SHUR

REED SEA
AREA

KADESH-
BARNEA

SUCCOTH?

ETHAM?

MT. HOR

EGYPT

W I L D E R N E S S E S

EZION-GEBER

MARAH

ELIM

LAND of
MIDIAN

LAND of
MIDIAN

WILDERNESS
OF SIN

REPHIDIM

MT. SINAI
(HOREB)

RED SEA

— — — — Alternate possible route from Sinai to Kadesh

6. How soon after the Exodus was the wilderness tabernacle completed?

7. Note how much Israelite history had transpired before the birth of Moses. Does this suggest to you any spiritual lessons?

D. GEOGRAPHY

Map F shows where the action of Exodus took place. Learn this geography so that you can visualize the book's narrative. Note the location of Goshen. This is where the Israelites were dwelling in Egypt. Read Exodus 8:22 and 9:26.

III. SURVEY

1. Begin your study of the text of Exodus by scanning the forty chapters of the book in one sitting. Look at each chapter just long enough to identify its general content. Don't read every verse, nor tarry over details. The first verse of each chapter is often a clue to the chapter's message. Also, your Bible may show general content at the top of each page. The purpose of this initial scanning is to get the "feel" of the book and observe its "flow" or progression. Always keep a pencil in your hand as you survey the text, and feel free to make notations in your Bible. Write down on a sheet of paper your impressions thus far, and record any key words or phrases that have stood out from the text.

2. Now go back to each chapter and secure from the text of each chapter a picturesque word or short phrase which will represent a leading thought in the chapter. Record your forty chapter titles on a chart similar to the following:

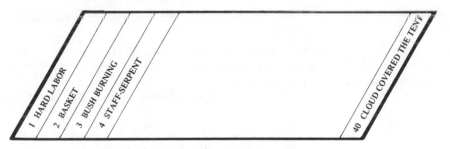

When you have done this, you will have a fair grasp of at least the large movements or groups of material in Exodus.

For help in completing the remaining study suggestions and questions, refer to these chapter titles as well as the text of the Bible.

3. Observe how the opening paragraph (1:1-7) records without

fanfare the emergence of a large nation of Israel from the small, original nucleus.[7] Compare the state of Israel in 1:8-14 with that suggested by the last five verses of chapter 40.

4. What are some of the major events in Exodus? Who is the main character? In what chapter is his birth recorded?

5. Often in the Bible a group of chapters (called a section) is about one common subject. In what sections are these subjects found (record approximate chapters):

plagues upon Egypt:

journey from Egypt to Sinai:

commandments of God:

specifications for the tabernacle:

construction of the tabernacle:

6. Geographically, Exodus is of three parts:

Israel in Egypt

Israel to Sinai

Israel at Sinai

At what place in the book (chapter, verse) do the Israelites begin their journey to Sinai? What verse reports the arrival of the Israelites at Sinai? (Note: An exhaustive concordance will answer this latter question quickly. Look up the word *Sinai*.)

7. The following two outlines represent the general contents of Exodus. At what chapter does the second division begin?

①	narrative	legislative
②	DELIVERANCE	WORSHIP

8. What chapter records the institution of the Passover sacrifices? Read the chapter and begin to ponder why this event was a turning point in Israel's experience.

9. Before you complete your study of Exodus you will want to

---

7. By the time of their departure from Egypt, the Israelites numbered over two million. This figure is based on Exodus 12:37 and Numbers 1:46. Here are the calculations, made with the two assumptions indicated by an asterisk (*):

603,550	(warriors over twenty)
+ equal number*	(all other males)
= at least one million	(total males)
+ equal number*	(total females)
= at least two million	(total population)

See C. F. Keil and F. Delitzsch, *The Pentateuch,* 3: 5-15; and Edward J. Young, *An Introduction to the Old Testament,* pp. 88-89, for a defense of the two million plus population of Israel during the wilderness journeys.

assign key words and key verses to the book. Have you decided on any of these yet?

10. Now refer to Chart 15 and view the total structure of this book of Exodus. Compare its outlines with the studies you have already made. Observe among other things that the book is of two main parts *and also* of three main parts. Are any spiritual lessons suggested by the things recorded on the chart? For example, is there any significance that the Israelites had wilderness experiences before receiving God's Law?

11. The dates shown at the bottom of Chart 15 are those used earlier in this chapter. How many chapters of Exodus represent about one year of Israel's experience? How many about eighty years? What is the time spread in chapter 1? What does this unequal assignment of reporting tell you about God's purposes in His written Word? For example, why so many chapters about the tabernacle, as compared with the single-verse reporting of the success story of 1:7?

12. On the basis of your study thus far, how would you state the theme of Exodus? Try to include in that theme the message of each of the two parts of the book, namely, *deliverance* and *worship*. For example, as a book about Israel's deliverance, Exodus describes the nation's redemption *from* the bondage of Egypt and *unto* a covenant relationship with God (cf. 19:5).

It is in Exodus that Israel emerges as God's covenant nation. Here is Archer's summary of the book:

> It relates how God fulfilled His ancient promise to Abraham by multiplying his descendants into a great nation, redeeming them from the land of bondage, and renewing the covenant of grace with them on a national basis. At the foot of the holy mountain He bestows on them the promises of the covenant, and provides them with a rule of conduct by which they may lead a holy life, and also with a sanctuary in which they may make offerings for sin and renew fellowship with Him on the basis of forgiving grace.[8]

13. You may want to refer to outside sources for detailed outlines of the Book of Exodus.[9]

IV. PROMINENT SUBJECTS

Eight words represent the multicolored narrative of Exodus: bondage, Moses, plagues, Passover, exodus, commandments, idolatry,

---

8. Gleason L. Archer, *A Survey of Old Testament Introduction*, p. 209.
9. Excellent outlines appear in ibid., pp. 209-10; Scroggie, 1:27-28; Philip C. Johnson, "Exodus," in *The Wycliffe Bible Commentary*, p. 52; J. C. Connell, "Exodus," in *The New Bible Commentary*, pp. 106-7.

tabernacle. A few study questions and suggestions are given below in connection with each of these subjects. These are not exhaustive, but they are intended to touch on some of the highlights. Look for spiritual applications as you study. Be sure to read the passages involved.

A. BONDAGE AND OPPRESSION (1:8-22)

Compare God and the king of Egypt in these verses. How do you reconcile the sovereignty of God with the vast powers of evil rulers in the world?

B. MOSES, LEADER OF ISRAEL (2:1—7:13)

Moses has been called "one of the most colossal and majestic characters in the history of the world."[10] Read this interesting account of his early life and ministry, and record the subject of each of these sections:

2:1-10
2:11-25
3:1-12
3:13-22
4:1-31
5:1—7:13

What prominent truths stand out in this story?

C. DEMONSTRATIONS OF GOD'S POWER (7:14—11:10; 12:29-36)

As you read this story, try to arrive at answers to these questions: What was the real issue of the confrontation between Moses and Pharaoh? What was the purpose of these miraculous signs? (Cf. 4:5,8, 30-31.) Why so many plagues? Why did the judgments of the first nine plagues not soften Pharaoh's heart? (Cf. 11:9-10.)

The passages describing the ten judgments are listed below:

1. blood (7:14-25)
2. frogs (8:1-15)
3. lice (8:16-19)
4. flies (8:20-32)
5. livestock pestilence (9:1-7)

6. boils (9:8-12)
7. hail (9:13-25)
8. locusts (10:1-20)
9. darkness (10:21-29)
10. death of firstborn (11:1-10; 12:29-36)

D. PASSOVER (12:1-28)

The night of the Passover sacrifices was a turning point in the history of Israel (see Chart 15). It was the beginning of a new era for the people of God, who had multiplied in number and now were about

---

10. Charles R. Erdman, *The Book of Exodus*, p. 7.

to be redeemed from the clutches of their oppressor (cf. 6:6-7). A new calendar was instituted (12:2), and the Israelites' experience was to be annually commemorated as a permanent ordinance (12:14). When the deep spiritual significance of the Passover is seen, one can well understand God's design in assigning crisis, pathos, awe, pageantry, and memorial status to the events beginning at the stroke of midnight.

The Passover chapter is also a key chapter of the whole Bible. As you read it, look for what is taught about divine holiness, election and grace, and man's sin and salvation. Why did God institute blood sacrifice as an atonement ritual? In answering this, relate blood to life (cf. Heb 9:22).

E. RED SEA DELIVERANCE AND WILDERNESS JOURNEY (12:37—18:27)

We saw in our survey study that the first eighteen chapters of Exodus relate Israel's *deliverance,* while the remaining chapters concern their *worship.* The deliverance was not in one isolated event. It involved God's preservation through bondage; provision of a leader; promotion of a spirit of hope of deliverance through promises; protection in the midst of severe plagues; power over the obstacle of the Red Sea; and provision in a strange and hostile wilderness. Such were the varied experiences of Israel over those many years. The latter two experiences are the subject of the present passage. As you read the passage, observe the many things which God taught His people through such trying circumstances. Record your observations on paper.

Red Sea Deliverance (13:1—15:21)
    Instructions   chap. 13
    Deliverance   chap. 14
    Song of Praise   15:1-21

Wilderness Journey (15:22—18:27)
    At Marah   15:22-26
    At Elim   15:27
    At the Wilderness of Sin   chap. 16
    At Rephidim   17:1—18:27

In what ways do you think the wilderness was a favorable place for God to mold and unify the hosts of Israelites into an organized nation of people before their journey onward to the land of Palestine?

F. LAW GIVEN AT SINAI (19:1—24:18)

This is the section of Exodus which contains the familiar Ten

Commandments.[11] Chapter 19 begins the last half of the book which we have called *worship* (Chart 15).

Worship is intimately related to law. For, to worship is to acknowledge a higher authority, and there is no authority where there is no law. So after God delivered His people from bondage, He began to spell out in detail how they should worship Him publicly, privately, and even in everyday living. These instructions were His laws. Their importance to Israel is seen by the space devoted to them in the Pentateuch: about half of Exodus, most of Leviticus, the first part of Numbers, and much of Deuteronomy. The importance of the Ten Commandments to the world is demonstrated by the fact that the legal codes of every civilized nation are based upon them.

Read the passage with the following outline in view. (You need only scan the long section of 20:18—23:19. Spend longer time with the other sections.)

The Setting
    Promise   19:1-6
    Preparation   19:7-15
    Phenomena   19:16-25
The Laws
    Basic Laws   20:1-17
    Laws in Detail[12]   20:18—23:19
The Promises 23:20-33
The Response 24:1-18[13]

The Ten Commandments of 20:1-17 are foundational and all-inclusive. Observe that the first four commandments tell man's duty toward God, and the last six, his duty toward his fellowman. After you have finished your study of chapters 19-24, answer this simple but basic question: Why did God impose these laws upon His people?

G. IDOLATRY AT SINAI (32:1—34:35)

We are bypassing chapters 25-31 at this time so that they may be studied last, in connection with the other chapters (35-40) about the tabernacle. See Chart 15 for the location of the idolatry section in the book's pattern.

Four words summarize the narrative chapters 32-34:

sin

judgment

---

11. The term "Ten Commandments" is a Bible term. See Exodus 34:28 and Deuteronomy 4:13; 10:4.
12. Some see the phrase "the book of the covenant" (Exod 24:7) as referring to this body of laws.
13. Of the ratification ceremony (24:4-8), Wood writes, "If one were to pick out a particular day when Israel became a true nation, this would be the day" (p. 145).

intercession

renewal

The people's sin was of the worst kind: spiritual idolatry and corruption (32:1-6). God's judgment was consuming, declared by a jealous Lord (32:7-10). Moses' intercession was desperate, appealing to God's mercy (32:11—33:23). And the consequent renewal of fellowship between Israel and God was conditional upon the people's repentance for sin and determination to obey the words of the covenant (34:1-35).

The cycle represented by the four words noted above was a constantly recurring sequence in Israel's history from this time forward. After coming to the place of renewal, the people would move back to the dwellings of sin again—and the cycle would repeat itself. That Israel was not ever utterly consumed is explained only by the mercy of God and by the ministry of prophets, judges, and men like Moses who pleaded with God in behalf of their brethren. That God was pleased to work through His chosen leaders is illustrated in these chapters by the experience of Moses, whose delay on the mountain was the occasion for his people to sin at the beginning of the narra-

PLAN OF THE JEWISH TABERNACLE   CHART 13

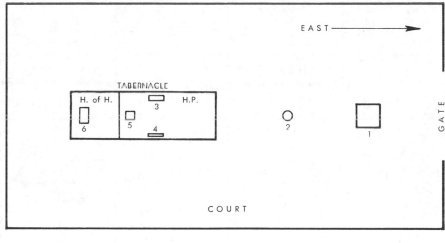

DIMENSIONS. (one cubit equals approximately 1 ½ feet).

    COURT.—100 BY 50 CUBITS.

    GATE.—20 CUBITS.

    TABERNACLE.—30 BY 10 BY 10 CUBITS.

    H. P.=HOLY PLACE.—20 BY 10 BY 10 CUBITS.

    H. of H.=HOLY OF HOLIES.—10 BY 10 BY 10 CUBITS.

FURNITURE.

    1. BRAZEN ALTAR.

    2. LAVER.

    3. TABLE OF SHEWBREAD

    4. GOLDEN CANDLESTICK.

    5. ALTAR OF INCENSE.

    6. ARK OF THE COVENANT.

EXODUS 25-31

CHART 14

INTRO: 25:1-9

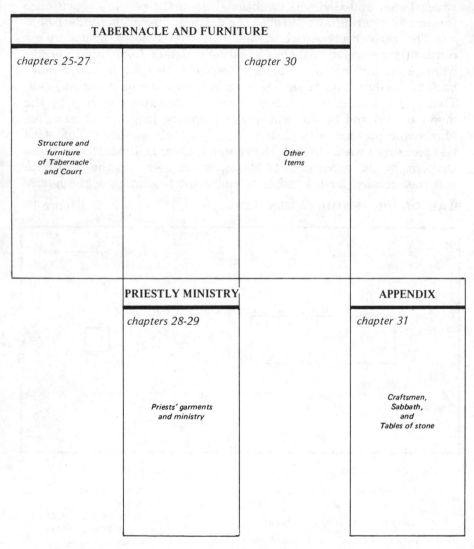

TABERNACLE AND FURNITURE

chapters 25-27

chapter 30

Structure and
furniture
of Tabernacle
and Court

Other
Items

PRIESTLY MINISTRY

chapters 28-29

Priests' garments
and ministry

APPENDIX

chapter 31

Craftsmen,
Sabbath,
and
Tables of stone

tive, but whose presence at the end of the narrative was an occasion of awe and respect—all because Moses spoke for God.

After you have read these three chapters, record your impressions and reflections, especially about human nature and the character of God.

H. TABERNACLE (25:1—31:18; 35:1—40:38)

Recall from Chart 15 that chapters 25-31 record God's specifications for the building of the wilderness tabernacle, and chapters 35-40 report the actual construction of that tabernacle.

The diagram of Chart 13 shows the plan and furniture of the tabernacle. Your reading of the Bible text will be enhanced if you first acquaint yourself with the names shown on this diagram.

I. SPECIFICATIONS OF THE TABERNACLE (25:1—31:18)

This section about the tabernacle is of four parts, shown by Chart 14.
As you read these chapters, refer to this chart for orientation. Otherwise the organization of the passage will be very elusive. Do not tarry over the details of the specifications. Rather, watch for statements of purpose (e.g., "that it may be a memorial," 30:16), and other phrases of explicit spiritual lessons (e.g., "every man that giveth willingly with his heart," 25:2, KJV).

According to Exodus 25:8, 22, what was the primary purpose of the tabernacle for the Israelites? Why do you think God gave such detailed specifications of the tabernacle, as far as the Israelites were concerned?

Read Hebrews 8:1-10:18. How is Christ shown here as the fulfillment of such Old Testament types as the tabernacle and the high priest?

J. CONSTRUCTION OF THE TABERNACLE (35:1—40:38)

Here is a brief outline of this passage:

35:1	36:8	39:43	40:1	40:34 40:38
Preparations	Items Made	Inspection	Tabernacle Erected	Glory of the Lord

If we compare the account of the tabernacle construction (chaps. 36-39) with the specifications given to Moses (chaps. 25-31), we observe that they correspond accurately (e.g., cf. 26:31 and 36:35). All things were done obediently, without question.

When the workmen had finished making the parts of the tabernacle, they brought everything to Moses (39:32-43); and Moses set up the structure, just one year after the Israelites had departed from Egypt (40:17). He carefully assembled every piece as directed, each article of furniture in its exact position (see 40:18-33). When all was done, a wonderful thing happened: God came down and filled the tabernacle with His glory (40:34-35). He had kept His word given earlier (cf. 25:8), and from that time on He would speak to them not from the fiery Mount Sinai, but from the hallowed tabernacle (cf. Lev 1:1). Young shows how the tabernacle pointed forward to Christ.

> The completion of the Tabernacle is an external pledge of the permanence of the Covenant of Grace. The God of deliverance (the Lord) has taken up His abode in the midst of His people. Yet, they are excluded from immediate access into His presence by the vail which shut off the most Holy place to all but the high priest and to him also, save on the Day of Atonement. Through endeavor to obey the Sinaitic legislation the people would be taught their need of a Mediator, a Mediator who would combine the prophetic office of Moses and the priestly office of Aaron. Thus, the arrangements of the Tabernacle were typical, preparatory for the one Sacrifice that has taken away the sins of the world.[14]

The key phrase of the closing paragraph of Exodus is "glory of the LORD." Whereas the book had opened on the grievous note of bondage, the people's groan has now been swallowed up in the Lord's glory. In the opening chapter of Exodus, the pressing need of the people was deliverance; in the closing chapters, the need is that of fellowship—fellowship with God for assurance, sustenance, and protection. To provide for all three, God gave the wilderness experiences for their testing, the Law for their living, and the tabernacle for their worship. In all, He proved Himself the gracious Redeemer.

V. KEY WORDS AND VERSES

One of the many key words of Exodus is "deliver." A key expression is "as the LORD commanded Moses." Two key verses suggested for this book are 3:8 and 12:51. What key words and key verses have impressed you in the course of your survey study?

VI. APPLICATIONS

You have been making spiritual applications along the way from time to time. Here are some further suggestions:

---

14. Young, p. 77.

1. What New Testament verses come to your mind that teach that salvation is not only a *deliverance from* (negative) but also an *entrance into* (positive)? Compare Deuteronomy 6:23.

2. What is the difference between ceremonial law and moral law? Which type, unchanged, applies today? Cite examples for your answers.

3. What did Jesus have in mind when He summed up the whole Law in the words of Matthew 22:37-40?

4. What do the laws of Scripture have to do with the person who is already saved?

5. Why did Christ have to die in order to save man? (See Matt 26:28; Rom 3:24-25; 5:9; Col 1:20; 1 Pet 1:18-19; Rev 1:5.)

6. What are some of the important truths which Exodus teaches about God? About man? Are these truths applicable today?

7. Why is it so important for God's authority to be recognized without reservation?

8. How would you describe the conversation between Moses and God? What lessons about prayer and fellowship can be learned from this?

9. God told Moses that He was the "I AM" (3:14). How does this identification relate to you, practically speaking?

10. What blessed truths about Christ and His ministry are foreshadowed in Exodus? Spend much time thinking about this.

11. What spiritual lessons about leadership may be learned from the example of Moses?

12. What does Exodus teach about obedience?

13. What view of miracles is a prerequisite for an understanding of the book of Exodus?

14. How do you define *worship*? What important truths about worship does Exodus teach?

15. Read Psalm 105. Why is praise to God so vital for the believer?

VII. FURTHER STUDY

Subjects suggested for further study are:

1. The chronology of the book of Exodus, including the date of the Red Sea crossing

2. The types and symbols of Exodus

3. God's laws and commandments

4. The ministry of Aaron

5. Word studies of the following key words of Exodus: covenant,

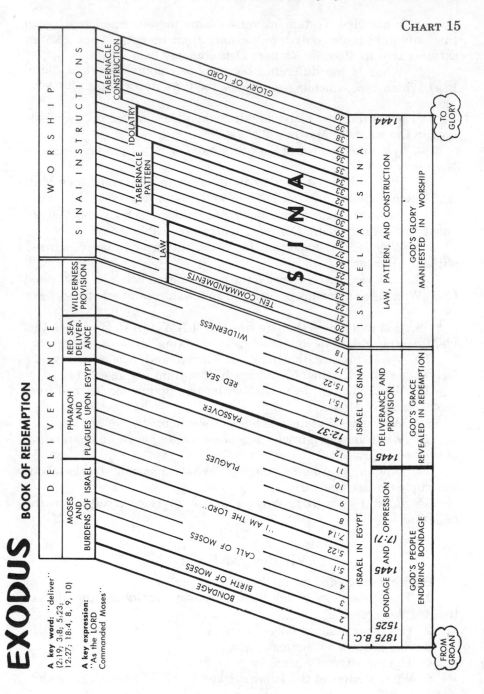

EXODUS
BOOK OF REDEMPTION

A key word: "deliver"
(2:19; 3:8; 5:23;
12:27; 18:4, 8, 9, 10)

A key expression:
"As the LORD
Commanded Moses"

	WORSHIP		DELIVERANCE			
	SINAI INSTRUCTIONS	WILDERNESS PROVISION	RED SEA DELIVERANCE	PHARAOH AND PLAGUES UPON EGYPT	MOSES AND BURDENS OF ISRAEL	

TABERNACLE CONSTRUCTION

GLORY OF LORD

IDOLATRY

TABERNACLE PATTERN

LAW

S I N A I

TEN COMMANDMENTS

WILDERNESS

RED SEA

PASSOVER

PLAGUES

"I AM THE LORD"

CALL OF MOSES

BIRTH OF MOSES

BONDAGE

40 39 38 37 36 35 34 33 32 31 30 29 28 27 26 25 24 23 22 21 20 19 18 17 15:22 15:1 14 12:37 12 11 10 9 8 7:14 5:22 5:1 4 3 2 1

ISRAEL AT SINAI — ISRAEL TO SINAI — ISRAEL IN EGYPT

1444 — 1445 — (7:7) — 1445 1525 1875 B.C.

LAW, PATTERN, AND CONSTRUCTION — DELIVERANCE AND PROVISION — BONDAGE AND OPPRESSION

GOD'S GLORY MANIFESTED IN WORSHIP — GOD'S GRACE REVEALED IN REDEMPTION — GOD'S PEOPLE ENDURING BONDAGE

TO GLORY

FROM GROAN

manna, sign, harden, fear, Passover, memorial, sanctify, altar, obey, testimony, worship, consecrate, Lord, glory

6. Verse studies of the following: 1:7; 2:24; 3:5, 8,12,14-15; 4:11; 5:2; 7:3; 8:19; 12:13-14; 12:41; 13:17-18; 14:31; 16:35; 19:5-6*a*; 20:1-17,20; 24:7; 31:18; 32:8, 10, 26, 31-32; 33:11, 13; 34:10, 28; 35:21; 40:17, 34, 38

VIII. SELECTED READING

CHRONOLOGY OF EXODUS

Archer, Gleason L. *Introductory Guide to the Old Testament,* pp. 204-23.

Unger, Merrill F. *Archaeology and the Old Testament,* pp. 140-52.

———. "Exodus." In *Unger's Bible Dictionary,* pp. 331-34.

Wood, Leon. *A Survey of Israel's History,* pp. 83-109.

HISTORICAL SETTING

Casson, Lionel. *Ancient Egypt.*

Free, J. P. *Archaeology and Bible History,* pp. 84-103.

Payne, J. Barton. *An Outline of Hebrew History,* pp. 49-51.

Pfeiffer, Charles F. "Exodus." In *The Zondervan Pictorial Bible Dictionary* pp. 267-69.

———. *Egypt and the Exodus.*

Schultz, Samuel J. *The Old Testament Speaks,* pp. 43-47.

Unger, Merrill F. *Archaeology and the Old Testament,* pp. 129-39.

———. *Unger's Bible Handbook,* pp. 84-89.

LAWS OF GOD

Erdman, Charles R. *The Book of Exodus,* pp. 87-104.

Goddard, Burton. "Law." In *The Zondervan Pictorial Bible Dictionary,* pp. 477-80.

Kelso, James L. *Archaeology and the Ancient Testament,* pp. 77-88.

Kline, M. G. "Ten Commandments." In *The New Bible Dictionary,* pp. 1251-52.

Manley, G. T. *The New Bible Handbook,* pp. 135-37.

Morgan, G. Campbell. *The Ten Commandments.*

Murray, J. "Law." In *The New Bible Dictionary,* pp. 718-23.

Sampey, John R. *The Heart of the Old Testament,* pp. 77-88.

Unger, Merrill F. "Decalogue," "Law," and "Law of Moses." In *Unger's Bible Dictionary,* pp. 256-57; 646-49.

Watson, Thomas. *The Ten Commandments.*

TABERNACLE

Erdman, Charles R. *The Book of Exodus,* pp. 105-44.

Gooding, D. W. "Tabernacle." In *The New Bible Dictionary,* pp. 1231-34.

Harrison, R. K. "Tabernacle." In *The Zondervan Pictorial Bible Dictionary,* pp. 821-24.

Kelso, James L. *Archaeology and the Ancient Testament,* pp. 88-98.

Levine, Moshe. *The Tabernacle.* Written from a Jewish non-Christian viewpoint.

Martin, W. S., and Marshall, A. *Tabernacle Types and Teachings.*

Soltau, Henry W. *The Tabernacle.*

Spink, James A. *Types and Shadows of Christ in the Tabernacle.*

Strong, James. *The Tabernacle of Israel.*

Unger, Merrill F. "Tabernacle of Israel." In *Unger's Bible Dictionary,* pp. 1059-66.

COMMENTARIES

Chadwick, G. A. *Exodus.* Expositor's Bible.

Driver, S. R. *Exodus.* The Cambridge Bible for Schools and Colleges.

Johnson, Philip C. "Exodus." In *The Wycliffe Bible Commentary.*

Mead, C. M. "Exodus." In *Lange's Commentary on the Holy Scripture.*

5

Leviticus: "Ye Shall Be Holy"

The book of Leviticus is God's manual for His people on how to approach Him and live pleasing in His sight. In the experience of the Israelites, encamped on Mount Sinai, the laws of Leviticus were the guideposts which they needed for life on the wilderness journey ahead, and for settling in Canaan. The key command, "Ye shall be holy," pervades the book, revealing something of the awesome message which God always wants all His people to hear and obey.

I. PREPARATION FOR STUDY

1. Leviticus continues the story of Exodus, even though there is very little narrative in it. Read Exodus 40:26-33, followed by Leviticus 1:1 2a. What is the common setting?[1]

2. Review the survey chart of Exodus (Chart 15). Where were the Israelites during chapters 19-40? What are the main subjects of those chapters?

3. The setting and contribution of Leviticus are suggested on Chart 16. Study the entries.
It might be said that Exodus records how Israel became a redeemed nation, while Leviticus concerns the cleansing, worship, and service of that redeemed nation. W. Graham Scroggie says, "EXODUS begins with sinners, but LEVITICUS begins with saints, that is, as to their standing."[2]

4. Sacrifice is a prominent subject in Leviticus. It will be very helpful for you to read about sacrifice in general, before studying the

---

1. The phrase, "all their journeys," in Exodus 40:36-38 refers to the wilderness journeys, which had not taken place as of Leviticus 1:1.
2. W. Graham Scroggie, *Know Your Bible,* 1:30.

LEVITICUS IN THE PENTATEUCH   CHART 16

GENESIS	EXODUS	LEVITICUS	NUMBERS	DEUTERONOMY
ORIGINS of the nation	DELIVERANCE of the nation	LIFE of the nation	TEST of the nation	REMINDERS to the nation
THEOCRACY BORN	THEOCRACY ESTABLISHED		THEOCRACY TESTED AND PREPARED FOR THE NEW HOME	
	COVENANT IS AMPLIFIED "Keep my cov- enant" to be a "peculiar treasure" "kingdom of priests" "holy nation" (Exodus 19:5-6)	LAWS ARE PRESCRIBED "which if a man do, he shall live in them: I am the LORD" (Lev. 18:5)		

many sacrifices in Leviticus. Consider such aspects as (1) meaning, (2) origin, (3) motives and purposes, and (4) types. (Recommended reading: Steven Barabas, "Sacrifice," in *The Zondervan Pictorial Bible Dictionary,* pp. 737-40; Edward J. Young, *An Introduction to the Old Testament,* pp. 85-87; and Merrill F. Unger, *Unger's Bible Handbook,* pp. 106-8.)

The sacrifices of Leviticus are many and varied. Keep the following classifications in mind as you study the book:

a) blood; or non-blood
b) for an individual; or for a group
c) confirming a relationship to God (e.g., praising God); or restoring relationship to God (e.g., atoning for sin)
d) animal; vegetable; liquid; or other object
e) ministered by a priest; or not ministered by a priest
f) wholly consumed on the altar; or partly consumed by the offerer
g) restitution involved; or no restitution involved

5. The basic principle of law undergirds all of the book of Leviticus. Consult various outside sources (e.g., *The International Standard Bible Encyclopedia,* 3:1879-80) for a discussion of this. Also read New Testament verses about the Old Testament Law. (A concordance will supply the verses containing the word "law.") Why is a correct view of law necessary for an appreciation and understanding of Leviticus?

II. BACKGROUND

A. NAME

It was the custom of the Jews to call each book of their Scriptures by its first word in the Hebrew text. For Leviticus this was *wayyiqra,* meaning "and he called." Obviously this title does not indicate what Leviticus is about. The Greek Septuagint version, which was the first translation of the Old Testament, assigned the title *Leuitikon,* meaning "that which pertains to the Levites." The reason for such a title is that much of the book concerns the ministry of the priests, who were an important segment of the tribe of Levi (cf. Heb 7:11). The Greek title was carried over into the Latin Vulgate as *Leviticus,* which was then adopted by the English Bible.

B. AUTHOR

As discussed earlier, Moses wrote all five books of the Pentateuch. Fifty-six times in Leviticus it is explicitly stated that the Lord gave the laws to His people through Moses. (Follow the name "Moses" in a concordance.) That Moses wrote the instructions in a book is stated in Ezra 6:18. Compare Jesus' reference to Moses in Matthew 8:2-4 with Leviticus 14:1-4.

C. DATE

First read the passages cited on Chart 17. Observe that God spoke the words of Leviticus during the first month of the second year after the Exodus. The Israelites were encamped on Mount Sinai (Lev 7:38; 27:34). Just when Moses wrote down the words we cannot be sure, but he may have done so before the wilderness journey of Numbers began, around the middle of the fifteenth century B.C. (based on the 1445 B.C. date for the Exodus from Egypt).

DATE OF LEVITICUS   CHART 17

EXODUS FROM EGYPT	COMMANDMENTS GIVEN at SINAI	TABERNACLE (portable) CONSTRUCTED	LEVITICAL LAWS GIVEN	PREPARATION for WILDERNESS JOURNEY
Exodus 12:41	Exodus 19:1	Exodus 40:17	————	Numbers 1:1
Beginning of the new calendar	First year; Third month	Second year; First month; First day	Second year; First month	Second year; Second month; First day

D. RELATION TO THE NEW TESTAMENT

The predictive symbols, types, and shadows found throughout this third book of the Bible find their fulfillments in the New Testament. For example, the blood sacrifices point to Christ as the Lamb of God. The priests typify Jesus as the Great High Priest. The worshipers in Leviticus foreshadow the New Testament Christians.

A list of the New Testament references to Leviticus is given later, under *Further Study*. The best biblical commentary on Leviticus is the book of Hebrews.

III. SURVEY

1. In your survey of Leviticus, follow the same study procedures described earlier. (To conserve space, these general procedures will not be repeated for the remainder of this study guide. However, individual steps of that general process will be suggested along the way.)

2. Observe among other things that Leviticus opens with an exhortation to voluntary consecration (freewill offering) and closes on a similar note (freewill vows).

3. Note especially groupings of chapters with similar subject matter. For example, the first seven chapters describe the laws of the five offerings.[3] After you have looked for other groupings, compare your findings with those shown on the survey Chart 22.

4. Study carefully the survey Chart 22. What one word represents the whole book? What outline divides the book into two parts?[4] Read 18:1-5 and notice how these words introduce a new theme, that of doing and living, or, *the walk with God*.

5. Study the outline shown just below the base line on Chart 22. How is holiness prominent in the outline? Scan the chapters in your Bible to see the bases for the groupings. This is an effective way of surveying the book.

6. Leviticus has a twofold theme, which may be stated thus: the way to God and the walk He demands. Keep surveying the book until it is clear to you that this theme represents its message.

IV. PROMINENT SUBJECTS

A. GOD'S HOLINESS AND MAN'S SINFULNESS

The inescapable fact of a dichotomy of God's holiness and man's

---

3. The section 6:8—7:38 gives additional rules concerning the five offerings described in 1:2—6:7.
4. Most expositors begin a main division at chapter 17, rather than 18. Either location can be justified. See *The International Standard Bible Encyclopedia*, 3:1871, for reasons supporting the division at chapter 18.

sinfulness is the universal basic problem confronting all people. The entire message of Leviticus is directed to it. The book's good news is that there are atonement and cleansing for man's sin to redeem him to God, and daily fellowship with God is possible for those who obey His directions. Keep this in mind as you read the Bible text.

B. LAWS

Leviticus is the most thoroughly legalistic book in the Bible.[5] The many laws which appear in its pages are of different kinds: general or specific; ceremonial, social, or moral; temporal or timeless; punitive or reparative. Burton Goddard writes:

> By means of the ceremonial law, God spoke in picture language of the salvation He was to effect through the life and death of the Incarnate Son. . . . The social legislation governing Israel was designed for a particular culture at a given period of history and so it . . . was but for a time, yet the principles which underlay it are timeless and applicable to all generations. God's moral law is in force everywhere and at all times, for it is a reflection of His very being.[6]

All the laws of Leviticus were designed by God for His glory and for man's good. Paul wrote that "the Law has become our tutor to lead us to Christ, that we may be justified by faith" (Gal 3:24). God's Law shows man his corruption, and is intended to bring conviction of sin. J. Gresham Machen comments, "A low view of law leads to legalism in religion; a high view of law makes a man a seeker after grace."[7]

Look for the purposes cited above as you study the laws of Leviticus.

C. THE FIVE OFFERINGS (1:1—7:38)

The five offerings described in these chapters were the major offerings of the Israelites' worship services. Below is listed what each offering meant to the people according to the specifications of Leviticus:

Burnt (1:3-17; 6:8-13): Voluntarily devoting all their very being and possessions to God, through purifying fire

Meal (2:1-16; 6:14-23): Thanking God and offering their lives for His service

Peace (3:1-17; 7:11-34): Participating in the blessings of fellowship with God

Sin (4:1—5:13; 6:24-30): Being forgiven because they were sinners

---

5. The few historical sections appear at these places: 8:1—10:7; 24:10-23.
6. Burton L. Goddard, "Law," in *The Zondervan Pictorial Bible Dictionary,* p. 480.
7. Quoted in *The Wycliffe Bible Commentary,* p. 1292.

Trespass (5:14—6:7; 7:1-10): Being forgiven for the sins they committed

Chart 18 identifies some of the Christian teachings derived from
these five offerings. Think about these, and add your own conclusions.

CHRISTIAN MESSAGE OF LEVITICUS' OFFERINGS   Chart 18

OFFERING			THE CHRISTIAN	C H R I S T
BURNT	(SWEET SAVOUR OFFERINGS)	IN COMMUNION WITH GOD	Consecration	He presented Himself to the Father, to do His will.
MEAL			Service	He served His Father and men as Son of Man.
PEACE			Fellowship	He is the common bond of fellowship between God and man.
SIN		FOR COMMUNION WITH GOD	Redemption for the sinner that he is	He atoned for the **guilt** of sin.
TRESPASS			Redemption for the sin he commits	He atoned for the **damage** of sin.

D. THE PRIESTHOOD (chap. 8-10; 21-22)

The inauguration of the Old Testament priestly ministry (Exod
28-29; Lev 8) began a new era in Israel's career, when God, through
clear and unmistakable signs, symbols, and events, daily showed
forth His righteousness, grace, and glory. Priests served especially as
mediators, to help maintain fellowship between the holy God and the
sinful people. Aaron and his four sons, Nadab, Abihu, Eleazar, and
Ithamar, were chosen of God to be Israel's first priests (Exod 28:1).
The qualifications of the priestly office matched the awesome responsibility which rested upon the priests' shoulders. It is not surprising,
therefore, that five chapters of Leviticus (8-10; 21-22) are devoted to
the consecration and holy disciplines of their ministry.

The Messianic typology of the Old Testament priesthood is rich,
as a reading of Hebrews 8:1—10:18 reveals. The one sinless, eternal
Mediator between God and man is Christ Jesus (1 Tim 2:5), and the
writer of Hebrews devotes many pages to exalt Him and His office

("we have *such* a high priest," Heb 8:1, italics added). Read and study Hebrews 8:1—10:18.

E. DAY OF ATONEMENT (chap. 16)

The Day of Atonement was the most important day of Israel's calendar, for it was then that the idea of atonement for sin reached its highest expression. Sin and burnt offerings were part of the day's ritual. Only on this day could the high priest enter into the most holy place of the tabernacle. This was the only day of the year for which fasting was required, in bold contrast to the atmosphere of rejoicing that attended the annual feasts. On no other day were the Israelites more strongly impressed with the *grace* of God in forgiving all their sins. The gospel of this day was a bright prophetic sign of the coming Gospel of the event of Calvary, when Jesus would sacrifice Himself for the sins of man, once for all. Oswald T. Allis sees the Day of Atonement as the peak of Leviticus.

> To understand Calvary, and to see it in its tragic glory, we must view it with all the light of sacred story centred upon it. With Isaiah, the "evangelical" prophet of the old dispensation, and with the writer of the Epistle to the Hebrews, we must turn to Leviticus and read of the great day of atonement, and of the explanation which is given of it there: "For the life of the flesh is in the blood: and I have given it to you upon the altar to make an atonement for your souls: for it is the blood that maketh an atonement for the soul" (Lv xvii.ii).[8]

F. HOLY TIMES (chaps. 23-25)

God instituted holy times (cf. *holi-days*) in the calendar of the Israelites so that His people would set aside many days of the year to meditate on who He was and what He had done for them. The convocations had a wholesome, positive purpose about them, to emphasize that believers were to be separated *unto* the Lord, as well as separated *from* evil. And what the Israelites learned and experienced at these holy seasons, they were to practice *daily,* step by step, throughout their life.

Chart 19 lists the holidays described in Leviticus 23-25. As you read the Bible text, look for the main purpose of each convocation, and observe the prominent truths revealed by each about God.

Charts 20*a* and 20*b* show how the feasts are distributed in the Hebrew calendar.[9]

---

8. Oswald T. Allis, "Leviticus," in *The New Bible Commentary*, p. 135.
9. See Guy B. Funderburk, "Calendar," in *The Zondervan Pictorial Bible Dictionary*, pp. 138-41, for a discussion of the Jewish calendar.

HOLY TIMES

CHART 19

LEVITICUS 23 — 25

PASSAGES	HOLY TIME	DATE	MAIN PURPOSE OF THE OBSERVANCE	GOD SEEN AS:
Lev. 23:3 Exodus 20:8-11 Deut. 5:12-15	SABBATH	7th day (weekly)	Rest from labor; worship of God	Creator, Lord
Lev. 23:5 Num. 28:16 Deut. 16:1-2	PASSOVER	1/14		
Lev. 23:6-8 Num. 28:17-25 Deut. 16:3-8	UNLEAVENED BREAD *	1/15-21		
Lev. 23:9-14 Exodus 23:16 Num. 28:26-31	FIRSTFRUITS	1/16		
Lev. 23:15-22 Exodus 34:22 Deut. 16:9-12	PENTECOST * (Harvest; Weeks)	3/6		
Lev. 23:23-25 Num. 29:1-6	TRUMPETS	7/1		
Lev. 23:26-32 Lev. 16 Num. 29:7-11	DAY of ATONEMENT	7/10		
Lev. 23:33-44 Num. 29:12-40 Deut. 16:13-15	TABERNACLES *	7/15-21		
Lev. 25:1-7 Exodus 23:10-11	SABBATICAL YEAR	every 7th year		
Lev. 25:8-55	JUBILEE	every 50th year		

*Observe from Exodus 23:14-17 and Deuteronomy 16:16-17 that three times yearly all the men of Israel were to make pilgrimages to the place of worship and to observe these feasts.

V. Key Words and Verses

Some of the most prominent key words and phrases of Leviticus are "holy" (about ninety times), "blood," "life," and "before the LORD" (about sixty times).

Key verses suggested for Leviticus are 17:11 and 19:2. Concerning the latter, compare 11:44-45 and 20:7, 26.

VI. Applications

1. With the five offerings of Leviticus 1-7 in mind, what do you think the Christian should be offering to God?

2. In what ways does Christ serve Christians as their High Priest?

3. The clear teaching of 1 John 1:8 is that all Christians do commit sins. Does this jeopardize the Christian's witness of the Gospel? Explain.

4. What do the chapters about the priests' consecration teach you about Christian service?

5. What is your personal testimony in connection with these two revealed truths:

a) The just penalty for sin is death through the shedding of blood, in which resides the life of the flesh.

b) God in His grace allows the death of an *acceptable substitute* as payment for sin's penalty. (Read the following verses: Matt 20:28; Rom 3:24-26; 1 Cor 15:3; Gal 1:4; Heb 7:25; 1 Pet 2:24.)

6 What are your thoughts about the following statements:

a) When man comes into fellowship with the holy God, he must live in the light of this new experience.

b) Offerings to God must be made willingly, in the spirit of obedience to His instructions.

7. The truth about holy living by God's people is taught in the New Testament as well as the Old. Apply these verses to your life: 1 Peter 1:13-16; Ephesians 1:4; Colossians 1:22; 1 Timothy 2:8; Titus 1:8; 1 John 1:6-7.

8. What do Christian holidays (e.g., Easter) mean to you?

9. What do you consider to be the most important practical teachings of Leviticus for today? Identify at least five.

VII. Further Study

1. Study these three subjects in the Bible: law, sacrifice, and offering.

2. Make word studies of the following: sin, atonement, holy. (See

CHART 20a

HEBREW CALENDAR (1-6)

ORDER IN SACRED CALENDAR	ORDER IN CIVIL CALENDAR	PREEXILIC NAME	POSTEXILIC NAME	EQUIVALENT	SEASON	FARMING	FESTIVALS	BIBLICAL REFERENCES
1	(7)	Abib	NISAN	Mar.-Apr.	Spring Equinox Latter rains	Barley harvest begins Flax harvest	(1: RELIGIOUS NEW YEAR'S DAY, Num. 28:11) 14: Passover (Exodus 12:18) 15-21: Unleavened Bread (Lev. 23:6) 16: Firstfruits (Lev. 23:10ff.)	Exodus 12:2 Neh. 2:1
2	(8)	Ziw	IYYAR	Apr.-May	Summer Dry season begins	Barley harvest	14: Later Passover (Num. 9:10-11)	I Kings 6:1, 37
3	(9)		SIVAN	May-June		Wheat harvest begins Early figs ripen	6: Pentecost (Lev. 23:15-21)	Esther 8:9
4	(10)		TAMMUZ	June-July		Wheat harvest Grape harvest		Ezek. 8:14
5	(11)		AB	July-Aug.		Principal fruit month: grape, fig, olive		
6	(12)		ELUL	Aug.-Sept.		Dates and summer figs		Neh. 6:15

HEBREW CALENDAR (7-12)

7	(1)	Etanim	TISHRI	Sept.-Oct.	Early Rains Seedtime	(Plowing and sowing)	(1: CIVIL NEW YEAR'S DAY) 1: Trumpets (Lev. 23:24; Num. 29:1) 10: Day of Atonement (Lev. 16:29ff.) 15-21: Feast of Tabernacles (Lev. 23:34ff.)	I Kings 8:2
8	(2)	Bul	HESHVAN	Oct.-Nov.		Wheat and barley sowing		I Kings 6:38
9	(3)		KISLEV	Nov.-Dec.	Winter begins (John 10:22)		22: Solemn Assembly (Lev. 23:36)	Neh. 1:1
10	(4)		TEBETH	Dec.-Jan.	Rainy winter months	Cultivation of Jordan valley begins	25: Feast of Dedication (Lights) (John 10:22)	Esther 2:16
11	(5)		SHEBAT	Jan.-Feb.		Almond blossoms Oranges ripen		Zech. 1:7
12	(6)		ADAR	Feb.-Mar.		Barley ripens Citrus fruit harvest		Ezra 6:15
13			ADAR SHENI	Intercalary month:			Added each year that the barley was not ripe on the 16th of Nisan. Two such years were not allowed in succession.	

Irving L. Jensen, *Enjoy Your Bible,* pp. 96-108, for help on how to study a word of the Bible.)

3. Compare the ministries of Aaron and Christ. Chart 21 suggests some comparisons.

AARON AND CHRIST, HIGH PRIESTS   Chart 21

Israel's high priest (Lev. 16)	Our High Priest (Heb. 9)
(1) Aaron, called of God from among men.	(1) Christ, called of God from among men (Heb. 5:4, 10).
(2) Had compassion for the wayward (Heb. 5:2).	(2) ·Prayed with tears (Heb. 5:7).
(3) In spotless purity of dress.	(3) In spotless purity of character.
(4) Entered the holy of holies.	(4) Entered heaven itself (Heb. 9:24).
(5) Made complete atonement (by offering the blood of a goat).	(5) Made complete atonement (by offering His own blood).
(6) For the whole nation (Israel) **and** for himself.	(6) For the whole human race (John 3:16); **not** for Himself.
(7) Offered continually, from year to year.	(7) Offered once, for all eternity (Heb. 9:25).

4. Study the book of Hebrews as it relates to Leviticus.[10]

5. With the help of outside sources, study the New Testament use of Leviticus.[11]

VIII. Selected Reading

GENERAL INTRODUCTION

Allis, Oswald T. "Leviticus." In *The New Bible Commentary;* pp. 134-35.

Erdman, Charles R. *The Book of Leviticus.*

Keil, C. F., and Delitzsch, F. *The Pentateuch,* 2: 261-64.

Kellogg, S. H. *The Book of Leviticus,* pp. 3-28.

OFFERINGS AND SACRIFICES

Archer, Gleason L. *A Survey of Old Testament Introduction,* pp. 228-32.

Barabas, Steven. "Sacrifice." In *The Zondervan Pictorial Bible Dictionary,* pp. 737-40.

Gardiner, Frederic. "Leviticus." In Lange's *Commentary on the Holy Scriptures,* pp. 9-19.

Schultz, Samuel J. *The Old Testament Speaks,* pp. 65-68.

Unger, Merrill F. *Unger's Bible Dictionary,* pp. 942-52.

---

10. See the survey chart of Hebrews, Chart 58, in Irving L. Jensen, *Jensen Bible Charts,* vol. 3.

11. A list of all the New Testament allusions to Leviticus appears in Irving L. Jensen, *Leviticus,* Self-Study Guide, pp. 72-74.

CHART 22

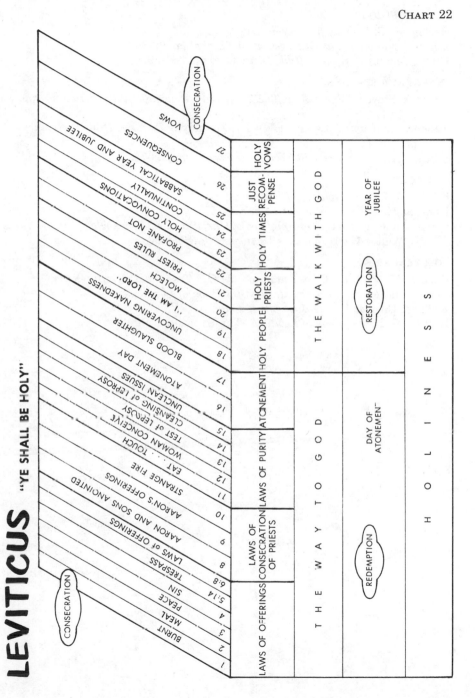

THE PRIESTHOOD

Heslop, W. G. *Lessons from Leviticus.*
Schultz, Samuel J. *The Old Testament Speaks,* pp. 62-65.
Unger, Merrill F. *Unger's Bible Dictionary,* pp. 881-89.

FEASTS AND SEASONS

Barabas, Steven. "Feasts." In *The Zondervan Pictorial Bible Dictionary,* pp. 280-81.
Funderburk, Guy B. "Calendar." In *The Zondervan Pictorial Bible Dictionary,* pp. 138-41.
Schultz, Samuel J. *The Old Testament Speaks,* pp. 68-73.

TYPOLOGY

Fairbairn, P. *The Typology of Scripture.*
Ironside, H. A. *Lectures on the Levitical Offerings.*
Spink, James F. *Types and Shadows of Christ in the Tabernacle.*
Wilson, Walter Lewis. *Wilson's Dictionary of Bible Types.*

COMMENTARIES

Barnes, Albert. *Bible Commentary on the Old Testament: Exodus-Ruth.*
Bonar, Andrew A. *A Commentary on the Book of Leviticus.*
Erdman, Charles R. *The Book of Leviticus.*
Kellogg, S. H. *The Book of Leviticus.* The Expositor's Bible.

6

Numbers: Journey to God's Rest Land

Numbers is the story of God leading His people, Israel, through wildernesses on their way to Canaan, the rest land He promised. The journey moves from Mount Sinai to the plains of Moab, opposite Jericho. First it is a brief journey in the dark unknown, demanding the utmost in trust and patience. Then it is a long, aimless wandering in judgment for unbelief, consuming all but a few of the original travelers. Finally, it is a new and swift journey by the next generation with a few of the old leaders, reviving the hopes of the nation to appropriate the original promise of a land of rest and blessing.

As the book of Numbers closes, the people can expect to hear the trumpet as the signal to cross over the Jordan into the land. They have to drive out the enemy, but success is assured, for their God has said, "I will give it [the land] to you" (10:29).

The five books of Moses (Pentateuch), as noted earlier, constitute a whole. Numbers, as the fourth part of that whole, makes its indispensable contribution. This may be seen in the following comparisons:

Book	Nation of Israel	Man	God
Genesis	Birth; infancy	His creation, Fall, hope	Sovereignty
Exodus	Delivered from Egypt	Deliverance	Mercy
Leviticus	Given Law of worship and living	Access to God, and fellowship with Him	Holiness
Numbers	Traveling to Canaan	Conditions for inheritance	Patience
Deuteronomy	Final preparations for entering Canaan	Consecration	Lordship

115

I. Preparation for Study

1. Acquaint yourself with the geography of the Numbers narrative. See Map F, studied earlier. It is very helpful to visualize *location* as you study *action* in any historical account. As indicated earlier, the story of Numbers moves from Mount Sinai to the plains of Moab, opposite Jericho.

2. Review the accounts of Exodus and Leviticus, which are the antecedents of the book of Numbers.

3. Be prepared to read about many supernatural works of God in behalf of the Israelites. These are a continuation of His mighty deeds recorded in Exodus. Do you know why God performed so many miracles in Old Testament times?

4. Be thinking of what the extent of the average Jew's acquaintance was with God at the beginning of the journey of Numbers.

II. Background

A. TITLE

This fourth book of Moses has had various titles (e.g., "Book of Journeyings," "Book of Murmurings"). According to the Hebrew custom of deriving its title from the first word of the Hebrew text, it has been called *Wayyedabber,* meaning simply, "And he said." When the Septuagint translators affixed a title to the book, they chose the Greek word *Arithmoi,* meaning "Numbers," the word being suggested by the two numberings, or censuses, of the people as recorded in the book (Num 1 and 26). The Latin Vulgate named it *Liber Numeri* ("Book of Numbers"), which was carried over into the English versions. It must be true that not a few readers and students of the Bible have passed by the fourth book of Moses because of the "dry" connotation of this title. But it is both an exciting and inspiring story, and all who spend time studying it receive much benefit.

B. AUTHOR

External and internal evidences point conclusively to Mosaic authorship of all five books of the Pentateuch, which includes Numbers. Moses certainly was a logical choice of God to write Numbers, since he was the chief eyewitness of its events.

C. DATE

Moses wrote Numbers when he was at Moab with his people, toward the end of his life at the close of the fifteenth century B.C.

III. SURVEY

1. Begin your survey study by scanning the thirty-six chapters of Numbers. Record on paper chapter titles similar to the ones shown on Chart 24.

2. Note on Chart 24 where the two main censuses are recorded in the book. The second census involves a different generation from the first. To understand the reason for a second count, read the pivotal chapters cited on the chart. (A pivot is a turning point in a book's structure. In the case of a historical account, the change that follows a pivot may be for the better or for the worse.)

3. According to the chart, how many major divisions comprise the book of Numbers? Study the various outlines showing this. Refer to your Bible text to support these outlines. For example, read 10:11-13 and 22:1, observing the geographical movements.

4. According to the chart, how much time is covered by each of the three divisions? (It should be noted here that, while the middle section covers a span of about thirty-nine years, there is scarcely any record of the events of these many years of wanderings. Most of the section deals with events immediately before and after the actual wanderings. This is a good example of the Holy Spirit's selectivity as to what He inspired the biblical authors to include and exclude.)

5. Read through Numbers again, referring to your chapter titles and the extended eight-point outline shown on the chart. This will give you a good overview of the book.

IV. PROMINENT SUBJECTS

A. THE CENSUSES (chaps. 1 and 26)

Both censuses of this book were counts of the fighting forces of Israel, not of the total population. On the basis of those censuses, the total population has been estimated to be around two million.[1] The people occupied a very large area as they traveled, and were miraculously fed and sustained along the way.

---

1. Refer back to footnote 7 of chapter 4, which showed how the two million count may be arrived at. For a defense of this two million figure, see the following: C. F. Keil and F. Delitzsch, *The Pentateuch,* 3:5-15; Edward J. Young, *An Introduction to the Old Testament,* pp. 88-89; and R. Laird Harris, "Book of Numbers," in *The Zondervan Pictorial Bible Dictionary,* p. 591. Some, who question the fact of such a large contingent of Israelites, interpret some Hebrew words not as numerical figures but as other designations. For example, it is contended that the consonants 1-p should be read as *allup,* translated "captain," and not as *elep,* translated "thousand." (See J. A. Thompson, "Numbers," in *The New Bible Commentary,* p. 169.)

B. FINAL INSTRUCTIONS BEFORE THE JOURNEY (5:1—10:10)

The first four chapters of Numbers record the directions which Jehovah gave Moses regarding preparations for the journey as related especially to the community of the camp as a whole. In chapter 1 the instruction was, "Count the warriors of the camp"; in chapter 2, "Arrange the tribes in the camp"; and in chapters 3 and 4, "Take care of the tabernacle of the camp." Beginning at chapter 5, the directions are aimed at individuals within the camp. Read these chapters with the following outline in mind:

1. Put out the unclean (5:1-4).
2. Judge the guilty (5:5-31).
3. Separate yourselves (Nazirite vow) (6:1-27).
4. Offer gifts (7:1-88).
5. Cleanse the Levites (7:89—8:26).
6. Keep the Passover (9:1-14).
7. Follow your leaders (9:15—10:10).

C. THE SPIES' REPORTS AND THE PEOPLE'S UNBELIEF (12:16—13:33)

Read the passage. As the Israelites approached the land of Canaan from the south (Map F), Moses sent spies ahead to see what the Israelite armies would be facing. God chose to use this situation as a terminal test of faith. He knew what the report would be—overwhelmingly fearful from a human standpoint. What God wanted to do was to face the people with the ultimate in the test of their faith: Would they move on in faith into the jaws of apparent annihilation?

Caleb's recommendation was to go in and possess the land, impregnable as it seemed. The other spies' conclusion was that a conquest of the land was impossible. In unbelief, all the people went along with the pessimistic report and rebelled against the Lord and His promises of deliverance. They cried out, "Let us appoint a leader and return to Egypt" (14:4).

Judgment by God was inevitable: death and disinheritance (14:11-12). Everyone who murmured against Jehovah would die in the wilderness in the course of forty years. Only Caleb and Joshua, along with the children of the murmuring Israelites, would enter Canaan at the end of the forty years.

D. DESERT WANDERINGS (15:1—19:22)

The next thirty-seven years or more were transitional years in the history of the nation of Israel. (When the commencement and closing days of the wilderness experiences are included, the total time period was forty years.) Read 15:1—19:22.

The history of Numbers records very few events of these transitional years, for in a real sense they were years of void; one generation of Israel's sacred history was quickly dying off, and its rising youth as yet had no history at all. But though the period lacked in events, it did not lack in its significance as a transitional period.

Geographically. The people neither advanced nor retreated geographically; rather, they wandered aimlessly about the wilderness and desert areas, between Kadesh and the Red Sea (14:25), consuming the years of God's calendar of judgment. Some of the names of the camping places are listed in 33:19-36. When the judgment years came to a close, the nation returned to Kadesh (20:1), ready then to advance toward Canaan.

Population. The thirty-seven years produced the major population change. The 600,000 warriors met their appointed death over the space of the years, some by violent causes (16:49), and were buried in the wilderness—daily reminders of God's great judgment. Children and youth under twenty years of age grew up, were married, and reared children; and by the end of the wandering years, a new generation of the seed of Abraham had appeared.

Spiritually. In a spiritual sense, new seeds of hope were sown, the original covenant and promise reaffirmed, and preparation for entering God's land renewed. For this spiritual ministry among the people, God still had His servants, Moses, Aaron, Aaron's sons, the Levites, Joshua, and Caleb. The next chapters of Numbers put into focus the major spiritual issues of these transitional years.

F AT THE GATE TO THE LAND (22:2—36:13)

The Israelites had now arrived at the gate to the promised land. Geographically, that gate is located in 22:1 as by "the plains of Moab beyond the Jordan opposite Jericho." For the Israelites, God would keep the gate closed until the day of entrance arrived. The delay was for the accomplishment of God's sovereign business at this crucial junction in the history of the Israelites. In the midst of new problems, the people would experience God's hand of vindication and judgment (22:2—25:18). For preparation for life in the new land, a new census must be taken, a new leader identified to succeed Moses, and the Law of God finalized (chaps. 26-30). (Actually, Deuteronomy contains the bulk of legislation given to the people at this time).

Good strategy called for completing the disposition of the Transjordan (land on the east side of the Jordan where the Israelites were now settled) before crossing into Canaan proper (chaps. 31-32). Finally, specifications were given as to the geographical distribution of the lands of Canaan, with an identification of cities of refuge, and a recognition of the stability of inheritances within the respective tribes (chaps. 34-36).

An important item of business at this time, as noted above, was the designation of a new leader to succeed Moses. After telling Moses to take one last view of the promised land before his death (27:12-14), the Lord instructed him to commission Joshua, son of Nun, as his successor (27:18-21).

And Moses, aged 120, a mature man of God and faithful leader of His people through agonizing years of tribulation, still in prime physical condition (Deut 34:7), who would have loved to be there when his brethren finally crossed the Jordan into the land of rest, unflinchingly obeyed his Master to the very end, and *"did just as the Lord commanded him"* (27:22, italics added). Before his death, recorded in Deuteronomy, Moses was to manifest this obedient attitude in a few more tasks as God's servant.

V. KEY WORDS AND VERSES

Note the key words cited on Chart 24. Refer to an exhaustive concordance, and read all the phrases where these words appear.

Two key verses suggested for Numbers are 10:9 and 10:29. Look for other key verses in the course of your study.

VI. APPLICATIONS

1. Numbers reveals much about God's character. Look for passages in which these attributes appear: unchanging faithfulness, omnipotence, holiness, justice, mercy, and sovereignty. Why is it important for you to keep learning about who God is?

2. Why did God perform such extreme miracles in the days of Numbers? Are such miracles generally observed today? Why or why not?

3. Numbers is like a mirror for man to look in. Especially in the middle section of the book, from chapters 10 through 21, man's heart is exposed with its many sinful tendencies. The prominent sin of Numbers, in the general category of unbelief and disobedience, is that of murmuring against God. The Israelites no sooner began the journey from Sinai to Canaan than they began to murmur. "Now the people became like those who complain of adversity in the hearing of the LORD" (11:1). This they did despite the fact that everything was to their advantage: (1) deliverance from Egypt's bondage; (2) no present problems on the start of the journey; (3) promise of sufficient help

from God for the successful arrival in Canaan (cf. 10:29). About what things are Christians tempted to murmur today?

4. The years of desert wanderings were literally years of waste and void, giving awesome testimony of the fact of divine judgment for sin. Is God still the Judge of all mankind? If so, what should the Christian's attitude be to this Judge?

5. Hebrews 3 and 4 apply Numbers to the Christian life, concerning victorious living. The main thrust of the Hebrews passage is shown below.

a) God offered the occupation of Canaan to His people, Israel.

b) They failed to enter the land because of unbelief (Heb 3:19).

c) Today God offers rest to the Christian if he will fulfill the conditions of belief and obedience. ("There remains therefore a Sabbath rest for the people of God," Heb 4:9.)

The "rest" spoken of in Hebrews does not refer to heaven, since the epistle teaches it is possible for a Christian to come short of it.

SUMMARY OF NUMBERS   CHART 23

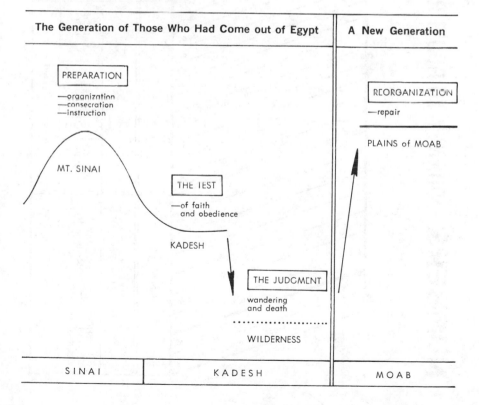

| The Generation of Those Who Had Come out of Egypt | A New Generation |

PREPARATION
—organization
—consecration
—instruction

REORGANIZATION
—repair

PLAINS of MOAB

MT. SINAI

THE TEST
—of faith
and obedience

KADESH

THE JUDGMENT
wandering
and death

WILDERNESS

| SINAI | KADESH | MOAB |

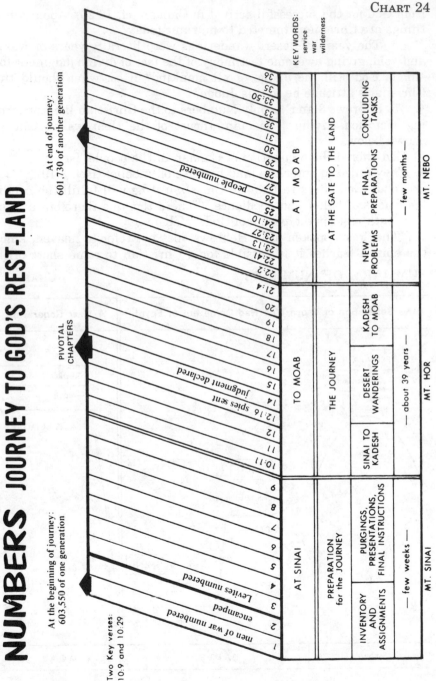

NUMBERS JOURNEY TO GOD'S REST-LAND

Two Key verses:
10:9 and 10:29

At the beginning of journey:
603,550 of one generation

At end of journey:
601,730 of another generation

PIVOTAL CHAPTERS

KEY WORDS:
service
war
wilderness

men of war numbered
encamped
Levites numbered

spies sent
judgment declared

people numbered

| | 2 | 3 | 4 | 5 | 6 | 7 | 8 | 9 | 10:1 | 11 | 12 | 12:16 | 14 | 15 | 16 | 17 | 18 | 19 | 20 | 21:4 | 22:2 | 22:41 | 23:13 | 23:27 | 24:10 | 25 | 26 | 27 | 28 | 29 | 30 | 31 | 32 | 33 | 33:50 | 35 | 36 |

| AT SINAI | | TO MOAB | | AT MOAB | |

| PREPARATION for the JOURNEY | | THE JOURNEY | | AT THE GATE TO THE LAND | |

| INVENTORY AND ASSIGNMENTS | PURGINGS, PRESENTATIONS, FINAL INSTRUCTIONS | SINAI TO KADESH | DESERT WANDERINGS | KADESH TO MOAB | NEW PROBLEMS | FINAL PREPARATIONS | CONCLUDING TASKS |

| — few weeks — | | — about 39 years — | | — few months — |

| MT. SINAI | | MT. HOR | | MT. NEBO |

("Let us fear lest, while a promise remains of entering His rest, any one of you should seem to have come short of it," Heb 4:1.) Therefore, this rest is a state of Christian living today, of victory and blessing, where Jesus has preeminence in the heart (hence, the fruits of *His* rest), and where the Holy Spirit continually fills the soul. Even as the Israelite needed to watch his life and keep right with God on his journey to Canaan if he would enter the land, so the Christian must "be diligent to enter that rest" (Heb 4:11). Spend time meditating on God's offer of spiritual *rest* to Christians who fulfill His conditions.

6. Although Moses was not granted entrance to the land because of his sin, nevertheless he was used of God in a mighty way to serve and lead Israel up to the hour of crossing the Jordan. This was partly because he did not murmur against God for judging his earlier sin. What spiritual lessons does this teach?

VII. Summary of the Book

Chart 23 serves as a review of the highlights of Numbers. Compare it with the survey Chart 24.

VIII. Further Study

1. Study carefully the Nazirite vow of chapter 6. Study similar vows in the Bible. Refer to Bible dictionaries and encyclopedias for help.

2. The real key to the successful conquest of Canaan and happy living within its borders was *continual fellowship with God*. Hence, it was that God at this time, by way of Moses, presented to the new generation a finalized and complete set of regulations for offerings, most of which had already been given at Sinai. Their observance would encourage an intimate worship of God by the people in the land (cf. Exod 23:14-17; 29:38-42; 31:12-17; Lev 23; Num 25:1-12). You may want to study these laws of offerings in chapters 28-30.

3. Read the commentaries of authors who reject the two million figure of Israel's population during the wilderness journeys. Evaluate the arguments advanced.

IX. Selected Reading

GENERAL INTRODUCTION
Allis, O. T. *God Spake by Moses,* pp. 107-28.
Archer, Gleason L. *A Survey of Old Testament Introduction,* pp. 233-34.
MacRae, A. A. "Numbers." In *The New Bible Commentary,* pp. 162-64.
Morgan, G. Campbell. *The Analyzed Bible,* pp. 42-50.

Ridderbos, N. H. "Book of Numbers." In *The New Bible Dictionary*, pp. 898-901.

GEOGRAPHY

Kraeling, Emil G. *Bible Atlas*, pp. 114-28.
Pfeiffer, Charles F., and Vos, Howard F. *The Wycliffe Historical Geography of Bible Lands*, pp. 88-92.

CENSUS

Archer, Gleason L. *A Survey of Old Testament Introduction*, pp. 234-38.
Mendenhall, G. E. "The Census Lists of Numbers 1 and 26." In *Journal of Biblical Literature*, pp. 52-66.

JOURNEYS

Jensen, Irving L. *Numbers, Journey to God's Rest-Land*. Everyman's Bible Commentary, pp. 49-92.
Schultz, Samuel J. *The Old Testament Speaks*, pp. 79-85.
Smick, Elmer. "Numbers." In *The Wycliffe Bible Commentary*, pp. 125-40.
Stevens, Charles H. *The Wilderness Journey*.
Wood, Leon. *A Survey of Israel's History*, pp. 137-67.

COMMENTARIES

Jamieson, Robert; Fausset, A. R.; and Brown, David. *A Commentary, Critical and Exploratory on the Old and New Testaments*, vol. 1.
Kerr, D. W. *Numbers*. The Biblical Expositor.
Mackintosh, C. H. *Notes on the Book of Numbers*.
Maclaren, Alexander. *Exposition of Holy Scriptures: Exodus, Leviticus and Numbers*.

7

Deuteronomy: Book of Remembrance

This last book of the Pentateuch records Moses' addresses to the nation of Israel as they prepared to enter the promised land of Canaan. "These are the words which Moses spoke to all Israel across the Jordan in the wilderness" (Deut 1:1). The closing words of the book are an epitaph memorializing the great patriarch's ministry:

> Since then [the time of Joshua] no prophet has risen in Israel like Moses, whom the LORD knew face to face, for all the signs and wonders which the LORD sent him to perform in the land of Egypt against Pharaoh, all his servants, and all his land, and for all the mighty power and for all the great terror which Moses performed in the sight of all Israel (34:10-12).

I. PREPARATION FOR STUDY

1. Read Deuteronomy 31:24-26. Where were the Levites instructed to deposit the Scriptures which Moses had written? Now read 2 Kings 22:1-13. This action took place more than seven hundred years after Moses wrote the scrolls. In what building were the writings found? What was the concern of King Josiah?

2. Read Exodus 20. The Ten Commandments were one portion of the earlier Scriptures which Moses repeated in his Deuteronomy addresses.

3. Read the last verse of Numbers (36:13). Compare it with the opening verse of Deuteronomy.

II. BACKGROUND

A. TITLE

Our English title *Deuteronomy* is traced back to the Greek

125

Septuagint version of the Old Testament, where the title was given as *Deuteronomion,* meaning literally, "second law." This latter title came from the Septuagint's mistranslation of the phrase "a copy of this law" (17:18) as *to deuteronomion touto,* "this second law." Actually, the book of Deuteronomy does not present another, or second, law, but repeats and amplifies the basic laws which had been given to the people on Mount Sinai.

B. AUTHOR AND DATE

Evidence for Mosaic authorship is overwhelming. At specific places in the text he is expressly identified as the author. (Read 1:1-6; 4:44-46; 29:1; 31:9, 24-26.) Jewish and Samaritan tradition has assigned the book to Moses. Jesus and New Testament writers, who quote from Deuteronomy more than from any other Old Testament book (about eighty times, e.g., Rom 10:6-8; Heb 12:29; 13:5; Matt 4:4, 7, 10; 22:37-38), associate the book with the Law. Internally, its message best fits the times and ministry of Moses. "The words are instinct with the warm solicitude of a great leader for the people whose experiences he had shared."[1]

Chapter 34, which records Moses' death, was written by another person. Of this, Gleason Archer writes, "The closing chapter furnishes only that type of obituary which is often appended to the final work of great men of letters."[2] Joshua, Moses' friend and successor, may have written the obituary.

As for the date of composition, Moses probably wrote the book soon after he delivered the addresses (1:3) and shortly before his death (1405 B.C.).

C. SETTING

The circumstances under which Deuteronomy was written are clear. Israel had reached the border of Canaan. Forty years earlier the nation had been on the border of the land, but because of unbelief and disobedience the people were not allowed to enter. This time they had to tarry on the banks of the Jordan until they learned this one lesson: They must obey their God. God was willing and ready to lead them on to victory and to give them the delights of the land, on the condition that they would bend their stubborn wills and surrender entirely to Him. Moses, the lawgiver, was about to leave them; so he gathered his beloved people around him for the last time and delivered his farewell address—Deuteronomy. (This took place on the plains of Moab. See Map G.)

1. G. T. Manley, ed., *New Bible Handbook,* p. 147.
2. Gleason L. Archer, *A Survey of Old Testament Introduction,* p. 244.

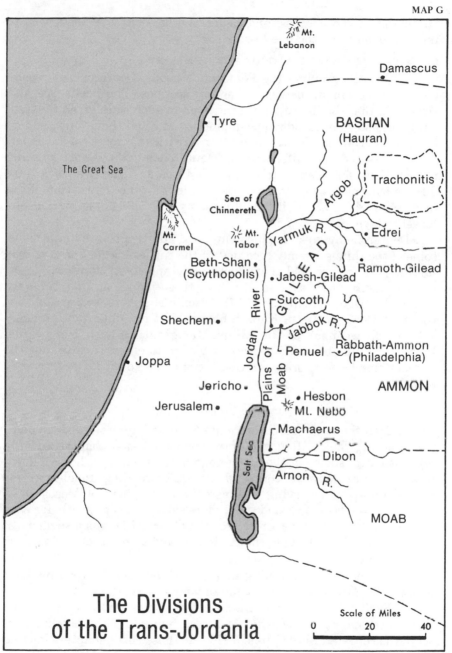

The Divisions
of the Trans-Jordania

His object in the address, and hence the object of the book, was to impress upon them the one lesson: *obey.*

D. COMPARISONS WITH LEVITICUS AND NUMBERS

Within the group of the Pentateuch books, Deuteronomy resembles Leviticus in its paucity of action sections. The books are also similar in that the instructions contained in each were given to Israel while they were in standby encampment—at Sinai (Leviticus), and on the plains of Moab (Deuteronomy). In Leviticus they were anticipating their wandering life, and in Deuteronomy they were making preparations for their settled life in Canaan. The two books are different in that Leviticus was given mainly for the instruction of the priests and Levites, while Deuteronomy was given to instruct the Israelite laymen.

Deuteronomy also supplements, by additions or explanations, some of the things already recorded in the earlier books. For example, in Numbers we are told that elders were appointed to assist Moses, but the instructions that Moses gave these judges at that time are recorded in Deuteronomy (1:16-17). Also, in Numbers we are told that the spies were sent from Kadesh-barnea, but not until Deuteronomy 1:19-23 do we hear of the request originating with the people. Further, in Numbers, Moses was forbidden to enter Canaan, but the conversation between him and God is not recorded until Deuteronomy 3:23-26.

III. SURVEY

1. Scan the book of Deuteronomy for first impressions. Include in the scanning the reading of the first verse of each chapter and the topic headings shown at the top of your Bible. Do not get bogged down in any details along the course of this quick reading. Read more for overall impressions, trying to sense the atmosphere of Moses' message. Scan the book a second time, more slowly. Record a title for each chapter of the book on paper. (Note that Chart 27 begins a segment at 4:44 instead of at 5:1. Read the Bible text and account for the division at this point.)

2. Compare the beginning and end of the book by reading 1:1-8 followed by 34:1-8. What are some of your observations?

3. Read 1:1—4:43, underlining strong words and phrases as you read. In chapters 1-3, of what is Moses reminding the people? (Observe the repeated word "Then.") How do those three chapters lead up to what Moses says in 4:1-43? Underline in your Bible all the imperative words which Moses spoke in chapter 4 (e.g., "listen," 4:1; and "keep," 4:6). How are chapters 1-4 represented on the survey

REMEMBRANCES OF THE PAST CHART 25

(Deuteronomy 1:1-4:43)

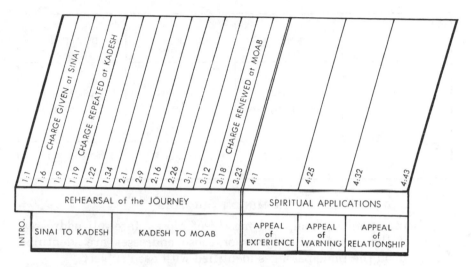

Chart 27? Use Chart 25 as an outline guide for your study of these chapters.

4. Note on Chart 27 how the division 4:44—26:19 is identified. In 4:44—11:32, Moses expounds and applies the Ten Commandments. In what chapter are those Ten Commandments quoted? How does 11:26-32 conclude this section?

5. In chapters 12-26, Moses cites related commandments which the people were to obey in their daily walk. Read these chapters. Observe the repeated phrase, "the LORD your God" in these chapters. Why did Moses not say "the LORD *our* God"? Read the concluding paragraph, 26:16-19. What does this reveal about the purposes of God's laws?

6. Read chapters 27-30, noting the many references to blessing and curse. What did Mount Gerizim represent (27:12)? What did Mount Ebal represent (27:13)? Why did God use object lessons like these? In your own words, what is the main point of these chapters?

7. The four concluding chapters of Deuteronomy are unusually interesting, partly because of the atmosphere of expectation. As you read and study these chapters, use Chart 26 as an outline guide. In your own words, list what these chapters contribute to the overall theme of Deuteronomy.

8. Spend more time studying the survey Chart 27. Account for the title "Book of Remembrance."

PARTING WORDS OF MOSES   CHART 26

(Deuteronomy 31:1-34:12)

31:1	31:30	33:1	34:1
CHARGE	SONG	BENEDICTION	DEPARTURE
CHALLENGE to DEVOTION	WITNESS of GOD'S JUDGMENTS	BLESSINGS on ISRAEL	CHANGE of LEADERSHIP
W O R D			EVENT

IV. PROMINENT SUBJECTS

Deuteronomy is composed mostly of Moses' farewell addresses. Some of the prominent subjects of those addresses are identified below. Read the Bible passages identified with each subject.

A. REMEMBRANCES OF THE PAST (1:1—4:43)

It was natural for Moses to refer to history first and let experience be a teacher. Not every event in Israel's journey from Egypt was reviewed, but only those from which Moses would draw his arguments. In substance, what he said was:

"You see how it has been for the past forty years. Whenever this nation obeyed God, it has been blessed; and whenever it has disobeyed Him, it has been punished. Therefore, in the future obey."

B. COMMANDMENTS FOR THE PRESENT (4:44—26:19)

Most of Deuteronomy records laws of God for Israel. God gave these as guides for leading His people into a faith relationship with Him, and to instruct them how to live their daily life acceptable to Him. Lest the people think lightly of that Law, Moses had reminded them of the great event at Sinai when the Maker of heaven and earth talked to them from the fiery, smoking, quaking mountain (read 4:32-33). And to guard against any idea that this Law had been given only to their fathers, and was therefore out-of-date and not binding upon this new generation, Moses reminded the people: "The LORD did not make this covenant with our fathers, but with us, with all those of us alive here today" (5.3).

Here is a brief general outline of these chapters:

1. Basic commandments (4:44—11:32)

2. Laws of worship and holy living (12:1-16:22)
3. Punishments for specific offenses (17:1—26:19)

C. OPTIONS AFFECTING THE FUTURE (27:1—30:20)

One of the first things Israel was to do on establishing themselves in the land of Canaan was to march to Mount Ebal and Mount Gerizim, two mountains in the center of the country (locate on Map H), and there set up great plastered stones on which the Law of God was to be written. Six tribes were to stand upon Mount Gerizim, to declare blessings upon the people for obedience to this Law, and the other six tribes were to stand upon Mount Ebal, to declare curses upon the people for disobedience.

The consequences of obeying this Law as well as the consequences of disobeying it are set forth in chapter 28. The first fourteen verses give a bright picture of the nation's future if they will take the path of obedience. From these verses we learn how blessed, rich, and powerful Israel could have been if they had been true to God. The tone changes at verse 15, and from there onward we have a picture of the black future awaiting the nation if they should take the path of disobedience.

A key subject of Deuteronomy is that of God's covenant. (The word "covenant" appears seven times in chap. 29.) Moses' addresses were delivered to Israel as a reaffirmation of the covenant relationship between God and His people. The pattern followed by Moses in delivering his message has been compared with the approach used by kings of Moses' day in addressing their subjects. Meredith Kline writes of this:

> Part of the standard procedure followed in the ancient Near East when great kings thus gave covenants to vassal peoples was the preparation of a text of the ceremony as the treaty document and witness. The book of Deuteronomy is the document prepared by Moses as witness to the dynastic covenant which the Lord gave to Israel in the plains of Moab (cf. 31:26).[3]

The prominence of the "covenant-concept" in Deuteronomy is underscored by Kline.

> Deuteronomy is the Bible's full scale exposition of covenant-concept and demonstrates that, far from being a contract between two parties, God's covenant with His people is a proclamation of His sovereignty and an instrument for binding His elect to Himself in a commitment of absolute allegiance.[4]

---

3. Meredith G. Kline, "Deuteronomy," in *The Wycliffe Bible Commentary*, p. 155.
4. Meredith G. Kline, "Deuteronomy," in *The Zondervan Pictorial Bible Dictionary*, p. 215.

Kline rightly observes that the sovereign character of God's covenant is not "an unconditional license to national privilege and prosperity."[5] The people were still responsible to choose to obey God.

Read chapters 29 and 30 carefully, and you will see how long-suffering and gracious God was in offering hope to Israel for loving Him and obeying His commandments.

D. PARTING WORDS OF MOSES (31:1—34:12)

The people who have been camping on the east side of the Jordan, waiting to cross over, are given (1) their final charges, (2) an interpretation of the philosophy of God's judgments in history, and (3) a reminder of the blessings awaiting the people in the land. The parting words of Moses are not bitter ones, but bright and warm and hopeful. This patriarch remained a spiritual giant to his dying day.

V. KEY WORDS AND VERSES

Note the key words and verses on Chart 27. Read the verses in your Bible, and study the key words in an exhaustive concordance.

VI. APPLICATIONS

1. Why should a Christian periodically look back to such important spiritual experiences as his conversion?

2. Why is it often easy to forget the Lord and His Word in one's daily walk? What helps to guard against this?

3. What do the Ten Commandments mean to you? Do they apply to your life? What about other Old Testament commandments, such as the ceremonial laws of burnt offerings?

4. Are the options of believing and not believing always offered to man? What about the invitation of the Gospel of salvation?

5. Does God's law of recompense still hold true (blessing for obedience and punishment for disobedience)? Support your answer with New Testament Scripture.

6. What does Deuteronomy teach you about God's sovereignty and holiness?

7. What spiritual lessons may a Christian learn from the life of Moses, as taught in Deuteronomy?

VII. FURTHER STUDY

1. Study the word "covenant" as it appears in both Testaments. (Refer to a concordance, Bible dictionary, and books on doctrine and theology.)

---

5. Ibid.

CHART 27

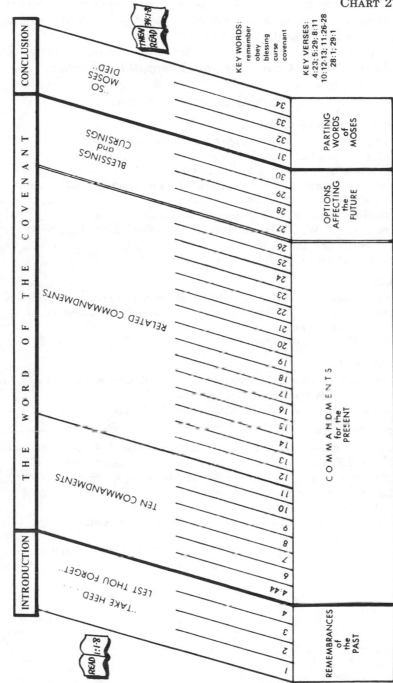

2. In Deuteronomy, God's laws are referred to by three words: judgments, statutes, commandments. Read G. T. Manley's discussion of this in *The New Bible Dictionary*.[6]

3. Read Gleason L. Archer's discussion of Deuteronomy's authorship and date in *A Survey of Old Testament Introduction*.[7]

VIII. SELECTED READING

GENERAL INTRODUCTION

Archer, Gleason L. *A Survey of Old Testament Introduction*, pp. 239-50.

Keil, C. F. and Delitzsch, F. *The Pentateuch*, 3: 269-77.

Manley, G. T. "Deuteronomy." In *The New Bible Commentary*, pp. 195-97.

Robinson, George L. "Deuteronomy." In *The International Standard Bible Encyclopedia*, 2: 835-40.

Schneider, Bernard N. *Deuteronomy*, pp. 12-24.

Schroeder, F. W. J. "Deuteronomy." In Lange's *Commentary on the Holy Scriptures*, pp. 39-45.

Schultz, Samuel J. *Gospel of Moses*.

AUTHORSHIP

Archer, Gleason L. *A Survey of Old Testament Introduction*, pp. 241-50.

Schroeder, F. W. J. "Deuteronomy." In Lange's *Commentary on the Holy Scriptures*, pp. 1-38.

Unger, Merrill F. *Introductory Guide to the Old Testament*, pp. 207-76.

COVENANT

Berry, George Richer. "Covenant (in the Old Testament)." In *The International Standard Bible Encyclopedia*, 2: 727-29.

Lockyer, Herbert. *All the Doctrines of the Bible*, pp. 146-51.

COMMENTARIES

Jamieson, Robert; Faucett, A. R.; and Brown, David. *A Commentary, Critical and Exploratory on the Old and New Testaments*, vol. 1.

Kline, Meredith G. "Deuteronomy." In *The Wycliffe Bible Commentary*.

Manley, G. T. *The Book of the Law*.

Reider, Joseph. *Deuteronomy*.

Schultz, Samuel J. *Deuteronomy*. Everyman's Bible Commentary.

---

6. G. T. Manley, "Deuteronomy," in *The New Bible Dictionary*, p. 309.
7. Archer, pp. 241-50.

Part 2

History of Israel

In and out of the Land of Canaan

The second main group of books in our English Old Testament is called the "Historical Books." The history which is involved begins with Israel's entrance into Canaan (reported by Joshua) and concludes with the nation's return to the land from exile, almost a thousand years later (reported by Nehemiah).

Joshua	2 Kings
Judges	1 Chronicles
Ruth	2 Chronicles
1 Samuel	Ezra
2 Samuel	Nehemiah
1 Kings	Esther

8

Joshua: Book of Conquest

Joshua is a book about a *land* and a *people*. The land is an inheritance promised by God, waiting to be occupied. The people are the elect nation of God, facing human obstacles in the way of taking the land. And the obstacles are the occasion for battle—a holy war—designed by God to oust the idolatrous and corrupt enemies from the land. It is for this that Joshua is called the "Book of Conquest."

Joshua's narrative about winning the rest land of Canaan resumes the history of Israel at the point where Deuteronomy ends. The sequence of the Pentateuch books is this: In Genesis, God brings Israel to birth,[1] and promises to give it the land of Canaan.[2] In Exodus, He delivers His people from oppression in a foreign land (Egypt), and starts them on their way to the promised land, giving them laws to live by (as recorded both in Exodus and Leviticus). Numbers records the journey of Israel through the wildernesses up to the gate of Canaan, while Deuteronomy describes final preparations for entering the land. At this point Joshua picks up the story, describing the conquest of the land and the division of its territories to the tribes of Israel. In a real sense, Joshua is the *climax* of a progressive history as well as the *commencement* of a new experience for Israel. Thus, its historical nexus gives it a strategic place in the Old Testament Scriptures.

I. PREPARATION FOR STUDY

1. Review the discussion in chapter 1 of the Old Testament canons of the Protestant and Hebrew Bibles. As noted there, the

---

1. To Abraham, God said, "I will make you a great nation" (Gen 12:2).
2. Genesis 12:7. God later gave further details of the promise (Gen 15:18-21).

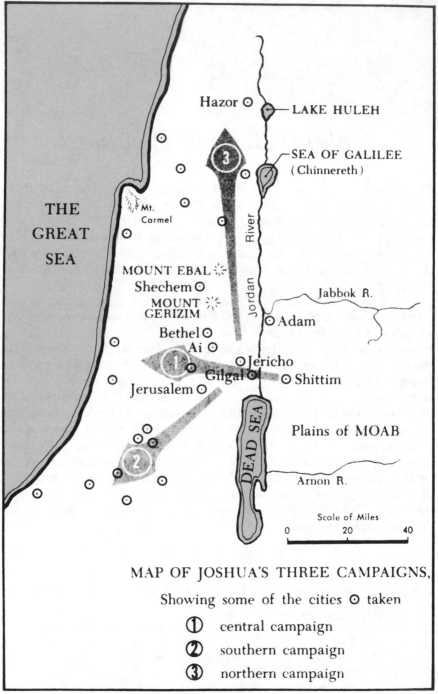

THE
GREAT
SEA

Hazor ⊙ ——— LAKE HULEH

③

——— SEA OF GALILEE
(Chinnereth)

Mt.
Carmel

MOUNT EBAL ☀
Shechem ⊙
MOUNT ☀
GERIZIM

Bethel ⊙
Ai ⊙
① ⊙Jericho
Gilgal⊙   ⊙ Shittim
Jerusalem ⊙

②

Jordan   River

Jabbok R.

⊙ Adam

DEAD SEA

Plains of MOAB

Arnon R.

Scale of Miles

0   20   40

MAP OF JOSHUA'S THREE CAMPAIGNS,

Showing some of the cities ⊙ taken

① central campaign

② southern campaign

③ northern campaign

arrangement of the thirty-nine books of the Protestant Old Testament can be traced back to the Greek Septuagint version (third and second centuries B.C.). The books are arranged in such an order that four groups appear: (1) Pentateuch, (2) history, (3) poetry and ethics, and (4) prophecy. In this arrangement, Joshua is the first of the twelve historical books.

It is helpful to have clear in one's mind the place which the book of Joshua occupies in the historical thread of the Old Testament books as concerns Israel. Simply stated, the Old Testament history of Israel is of three eras,[3] centered around a *land* (Canaan) and a *government* (theocracy [God as Ruler]), as shown by Chart 28.

CHART 28

ISRAEL AND THE LAND OF CANAAN		
I	II	III
TO THE LAND	IN THE LAND	FROM THE LAND
promises of, and journey to the land and theocracy	entry into and living in, the land and theocracy	taken from the land to captivity; theocracy dissolved

As noted in chapter 1, the arrangement of the Hebrew Old Testament is vastly different from that of the Protestant Old Testament, though the text content is identical. The Hebrew Old Testament contains three groups, namely, Law, Prophets, and Writings. The Prophets section is divided into two parts: Former and Latter. Joshua is the first book of the Former Prophets, followed in order by Judges, Samuel (1 and 2 Samuel), and Kings (1 and 2 Kings). Placing Joshua among prophetical books may have been because its author was considered to hold the office of prophet; more likely it was because the historical record illustrated the great principles which prophets preached.[4]

2. Before you study the Bible text of Joshua, become acquainted with the geography involved in the narrative. Map H marks the major movements of the Israelite hosts against the enemies, which fall naturally into three general campaigns:

a) the central campaign—to secure a bridgehead for the Israelites in the center of the land, from which to spread out

---

3. More accurately, there were four eras, when one considers the restoration period (e.g., under Nehemiah). Since this was a brief period of revival, with hearts returning to "stone" by the time of Malachi, the simplified threefold outline holds.

4. F. F. Bruce, *The Books and the Parchments*, p. 92.

MAP I

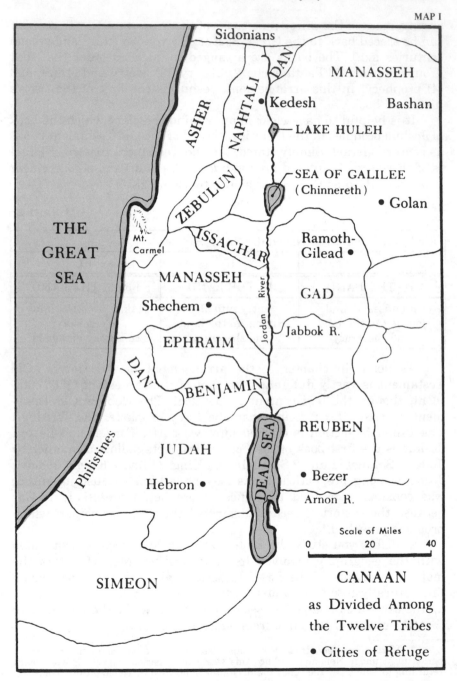

CANAAN

as Divided Among
the Twelve Tribes

• Cities of Refuge

b) the southern campaign—to rout the nearest foes
c) the northern campaign—to gain control of the distant territory

Map I shows how Joshua divided the land of Canaan among the twelve tribes after the major campaigns were completed.

The land originally promised to Abraham's seed extended from the "river of Egypt"[5] to the "great river" Euphrates (Gen 15:18). The same promise was confirmed to the Israelites in the days of Moses (Exod 23:31), and again to Joshua (Josh 1:4). These were the two ideal limits of influence, from Egypt, the one world power on Palestine's southwestern border, to Babylon, the power on its eastern side. One can easily recognize the strategic location of Canaan with reference to the rest of the world of Israel's day. It was the connecting link, the point of balance and the spot on which the major land and sea routes converged.[6] The explicit details of the geographical boundaries of the Canaan[7] to be possessed were described by the Lord to Moses on the eve of Israel's entry into the land (Num 34:1-15). At that time also, Joshua and Eleazar were appointed to the task of apportioning the territories to the different tribes. The accomplishment of this business is recorded in Joshua 13-19.

It is to be noted that all the enemies were not routed immediately; some cities within the boundaries were not taken until the days of David and Solomon. This piecemeal conquest can be attributed partly to the failure of the Israelites to fully obey God's conditions. Another factor was the divine timetable of designed delay, to spare the land from sudden desolation by nature itself: "I will not drive them out before you in a single year, that the land may not become desolate, and the beasts of the field become too numerous for you. I will drive them out before you little by little, until you become fruitful and take possession of the land" (Exod 23:29-30).

3. Do you recall from your earlier studies of Numbers and Deuteronomy who were the ones of Israel allowed by God to enter the promised rest land?

---

5. The "river of Egypt" is either (1) the Wadi el Arish, or "brook of Egypt" (Josh 15:4,47), which was the boundary line between Egypt and the southern deserts of Canaan, or (2) the Nile River. In either case, the land limit is *Egypt*.

6. See Denis Baly, *The Geography of the Bible,* p. 5.

7. The name Canaan in the Bible, especially when used in the phrase "land of Canaan" (as in Num 34:2), usually refers to the combined areas known today as Palestine and Syria, rather than to the smaller coastal territory of the heathen people called Canaanites. It is in this large sense that the term "Canaan" is used also in this book, unless otherwise specified.

II. BACKGROUND

A. AUTHOR

The author of the book of Joshua is not explicitly identified. But the following facts are known about its authorship:

1. The general tenor of the book indicates that the author was an eyewitness of most of the events, which are described with great vividness and minuteness of detail, and occasionally in the first person ("we" and "us", e.g., 5:6).

2. The unity of style in the organization of the book indicates that one author wrote the bulk of the work.

3. Joshua is *specifically* identified as the author of some writings. He wrote the words of a covenant which he shared with Israel "in the book of the law of God" (24:26), which was born of his farewell charge in chapter 24. Also, Joshua was responsible for the land survey of Canaan, which he caused to have recorded in a book (18:9).

4. Some small parts of the book could not have been written by Joshua. Such sections include the references to his death (24:29-30) and to the faithfulness of Israel during the years after his death (24:31). It is possible that these sections were added by Eleazar the priest, and that the note of Eleazar's death (24:33) was in turn recorded by Phinehas, his son.

Jewish tradition, both ancient and modern, has consistently ascribed the authorship of the book to Joshua. Among conservative Christians today, opinion is perhaps equally divided.[8] Internally, there is nothing to deny the bulk of the book to Joshua's pen. The important thing to recognize is that the identification of the author is not a crucial factor in studying the Bible text.

B. DATE

The book was written not long after the events themselves had transpired. If the conquest of Canaan was completed around 1400 B.C., the book was written soon after this date. (Note: Concerning dates of this period of Old Testament history, see John C. Whitcomb's chronological chart, *Old Testament Patriarchs and Judges*.)

About twenty-four years are covered by the narrative of Joshua. After the Canaanites were conquered, Joshua divided the land, settled the tribes in their respective places, and looked after the affairs of the nation until his death.

---

8. Here are three representative positions by conservatives on the Joshua authorship: "yes": Gleason L. Archer, *A Survey of Old Testament Introduction*, p. 252; "no": Robert Jamieson, A. R. Fausset, and David Brown, *A Commentary, Critical and Exploratory on the Old and New Testaments*, 2:210; "possibly": Merrill F. Unger, *Introductory Guide to the Old Testament*, p. 281.

III. SURVEY

1. First, scan the book of Joshua in one sitting, if possible.

2. Jot down on paper your impressions from this first reading (e.g., which part of the book is mostly narrative?).

3. If your Bible identifies main content at the top of each page (or at the beginning of each chapter), read this sequence now, for the whole book. Also, you may want to read the first verse of each chapter.

4. Now return to the beginning of the book, and assign a title to each of the twenty-four chapters. Record on paper. (Note that Chart 32 shows a segment beginning at 11:16 instead of at 12:1.)

5. Read the first paragraph of the book (1:1-9) and the last three paragraphs (24:19-33). Make comparisons.

6. Before studying the survey Chart 32, try to group chapters into sections of similar content. For example:
What chapters are mainly of *action?*
What chapters record mainly the allotments of territory?

STRUCTURAL OUTLINE OF JOSHUA   CHART 29

"Cleave unto Jehovah . . . , as ye have done unto this day" (23:8)

"So Joshua took the whole land" (11:23)

CONSECRATION

for continued blessing

INHERITANCES

land allotments

CONQUEST

the campaigns

PREPARATION

for war

1:1   6:1   13:1   22:10

ACTION   BUSINESS   APPEAL

What chapters report preparations for conquest, and what chapters report the battles themselves?

7. When you read the text in more detail, look for references to important experiences of the Israelites, such as altars. Are there many references in the book to sin of God's people, and judgments reaped?

8. The account of the book of Joshua is presented in a logical sequence of four sections, as shown on Chart 29.

The first two sections, comprising the *action* section of the book, lead up to a peak of attaining the promised goal, as represented by a phrase of the key verse, "So Joshua took the whole land" (11:23). From this midpoint of the book, the account levels off to a plateau, as it were, to present the immediate business of Joshua, that of dividing the inheritance of land among the tribes. This is followed by a fitting intense appeal and exhortation to the people, to fulfill the conditions for anticipated heights of continued blessing in God's rest land.

9. Study the survey Chart 32. Note the similarities to Chart 29. How does the survey chart divide the book of Joshua into two main parts? Find a phrase in 11:16-23 which summarizes the successful engagements of Joshua and his army. Note the two anticipatory sections.

10. To conclude your survey, read the last three chapters of Joshua, keeping the survey chart in mind as you read.

IV. PROMINENT SUBJECTS

A. THE MAN JOSHUA

The prominent person of this book is the man Joshua. A few of the many things revealed about him are cited below. Read all the Bible passages involved.

1. His name. Joshua's original name was Hoshea (Num 13:8; Deut 32:44), which literally means "salvation." During the wilderness journey, Moses changed the name to Jehoshua (Num 13:16, KJV), meaning, "Jehovah is salvation." (Joshua is a contracted form of Jehoshua.) What is the significance of this change of name?

2. His association with Moses. Joshua was a young man when Moses appointed him as one of his ministers, or attendants, during the wilderness journey. Read the following passages which tell of some of his services during those years: Exodus 17:8-16; 24:12-13; Numbers 13:1-16; 14:26-35. At the close of Moses' career, God chose Joshua to be his successor (Num 27:18), and Moses transferred the mantle of leadership to his faithful attendant and friend (Deut 34:9).

3. His character. Read what God said of Joshua in Numbers 27:18 (cf. Deut 34:9). Joshua feared God, believed God, obeyed God, and glorified God. He was a great ruler, commanding the respect of all his subjects (Deut 34:9), maintaining order and discipline, putting the worship of God central in the nation's government, encouraging his people to press on to claim God's best. He was also a great military leader, using his God-given traits of wisdom, confidence, courage, and a spirit of challenge to manipulate his army in strategies that consistently led to triumph. And Joshua was a humble man who thought highly of others and most gloriously of God.

B. THE LORD GOD

One writer has commented that "the criterion of the religious value of any book is, What does it tell us about God?"[9] The book of Joshua reveals much about the person and work of God. Look up the names "Lord" and "God" in an exhaustive concordance and observe that the Lord was actively and incessantly involved in the battles and business of the leaders and people. Three attributes of God especially prominent in the book are His holiness,· faithfulness, and saving grace.

C. THE MAJOR TASKS

The book of Joshua reports the essential details of four major tasks or experiences of Israel in occupying the promised rest land: preparation, conquest, allocating the land parcels, and consecration.

1. Preparation (1:1—5:15). The first five chapters of Joshua concern the preliminary stages of the Israelites' conquest of Canaan, as they prepared and positioned themselves for the battles against their enemies. Read the passage, referring to this condensed outline as you read:

Chapter	Event	Significance
1	Charge to Joshua	Task identified
2	Spying Jericho	Enemy studied
3	Crossing Jordan	Leader magnified
4	Stones set up	Deliverance memorialized
5	Circumcision and Passover	Hearts prepared

2. Conquest (6:1—12:24). To possess Canaan meant to drive out the enemy. But the enemy was many—Hittites, Amorites, Perizzites,

---

9. Hugh J. Blair, "Joshua," in *The New Bible Commentary*, p. 225.

Jebusites, and others—each to be reckoned with as Joshua planned his strategy of conquest. There is no record of God explicitly instructing Joshua as to the pattern of that strategy, though the divine direction was ever present. Actually, the geographical location of entrance into the north-south-oriented Canaan, at Jericho, determined the plan. See Map H for the general movements of the central, southern, and northern campaigns. The strategy was simply to (1) gain the bridgehead at Jericho; (2) extend the battle in this central region to effect a wedge between the northern and southern armies; (3) then engage each, one after the other, the nearer armies (southern) first. The account of the book of Joshua follows the sequence of that plan in recording the highlights[10] of Israel's conquest of the enemies in Canaan. Chart 30 outlines this section of Joshua. Study the chart as you read the Bible text.

THE CONQUEST OF CANAAN   CHART 30

(Joshua 6:1-12:24)

6:1			9:1	11:1	11:16 / 12:24
CENTRAL CAMPAIGN			SOUTHERN CAMPAIGN	NORTHERN CAMPAIGN	SUMMARY
Victory Through Faith	7:1 Defeat Through Sin	8:1 Restoration	Progressive Conquests		

3. Allocations (13:1—21:45). The activities of Israel during the years of chapters 1-12 were not terminal in themselves. The terminus was reached when it could be said that "Joshua took the whole land" (11:23) and that he could now divide the land "for an inheritance to

_____

10. As with all history in the Bible, selectivity, not exhaustiveness, is the aim. Those events are recorded which retain the unity of the narrative and serve the underlying purposes of the divine revelation. In the book of Joshua, not all the events but the highlights of the campaigns are recorded.

Israel according to their divisions by their tribes" (11:23). The action of the unhappy though necessary wars was the prelude to the gratifying and pleasant business of the allotment of the lands to the Israelites.

Chart 31 shows how these chapters report the various allocations made to the tribes and individuals.

LAND ALLOCATIONS   CHART 31

(Joshua 13-21)

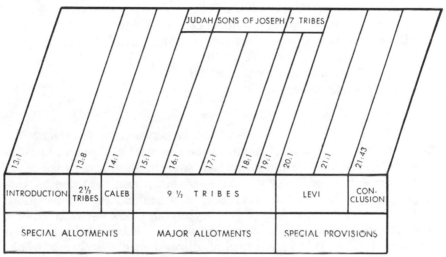

While there is no record of any pageantry or colorful ceremony attending the drawing of lots for the land assignments for each tribe, the importance of such allotments cannot be overstated. This was the climactic moment in Israel's young life, when for the first time she could claim a land as her own, given by God. In the days of the patriarchs—Abraham, Isaac, Jacob, and Joseph—the land was too large for total claim. When by propagation Israel grew to the size of a formidable nation, the people were dwelling in bondage in a foreign land, Egypt. The wilderness years were spent on the way to the land. The seven years of fighting after crossing the Jordan were used to conquer the land. Now the hour had come to claim the land, build homes, and live with God in peace. The day of land allotment was truly a happy day for Israel.

4. *Consecration (22:1—24:33)*. The first five chapters of Joshua, the *Preparation* section, are chapters of anticipation of conquest. The last three chapters, this *Consecration* section, are chapters of antici-

pation of continued dwelling in God's rest land. The intense action of the first half of the book, which reached a plateau in the business of land allotments, now gives way to relatively quiet but emotion-filled moments of crisis, when Joshua appeals for total commitment, and elicits Israel's consecration to God, a heartwarming climax to the years of his ministry among them.

Here is a brief outline of these concluding chapters:

I.   Consecration of Eastern Tribes (22:1-34)
     A. Joshua's Charge (22:1-9)
     B. Tribes' Altar of Witness (22:10-34)
II. Consecration of Western Tribes (23:1—24:28)
     A. Joshua's Charge (23:1-16)
     B. Covenant Renewed (24:1-28)
III. Appendix (24:29-33)

D. TYPES AND SYMBOLS

There is a remarkable correspondence between the experiences of Israel, from the bondage of Egypt to the conquest of Canaan, and the spiritual experiences of the individual soul. In Exodus we read of (1) Israel's condition in Egypt (bondage, poverty, imminent death), corresponding to the spiritual condition of a soul before regeneration; and (2) Israel's Exodus from Egypt, typifying God's deliverance of a soul, bringing salvation. In Numbers we read of Israel's backslidden condition in the wilderness (unbelief, disobedience, discontent, weakness), picturing a soul regenerated but out of fellowship with God.

The close of the book of Joshua shows the commencement of Israel's life in Canaan to be one of peace, joy, wealth, power, and victory, typifying a saved soul wholly surrendered to God.

Three prominent types in Joshua are identified below.

1. Joshua, leader of the host of Israel, is a type of Christ, the "captain of . . . [our] salvation." (Read Heb 2:10-11, KJV; cf. Rom 8:37; 2 Cor 1:10; 2:14.)
2. The crossing of the Jordan is a type of the Christian's dying with Christ. (Read Rom 6:6-11; Eph 2:5-6; Col 3:1-3.)
3. Israel's conquest of Canaan typifies the Christian's victories over the enemies of his soul (e.g., 2 Cor 10:3-6).

V. KEY WORDS AND VERSES

On the basis of your study thus far, choose key words and verses from the Bible text which represent the theme of Joshua. Chart 32 suggests one of each.

VI. APPLICATIONS

1. What makes Joshua so practical for the Christian is that its major application concerns the Christian's pursuit of that abundant life which Christ talked about when He said, "I have come for people to have life and have it till it overflows" (John 10:10, Williams). Israel dwelling in the rest land of Canaan is a vivid type of the Christian living in intimate relationship to Christ, abiding in Him (John 15:4), and being filled with His joy (John 15:11). The Christian's rest is a peace that comes out of victory over the soul's enemies, through the power and help of God (Heb 4:9-10). While it is true that the blessings of abiding in Christ originate in the divine act of regeneration, they are contingent upon the Christian's diligence to enter into that abiding life. (Read Heb 4:11.)

2. Much can be learned from the book of Joshua about the Christian's call to service for God. Hugh J. Blair writes this about Joshua: "His supreme qualification lay in the fact that all his gifts and training and experience were fused into a dynamic force by the touch of God. It was at the call of God that all his potentialities were called forth."[11] What different things are involved in a Christian's call to service?

3. Why are the wars of Joshua called "holy wars"? Is war ever justifiable today? (Give biblical support to your answer.) The book of Revelation prophesies many wars of God in last times. Refer to the book and try to derive some basic principles about "holy wars."

4. Make a list of other practical truths taught by this book, for example, concerning blessing, judgment, and the Word of God.

VII. FURTHER STUDY

1. Read outside sources on the life and religion of the various Canaanite peoples who were dwelling in the land when Joshua began his campaigns.[12]

2. Study in more detail the land allotments to the tribes.[13]

3. Read various discussions concerning whether war is justifiable.[14] Base your own conclusion on what you believe the Bible teaches on this vital subject.

4. Make a biographical study of the man Joshua.

---

11. Blair, p. 223.
12. See *The Wycliffe Bible Commentary*, p. 206; Howard F. Vos, *Genesis and Archaeology*, pp. 85-91; K. A. Kitchen, "Canaan," in *The New Bible Dictionary*, pp. 183-86; Samuel J. Schultz, *The Old Testament Speaks*, pp. 89-93.
13. Leon Wood, *A Survey of Israel's History*, pp. 185-92. Also see Irving L. Jensen, *Joshua: Rest-land Won*, Everyman's Bible Commentary, pp. 97-115. A chart of land allotments appears on p. 113.
14. For example, read Blair, p. 225.

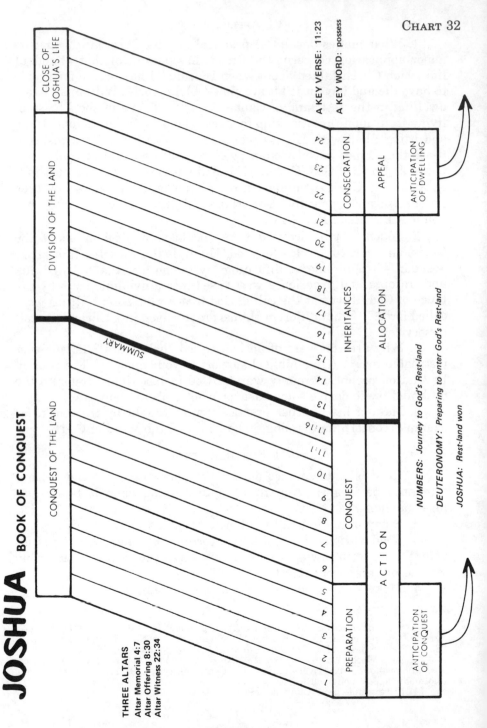

CHART 32

JOSHUA BOOK OF CONQUEST

CLOSE OF JOSHUA'S LIFE

DIVISION OF THE LAND

CONQUEST OF THE LAND

SUMMARY

THREE ALTARS
Altar Memorial 4:7
Altar Offering 8:30
Altar Witness 22:34

A KEY VERSE: 11:23

A KEY WORD: possess

CONSECRATION

APPEAL

ANTICIPATION OF DWELLING

INHERITANCES

ALLOCATION

CONQUEST

PREPARATION

ANTICIPATION OF CONQUEST

ACTION

NUMBERS: Journey to God's Rest-land

DEUTERONOMY: Preparing to enter God's Rest-land

JOSHUA: Rest-land won

VIII. SELECTED READING

GENERAL INTRODUCTION

Archer, Gleason L. *A Survey of Old Testament Introduction,* pp. 251-61.

Blair, Hugh J. "Joshua." In *The New Bible Commentary,* pp. 223-26.

Jensen, Irving L. *Joshua: Rest-land Won.* Everyman's Bible Commentary, pp. 8-26.

Keil, Carl F. "Joshua." In *Joshua, Judges, Ruth,* pp. 13-27.

Pink, Arthur W. *Gleanings in Joshua,* pp. 9-22.

Wood, Leon. *A Survey of Israel's History,* pp. 168-70; 192-202.

WAR

Archer, Gleason L. *A Survey of Old Testament Introduction,* p. 261.

Blair, Hugh J. "Joshua." In *The New Bible Commentary,* p. 225.

Unger, Merrill F. "War." In *Unger's Bible Dictionary,* pp. 1161-63.

COMMENTARIES

Blaikie, William G. *The Book of Joshua.*

Edersheim, Alfred. *The Bible History—Old Testament,* 3:46-104.

Henry, Matthew. *Commentary on the Whole Bible.*

Pink, Arthur W. *Gleanings in Joshua.*

Rea, John. "Joshua." In *The Wycliffe Bible Commentary.*

9

Judges: Apostasies of God's People

The book of Judges is one of the saddest parts of the Bible, humanly speaking. Some have called it the "Book of Failure." The last chapter of the preceding book, Joshua, anticipates continued blessing upon God's people in the rest land of their inheritance. (Read Joshua 24:19-28.) But one does not proceed far into the account of Judges before he senses that all is not well. While there are deliverances along the way, the tone of the book is predominantly one of oppression and defeat because "everyone did what was right in his own eyes" (21:25). When the gospel of God's grace does appear in the book, it shines forth in sharp brightness because of the contrast of this dark setting. As in all books of the Bible, God does not furnish a diagnosis of sin and guilt unless He also prescribes a cure.

I. PREPARATION FOR STUDY

1. Read Exodus 18:21-26. The judges referred to here were civil magistrates, fulfilling the judicial functions usually associated with the office of judge. These magistrates should not be confused with the judges of the book bearing the name Judges. The latter are *shophetim* (Heb.), commissioned by God to deliver the Israelites from the oppression of their enemies, usually by war, and then to rule the people during the era of peace. Read Judges 2:16; 3:9. Refer to a Bible dictionary for a description of both types of judges.

2. The era of judges during Israel's occupation of Canaan was one of many important phases of the nation's history. Study carefully Chart 33, which represents all of Israel's history from Genesis through Malachi. Observe the duration of the period of judges. (The bottom of the chart indicates the Bible's coverage of this history.)

THE PERIOD OF JUDGES
IN OLD TESTAMENT HISTORY

CHART 33

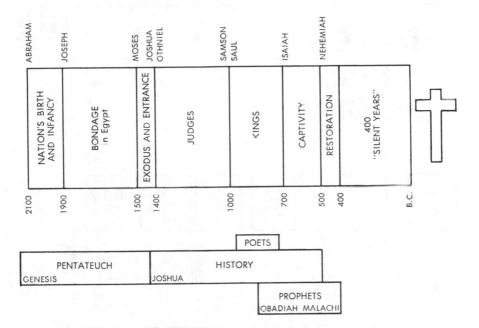

3. Now observe on Chart 34 the order and dates of the judges' reigns. (Note: Eli, a priest-judge, and Samuel, a prophet-judge, do not appear in the Bible until 1 Samuel.)

Begin now to become acquainted with the names of these judges, for they are the main characters of this Bible book.

4. Review your study of Joshua. Many comparisons may be made between the books of Joshua and Judges, some of which are listed here:

JOSHUA	JUDGES
Upward trend, spiritually	Downward trend, spiritually
One man is prominent	No one man is prominent
Israel as a tutored child	Israel as an adult
Victory	Defeat
Fidelity	Apostasy

As the book of Joshua closes, Israel is shown taking a stand for

CHART 34

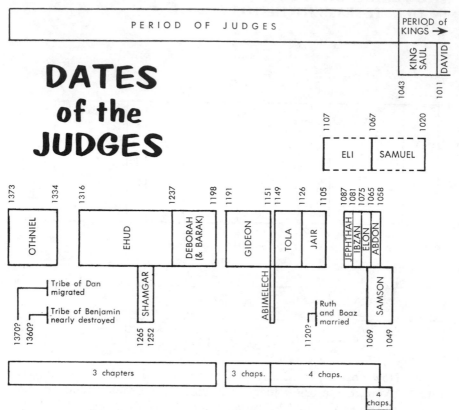

God. Thus they entered into the promised blessings of the inheritance—victory, prosperity, and happiness—which is the life God would always have His people lead. They were still surrounded by enemies; indeed, some enemies still lived within their boundaries. But if they would obey God's commands concerning these enemies, they would have the power of the Almighty with them.

In the book of Judges we shall see Israel turning away from God and doing the very things which God through Moses and Joshua had repeatedly besought them not to do.

II. BACKGROUND

A. TITLE

The title of the book is Judges, named after the judges *(shophetim)* who are the leading characters of the book.

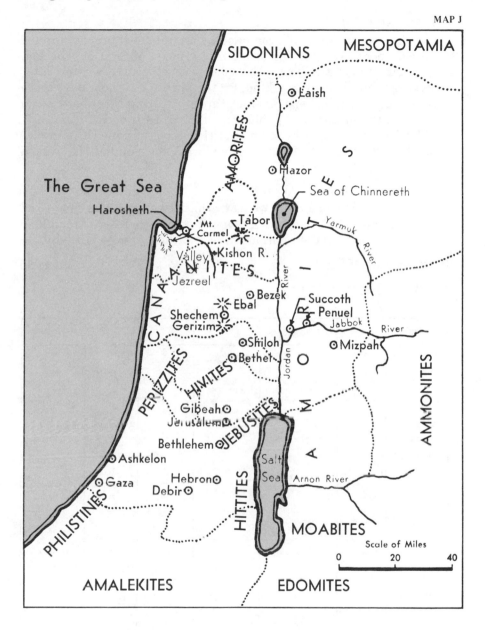

**ENEMIES DWELLING IN CANAAN
DURING THE TIMES OF THE JUDGES**

B. DATE AND AUTHOR

Judges was written and compiled by an unnamed prophet around 1000 B.C., not long after the death in 1051 B.C. of Samson, the last main character of the book. The book was obviously written after Israel began to be ruled by a king, for the phrase, "in those days there was no king in Israel," appears four times, implying that there was a king when the history was published (cf. 17:6; 18:1; 19:1; 21:25).

Jewish and early Christian tradition have assigned this book's authorship to Samuel. If the author was not Samuel, he was a contemporary of Samuel.

C. ENEMIES DWELLING IN CANAAN

From Joshua and Judges we learn that although Israel conquered the whole land of Canaan in a general sense, there still remained pockets of enemy heathen nations here and there. These proved to be

JUDGES OF ISRAEL   CHART 35

(cited in Judges)

NAME	TRIBE	IDENTIFICATION	ENEMY	YEARS OF OPPRESSION	YEARS OF PEACE	REFERENCES
1. OTHNIEL	Judah	nephew of Caleb	Mesopotamians (king Chushan)	8	40	3:9-11
2. EHUD	Benjamin	left-handed an assassin	Moabites (king Eglon)	18	80	3:12-30
3. SHAMGAR	Nephtali?	used ox goad	Philistines	?	?	3:31
4. DEBORAH	Ephraim	only woman judge	Canaanites (king Jabin)	20	40	4:4-5:31
5. GIDEON	Manasseh	of an obscure family sought a sign	Midianites	7	40	6:11-8:35
6. TOLA	Issachar				23	10:1-2
7. JAIR	Gilead	30 sons, 30 cities			22	10:3-5
8. JEPHTHAH	Gilead	made rash vow	Ammonites	18	6	11:1-12:7
9. IBZAN	(Bethlehem)	30 sons, 30 daughters			7	12:8-10
10. ELON	Zebulun				10	12:11-12
11. ABDON	Ephraim				8	12:13-15
12. SAMSON	Dan	Nazirite from birth strongest man	Philistines	40	20	13:2-16:31

real tests for the tribes of Israel as to whether they would obey God's command to utterly subdue them. Those were enemies within the boundaries of their inheritances. In addition to this, enemy nations from without also plagued the Israelites. The book of Judges shows how God used His appointed judges to conquer them. Refer to Map J for the locations of these enemy nations.

D. DESCRIPTIONS OF THE JUDGES

Chart 35 gives brief descriptions of the twelve judges appearing in the book of Judges. Acquaint yourself with each of these now, and your later survey will be more effective. Read the Bible references.

III. SURVEY

1. First, swiftly scan the pages of the Bible text, reading at least the first and last sentences of the chapters and also the chapter headings in your Bible. The purpose of this exercise is merely to catch highlights of the book and to sense something of the tone of its message. Follow with a second, slower scanning of the book.

2. Next, choose a chapter title for each chapter and record them on paper. (Note on Chart 36 the special segment divisions at 2:6; 3:7; and 12:8. Mark these divisions in your Bible before you get your chapter titles.)

3. Refer to Chart 35 and note the chapter spread of the references to the judges. Where on Chart 36 does this grouping appear?

4. Study the survey Chart 36 carefully. Read 1:1—3:6 and observe how these chapters serve as an introduction to the main body of the book. Why is a main division made at 3:7?

5. According to Chart 35, who is the last judge appearing in this book? What chapter is the last to report about him? Use this as a clue to explain why a new division is made at chapter 17 on the chart.

6. The long section 3:7—16:31 is one continuous story of deliverances and setbacks. How does the bottom of the chart relate 1:1—3:6 and 17:1—21:25 to this?

7. Note the contrast between the beginning of the book—fighting the enemy—and the end—fighting a brother.

IV. PROMINENT SUBJECTS

A. THE JUDGES (3:7—16:31)

According to Chart 36, a comparatively large space of the Bible text is devoted to three judges, Deborah, Gideon, and Samson. Many are the Bible stories which have been written about these interesting leaders. But all the judges of Israel had the equally responsible task of delivering the nation from six successive foreign oppressions. These are cited in the next section (B).

B. THE CYCLE OF ISRAEL'S RELIGIOUS EXPERIENCE

A pattern of religious experience, which might be called a cycle, appears again and again in the book of Judges. The following diagram illustrates this cycle.

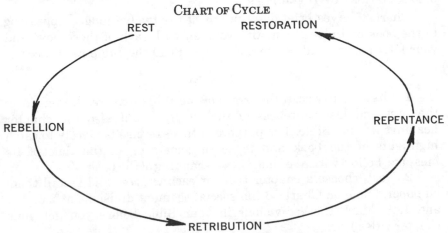

CHART OF CYCLE

Read 2:16-19 to see the pattern of this cycle.

1. Rest. During Joshua's lifetime and for some years afterward, Israel served God and enjoyed the blessings of their rest land. This is where the book of Judges begins.

2. Rebellion. When a new generation arose, they divorced themselves from God and, in rebellion against Him, took on the ways of the idolatrous Canaanites.

3. Retribution. Just as He had said He would, God withdrew His protection and power from Israel and delivered them into the hands of foreign oppressors.

4. Repentance. Then the Israelites repented of their sin and cried to God for help. (In 2:16 this is only inferred; read 3:9 for a fuller statement. Read also 10:10, KJV, to see what was involved when they "cried unto the LORD.")

5. Restoration. God raised up a judge to deliver His people from their oppressor and to lead them back to a life of fellowship with Him—back to the beginning of the cycle, *rest.*

The cycle accentuates two prominent lines of truth: (1) the desperate sickness of the human heart, revealing its ingratitude, stubbornness, rebellion, and folly; and (2) God's long-suffering, patience, love, and mercy. (The prominence of the Lord in the narrative of Judges is shown by the fact that the name "LORD" appears 178 times and "God" 62 times in the book.)

The passages of Judges which report the occurrences of this cycle are listed below. Read the Bible text to see the pattern.

CYCLE	PASSAGE	OPPRESSORS	JUDGES
I	3:8-11	Mesopotamians	Othniel
II	3:12-31	Moabites	Ehud Shamgar
III	4:1—5:31	Canaanites	Deborah with Barak
IV	6:1—10:5	Midianites	Gideon Tola Jair
V	10:6—12:15	Ammonites	Jephthah Ibzan Elon Abdon
VI	13:1—16:31	Philistines	Samson

V. KEY WORDS AND VERSES

Read 2:19 and 17:6 as key verses of Judges. A key phrase suggested for the book is "did evil."

VI. APPLICATIONS

Answer the following questions on the basis of your study of Judges.

1. Why do Christians disobey the Word of God, even though they know the promised blessings for obedience? What are the consequences of disobedience?

2. What is apostasy? (Refer to a dictionary for a definition of the word.) Can Christians be guilty of this?

3. How long-suffering is God? Does God overlook sin in His long-suffering and mercy?

4. God's people often live far below their privileges. What are some privileges and blessings which Christians may forfeit?

5. Only God can give spiritual victory. Why?

6. God uses weak vessels to accomplish His divine work (1 Cor 1:26). Why?

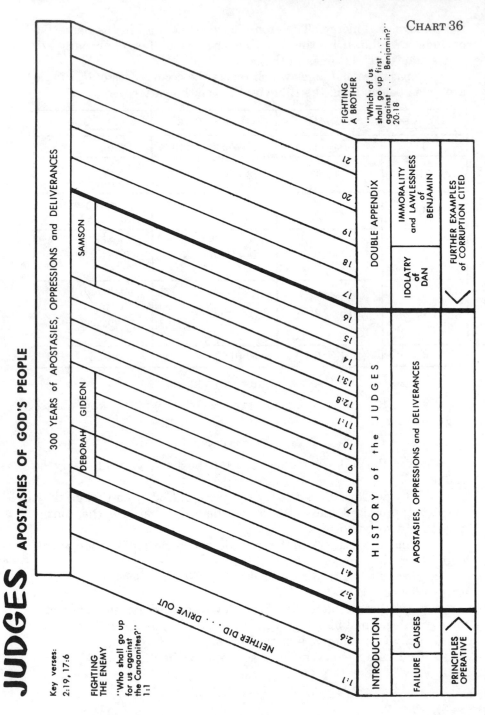

CHART 36

JUDGES APOSTASIES OF GOD'S PEOPLE

Key verses:
2:19, 17:6

FIGHTING
THE ENEMY

"Who shall go up
for us against
the Canaanites?"
1:1

FIGHTING
A BROTHER

"Which of us
shall go up first . . .
against . . . Benjamin?"
20:18

300 YEARS of APOSTASIES, OPPRESSIONS and DELIVERANCES

DEBORAH   GIDEON   SAMSON

NEITHER DID . . . DRIVE OUT

	1:1	2:6	3:7	4:1	5	6	7	8	9	10	11:1	12:8	13:1	14	15	16	17	18	19	20	21
	INTRODUCTION		HISTORY of the JUDGES														DOUBLE APPENDIX				
	FAILURE	CAUSES	APOSTASIES, OPPRESSIONS and DELIVERANCES														IDOLATRY of DAN		IMMORALITY and LAWLESSNESS of BENJAMIN		
	PRINCIPLES OPERATIVE																FURTHER EXAMPLES of CORRUPTION CITED				

7. The Israelites were to expel the idolatrous nations from the land of Canaan. Does this mean that God did not want the Israelites to have any evangelistic ministry with these people at a later time? What should be the Christian's attitude toward very worldly sinners?

8. What are some other practical lessons which you have learned from Judges?

VII. FURTHER STUDY

Four subjects suggested for extended study are:

1. the various appearances in Judges of the religious cycle cited earlier in the chapter

2. biographical studies of Gideon and Samson

3. war

4. the long-suffering of God

VIII. SELECTED READING

GENERAL INTRODUCTION

Bruce, F. F. "Judges." In *The New Bible Commentary*, pp. 236-38.
Cundall, Arthur E. *Judges and Ruth*, pp. 15-49.
Eason, J. Lawrence. *The New Bible Survey*, pp. 120-27.
Morgan, G. Campbell. *The Analyzed Bible*, pp. 70-77.
Payne, J. Barton. "Book of Judges." In *The New Bible Dictionary*, pp. 676-79.
Unger, Merrill F. *Introductory Guide to the Old Testament*, pp. 286-92.

OPPRESSIONS OF ISRAEL

Edersheim, Alfred. *The Bible History-Old Testament*, 3:105-77.
Purkiser, W. T.; Demaray, C. E.; Metz, Donald; and Stuneck, Maude A. *Exploring the Old Testament*, pp. 150-59.
Wood, Leon. *A Survey of Israel's History*, pp. 211-26.
Young, Edward J. *An Introduction to the Old Testament*, pp. 168-72.

COMMENTARIES

Baxter, J. Sidlow. "Judges to Esther." In *Explore the Book*, vol. 2.
Burney, C. F. *The Book of Judges.*
Cook, G. A. *The Book of Judges.* The Cambridge Bible for Schools and Colleges.
Moore, George F. *A Critical and Exegetical Commentary on Judges.* The International Critical Commentary.
Watson, Robert Addison. *Judges and Ruth.* The Expositor's Bible.

10

Ruth: Kinsman-Redeemer Gives Rest

The short story of Ruth is one of the beautiful love stories of the Bible. Boaz, a type of Christ the Redeemer, woos and marries Ruth, a type of Christ's Church. The events took place "in the days when the judges governed" (1:1). In chapter 9 it was shown that the period of judges, extending from about 1375 to 1050 B.C., was mainly one of apostasy, unrest, wars, and judgments. But there were temporary periods of deliverance and peace from the harassments of the enemies. The book of Ruth relates one of the stories of the brighter years, reminding us—among other things—that all was not black darkness during those years.

This account of a godly family from Bethlehem reveals something of God's mysterious and wonderful ways of sovereign grace in fulfilling His divine purposes through a believing remnant. G. T. Manley comments:

> The absence of any reference to the "shield, the sword and the battle," the atmosphere of simple piety that pervades the story, the sense throughout of an overruling providence, and the setting in that quiet corner of Judah all conspire to remind us that the story comes straight from the heart of that Hebrew consciousness of *divine destiny* which was later to reach so glorious a fulfilment.[1]

The chief purpose of the book is to be found in the genealogical table at the end (4:17-22): "And to Obed was born Jesse, and to Jesse, Dàvid." G. Campbell Morgan comments, "In this final word of the book there is manifest the Divine moment in the history of the chosen people. Thus the kingly line was ordered in the midst of infidelity,

---

1. G. T. Manley, ed., *The New Bible Handbook*, p. 166.

162

through faithful souls."[2] God was soon to allow Israel to have kings, and so, by way of preparation, the book of Ruth introduces the kingly line, Boaz and Ruth being the ancestors of King David, through whom came the Saviour-King.

I. PREPARATION FOR STUDY

1. Read Matthew 1:1-17. Observe especially the names given in verses 3-6. Compare these with the names of Ruth 4:18-22. What name begins Matthew's genealogy?[3] Account for this, in view of the fact that Matthew's gospel was written especially with the Jew in mind.

2. Consult an outside source on the subject of typology.[4] Determine the purpose of Old Testament types, and how to interpret them.

3. Refer to Chart 34. Observe on the chart the suggested date for the marriage of Ruth and Boaz.

4. Locate on a map the region of Moab and the city of Bethlehem. This is the geography of the book of Ruth.

II. BACKGROUND

A. TITLE

The book is named after its heroine, Ruth. The name Ruth may be a Moabite modification of the Hebrew *reeiut,* meaning "friendship, association."

B. DATE AND AUTHOR

The author is not known. The book may have been written some time during the reign of King David (1011-971 B.C.). It could not have been written before then because David's name appears in 4:17,22. It may have been written before the time of Solomon, David's successor on the throne, since Solomon's name is not included in the genealogy of 4:18-22. It is very likely that the author was a contemporary of David.

C. PLACE IN THE CANON

The book of Ruth follows Judges in our canon, placed there to fit the chronological sequence. In the Hebrew Bible, it appears in the third division ("Writings") of the threefold canon, under the group of five *Megilloth* books (Song of Solomon, Ruth, Lamentations, Ecclesiastes, Esther). As noted in earlier chapters, these books are

---

2. G. Campbell Morgan, *The Analyzed Bible,* p. 83.
3. The list of Matthew's genealogy is only partial, but the hereditary connections are accurately represented.
4. For example, Bernard Ramm, *Protestant Biblical Interpretation,* pp. 196-219.

read by the Jews at annual feasts or holidays of the Jewish calendar. The harvest field setting of Ruth makes it an appropriate liturgy for the harvest festival (Pentecost).

III. SURVEY

1. First, read through the four chapters at one time. If possible, read aloud. Familiarity with the text is the first law of Bible study. Have pencil or pen in hand as you read so you can make notations in your Bible along the way.

2. Assign chapter titles, and record them on paper.

3. Observe these items in the story: people, places, actions, things. Record outlines of these on paper.

4. Observe all the questions in the book. Also, note the many references to "God" and "LORD."

5. Study the survey Chart 37. Compare its outlines with the observations you have already made in the Bible text.

6. Thus far you have concentrated on observing the facts of the narrative. This is the basis for moving on to interpretation and application. In the remainder of your study you will want to see especially the Messianic character of the book.

IV. MAIN PURPOSES

Four of the book's main purposes are cited below.

1. Genealogy. The book introduces a few of the ancestors of David, the royal lineage of Christ the Messiah. Prominent is the inclusion of a non-Israelite person (Moabitess Ruth) in this line.

2. Typology. The kinsman-redeemer (Boaz) is the prominent Messianic type. Ruth, then, is the type of the Church, the Bride of Christ. Some Bible students view Naomi as a prominent type of Israel.[5] Other types may be seen in the book.

3. Theology. Underlying the entire book is its revelation of the character and ways of God: His providence, sovereignty, grace, holiness, and His invitation of salvation to all peoples.

4. History. As noted earlier, the book describes a few intimate experiences of a godly family of Bethlehem during the period of the judges.

V. PROMINENT SUBJECTS

A. MAIN CHARACTERS

The main characters of the story are:

---

5. For a description of this interpretation, see Merrill F. Unger, *Unger's Bible Handbook*, pp. 181-85.

Naomi ("pleasant one"[6])—a Jewess of Bethlehem, wife of Elimelech, and mother of two sons, Mahlon and Chilion.

Orpah ("neck")—wife and widow of Chilion.

Ruth ("friendship")—widow of Mahlon, who later married Boaz.

Boaz ("in him is strength")—a wealthy Bethlehemite, distant relative of Mahlon, who married Ruth.

B. KINSMAN-REDEEMER

Two key words of the story are "kinsman" and "redeem," which have given Boaz the classic title, "kinsman-redeemer."

Kinsman. This word (Heb., *gô-ēl*) appears thirteen times in Ruth. It basically means "one who redeems," and in the setting of Ruth refers to the near male relative of a deceased man who had the right and duty to buy back (i.e., redeem) land which had been sold to another family, thus preventing the alienation of the land and the extinction of the family. If the nearest kinsman could not fulfill such a redemption, the next of kin had the opportunity. The sequence of the story is described below:

1. When Naomi returned from Moab, she sold her deceased husband's property, probably under pressure of poverty. A. Macdonald writes: "Either Elimelech sold the land before he went to Moab and the year of jubilee came in the interval so that the land reverted to Naomi—see Lev 25:8ff.—or the land was for the last ten years left in the care of a friend."[7]

2. It was necessary for a *gô-ēl* to redeem the land in order to keep it in the family name. By buying it back, however, "the *gô-ēl* would not come into possession of the land himself, but would hold it in trust for his son by Ruth, who would inherit the name and patrimony of Mahlon (her first husband)."[8] In this connection it should be noted that it was Naomi who had prior claim upon the *gô-ēl* but she surrendered it in favor of Ruth.

3. As it turned out, the nearest kinsman wanted the land (4:4*b*) but not Ruth, and so he would not gain by the transaction. Boaz wanted Ruth, not the land, and had the money to transact the business. (Read the following references to a kinsman and his right to redeem: Lev 25:25-31, 47-55; Deut 25:5-10; Job 19:25.)

Redeemer. In view of the above description, it may now be seen why Boaz is called a kinsman-redeemer. The two words are essentially synonymous, but the word "redeemer" is added since our En-

---

6. This is the literal meaning of the Hebrew name.
7. A. Macdonald, "Ruth," in *The New Bible Commentary*, p. 261.
8. Charles F. Pfeiffer and Everett Harrison, eds., *The Wycliffe Bible Commentary*, p. 271.

glish word "kinsman" usually suggests only the idea of family relationship. Notice the seven occurrences of the word "redeem" in chapter 4. It translates the same Hebrew root as *gô-ēl*.

C. MESSIANIC TYPES

Since we now have the New Testament with its antitypes (antitypes are the fulfillments of the types), it is usually not too difficult
to identify types which reside in various persons, things, and events
of Old Testament history. (Note: In a study of types, one should
always be careful to make the antitype, not the type, the preeminent
fact; and also to avoid forcing types for the mere sake of typology.)

There is a rich underlying typology in the book of Ruth. The
major groups are described below.

1. Ruth, representing the Church, the body of believers. Follow
this theme through from Ruth's lost condition in chapter 1 to her
salvation in the later chapters. G. Campbell Morgan suggests an
outline: The Choice of Faith (1-2); The Venture of Faith (3); The
Reward of Faith (4).[9]

2. Boaz, representing Christ, the Kinsman-Redeemer. Gleason L.
Archer says that "the little book of Ruth is one of the most instructive
in the Old Testament concerning the mediatorial work of the Lord
Jesus."[10] He cites some of the qualifications and functions of the *gô-ēl*.
a) He must be a blood relative.
b) He must have the money to purchase the forfeited inheritance.
c) He must be willing to buy back that forfeited inheritance.
d) He must be willing to marry the wife of a deceased kinsman.

Pursue this study further, observing how Christ as the believer's
Kinsman-Redeemer fulfills the above qualifications.

D. GENEALOGY OF THE MESSIAH

The concluding verses (4:17-22) of the book of Ruth are very
significant, for, as one writer has said, "a genealogy is a striking way
of bringing before us the continuity of God's purpose through the
ages."[11] As to the uniqueness of this particular genealogy, A. Macdonald comments:

> The reader is here constrained to face the vital matter that is behind
> the story, namely the genealogy of the Messiah, for every Israelite
> knew that the Messiah was to spring from David. Ruth the Moabitess is
> seen no longer as the courageous stranger who came to Bethlehem, but

9. Morgan, p. 78.
10. Gleason L. Archer, *A Survey of Old Testament Introduction*, p. 269.
11. Leon Morris, *Judges and Ruth*, p. 318.

CHART 37

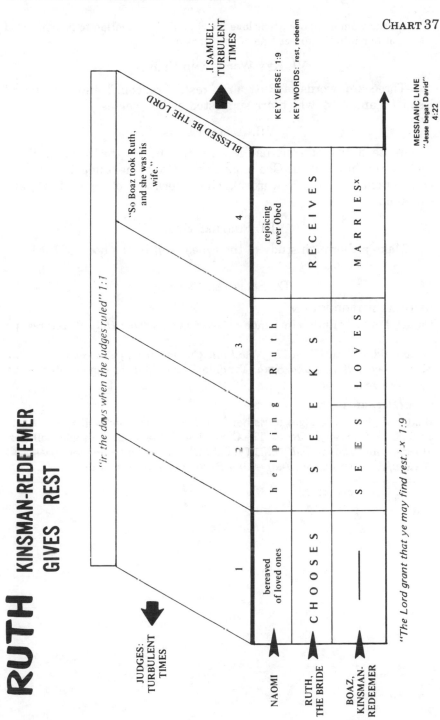

RUTH **KINSMAN-REDEEMER GIVES REST**

"in the days when the judges ruled" 1:1

BLESSED BE THE LORD

JUDGES: TURBULENT TIMES

I SAMUEL: TURBULENT TIMES

KEY VERSE: 1:9

KEY WORDS: rest, redeem

MESSIANIC LINE "Jesse begat David" 4:22

	1	2	3	4
	bereaved of loved ones	helping Ruth		rejoicing over Obed
NAOMI	C H O O S E S	S E E K S		R E C E I V E S
RUTH, THE BRIDE		S E E S	L O V E S	M A R R I E S x
BOAZ, KINSMAN-REDEEMER				

"So Boaz took Ruth, and she was his wife."

"The Lord grant that ye may find rest." x 1:9

as the woman whose great love for Naomi and devotion to Naomi's God put her into the direct line of the Messiah.[12]

VI. KEY WORDS AND VERSES

Three key words of Ruth are "rest," "redeem," and "kinsman." Read 1:9 and 4:14, which are suggested as key verses.

VII. APPLICATIONS

Write a list of spiritual lessons taught by the book of Ruth. Include teachings about God (e.g., as the Holy One, Judge, worshiped One, gracious Lord, Rewarder); characteristics of man; faith and salvation.

VIII. FURTHER STUDY

Make a thorough study of the types seen in the book of Ruth.

IX. SELECTED READING

GENERAL INTRODUCTION

Cassel, Paulus. "Ruth." In Lange's *Commentary on the Holy Scriptures*, pp. 3-10.

Macdonald, A. "Ruth." In *The New Bible Commentary*, pp. 258-59.

Morris, Leon. *Judges and Ruth*. Tyndale Old Testament Commentaries, pp. 229-43.

COMMENTARIES

Baxter, J. Sidlow. "Judges to Esther." In *Explore the Book*, vol. 2.

Cook, G. A. *The Book of Ruth*. The Cambridge Bible for Schools and Colleges.

Morris, Leon. *Judges and Ruth*. Tyndale Old Testament Commentaries.

Watson, Robert Addison. *Judges and Ruth*. The Expositor's Bible.

---

12. Macdonald, p. 261.

11

1 and 2 Samuel: The First Two Kings of Israel

The books of 1 and 2 Samuel continue the history of Israel from the point where Judges leaves it. The last verse of Judges sums up the spiritual life of Israel at that time: "In those days there was no king in Israel; everyone did what was right in his own eyes" (Judg 21:25). That is, no man was the head of the nation, no voice commanded the obedience of the people, no prince served as commander in chief of all the tribes at one time in a nationwide program to subdue the enemies, and no one monarch unified the people under the banner of their sovereign Lord God.

It was always God's purpose to reign as King in the hearts and lives of the Israelites. A government so ordered is called a *theocracy* (from the Greek *theos*, "God"). Furthermore, in terms of organization, God desired to preserve the unity of His chosen people through the leadership of *one* ruler over all. That is what is called *monarchy* (from the Greek *monos*, "one"). God's design, therefore, called for the combination theocracy-monarchy (theocratic monarchy, or monarchic theocracy).

The years of the judges were years of spiritual decline for Israel, because the nation was increasingly putting God out of their lives. Thus they were untheocratic. When the time came (1 Sam 8) that they felt their need of a king (monarchy), they had rejected the idea of God on the throne (theocracy). God objected to their request for a king, not because He was against kingship (monarchy), but because of their rejection of Him (theocracy): "They have rejected me, that I should not reign over them" (1 Sam 8:7, KJV).

God granted Israel's request for rulership by kings, but not without warning of consequences for dethroning Him as their King (1 Sam 8:7-9). Then, in His mysterious workings of grace and might, as God of history He used the people's kings as His channels of revelation, service, blessing, and justice. One of those whom He anointed as king was David, "a man after His own heart" (1 Sam 13:14), who would be the grand type and forerunner of the Messianic King. The two books of 1 and 2 Samuel describe the establishing of this Davidic kingdom in Israel.

I. Preparation for Study

1. It will be of help to you as you begin your study of 1 and 2 Samuel to see their place among the Old Testament books that describe Israel's history. Broadly speaking, the history of Israel as given in the Old Testament falls into four periods, which someone has identified by the words *camp, commonwealth, crown, captivity.* See Chart 38.

ISRAEL'S HISTORY BY PERIODS   Chart 38

IN EGYPT AND THE WILDERNESS	IN CANAAN UNDER JUDGES	IN CANAAN UNDER KINGS	IN ASSYRIA AND BABYLON
CAMP	COMMONWEALTH	CROWN	CAPTIVITY
660 YEARS	360 YEARS	460 YEARS	160 YEARS
PENTATEUCH	JOSHUA JUDGES RUTH	I and II SAMUEL KINGS CHRONICLES	EZRA NEHEMIAH ESTHER

a) The *Camp* period extended from the call of Abraham, the founder of the nation, to Moses' bringing the people up to the "gate" of Canaan, a period of about 660 years. This history is recorded in the Pentateuch.

b) The *Commonwealth* period extended from their entrance into Canaan under Joshua to the crowning of their first king, Saul, a period of about 360 years, the history of which is given in Joshua, Judges, and Ruth.

c) The *Crown* period extended from the crowning of their first king, Saul, to the Babylonian Captivity, a period of about 460 years. This history is given in the six books of Samuel, Kings, and Chronicles.

d) The *Captivity* period, including the restoration, extended from the Babylonian Captivity to the end of the Old Testament history, a period of about 160 years. Ezekiel and Daniel were prophets during this period. The historical books of Ezra, Nehemiah, and Esther report some events of this period, especially the return from captivity.

You will find interesting descriptions of these four periods of Israel's history in Psalms 78 and 79, as follows: under Moses, 78:5-54; under Joshua, 78:55; under the judges, 78:56-64; under the kings, 78:65-72; in captivity, 79:1-13.

2. Acquaint yourself with the geographical setting of 1 and 2 Samuel. Study Map K now, and refer to it as you read the action of the books.

II. BACKGROUND

A. TITLE

The Jews probably assigned the name Samuel as a title for these books for various reasons: (1) the man Samuel was the key character of the books; (2) he was the "king-maker," anointing the two other main characters, Saul and David, to be king; (3) the Jews regarded him as a national leader, second only to Moses. Of this, A. M. Renwick writes:

> As Moses delivered Israel from Egypt, gave them the law, and brought them to the very borders of the promised land, so Samuel was sent of God to deliver Israel when the nation's fortunes seemed almost hopeless. Spiritually and politically, the nation appeared virtually lost at the end of Eli's judgeship (cf. 1 Sam. 4:12-22; Ps. 78:59-64; Jer. 26:6). Under Samuel came a wonderful spiritual renovation and a new hope (1 Sam. 7).[1]

B. PLACE IN THE CANON

In our English Bible, 1 and 2 Samuel appear among the historical books. The earliest Hebrew Bibles considered the two books as one, among the Former Prophets (Joshua, Judges, Samuel, Kings). Notice the changes made over the years of the Samuel and Kings books:
Hebrew Bible (B.C.): Samuel; Kings (two books)

---

1. A. M. Renwick, "I and II Samuel," *The New Bible Commentary*, pp. 262-63.

The Great Sea

PHOENICIANS

Sea of Chinnereth

Mt. Carmel

ISRAEL

CANAANITES

Jordan River

Jabesh-Gilead

Aphek

Mahanaim

AMMON

Bethel

Shiloh

GILEAD

Mizpeh

Michmash

Gibeon

Geba

Gilgal

Gibeah

Ramah

Kirjath-Jearim

Nob

Jerusalem

Ekron

Beth-shemesh

Bethlehem

Ashdod

Gath

Ashkelon

Keilah

Salt Sea

Gaza

Hebron

Ziklag

En-gedi

PHILISTIA

Beersheba

MOAB

JUDAH

Scale of Miles

0   20   40

GEOGRAPHY of FIRST and SECOND SAMUEL

Septuagint (B.C.): 1,2 Kings; 3,4 Kings (four books)
Vulgate (A.D.): 1,2 Kings; 3,4 Kings (four books)
English Bible (A.D.): 1,2 Samuel; 1,2 Kings (four books)

The intimate structural connection of 2 Samuel with 1 Samuel is shown by the accompanying outline. Note especially that the last half of 1 Samuel and the first chapter of 2 Samuel are part of one section in the outline for the simple reason that the story of Saul does not end until chapter 1 of 2 Samuel.

FIRST AND SECOND SAMUEL

ELI, the ARK, and SAMUEL	SAMUEL and SAUL	SAUL and DAVID	DAVID, KING over JUDAH	DAVID, KING over ALL ISRAEL
I SAM. 1	9	16	II SAM. 2	5 24

C. AUTHOR AND DATE

It is difficult to identify the author (or authors). Various suggestions of authorship or coauthorship include Abiathar, an attendant of David; Nathan and Gad (cf. 1 Chron 29:29); and pupils from Samuel's school of the prophets. The detailed and vivid account of the happenings, with which these books abound, indicates that most of the narrative was written by men living at the time these things occurred rather than at a much later date.

The fact of joint authorship does not take away from the unity of the books as to theme. Concerning all the writings of Scripture, one must continually recognize the supernatural moving of the Holy Spirit in the hearts and minds of the human writers, whoever and however many they were, to compose the holy writings.

If Samuel was one of the authors, he could only have narrated the events that preceded his death (which is recorded in 1 Sam 25).[2] He would have done his writing sometime between 1025 and 900 B.C.

D. THE THREE LEADING CHARACTERS OF 1 AND 2 SAMUEL

1. Samuel. The name Samuel is from a Hebrew word which has been variously translated as: "the name of God," "his name is God," "his name is mighty," or "heard of God."

One is not surprised that the Jews have esteemed Samuel second to Moses among their leaders. The psalmist (Psalm 99:6), and God speaking to Jeremiah (Jer 15:1), classified Samuel with Moses as an interceding priest. Samuel held the honor of being the last of the

---

2. That Samuel was a writer of at least one work is indicated by 1 Samuel 10:25.

judges (1 Sam 7:6, 15-17) and the first of the new order of prophets (1 Sam 3:20; Acts 3:24; 13:20). The stature of the prophetic office during the years of the kingdoms can be traced back to Samuel's life and ministry. He probably was the founder of a school of prophets (cf. 1 Sam 10:5).[3]

2. *Saul.* Saul (Heb., *Sa-ul*, "asked," i.e., of God) was the first king of Israel; son of Kish, of the tribe of Benjamin. He was a choice young man in the prime of life when he was placed on the throne. He was a physical "giant" (1 Sam 10:23), industrious, generous, honest, and modest. God chose him to institute Israel's monarchy, but three times during his reign he disqualified himself from the high office. The story of Saul (1 Sam 9-31) is one of the most pathetic accounts of God's servants. J. Barton Payne cites four degenerations in Saul's experience:[4]

GOOD POINTS	DEGENERATED INTO
striking appearance, 9:2	pride, 18:8
initiative, 11:7	rebellion, 20:31
bravery, 13:3	recklessness, 14:24
patriotic Spirit-filling, 11:6	demon possession, 16:14

3. *David.* David, son of Jesse, was a man after God's heart, and in a life-span of about seventy years, he "served his own generation by the will of God" (Acts 13:36, KJV). T. H. Jones describes David:

> He stood out as a bright and shining light for the God of Israel. His accomplishments were many and varied; man of action, poet, tender lover, generous foe, stern dispenser of justice, loyal friend, he was all that men find wholesome and admirable in man, and this by the will of God, who made him and shaped him for his destiny.[5]

David was Israel's greatest king, designated by God as the Messianic forerunner of Christ. He is the only person in Scripture with the name David. There are fifty-eight New Testament references to him. (Read Rom 1:3 and Rev 22:16 for two examples.)

---

3. The Old Testament (e.g., 1 Sam 10:5) makes only a reference to a "group" of prophets. It is not known if such groups had any formal organization. The word "school" is still probably an accurate designation. See Edward J. Young, "Prophets," *The Zondervan Pictorial Bible Dictionary*, p. 687.

4. J. Barton Payne, *An Outline of Hebrew History*, p. 96. ©1954 by Baker Book House. Used by permission.

5. T. H. Jones, "David," in *The New Bible Dictionary*, p. 296.

David's career was marred by heinous sins, but his honesty and contrition in acknowledging and confessing those sins brought God's forgiveness. (Read his prayer of Psalm 51.)

E. FIRST TWO KINGS OF ISRAEL

Saul and David were the first two kings of Israel, followed by Solomon, the third king. For orientation in your study of 1 and 2 Samuel, keep in mind the simple outline of Chart 39.

THE FIRST THREE KINGS OF ISRAEL   CHART 39

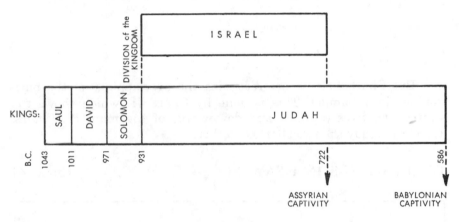

III. SURVEY OF 1 SAMUEL

1. First note on the survey Chart 42 that most of the thirty-one chapters are individual segments of study. Mark your Bible to show that extra segments begin at 2:11 and 21:10; and that 4:1*b*; 7:3; and 28:3 replace 4:1; 7:1; and 28:1 as starting points.

2. Scan the thirty-one chapters in your Bible. Make notations (e.g., underline strong phrases) in your Bible as you read. Record segment titles on paper.

3. Read your segment titles and try to recall the general movement of the narrative from chapter to chapter.

4. Try to determine what chapters of 1 Samuel might be grouped together according to similar content. Look especially for grouping according to main characters. Is there any overlapping?

5. Observe the important places of chapters 9 and 16 in the book: Samuel gives way to Saul in chapter 9; Saul is rejected in favor of David in chapter 16. This is diagrammed on Chart 40.

MAIN CHARACTERS OF I SAMUEL   CHART 40

1	9	16	31
SAMUEL —prophet, priest, judge	SAUL —man after man's heart	DAVID —man after God's heart	
—birth —childhood —judgeship	—choice —reign —rejection	—anointing —pursuit —exile	

But Chart 40 does not recognize the overlappings of the biographies in 1 Samuel. This is done by Chart 41, which shows the contrasting lives (upward and downward) of the main characters. Carefully study the two charts together.

OVERLAPPINGS IN I SAMUEL   CHART 41

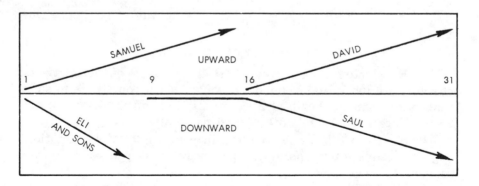

6. Compare the beginning and ending of the book.

7. Before you finish your survey study, try to suggest a theme for 1 Samuel. Write out a few important truths which you have already observed in your study.

8. Study the survey Chart 42. Compare its outlines with what you have already observed. How does the chart show 1 Samuel to be a connecting link between the books of Judges and 2 Samuel?

CHART 42

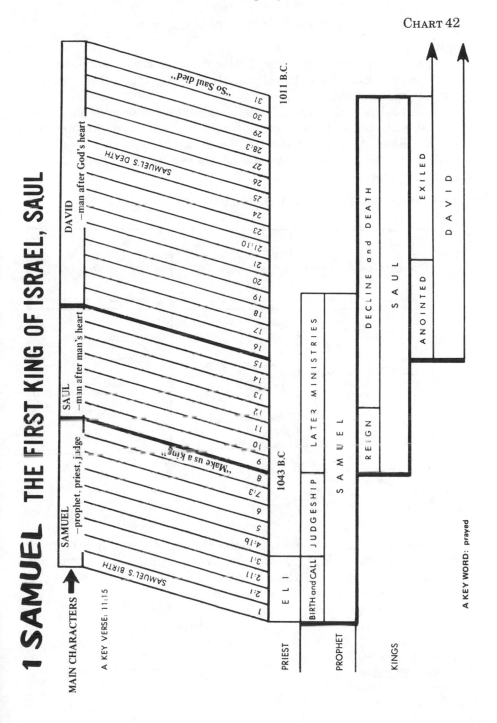

1 SAMUEL THE FIRST KING OF ISRAEL, SAUL

MAIN CHARACTERS

A KEY VERSE: 11:15

SAMUEL'S BIRTH

SAMUEL — prophet, priest, judge

"Make us a king"

SAUL — man after man's heart

DAVID — man after God's heart

SAMUEL'S DEATH

"So Saul died."

1043 B.C.

1011 B.C.

| | | 1 | 2:1 | 2:11 | 3:1 | 4:1b | 5 | 6 | 7:3 | 8 | 9 | 10 | 11 | 12 | 13 | 14 | 15 | 16 | 17 | 18 | 19 | 20 | 21 | 21:10 | 23 | 24 | 25 | 26 | 27 | 28:3 | 29 | 30 | 31 |

PRIEST — ELI

PROPHET — BIRTH and CALL | JUDGESHIP | LATER MINISTRIES

SAMUEL

REIGN | DECLINE and DEATH

KINGS — SAUL

ANOINTED | EXILED

DAVID

A KEY WORD: prayed

IV. PROMINENT SUBJECTS OF 1 SAMUEL

A. HISTORY

First Samuel records the transition from the era of judges to that of the monarchy. (Read Acts 13:20-21, noticing these three words: judges, prophet, king.)

The book also describes Samuel's influences, as prophet-judge, on the life of Israel and many of its leaders. Chart 43 shows how the story of Samuel is told in the first eight chapters of 1 Samuel. (He continued to serve after 1 Samuel 8:22, but beginning at chapter 9 the head of the nation is a king, Saul.)

THE MAN SAMUEL IN I SAMUEL 1-8   CHART 43

1:1	4:1b	7:3 8:22
SAMUEL'S BIRTH and CALL	ARK of the LORD	SAMUEL the JUDGE
(Samuel the main character)	(no mention of Samuel)	(Samuel the main character)

CHILDHOOD YEARS
(1-12 yrs. old)

SILENT YEARS
(12-32 yrs. old)

PUBLIC MINISTRY
(32 to an old age)

PRESENTED
to GOD
as a NAZARITE

COMMISSIONED
by GOD
as a PROPHET

SERVING
GOD
as a JUDGE

Most of 1 Samuel reports the highlights of the tragic reign of Saul, Israel's first king. Overlapping this account is the setting for the reign of David as described in 2 Samuel.

Read 1 Samuel with this outline in mind:

1. Samuel's Birth and Call   (1:1—4:1a)
2. The Ark of the Lord   (4:1b—7:2)
3. Samuel the Judge   (7:3—8:22)
4. Saul the King   (9:1—12:25)
5. Saul Rejected   (13:1—15:35)

6. David Anointed	(16:1—17:58)
7. David Flees Saul	(18:1—21:9)
8. David in Exile	(21:10—28:2)
9. Last Days of Saul's Reign	(28:3—31:13)

B. TYPES AND SYMBOLS

The books of Samuel are rich in typical or symbolic truths. In many ways this Old Testament book foreshadows Christ in the offices of prophet, priest, and king.

C. SOME DISTINCTIVE POINTS OF 1 SAMUEL

The book of 1 Samuel contains many unique items. Some of them are:

1. The sources of the oft-quoted words, "Ichabod" ("The glory is departed" or "Where is the glory?") 4:21 (KJV); "Ebenezer" ("Hitherto hath the LORD helped us") 7:12 (KJV); "God save the king," 10:24 (KJV).

2. Reference to the school of the prophets, probably founded by Samuel (10:5; 19:18-24).

3. First Old Testament book to use the phrase "LORD of hosts" (appears eleven times in the two books of Samuel; e.g., 1 Sam 1:3).

4. Important place given to the Holy Spirit and prayer.

5. As in the book of Judges, explicit reference to the Law of Moses is lacking. But many of the items and activities inherent in the Law (e.g., offerings, tabernacle, ark, Aaron, Levites) appear frequently.

6. In the early chapters, much light is shed on Shiloh as the focal place of the national religion.

V. KEY WORDS AND VERSES OF 1 SAMUEL

After you have finished your survey of 1 Samuel, choose key words and verses which represent its story. Also, assign a title to the book. Note the title given on Chart 42. Compare this with the one assigned to 2 Samuel (Chart 44).

VI. APPLICATIONS OF 1 SAMUEL

1. Among other things, 1 Samuel teaches much about prayer. Read the following verses, and apply them to your own life: 1:10-28; 7:5-10; 8:5-6; 9:15; 12:19-23; 28:6.

2. What constitutes a call to Christian service?

3. In what sense does a Christian need and enjoy the presence of the Lord?

4. Why does God sometimes let His people have the things they

request, even though the thing desired is evil (1 Sam 8:6-9)? Is judgment for such an evil request inevitable? (Cf. Psalm 106:15.)

5. What are some causes of spiritual backsliding? Trace the downward path in Saul's life.

6. List some spiritual lessons taught by the story of David in 1 Samuel.

7. What do you learn here about jealousy and hate, and about faithful friendship?

8. What does the book teach about God?

VII. FURTHER STUDY OF 1 SAMUEL

1. Make biographical studies of Eli, Samuel, and Saul.

2. Critics of the Bible text see two conflicting reactions by God concerning Israel's request for a king. They see God condemning in chapters 7 and 8; and God favoring in chapter 9 (especially v. 16). Read these chapters. Is there contradiction here? Support your answer.

3. Study the origin of the ministry of prophet. Look into the schools of prophets of those early days.[6]

VIII. SURVEY OF 2 SAMUEL

1. Survey 2 Samuel, using procedures followed for 1 Samuel.

2. Who is the main character of the book? Is he still living when the book closes?

3. Read 1 Samuel 31 immediately followed by 2 Samuel 1. What is the continuity?

4. Carefully study Chart 44. Compare its outlines with what you have already observed in your scanning of the book.

5. The pivotal point of the book is 11:1—12:31. Read the two chapters. Note on the chart the contrast before and after this turning point.

6. The last four chapters are appendixes, recording some of David's last acts and words. Read these chapters, and relate them to the main body of the book.

IX. PROMINENT SUBJECTS OF 2 SAMUEL

Of the many ingredients of this narrative of 2 Samuel,[7] four are given prominence:

a king—David (e.g., 2:4)

---

6. See *The Zondervan Pictorial Bible Dictionary*, p. 687.
7. Much of 2 Samuel is reported in 1 Chronicles.

a city—Jerusalem (5:6-12)
   —Zion (5:7; 6:1-17)
a covenant—Davidic (7:8-17)
a kingdom—everlasting (7:16; 23:1-7)
Read the passages cited above, and look for other references in the book to those subjects.

A. SOME HIGHLIGHTS OF DAVID'S REIGN

This history book does not intend to be exhaustive in its contents. The authors, under the guidance of the Holy Spirit, selected those events from this period of David's life which would serve to impart the message God intended for the reader. Some events not recorded here, but occurring about the same time, are found in other books, such as 1 Chronicles.

The following brief outline shows some of the highlights of David's reign as recorded in 2 Samuel.

1. David's Lament over the Death of Saul and Jonathan (1:1-27)
2. David's Reign over Judah (2:1—4:12)
3. David's Reign over All Israel (5:1—10:19)
4. David's Sins (11:1—12:31)
5. David's Troubles (13:1—20:26)
6. Appendixes (21:1—24:25)
   a) Famine (21:1-14)
   b) Philistine Wars (21:15-22)
   c) Psalms of Thanksgiving (22:1—23:7)
   d) David's Mighty Men (23:8-39)
   e) Census and Pestilence (24:1-25)

B. THE TEMPLE AND THE COVENANT

God refused David's offer to build Him a house, but He spoke His refusal in such a burst of grace and glory and revelation that David could only marvel at God's greatness and goodness. It was not that God was displeased with David's desire to build Him a house; indeed, He said, "You did well that it was in your heart" (1 Kings 8:18). But God had another plan for His beloved servant. God would build a "house" for *David*. God was reaffirming the covenant He had originally made with Abraham, a covenant promising an everlasting Kingdom, with Christ on its throne.

David wanted to build a temple for God, but Solomon was given the privilege. David's wars cleared the way for another man to lay the foundation of that house of worship (1 Chron 22:18; cf. 22:8-10). After the warring was over, Solomon erected the Temple from materials which David had prepared.

C. DAVID'S SINS (11:1—12:31)

David had not reigned long in Jerusalem as king of all Israel before he came to a tragic turning point in his career. There had been other times in his experience when he left his usual high plane of living and descended into the valley, yielding to such things as unbelief, fear, falsehood, deceit, pride, and anger. But the sins of this day—adultery involving Bathsheba and the murder of Uriah—were all the more conspicuous because they were committed at the height of his reign.

David was never the same again. As long as he lived, troubles kept arising to plague him.

D. DAVID'S TROUBLES (13:1—20:26)

David's sins against Bathsheba and Uriah were forgiven by God when he confessed in repentance, but the bitter fruits of his sins were inevitable. Read these chapters with this brief outline in view:

1. Family Troubles (chaps. 13-14)
2. Absalom's Rebellion (15:1—19:8)
3. David's Restoration (19:9-40)
4. Further Strife and Rebellion (19:41—20:26)

X. KEY WORDS AND VERSES OF 2 SAMUEL

Read 5:4 and 7:25-26 as key verses of 2 Samuel. Choose others from the Bible text. The phrase "before the LORD" is a key phrase of the book. Consult an exhaustive concordance to see its uses.

XI. APPLICATIONS OF 2 SAMUEL

1. What does the book teach about the following:
a) sin and its workings, punishment, confession, and pardon
b) God and His relationship to the believer
c) the believer's dependence on God (see 2:1; 5:3; 6:16,21: 7:18; 8:6,14: 12:16; 22:1).
d) the will of God
e) rewards of God

　　2. Read Galatians 6:7. Apply its teaching to the life of David.

　　3. How important is the ministry of the Holy Spirit in the daily walk of the believer? What are His ministries?

　　4. Study the contrasts (page 184) about *control* in David's life, as J. Barton Payne has observed these in the books of Samuel.[8]

XII. FURTHER STUDY OF 2 SAMUEL

　　1. Make a biographical study of David. The Bible passages about

---

8. J. Barton Payne, *An Outline of Hebrew History*, p. 110. ©1954, Baker Book House. Used by permission.

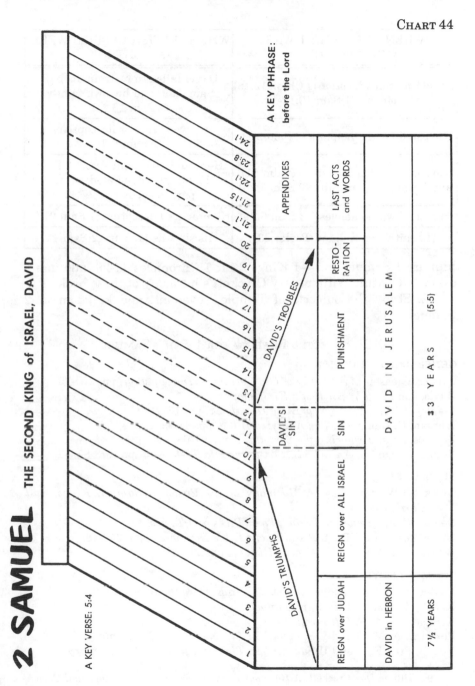

2 SAMUEL THE SECOND KING of ISRAEL, DAVID

A KEY VERSE: 5:4

A KEY PHRASE: before the Lord

DAVID'S TRIUMPHS

DAVID'S TROUBLES

REIGN over JUDAH	REIGN over ALL ISRAEL	DAVID'S SIN	PUNISHMENT	RESTO-RATION	APPENDIXES
		SIN			LAST ACTS and WORDS

DAVID in HEBRON

DAVID IN JERUSALEM

7½ YEARS

33 YEARS (5:5)

1 2 3 4 5 6 7 8 9 10 11 12 13 14 15 16 17 18 19 20 21:1 21:15 22:1 23:8 24:1

WHEN GOD'S SPIRIT WAS IN CONTROL	WHEN SELFISH DESIRES WERE IN CONTROL
David had men's devotion (1 Chron 12:18) and women's (1 Sam 19:12-13)	David failed to restrain Joab (2 Sam 3:39) and his own family (2 Sam 13:21)
He cared for the helpless (2 Sam 9:1)	He was brutal with captives (2 Sam 8:2)
He confessed his own sins (Psalm 51) and his enemies' nobility (2 Sam 1:23)	He would not admit error (2 Sam 19:29) and repudiated former pardons (1 Kings 2:8-9)
His piety was shameless (2 Sam 6:21)	He practiced deception (1 Sam 21:2)
His faith was radiant (Psalm 23)	His sin was heinous (2 Sam 11)

him are 1 Samuel 16:1—1 Kings 2:11; 1 Chronicles 11-29; and many psalms. (Consult William Day Crockett's harmony of these books.)[9]

2. Study the subjects of Temple, covenant, and kingdom in 2 Samuel.

XIII. Selected Reading for 1 and 2 Samuel

GENERAL INTRODUCTION

Archer, Gleason L. *A Survey of Old Testament Introduction*, pp. 270-75.
Davis, John D. *The Birth of a Kingdom*.
Manley, G. T., ed. *The New Bible Handbook*, pp. 167-72.
Morgan, G. Campbell. *The Analyzed Bible*, pp. 84-99.
Phillips, John. *Exploring the Scriptures*, pp. 61-66.
Young, Edward J. *An Introduction to the Old Testament*, pp. 173-83.

BIOGRAPHY

Crockett, William Day. *A Harmony of the Books of Samuel, Kings, and Chronicles*.
Deane, W. J. *Samuel and Saul: Their Lives and Times*.
Unger, Merrill F. "David." In *Unger's Bible Dictionary*, pp. 242-48.
Wood, Leon. *A Survey of Israel's History*, pp. 237-86.

COMMENTARIES

Baxter, J. Sidlow. "Judges to Esther." In *Explore the Book*, vol. 2.
Keil, C. F., and Delitzsch, F. *Samuel*.
Kirkpatrick, A. F. *I, II Samuel*.
Renwick, A. M. "I and II Samuel." In *The New Bible Commentary*.
Young, Fred E. "I and II Samuel." In *The Wycliffe Bible Commentary*.

---

9. William Day Crockett, *A Harmony of the Books of Samuel, Kings and Chronicles*.

12

1 and 2 Kings: From Glory to Captivity

The story of 1 and 2 Kings is basically one of failure: a nation passes "from affluence and influence to poverty and paralysis."[1] The opening chapters of 1 Kings describe the glory attending Solomon's reign, but by the middle of the book antagonisms between the ten northern tribes and the two southern tribes bring on a split in the

THE DOWNWARD MOVEMENT OF 1 AND 2 KINGS

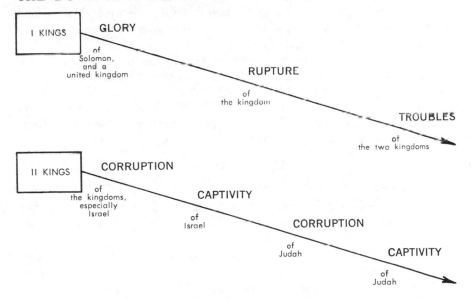

I KINGS — GLORY of Solomon, and a united kingdom — RUPTURE of the kingdom — TROUBLES of the two kingdoms

II KINGS — CORRUPTION of the kingdoms, especially Israel — CAPTIVITY of Israel — CORRUPTION of Judah — CAPTIVITY of Judah

---

1. G. Campbell Morgan, *Living Messages of the Books of the Bible*, p. 177.

kingdom. The troubles of the two new kingdoms (Israel and Judah) carry over into the narrative of 2 Kings, climaxing in the fall and captivity of both. The accompanying diagram shows the downward movement in both books.

By revealing the failure of man and of human governments, 1 and 2 Kings point forward to that age when God will set up His own Kingdom, with the greater Son of David as its sovereign Head, and all nations subject to Him.

I. Preparation for Study

1. Review the four periods of Israel as shown on Chart 38.

2. Study carefully Chart 45. Read the explanation furnished on the chart. Note especially the reference to three periods of Israel's history: united kingdom, divided kingdom, and surviving kingdom. Account for the words *united*, *divided*, and *surviving*. Where on the chart does each period begin?

Observe the prominence of the prophets during the kingdom years. The prophets of the first half of the divided kingdom period, among whom were Elijah and Elisha, did not write any prophetical books of the Old Testament. They were succeeded in the prophetic office by such great prophets as Isaiah and Jeremiah. Kings and Chronicles furnish a background for the prophetic utterances, and the prophetic books shed much light on Kings and Chronicles.

3. Before reading each of the Kings books, acquaint yourself with the geography involved. Map L shows the geography of 1 Kings, and Map M that of 2 Kings.

4. Consult the Appendix (Charts 118 and 119) for a listing of the kings of Israel and Judah. You will want to refer to these charts from time to time as you survey the books of Kings.

II. Background

A. TITLE AND PLACE IN THE CANON

The title "Kings" is very appropriate for these books, since they record events in the careers of the kings of Judah and Israel from Solomon to Zedekiah, the last king.

Chart 46 shows the locations of the four books of Kings and Chronicles in the early Hebrew canon, in the Greek Septuagint listing, and in our present English Bible. As the chart shows, 1 and 2 Kings were one book in the early Hebrew Bibles. When the Septuagint translators translated this one book into Greek, they made two books out of it. The reason was that of convenience of handling the

MAP L

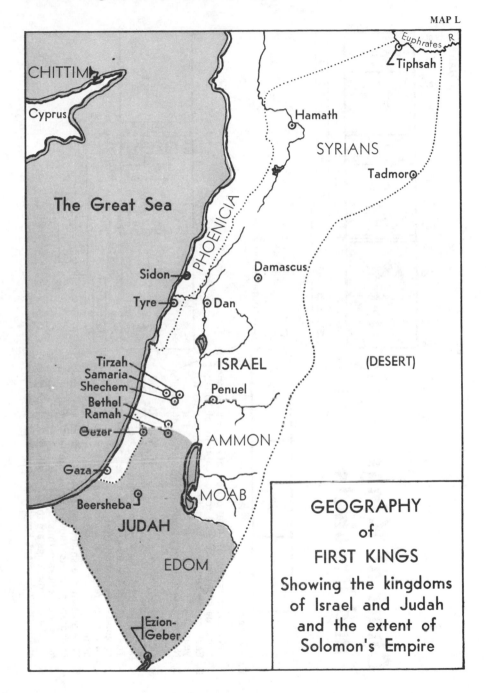

CHITTIM

Cyprus

The Great Sea

PHOENICIA

Sidon—

Tyre—

Dan

Tirzah
Samaria
Shechem
Bethel
Ramah
Gezer—

Gaza—

Beersheba

JUDAH

EDOM

Ezion-
Geber

Euphrates R

Tiphsah

Hamath

SYRIANS

Tadmor

Damascus

(DESERT)

ISRAEL

Penuel

AMMON

MOAB

GEOGRAPHY
of
FIRST KINGS
Showing the kingdoms
of Israel and Judah
and the extent of
Solomon's Empire

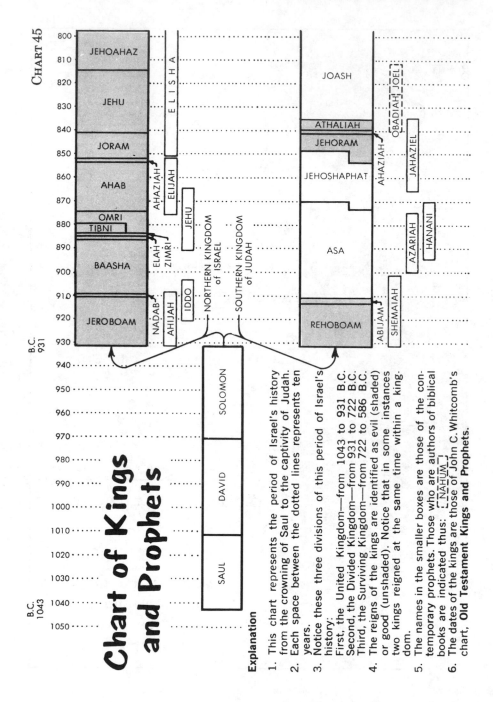

Chart of Kings and Prophets

Explanation

1. This chart represents the period of Israel's history from the crowning of Saul to the captivity of Judah.

2. Each space between the dotted lines represents ten years.

3. Notice these three divisions of this period of Israel's history:
   First, the United Kingdom—from 1043 to 931 B.C.
   Second, the Divided Kingdom—from 931 to 722 B.C.
   Third, the Surviving Kingdom—from 722 to 586 B.C.

4. The reigns of the kings are identified as evil (shaded) or good (unshaded). Notice that in some instances two kings reigned at the same time within a kingdom.

5. The names in the smaller boxes are those of the contemporary prophets. Those who are authors of biblical books are indicated thus: [NAHUM].

6. The dates of the kings are those of John C. Whitcomb's chart, **Old Testament Kings and Prophets**.

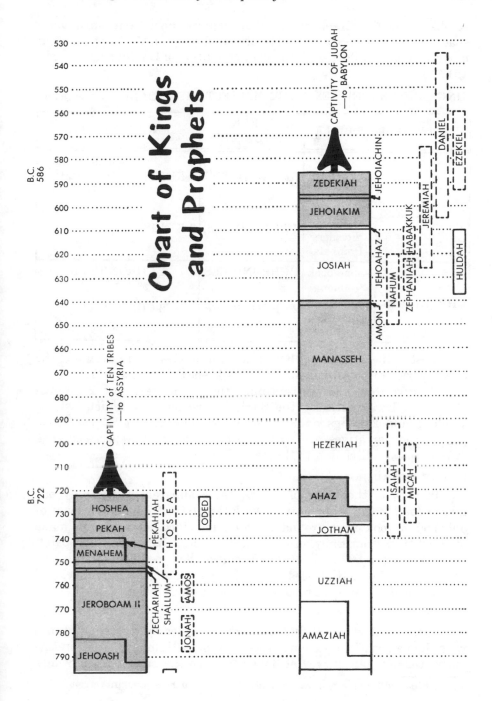

Chart of Kings and Prophets

scrolls, since the Greek translation requires about one-third more space than the Hebrew text. This twofold division first appeared in modern Hebrew Bibles with the printed edition of Daniel Blomberg in 1517.

KINGS AND CHRONICLES IN THE OLD TESTAMENT CANONS CHART 46

EARLY HEBREW BIBLE	GREEK SEPTUAGINT	ENGLISH BIBLE	
KINGS { —one book	III KINGDOMS[2]	1 KINGS	—among the Historical Books
—among the Former Prophets	IV KINGDOMS	2 KINGS	
CHRONICLES { —one book	1 CHRONICLES	1 CHRONICLES	
—among the Historical Writings	2 CHRONICLES	2 CHRONICLES	

Most of the chapters of Kings and Chronicles relate events of the crown period of Israel and Judah. This is shown by Chart 47.

Observe that 1 Kings continues the narrative where 2 Samuel stops, and Ezra continues the narrative where 2 Chronicles stops. While 1 and 2 Kings and 2 Chronicles generally cover the same period, the narratives are written from different perspectives. The differences are discussed in the next chapter.

B. DATE AND AUTHOR

In view of the unity of Kings, there apparently was only one author for 1 and 2 Kings. Since the latest item of 2 Kings (release of Jehoiachin) took place around 562 B.C., and since no mention is made of the return from Babylon (536 B.C.), 1 and 2 Kings were probably written between 562 and 536 B.C. Tradition has assigned Jeremiah as the author. Most authorities prefer the viewpoint of anonymity, and agree that the writer was a Jewish captive in Babylon.

C. SETTING

Just as the study of Judges is made easier by an acquaintance with the names of the various judges, so you will find it helpful in this early stage of your survey of Kings to learn the names of the kings.

---

2. First and 2 Samuel were called I and II Kingdoms in the Septuagint version.

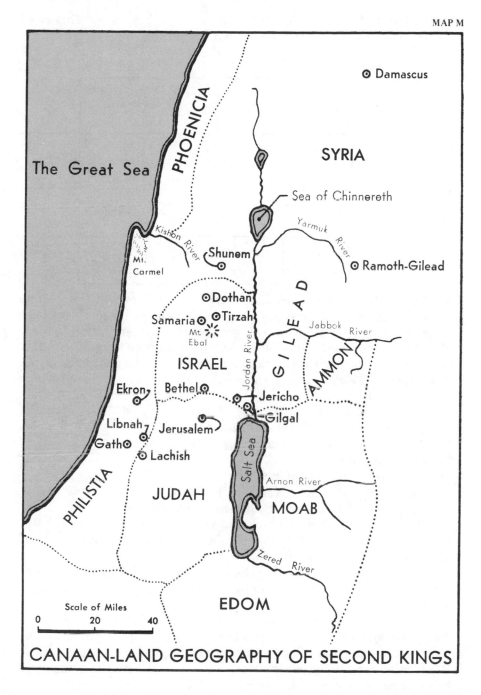

CANAAN-LAND GEOGRAPHY OF SECOND KINGS

COVERAGE OF THE BOOKS OF SAMUEL, KINGS AND CHRONICLES

CHART 47

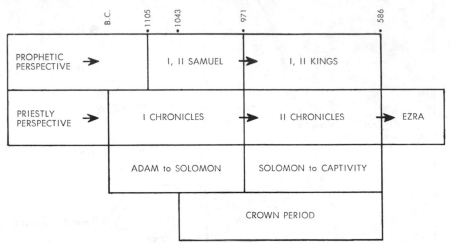

Study the lists in the Appendix, where the nineteen kings (plus one queen) of Judah and nineteen kings of Israel are listed chronologically. Some names appear in both groups but represent different men. Note the words "good" and "bad" designated for each king. It was part of the biblical writer's aim to issue a verdict on the character of the leadership of the kings. Keep these lists before you as you read Kings (and Chronicles).

Next study the accompanying Chart 48 entitled "The Setting of Kings and Chronicles." Observe the following:

1. Note the key historical *events* of this period:

1043 B.C. First King

931 B.C. Division of the Kingdom

722 B.C. Fall of Samaria (Northern Kingdom)

586 B.C. Fall of Jerusalem (Southern Kingdom)

2. Note where 1 Kings picks up the narrative. Note also that 2 Kings concludes at the fall of Jerusalem, but that it includes a brief epilogue (25:27-30) of a later date.

3. Observe that 2 Kings picks up the narrative from 1 Kings at an uneventful junction. This confirms the approach to 1 and 2 Kings as one unified narrative.

4. Note that Elijah and Elisha are prominent characters in Kings. Look at Chart 45 and note that almost all of the prophets who lived after Elijah and Elisha were authors of prophetical books of the Bible. Why was the prophet's work so important for the kingdoms? What three periods of kingdom history are covered by Kings?

CHART 48

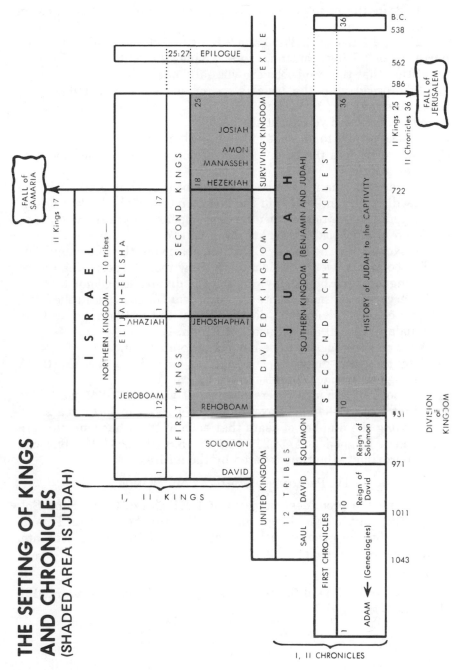

THE SETTING OF KINGS
AND CHRONICLES
(SHADED AREA IS JUDAH)

III. SURVEY OF 1 KINGS

1. Scan the chapters of 1 Kings, and record chapter titles on paper.

2. Read 1 Kings 22:37-53 and 2 Kings 1:1-4 and observe how the narrative of 1 Kings continues into 2 Kings without any real break, indicating that the two books are virtually one unit.

3. Proceed with the usual steps of survey study, and answer these questions:

a) What impressed you about the book?

b) What appeared to be some of the highlights?

c) How much does the book contain of action, description, and conversation?

d) Who are the main characters of the book? What prophet is the leading servant of God in the last chapters of the book? Consult a concordance to see when he first appears in the story.

e) Where is the book's critical turning point?

4. Now study the survey Chart 49, observing the following:

a) The book has twenty-two chapters. How many concern the united kingdom, and how many concern the divided kingdom?

b) Observe where these events are recorded: David's death; the Temple chapters; Solomon's death; split of the northern tribes from Judah; the call and ministry of Elijah.

c) What do you consider to be key chapters in 1 Kings?

d) Note the title given to 1 Kings, as shown on the chart: "A Kingdom Divided Against Itself."

e) The book of 1 Kings covers about 130 years (971-841 B.C.). The first eleven chapters cover Solomon's reign of forty years. By adding the number of years that each of the other four kings in Judah reigned (see 14:21; 15:1-2; 15:8-10; 22:41-42), one can approximate the time covered by the entire book.

IV. PROMINENT SUBJECTS OF 1 KINGS

Among the prominent subjects of 1 Kings are these: King Solomon, the split of the kingdom, and the prophet Elijah. This is suggested by the general outline (page 196) of the book's contents, around the pivotal chapter 12.

A. SOLOMON

Make an outline of Solomon's early life and reign as recorded in chapters 1-4.

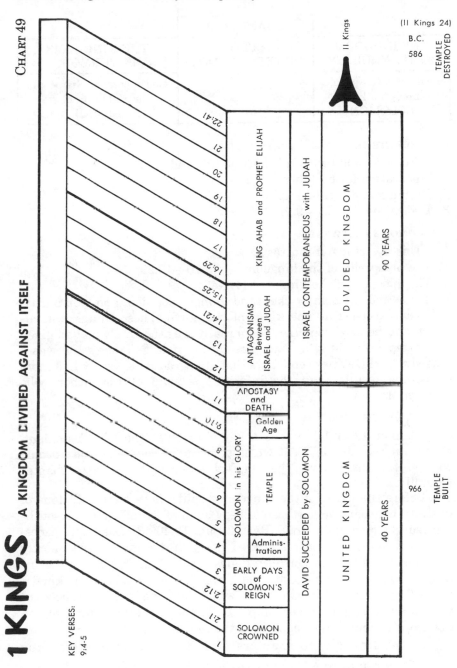

CHART 49

1 KINGS   A KINGDOM DIVIDED AGAINST ITSELF

KEY VERSES:
9:4-5

SOLOMON
CROWNED

EARLY DAYS
of
SOLOMON'S
REIGN

SOLOMON in his GLORY

Administration

TEMPLE

Golden
Age

APOSTASY
and
DEATH

ANTAGONISMS
Between
ISRAEL and JUDAH

KING AHAB and PROPHET ELIJAH

DAVID SUCCEEDED by SOLOMON

ISRAEL CONTEMPORANEOUS with JUDAH

UNITED KINGDOM

DIVIDED KINGDOM

40 YEARS

90 YEARS

2:1   2:12   3   4   5   6   7   8   9:10   11   12   13   14:21   15:25   16:29   17   18   19   20   21   22:41

966

TEMPLE
BUILT

II Kings

(II Kings 24)

B.C.

586

TEMPLE
DESTROYED

	CHAPTER 12	
THE KINGDOM IN TRANQUILITY	SPLIT OF THE KINGDOM	THE KINGDOMS IN TURMOIL
God rules His people through a king: SOLOMON		God speaks to His people through a prophet: ELIJAH

B. SOLOMON'S TEMPLE

Study 5:1—9:9 with this outline in mind:
1. Preparation for building   (5:1-18)
2. Building and furnishings   (6:1—7:51)
3. Dedication   (8:1—9:9)

C. SOLOMON'S LAST YEARS

This is a study of contrasts:
1. The prosperity of the kingdom   (9:10—10:29)
2. The apostasy of the king   (11:1-43)
In fame and wisdom, riches and honor, position and popularity, Solomon exceeded all the kings of the earth. These things won his heart, and he forgot the Lord, who really was the One who had given him every good thing he had. The last part of Solomon's life was a tragedy. Carl DeVries comments that "his gradual apostasy had more disastrous results than the infamous scandal of his father, who sincerely repented."[3]

D. SPLIT OF THE KINGDOM

Chapter 12 of 1 Kings is a key chapter in the Old Testament, because it records the event which steered the course of God's people through the remainder of the Old Testament days. Study the chapter carefully.

Before the event of the kingdom's split, there were occasions of hostility between the northern tribes ("men of Israel") and the southern tribes ("men of Judah"). (Read 2 Sam 19:40-43.) Solomon's excessive taxation of the people stirred up such discontent that shortly after his death the ten northern tribes revolted against the authority of Solomon's son Rehoboam, and formed another kingdom, known thereafter as Israel. The two tribes which remained true to Rehoboam were known as Judah (see Map L). This was the beginning of the divided kingdom. Who was king of the northern group?

In the first eleven chapters of 1 Kings the narrative runs

---

3. Carl E. DeVries, "Solomon," in *The Zondervan Pictorial Bible Dictionary*, p. 802.

smoothly because only one kingdom (all the tribes of the united or undivided kingdom) is involved. From 1 Kings 12 to 2 Kings 17, however, with the two kingdoms (Israel, north and Judah, south) existing side by side, the account reads with more difficulty, because the author has chosen to shift the narrative from the one kingdom to the other, in order to synchronize the histories. Then at 2 Kings 18 to the end, there is a return to the smooth flow again, since only the one surviving kingdom (Judah) is involved. This alternation of kingdoms in the narrative of 1 Kings 12-22 is shown by the following outline:[4]

I. The Kingdom of Judah (12:1-19).
    A. Accession and Folly of Rehoboam (12:1-15; cf. 2 Chron 10:1-11).
    B. Rebellion of the Ten Tribes (12:16-19; cf. 2 Chron 10:12-19; 11:1-4).
II. The Kingdom of Israel (12:20—14:20).
    A. Accession and Sin of Jeroboam (12:20-33).
    B. God's Interposition (13:1-32).
    C. Jeroboam's Continued Sin and God's Message (13:33—14:18).
    D. Jeroboam's Death (14:19-20).
III. The Kingdom of Judah (14:21—15:24).
    A. Judah's Sin and Idolatry (14:21-24; cf. 2 Chron 12:1).
    B. God's Chastisement and Mercy (14:25-30; cf. 2 Chron 12:2-12).
    C. Death of Rehoboam (14:31; cf. 2 Chron 12:13-16).
    D. Abijah (15:1-8; cf.2 Chron 13:1-2).
    E. Asa (15:9-24; 2 Chron 14·1; 16:1-6, 12 14).
IV. The Kingdom of Israel (15:25—22:40).
    A. Nadab (15:25-26).
    B. Baasha (15:27-34).
    C. God's Message (16:1-7).
    D. Elah (16:8-10).
    E. Zimri (16:10-20).
    F. Omri (16:21-28).
    G. Ahab (16:29—22:40).
V. The Kingdom of Judah (22:41-50).
    A. Jehoshaphat (22:41-50; 2 Chron 17:1—21:1).
VI. The Kingdom of Israel (22:51-53).
    A. Ahaziah (22:51-53).

E. ELIJAH

    Elijah is the main character of 16:29—19:21. As you study these

---

4. Coverage by 2 Chronicles is included in the outline, for future reference.

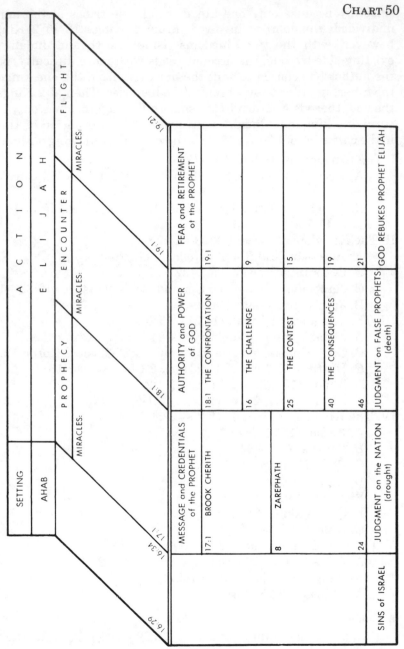

THE PROPHET ELIJAH
I KINGS 16:29—19:21

		ACTION		
SETTING		ELIJAH		
		PROPHECY	ENCOUNTER	FLIGHT
AHAB		MIRACLES:	MIRACLES:	MIRACLES:
		18:1	19:1	19:21
	16:34	17:1		
	MESSAGE and CREDENTIALS of the PROPHET	AUTHORITY and POWER of GOD	FEAR and RETIREMENT of the PROPHET	
	17:1 BROOK CHERITH	18:1 THE CONFRONTATION	19:1	
	8 ZAREPHATH	16 THE CHALLENGE	9	
		25 THE CONTEST	15	
		40 THE CONSEQUENCES	19	
	24	46	21	
SINS of ISRAEL	JUDGMENT on the NATION (drought)	JUDGMENT on FALSE PROPHETS (death)	GOD REBUKES PROPHET ELIJAH	
16:29				

chapters, use the outlines of Chart 50 to help in your observations and conclusions.

V. KEY WORDS AND VERSES OF 1 KINGS

Consider 9:4-5 as key verses for this book. Look for other key verses. A key phrase is "David his father" (also "David my father"). A concordance shows how often the phrase appears.

VI. APPLICATIONS OF 1 KINGS

1. Look in 1 Kings for spiritual applications concerning the following:

prayers; warnings; exhortations
the Lord's justice and righteousness; His judgments
the Lord's mercy
the church as God's house
worship and praise
the voice of God
successful leadership
causes of apostasy
the hand of God in the experiences of individuals and nations (cf. Dan 4:25, 34, 35)

2. What part should Christians play in government today?
3. What is true worship?

VII. FURTHER STUDY OF 1 KINGS

Study the character and career of Solomon. Include the subject of Solomon's Temple. Among other things, compare this Temple with the earlier wilderness tabernacle.

VIII. SURVEY OF 2 KINGS

1. First review Chart 44, observing the general movement of 2 Kings' story.

2. Scan the entire book of 2 Kings in one sitting, if possible. Do not tarry over details.

3. Record a title for each segment on paper. (Note: In some instances Chart 52 shows a segment to comprise a group of chapters, or part of a chapter.)

4. What are your first impressions after making this survey?

5. Did you notice any important key words or phrases? If not, be on the lookout for these as you proceed with your survey. The identification of key words and phrases in a book is often the best clue to the theme of the book.

6. Did you notice any turning point in the book? Any climax? Compare the beginning and ending of the book.

7. Study carefully the survey Chart 52. Recall from your earlier studies that 2 Kings is a continuation of the story of 1 Kings.

8. The two main divisions of the book are marked by a heavy line between chapters 17 and 18, the first division being "The Divided Kingdom," chapters 1-17; and the second division being "The Surviving Kingdom," chapters 18-25. (Scan the Bible text to observe that up to the end of chapter 17 both the kingdoms of Israel and of Judah are under consideration, as they have been since 1 Kings 12. Beginning at chapter 18, only the closing years of Judah are reported.)

9. As the chart shows, the book of 2 Kings covers a period of about 265 years. The first division, chapters 1-17, covers about 130 years, while the second division, chapters 18-25, covers about 135 years.

10. Observe which chapters record the two critical events of the judgments of Israel and Judah. What are those judgments? Read the two passages carefully.

11. Note which chapters are devoted to the ministry of Elisha. Observe also that the last of Elijah's ministry is the subject of the opening chapter of the book.

12. The large proportion of space devoted to the ministries of Elijah and Elisha suggests the importance of these men during this era of God's people. The time period covered by 2 Kings has been called the great prophetic period. Refer to the "Chart of Kings and Prophets" (Chart 45) and identify the various prophets who served between the dates 850 and 586 B.C.

13. Note from the survey chart the arrangement of 2 Kings' record of the reign of the kings of Israel and Judah.

14. The title given to 2 Kings is "Kingdoms Taken Captive." Compare this with the title of 1 Kings.

15. Read the epilogue (25:27-30). Refer to Chart 48 and note that the events of this epilogue happened some years later than the fall of Jerusalem (586 B.C.).

16. Since 2 Kings completes the narrative begun in 1 Kings, it will be of interest to compare the beginning of 1 Kings with the end of 2 Kings (not considering the epilogue). Recalling your survey of 1 Kings, observe such contrasts as these:

a) First Kings begins with a kingdom established in glory; 2 Kings ends with a kingdom dissolved in shame.

b) First Kings begins with bright prospects for obedience; 2 Kings ends with tragic judgments for disobedience.

c) First Kings begins with the dazzling splendor of the Temple; 2 Kings ends with the smoke and flames of the Temple in ruins.

IX. PROMINENT SUBJECTS OF 2 KINGS

A. ELISHA

The prophet Elisha is the key person of 2 Kings, even as Elijah is the central figure of 1 Kings. Both were God's spokesmen to the Northern Kingdom of Israel. Interesting comparisons may be made of these two representatives of God. Elijah is noted for great public acts, and Elisha is known for the large number of miracles he performed, many of them for individual needs. Elijah's ministry emphasized God's Law, judgment, and severity. Elisha supplemented this by demonstrating God's grace, love, and tenderness. Elijah was like John the Baptist, thundering the message of repentance for sin. Elisha followed this up by going about, as Christ did, doing deeds of kindness and miracles attesting that the words of the prophets were from God.

The religious climate in the Northern Kingdom of Israel during Elisha's ministry was very bad. Never since the kingdom was formed under Jeroboam had the people of these ten tribes availed themselves of the Temple worship at Jerusalem. Neither had they had the ministry of the priests and Levites, because these servants of God, together with many devout worshipers of God, had fled into Judah under the persecution of Jeroboam (see 2 Chron 11:13-16).

However, the schools of the "sons of the prophets" were evidently a power for righteousness in Israel. These schools of the prophets were colleges for instruction in the Law of God, and no doubt the prophets taught the people what they themselves had learned. A prophet is a spokesman for God, not only a *foreteller* of future events but also a *forthteller* of the truth. The prophets performed somewhat the same services for the Northern Kingdom which the priests did for the Southern Kingdom.

Elisha was the acknowledged head of the prophetic body, and he journeyed up and down throughout the land, making frequent visits to each of these schools. It was while he was engaged in these duties that many of his miracles were performed. In fact, one of his miracles was performed for the benefit of one of the sons of the prophets (6:1-7).

Make a list of all of Elisha's miracles recorded in 1:1—8:15.

B. FALL OF SAMARIA (17:1-41)

Hoshea was the last ruler of the Northern Kingdom, and at the close of his short reign, Samaria, the capital of Israel, fell, and the ten

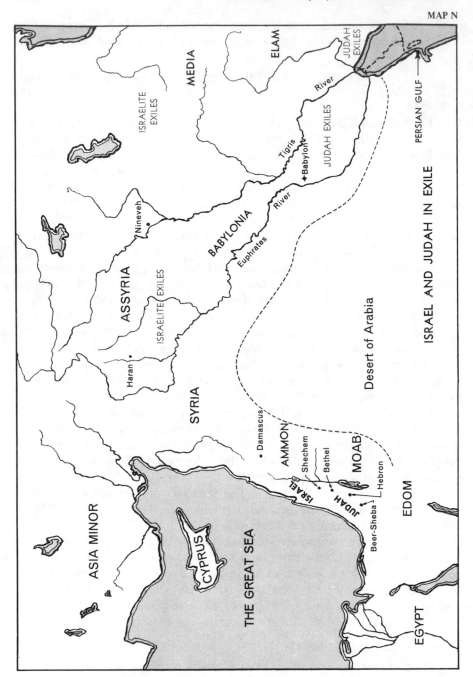

ISRAEL AND JUDAH IN EXILE

tribes were carried away into captivity by the Assyrians. See Map N, "Israel and Judah in Exile." The *immediate* cause which brought on the kingdom's overthrow was Hoshea's conspiracy against the king of Assyria, to whom he had become a vassal some time earlier. The *underlying* cause of Israel's overthrow was their persistent sin of rejection of God. Study carefully God's arraignment of His apostate people, recorded in 17:7-23.

C. HEZEKIAH (18:1—20:21)

After the fall and captivity of Israel, the kingdom of the south (Judah) was left alone to perpetuate a testimony for God. Ahaz, co-regent with Hezekiah over Judah at the time of Israel's fall,[5] did not champion God's cause because he was an evil king. But Hezekiah, his son, was a God-fearing young man whom God used to purge the corruptions of Ahaz and restore true worship to the kingdom. Study the ministries and trials of Hezekiah in 18:1—20:21.

D. FALL OF JERUSALEM (25:1-26)

The fall of Jerusalem in 586 B.C. is the last tragic event reported in 2 Kings. God had waited and pleaded long with the people to turn from sin to Him, but they would not. The king, the priests, and the people were utterly corrupt. And so the Babylonian captors came and

SETTING OF THE SURVIVING KINGDOM OF JUDAH CHART 51

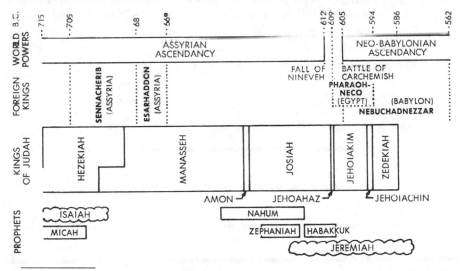

5. Some Bible students hold that Hezekiah began reigning *after* Israel's fall. Refer to outside sources for a discussion of this question. What view does Chart 45 represent?

demolished the city and Temple, and took the people captive. Read this key chapter carefully.

Three influences listed below might have spared Judah from the fate already suffered by Israel.

1. The example of Israel. Israel's captivity by a foreign power was really a judgment for Israel's sins against God. Israel worshiped other gods, and so did not look to God for deliverance from Assyria. Was Judah guilty of the same sins? The threat from outside was a situation very similar to that of Israel. Chart 51 shows the names of some of the foreign kings which played a part during these closing centuries of Judah. (Compare Chart 4.)

2. The reform programs of Judah's kings. There were two good kings of the surviving kingdom of Judah: Hezekiah and Josiah. Both instituted extensive religious reforms, though the benefits were only temporary (Charts 45 and 51). See 18:1-8 and 22:1—23:30.

3. The ministries of the prophets. The prophets are shown on Chart 51. Isaiah and Jeremiah were the key prophets of this period. Their message was mainly one of denunciation of sin and warning of judgment. It could not be said of Judah, as it also could not be said of Israel, that the people were not given many warnings to repent of their evil ways.

But the people "mocked the messengers of God, despised His words, and scoffed at His prophets, until the wrath of the LORD arose against His people, until there was no remedy" (2 Chron 36:16).

The accompanying diagram represents the crucial experiences of God's people, beginning with the institution of rule by kings. Identify each of the four crucial events (see Chart 45).

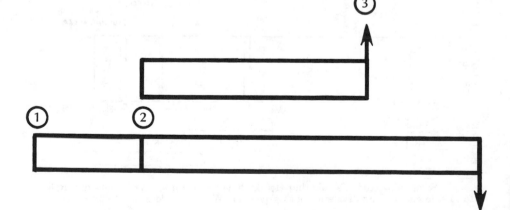

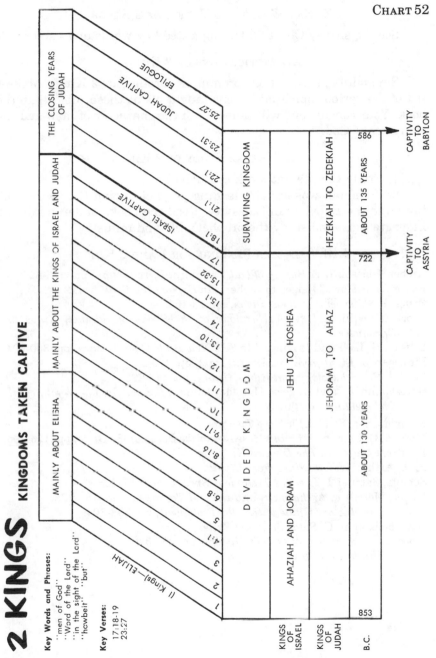

2 KINGS KINGDOMS TAKEN CAPTIVE

Key Words and Phrases:
"men of God"
"Word of the Lord"
"in the sight of the Lord"
"howbeit" "but"

Key Verses:
17:18-19
23:27

(1 Kings)—ELIJAH

MAINLY ABOUT ELISHA

MAINLY ABOUT THE KINGS OF ISRAEL AND JUDAH

THE CLOSING YEARS OF JUDAH

ISRAEL CAPTIVE

JUDAH CAPTIVE

EPILOGUE

4:1 | 6:8 | 8:16 | 9:11 | 10 | 11 | 12 | 13:10 | 14 | 15:1 | 15:32 | 17 | 18:1 | 21:1 | 22:1 | 23:31 | 25:27

DIVIDED KINGDOM

SURVIVING KINGDOM

KINGS OF ISRAEL

AHAZIAH AND JORAM

JEHU TO HOSHEA

KINGS OF JUDAH

JEHORAM TO AHAZ

HEZEKIAH TO ZEDEKIAH

ABOUT 130 YEARS

ABOUT 135 YEARS

CAPTIVITY TO ASSYRIA

CAPTIVITY TO BABYLON

B.C. 853 | 722 | 586

X. KEY WORDS AND VERSES OF 2 KINGS

See the survey Chart 52 for suggested key words and verses.

XI. APPLICATIONS OF 2 KINGS

Sin and its judgment are prominent throughout 2 Kings. Make a list of the various spiritual lessons taught about these subjects in the book. Your conclusions will reflect both the character of man and the character of God.

XII. FURTHER STUDY OF 2 KINGS

1. Study the life and work of Elisha.
2. Jeremiah was Judah's leading prophet during the years leading up to the Babylonian Captivity. Read the books of Jeremiah and Lamentations, and study the prophet's life and ministry.

XIII. SELECTED READING FOR 1 AND 2 KINGS

Archer, Gleason L. *A Survey of Old Testament Introduction*, pp. 275-82.
Baxter, J. Sidlow. "Judges to Esther." In *Explore the Book*, vol. 2.
Bruce, F. F. *Israel and the Nations*, pp. 13-104.
Crockett, William Day. *A Harmony of the Books of Samuel, Kings and Chronicles*.
Ellison, H. L. "I and II Kings." In *The New Bible Commentary*, pp. 300-301.
Finnegan, J. *Light from the Ancient Past*, pp. 129-91.
Free, J. P. *Archaeology and Bible History*, pp. 146-225.
Gates, John T., and Stigers, Harold. "1 and 2 Kings." In *The Wycliffe Bible Commentary*, pp. 307-9.
Krummacher, F. W. *Elijah the Tishbite*.
Morgan, G. Campbell. *Living Messages of the Books of the Bible*, pp. 176-206.
Pfeiffer, Charles F. *The Divided Kingdom*.
Pink, Arthur W. *Gleanings from Elisha*.
Schultz, Samuel J. *The Old Testament Speaks*, pp. 141-228.
Unger, Merrill F. *Archaeology and the Old Testament*, pp. 188-288.
———. *Introductory Guide to the Old Testament*, pp. 298-304.
Whitcomb, John C. *Solomon to the Exile*.
Wood, Leon. *A Survey of Israel's History*, pp. 287-376.
———. *Elijah, Prophet of God*.

13

1 and 2 Chronicles: Judah During the Years of Monarchy

The two books of Chronicles focus primarily on the religious foundations and fortunes of Judah, the covenant people of Jehovah, during the years of the kings. Their content is solid history, but the selective character of that content reveals a thoroughgoing theological and spiritual purpose in all the books' pages. Of that purpose Gleason Archer writes that the books were

> composed with a very definite purpose in mind, to give to the Jews of the Second Commonwealth the true spiritual foundations of their theocracy as the covenant people of Jehovah. This historian's purpose is to show that the true glory of the Hebrew nation was found in its covenant relationship to God, as safeguarded by the prescribed forms of worship in the temple and administered by the divinely ordained priesthood under the protection of the divinely authorized dynasty of David. Always the emphasis is upon that which is sound and valid in Israel's past as furnishing a reliable basis for the task of reconstruction which lay ahead. Great stress is placed upon the rich heritage of Israel and its unbroken connection with the patriarchal beginnings (hence the prominence accorded to genealogical lists).[1]

If the books of Chronicles were written after the Babylonian Captivity was over, one can see why the writer emphasized such things as heritage, covenant, Temple, dangers of apostasy, and Messianic hopes in the Davidic line. For now that the Jews had returned to their homeland under Ezra's leadership, they needed every encouragement and persuasion to rebuild the theocracy that had collapsed over a hundred years earlier. The books of Chronicles are a "clear

---

1. Gleason L. Archer, *A Survey of Old Testament Introduction*, p. 389.

warning to the people never again to forsake the temple and the
worship of the living God."[2]

I. PREPARATION FOR STUDY

Review the general contents of 2 Samuel and the two books of
Kings, since much of their reporting is duplicated in Chronicles.
(More than half of the content of Chronicles is included in Genesis, 2
Samuel, and Kings.) Despite the duplication, do not consider your
study of Chronicles as a repeat exercise. Like all other books of the
Bible, 1 and 2 Chronicles serve a distinct function in the canon of
Scripture. For example, the books of Kings narrate the political and
royal fortunes of God's elect people, and 1 and 2 Chronicles look at
these in the light of the sacred and ecclesiastical. This is something
like one's study of John's gospel, where it is found that John repeats
much of the narrative of the other three gospels, but he emphasizes
interpretation and reflection.

II. BACKGROUND OF 1 AND 2 CHRONICLES

A. TITLE

In the Hebrew Bible the books of Chronicles are one, carrying the
title "The accounts of the days." Jerome viewed the text as a *chronicle*
of the entire divine history, and his Latin titles were translated for
the later English Bibles as 1 and 2 Chronicles.[3]

B. DATE AND AUTHOR

Chronicles was written in the latter half of the fifth century B.C.,
probably between 450 and 425. Some Bible students suggest that
Chronicles and Ezra were originally one consecutive history (e.g.,
compare 2 Chron 36:22-23 and Ezra 1:1-3a). It is very likely that Ezra
was the author.

C. PLACE IN THE CANON

Observe on Chart 1 that Chronicles is the last book listed in the
Hebrew Bible. (See Chart 46.) Note that it appears in the list long
after Kings. This suggests that the early Jews looked upon it as very
distinct from Kings, despite the similar historical reporting.

In our English Bible, 1 and 2 Chronicles appear immediately
after the books of Kings (just as the four gospels appear together).

D. CHRONICLES COMPARED WITH KINGS

As noted earlier, Chronicles and Kings have much in common, as

---

2. John Phillips, *Exploring the Scriptures*, p. 84.
3. The word "chronicles" appears often in 1 and 2 Kings, and once in Chronicles (1
Chron 27:24).

to content. But the differences are very clear and consistent. The following tabulation shows various contrasts:

KINGS	CHRONICLES
1. prophetic perspective (e.g., judgments)	priestly perspective (e.g., hopes)
2. wars very prominent	Temple very prominent
3. the fortunes of the thrones	continuity of the Davidic line
4. record of both Israel and Judah	record primarily of Judah
5. morality	redemption

On the different perspectives noted above, see Chart 47.

The books of Chronicles are more selective than Kings, illustrated in the fact that the Northern Kingdom of Israel is hardly mentioned. The author makes prominent the unbroken (though at times slender) thread of the covenant promise from the earliest days and through the Davidic dynasty, represented by the house of Judah (cf. 1 Chron 28:4). Hence the inclusion of:

a) The genealogies (1 Chron 1-9), where the Davidic line, the descendants of Levi and the two tribes of Judah and Benjamin are of chief interest.

b) The high points of Judah's history up to the captivity.

c) The prominent place given to the Temple, priesthood, and other worship items.

III. Survey of 1 Chronicles

1. Follow the procedures of survey study suggested in the preceding chapters.

2. What strikes you about the first nine chapters?

3. Who is the main character of chapters 10-29?

4. What chapters have much to say about the Temple? (Note: The phrase "house of God" or "house of the Lord" is the usual designation for the Temple in Chronicles.) Is the Temple built during the years of these chapters?

5. Read 29:22b-30. How is this an appropriate conclusion to the book? Compare "Adam" (1:1) with "all the kingdoms of the lands" (29:30).

6. Study carefully the survey Chart 53. In what sense are chapters 1-9 *introductory* to chapters 10-29?

7. Note the two-part outlines.

1 CHRONICLES HIGHLIGHTS OF DAVID'S REIGN

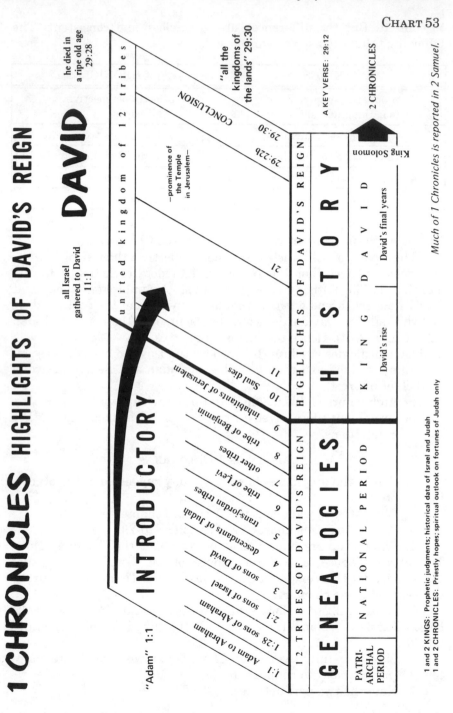

"Adam" 1:1

INTRODUCTORY

1:1	1:28	2:1	3	4	5	6	7	8	9	10	11
Adam to Abraham	sons of Abraham	sons of Israel	sons of David	descendants of Judah	trans-jordan tribes	tribe of Levi	other tribes	tribe of Benjamin	inhabitants of Jerusalem	Saul dies	all Israel gathered to David 11:1

DAVID

he died in a ripe old age 29:28

united kingdom of 12 tribes

—prominence of the Temple in Jerusalem—

CONCLUSION

21   29:22b   29:30

"all the kingdoms of the lands" 29:30

A KEY VERSE: 29:12

12 TRIBES OF DAVID'S REIGN — **GENEALOGIES** — NATIONAL PERIOD

PATRI-ARCHAL PERIOD

HIGHLIGHTS OF DAVID'S REIGN — **HISTORY**

KING DAVID

David's rise

David's final years

King Solomon

2 CHRONICLES

Much of 1 Chronicles is reported in 2 Samuel.

1 and 2 KINGS: Prophetic judgments; historical data of Israel and Judah
1 and 2 CHRONICLES: Priestly hopes; spiritual outlook on fortunes of Judah only

8. According to the chart, how is the book organized around the subject *David*?

IV. Prominent Subjects of 1 Chronicles

A. GENEALOGIES (1:1—9:44)

The genealogies of 1 Chronicles are not exhaustive, but rather selective, to support the main purposes of the book cited earlier. H. L. Ellison cites a few examples of this selectivity.

> It is plain that the Davidic line and the descendants of Levi are the chief interest (note the pointed omission of the house of Eli, which did not serve the Jerusalem temple). Next in importance are the two tribes especially connected with the monarchy, Judah and Benjamin.[4]

B. DAVID'S REIGN AND THE TEMPLE PLANS (10:1—29:30)

Review what you studied in 2 Samuel and 1 Kings about these two subjects. Then observe what new material is added by 1 Chronicles. Account for the additions, in view of Chronicles' purposes.

V. Applications of 1 Chronicles

1. Many spiritual lessons can be learned from the genealogies of this book (chaps. 1-9). See how many you can find. (Sometimes the lessons are only implied.)

2. Practical truths abound in the stories of chapters 10-29. Write a list of these.

VI. Further Study of 1 Chronicles

1. Compare the genealogical lists of 1 Chronicles with those interspersed throughout Genesis.

2. Read various books which treat the subjects of Chronicles' authorship, trustworthiness, and sources of material.[5]

VII. Survey of 2 Chronicles

1. Follow the usual survey procedures.

2. Who is the main character of chapters 1-9? What chapters concentrate on the Temple?

3. Who was Solomon's successor? What is the main content of chapters 12:1—36:16?

---

4. H. L. Ellison, "I and II Chronicles," in *The New Bible Commentary*, p. 341.
5. Reference works are cited under *Selected Reading*.

4. What two very tragic events are recorded in this book, as far as the nation of Judah was concerned? What chapters report these?

5. Read 36:17-23. How do these verses conclude the book?

6. Study the survey Chart 54. Note the simple outline at the top which divides the book into two major parts.

7. Note how the verses 1:1 and 36:22 are compared.

8. Study carefully the outline about the Temple, at the bottom of the chart. G. Campbell Morgan sees the Temple as *the* key to Chronicles.

> In the books of Chronicles, Israel, the Northern Kingdom, is out of sight. There are references to it, but only when it is absolutely necessary to show relationship to Judah. Judah is in view, only to fix attention upon David. David is the central personality. . . . Yet the purpose of the writer was not that of dealing with Judah or with David, BUT OF DEALING WITH THE TEMPLE OF GOD.[6]

9. Note on the chart the references to four reformations. Read the Bible passages.

VIII. PROMINENT SUBJECTS OF 2 CHRONICLES

A. SOLOMON'S REIGN AND THE TEMPLE PROJECT (1:1—9:31)

The extent of Solomon's domination was far-reaching: from the Euphrates River in the east and north, to the border of Egypt in the west and south. (See Map L.) This may have represented as much as fifty thousand square miles. John Gates writes:

> It might seem impossible . . . with two such strong contending powers as Egypt to the south and Assyria to the north . . . to build so large an empire, but such was the case at the beginning of Solomon's reign. At this time, the kingdom of Egypt was ruled by the weak and inglorious Twenty-first Dynasty; and the power of Assyria was in a state of decline.[7]

Solomon was an expert in such fields of knowledge as botany and zoology. God used this to His own glory when He inspired Solomon to write books like Proverbs, where spiritual truths are illustrated by the pictures afforded by the physical world. Read some of the Proverbs, keeping this background in mind. (It should be noted here that Solomon's biblical writings—Proverbs, Ecclesiastes, Song of Solomon, and at least two psalms, 72 and 127—comprised an important part of

---

6. G. Campbell Morgan, *Living Messages of the Books of the Bible,* p. 210.
7. John T. Gates, "1 Kings," in *The Wycliffe Bible Commentary,* p. 314.

his ministry, even overshadowing, in the perspective of the ages, the part he played in building the Temple.)

The Temple which Solomon built was the first large single structure undertaken by any Israelite ruler. The king realized something of the importance of this building he was about to erect, and also something of his own insignificance (2 Chron 2:4-6). The Temple was to be not only a central place of worship but the actual dwelling place of Almighty God. That is why Solomon called the house "great" (see 2 Chron 2:5). And David had said of it: "The house that is to be built for the LORD shall be exceedingly magnificent, famous and glorious throughout all lands" (1 Chron 22:5).

Some of the prominent features of the Temple, including its size, layout, furniture, and associated buildings, are noted below.

1. The erection of the Temple was begun in 966 B.C., in the fourth year of Solomon's reign, 480 years after the Exodus from Egypt. The Temple took seven years to build. This was a comparatively short time for such a spectacular work, but, as *The Wycliffe Bible Commentary* points out, (1) much of the preparation had been completed beforehand; (2) the building was relatively small, though very ornate; (3) a huge personnel was employed in the task.[8]

2. The pattern for this building had been given David by the Lord (1 Chron 28:19), and David had given the pattern to Solomon (1 Chron 28:11-12; 2 Chron 3:3). The divine origin of the blueprints is not contradicted by the similarities to Phoenician architecture of that day.

3. The Temple was similar to the tabernacle in its overall layout. Both the Temple and the tabernacle had two prominent areas, known as the "holy place" and the "most holy place" or "holy of holies." In the text of Kings and Chronicles, these Temple areas are called by the following names:

	1 Kings 6:17,20	2 Chron 3:5, margin, 8
the holy place	"the house"	"the great house"
the most holy place	"the inner sanctuary"	"the room [lit., house] of the holy of holies"

Great as was Solomon's task in overseeing the construction of the Temple, his greater responsibility was his spiritual leadership of the people. God said that His dwelling among the children of Israel

8. *The Wycliffe Bible Commentary*, p. 317.

depended upon Solomon's faithfulness. But Solomon, great and wise as he was, failed in his faithfulness to God, and the idolatry which he later introduced (1 Kings 11:1-13) caused the whole nation to be unfaithful to God.

B. SPLIT OF THE KINGDOM (2 Chron 10:1-19)

Read this chapter and compare it with 1 Kings 12. Also review your earlier studies of this subject (chap. 13).

C. FALL OF JUDAH AND CAPTIVITY TO BABYLON (2 Chron 36:1-21)

Read this passage, and compare it with the reporting by 2 Kings 25:1-26.

D. DECREE OF CYRUS (2 Chron 36:22-23)

The book of 2 Chronicles ends on a bright note. Read the verses, noting the prominence of the Temple. Compare the decree to rebuild (36:23) with the reporting of the destruction (36:19). How many years had transpired between these events? (See Chart 48.) Read Isaiah 45:1-7, 13, which is Isaiah's earlier prophecy that it would be King Cyrus who would free God's exiles and encourage them to return to their homeland.

IX. KEY WORDS AND VERSES OF 2 CHRONICLES

Read the key phrases and verses cited on Chart 54. Add others which you may have observed in your studies.

X. APPLICATIONS OF 2 CHRONICLES

1. List at least five spiritual lessons learned from the life of Solomon.

2. What does the book teach about God?

3. Look for various applications of the accounts of the four reformations listed on Chart 54.

4. What do the last two verses teach you?

XI. FURTHER STUDY OF 2 CHRONICLES

Compare the parallel accounts of 2 Chronicles and the Kings books.

XII. SELECTED READING FOR 1 AND 2 CHRONICLES

GENERAL INTRODUCTION

Archer, Gleason L. *A Survey of Old Testament Introduction*, pp. 389-95.

Beecher, Willis J. "Chronicles." In *The International Standard Bible Encyclopedia*, 1:629-35.

CHART 54

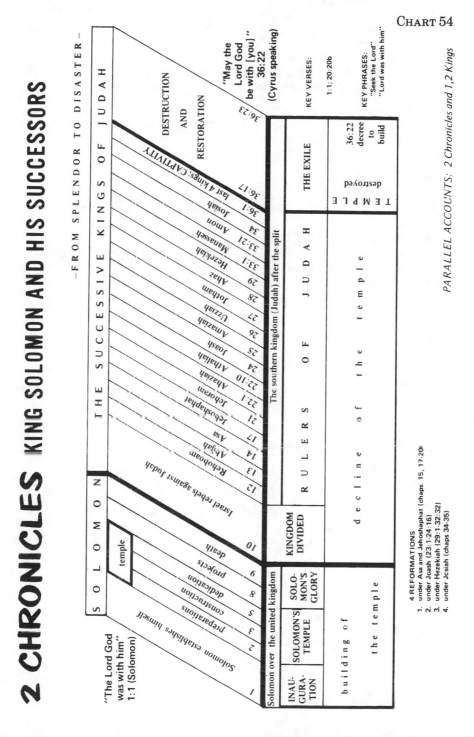

2 CHRONICLES KING SOLOMON AND HIS SUCCESSORS

— FROM SPLENDOR TO DISASTER —

THE SUCCESSIVE KINGS OF JUDAH

SOLOMON

"The Lord God was with him" 1:1 (Solomon)

DESTRUCTION AND RESTORATION

"May the Lord God be with [you]" 36:22 (Cyrus speaking)

36:23

last 4 Kings: CAPTIVITY

36:17

	36:1
Josiah	
Amon	34
Manasseh	33:21
Hezekiah	33:1
Ahaz	29
Jotham	28
Uzziah	27
Amaziah	26
Joash	25
Athaliah	24
Ahaziah	22:10
Jehoram	22:1
Jehoshaphat	21
Asa	17
Abijah	14
Rehoboam	13
Israel rebels against Judah	12

Solomon establishes himself

preparations — 2
construction — 3, 5
dedication — 8
projects — 9
death — 10

temple

KEY VERSES:

1:1; 20:20b

36:22 decree to build

KEY PHRASES:
"Seek the Lord"
"Lord was with him"

THE EXILE	JUDAH		
RULERS	OF	JUDAH	
	decline	of	the temple
KINGDOM DIVIDED			
SOLO-MON'S GLORY			
INAU-GURA-TION			

Solomon over the united kingdom

The southern kingdom (Judah) after the split

TEMPLE destroyed

building of the temple

PARALLEL ACCOUNTS: 2 Chronicles and 1,2 Kings

4 REFORMATIONS
1. under Asa and Jehoshaphat (chaps. 15, 17-20)
2. under Joash (23:1-24:16)
3. under Hezekiah (29:1-32:32)
4. under Josiah (chaps 34-35)

Crockett, William Day. *A Harmony of the Books of Samuel, Kings and Chronicles.*

McClain, Alva J. *The Greatness of the Kingdom.*

Morgan, G. Campbell. *Living Messages of the Books of the Bible*, pp. 208-35.

Young, Edward J. *An Introduction to the Old Testament*, pp. 381-95.

TEMPLE

Heaton, E. W. *The Hebrew Kingdoms*, pp. 133-64. This is a chapter on Israel's worship.

Smith, Arthur E. *The Temple and Its Teaching.*

COMMENTARIES

Baxter, J. Sidlow. "Judges to Esther." In *Explore the Book*, vol. 2.

Ellison, H. L. "I and II Chronicles." In *The New Bible Commentary*, pp. 339-64.

Keil, C. F. *The Books of the Chronicles.*

Payne, J. Barton. "First and Second Chronicles." In *The Wycliffe Bible Commentary*, pp. 367-421.

Whitcomb, John C. *Solomon to the Exile.*

14

Ezra, Nehemiah and Esther: Return of the Jewish Remnant from Exile

Ezra, Nehemiah, and Esther are the last three books classified under the historical section of our English Old Testament. The first two report the fulfillment of the earlier prophecies that after seventy years of captivity God would gather His people and bring them back to the land of Canaan (e.g., Jer 29:10-14).[1] Thus, the historical portion of the Old Testament ends on a bright note.

The restoration of Israel, in their regathering to the homeland of Canaan, was important for various reasons. For Israel, it showed that God had not forgotten His promise to Abraham concerning the land of Canaan (e.g., read Gen 13:15 and note the strength of the phrase "forever"). Hence, the *relocation* of a returning remnant. Hope for a missionary outreach to Gentiles was stirred up in the *revival* of true worship, for a key mission of Israel was to show heathen nations of the world what true worship of the true God was. And then, the restoration was directly related to the life and ministry of the coming Messiah, in the *renewal* of the Messianic promises. For example, Bethlehem, Nazareth, and Zion were some of the geographical places woven into the promises concerning Jesus' coming. In about four hundred years Jesus would be born of the seed of David in *Bethlehem*, *not* in Babylon. The Holy Land of *promise*, *not* a land of captivity, was where His people would be dwelling when He would come unto them, "His own" (John 1:11).

---

1. Although the book of Esther is not about this return, its story is dated during the time span of Ezra, as will be seen later.

I. Preparation for Study

1. Note the location of these books in the Old Testament canon. Chronologically, the group is correctly located in our Bibles, because here are recorded the last events of Old Testament history (i.e., up to about 425 B.C.). But the historical setting of these books is often obscured in the mind of the Bible reader, because the books that follow them (poetical and prophetical books, through Zephaniah) in our present Bible arrangement actually revert back in time. Chart 55 shows the chronological setting of these last three historical books (Ezra, Nehemiah, Esther).

LOCATION OF EZRA-NEHEMIAH-ESTHER   Chart 55
IN THE OLD TESTAMENT CANON

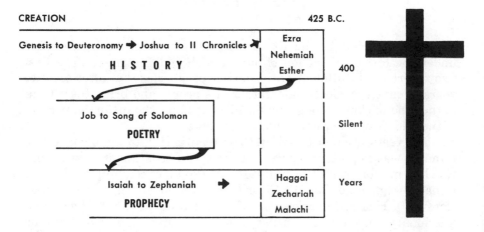

2. The best preparation for the study of Ezra, Nehemiah, and Esther is a review of the books immediately preceding them: Kings and Chronicles. Recall that these latter books record the successes and failures of the two kingdoms of God's chosen people—Israel and Judah—and of their eventual fall and captivity in foreign lands as a divine judgment for sin. The overall account is a classic illustration of the eternal law of returns, a law of cause and effect. The effect was judgment; the cause was sin.

When we come to Ezra and Nehemiah, we are in a new and bright era of Israel's history—the period of *restoration*, involving a return from captivity to the homeland of Canaan. Fix in your mind the following simple outline of the context of Ezra and Nehemiah as you prepare to survey the books.

Kings and Chronicles		Ezra, Nehemiah
CAUSE	EFFECT	SEQUEL
SIN	JUDGMENT	RESTORATION
(during the kingdom years)	(captivity)	(return to the land)

There would have been no restoration for Israel were it not for the grace of God. The restoration was surely not deserved. And before there was even a captivity, the restoration was scheduled on a prophetic timetable by a gracious God who, in the forthcoming captivity period, would be calling out of the communities of Jewish exiles in Babylon a remnant of believers whom He could bring back to the promised land. With these He would perpetuate His covenanted blessings for the generations to come.

3. Read Jeremiah's earlier prophecies about captivity and return in Jeremiah 25:11-14 and 29:10-14.

. 4. Spend time acquainting yourself with the following historical antecedents of these books. Some of this material will be review of things studied earlier.

THE TWO CAPTIVITIES   CHART 56

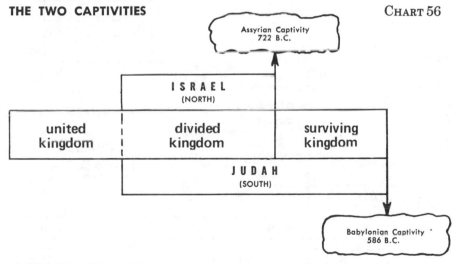

a) The Two Captivities

The word "restoration," as applied to Ezra's day, refers to the *return* of God's people to Canaan *from captivity.* That captivity took place in two stages, which are known as the Assyrian and Babylonian captivities. See Chart 56.

HISTORICAL SETTING OF
EZRA-NEHEMIAH-ESTHER

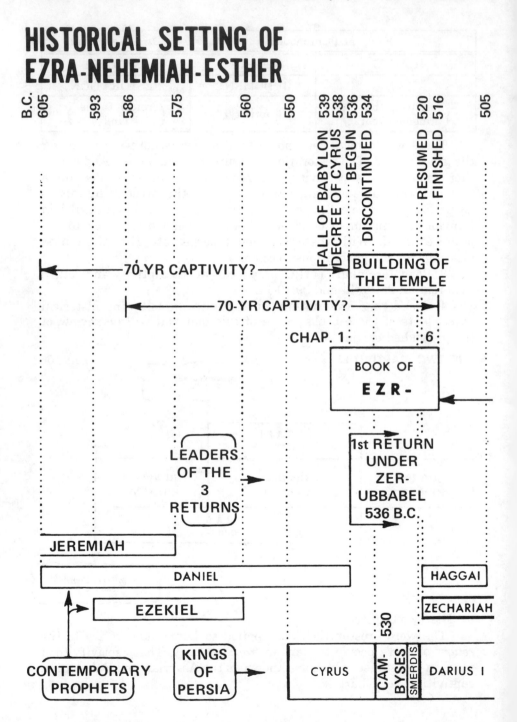

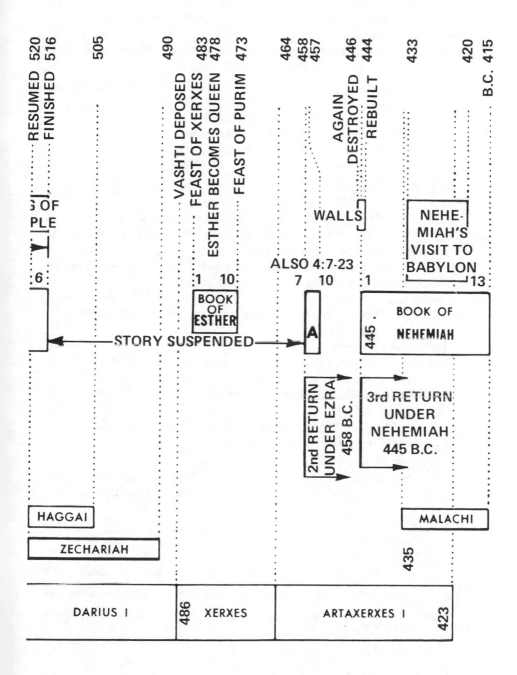

1) Assyrian Captivity (fall of Samaria, 722 B.C., recorded in 2 Kings 17)

Most of the people and rulers of the ten tribes of the Northern Kingdom of Israel were deported to Assyria and scattered among the inhabitants there. (Locate Assyria on Map O.) *The Zondervan Pictorial Bible Dictionary* comments on what happened to these people and their offspring in the years that followed:

> The Ten tribes taken into captivity, sometimes called the Lost Tribes of Israel, must not be thought of as being absorbed by the peoples among whom they settled. Some undoubtedly were, but many others retained their Israelitish religion and traditions. Some became part of the Jewish dispersion, and others very likely returned with the exiles of Judah who had been carried off by Nebuchadnezzar.[2]

2) Babylonian Captivity (fall of Jerusalem, 586 B.C., recorded in 2 Kings 25)

The fall of Jerusalem in 586 B.C. sealed the fate of the two tribes of the Southern Kingdom of Judah. Nebuchadnezzar was the captor, and Babylon was the place of exile. Second Kings closes with an account of this tragic event in Judah's history. Read chapter 25 again to appreciate the theme of the restoration books.

(Note: Unless otherwise stated, the names "Israel" and "Judah," denoting the chosen people of God, will be used interchangeably throughout the next chapters.)

b) Duration of the Babylonian Captivity

Before Judah was taken captive, Jeremiah had prophesied that the duration of exile would be seventy years[3] (read Jer 25:11-12; 29:10; 2 Chron 36:21). The exile began with Nebuchadnezzar's first invasion of Judah in 605 B.C. (2 Chron 36:2-7), and ended with the first return of the Jews to Canaan in 536 B.C.[4] (Ezra 1). See Chart 57.[5] Keep this chart before you while you are surveying the three books.

c) Contemporary Rulers

The Jews in exile in Babylonia were subject to the kings of the Neo-Babylonian Empire, such as Nebuchadnezzar. When Cyrus, king

---

2. Steven Barabas, "Captivity," in *The Zondervan Pictorial Bible Dictionary*, p. 147. Read Ezekiel 36:24, which clearly teaches that the Jews who eventually returned to Canaan were gathered from many countries.

3. The number seventy may have been a round number, as is often the case in Scripture.

4. If Jeremiah's prophecy is interpreted from an ecclesiastical standpoint, with the Temple as the key object, then the seventy-year period extended from the destruction of the Temple in 586 B.C. to the year of completion of its reconstruction, which was 516 B.C.

5. Most of the dates of Chart 57 are those of John C. Whitcomb's *Chart of Old Testament Kings and Prophets*.

of Persia, overthrew Babylon in 539 B.C., the rule of Babylonia was transferred to the Persian Empire. Cyrus's policy of liberation for the exiles in Babylonia brought about the first return of Jewish exiles to the land of their fathers. Observe the names of the Persian kings who succeeded Cyrus on Chart 57. The names of Darius and Artaxerxes appear frequently in the books of Ezra and Nehemiah. (Observe this in an exhaustive Bible concordance.)

d) Jewish Leaders of the Restoration

The three key leaders of the returning Jews were Zerubbabel, Ezra, and Nehemiah. Zerubbabel and Nehemiah were appointed by Cyrus and Artaxerxes, respectively, as governors of the Jewish returnees. Ezra, a leading priest of the Jews, was not only the leader of the second return but also a co-worker with Nehemiah on the third. Locate the names of Zerubbabel,[6] Ezra, and Nehemiah on Chart 57. Note also the dates associated with each of the three returns to Judah:

536 B.C. First return—under Zerubbabel
458 B.C. Second return—under Ezra
445 B.C. Third return[7]—under Nehemiah

Fix in your mind the other dates and events cited on the chart.

The preaching and teaching ministries of three prophets during the restoration period should not be overlooked. Observe on Chart 57 when Haggai, Zechariah, and Malachi ministered. Read Ezra 5:1 and 6:14 for brief but important mention of the influence of Haggai and Zechariah. The name Malachi does not appear in these or any other historical books. Observe on the chart that most of Malachi's ministry took place during Nehemiah's return visit to Babylon. Those were years of backsliding on the part of the Jews in Canaan, when the first spiritual zeal had subsided. Hence, the message of Malachi was mainly about sin and judgment because of sin.

The prophet Daniel went into exile with the first contingent of Jews in 605 B.C. and was ministering in Babylon in the service of Darius the Mede (who was made king of Babylon by Cyrus, Dan 5:31; 9:1) when the exiles received permission to return (cf. Dan 1:21; 6:28). Though aged Daniel did not return to Jerusalem with the exiles, he supported the project in spirit (see Dan 9:1-25).

5. Observe on Chart 57 the periods covered by each of the three books of Ezra, Nehemiah, and Esther. Note the suspension of the story of Ezra for a number of years. Note also that Esther chronologi-

---

6. Zerubbabel is probably the Sheshbazzar referred to in Ezra 1:8,11.
7. No large contingent of Jews was involved in this return.

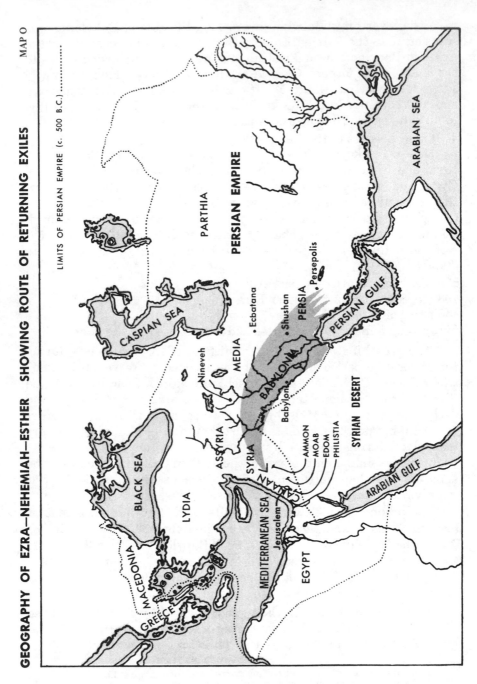

GEOGRAPHY OF EZRA–NEHEMIAH–ESTHER SHOWING ROUTE OF RETURNING EXILES

MAP O

LIMITS OF PERSIAN EMPIRE (c. 500 B.C.)

ARABIAN SEA

PERSIAN EMPIRE

PARTHIA

CASPIAN SEA

Ecbatana

Shushan

PERSIA

Persepolis

MEDIA

PERSIAN GULF

Nineveh

BABYLONIA

Babylon

ASSYRIA

SYRIAN DESERT

SYRIA

AMMON
MOAB
EDOM
PHILISTIA

CANAAN

ARABIAN GULF

BLACK SEA

LYDIA

MEDITERRANEAN SEA

Jerusalem

MACEDONIA

EGYPT

GREECE

cally fits between chapters 6 and 7 of Ezra, during the reign of Xerxes.

6. Study the two maps related to the story of these books. Map O shows the route of the returning exiles, and Map P shows the major places of postexilic Palestine, when the Jews settled down in their homeland.

II. BACKGROUND OF EZRA

A. TITLE AND PLACE IN THE CANON

The book of Ezra is named after its principal character. (If Ezra was its author, this would also account for the title.) Actually, the name Ezra does not appear in the story until 7:1, but he still may be regarded as the key person in the book.

In our English Bible, Ezra follows 2 Chronicles, picking up the story where 2 Chronicles leaves it (cf. 2 Chron 36:22-23 with Ezra 1:1-3). In the Hebrew canon, Ezra and Nehemiah were considered as one historical book[8] and were located just before Chronicles.

B. DATE AND AUTHORSHIP

The traditional view is that Ezra wrote the book which bears his name. If he also wrote 1 and 2 Chronicles, which is very possible, then we have in these three books a continuous historical record by the one author. (Compare the third- and first-person references to Ezra in such verses as 7:1,11,25,28; 8:15,16,17,21.)

Ezra may have written this book at about 450 B.C., soon after he arrived in Jerusalem (458 B.C.).

C. THE MAN EZRA

Ezra has always been considered a key figure in Jewish history. Just as Moses led Israel from Egypt to Canaan, Ezra led the Jews from Babylon to the land of their fathers. Ezra's name means "helper" (from the Hebrew *'ezer,* "help"). He ministered to his fellow Jews in captivity, and he led a group of them back to Jerusalem in 458 B.C. When Nehemiah arrived in Jerusalem thirteen years later, Ezra helped him in ministering to the people about spiritual matters (cf. Neh 8:9).

Ezra is referred to in the Bible as a priest and scribe (e.g., Ezra 7:6, 21).[9] One of his key ministries was to revive the people's interest in the Scriptures. Some believe that Ezra was the author of Psalm

---

8. The first division into two books in the Hebrew Bible was made in A.D. 1448.
9. The phrase "scribe skilled" (Ezra 7:6) is translated by the Berkeley Version as "scribe, well versed."

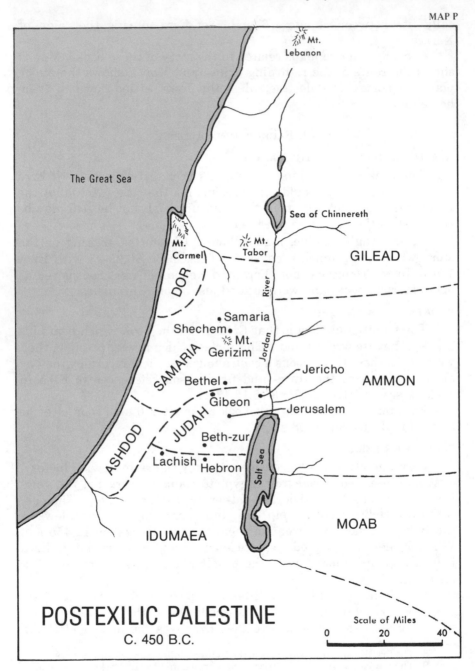

The Great Sea

Mt.
Lebanon

Sea of Chinnereth

Mt.
Carmel

DOR

Mt.
Tabor

GILEAD

Jordan River

Samaria

Shechem

Mt.
Gerizim

SAMARIA

Jericho

AMMON

Bethel

Gibeon

Jerusalem

ASHDOD

JUDAH

Beth-zur

Lachish

Hebron

Salt Sea

IDUMAEA

MOAB

POSTEXILIC PALESTINE
C. 450 B.C.

Scale of Miles

0   20   40

119, the great "Word" psalm. In any case, he loved the Word and loved to teach it.

Hebrew tradition says that Ezra served in Babylon as a high priest, that he originated the Jewish synagogue form of worship, and collected the Old Testament books into a unit. Read Ezra 7:1-5 and observe that Ezra was a descendant of Aaron, the high priest of Moses' day.

D. HISTORICAL BACKGROUND

Read Ezra 1:1; 4:5, 24, and 7:1 for the references to three important kings of Persia: Cyrus, Darius, and Artaxerxes.[10] You will recall these names from your study of Chart 57. How the account of Ezra proceeds chronologically with reference to these kings is shown on Chart 58.

It can be seen from Chart 57 how Ezra is not a continuous or complete historical record of any one period, but follows the principle of selectivity. For example, its author passes over the period from the completion of the Temple (516 B.C.) to Ezra's journey to Jerusalem (458 B.C.).[11] Bible authors were inspired to select only those materials of the historical record which had a bearing on the subject being discussed. This should always be kept in mind when studying Bible history. (It may be observed here also that the two books of Ezra and Nehemiah contain practically all that is known of the history of the Jews between 538 and about 425 B.C.)

E. PURPOSES OF THE BOOK OF EZRA

The book of Ezra shows how the Lord fulfilled His promises, given through His prophets, to restore Israel to their own land.[12] He moved heathen monarchs to show favor to the Jews, and raised up leaders (Zerubbabel and Ezra) and prophets (Haggai and Zechariah) for the grand task of restoration. The restoration involved the physical aspect—moving back to the land of Canaan and rebuilding the Temple buildings; and, more vital, the spiritual aspect—restoring true worship, reestablishing the authority of God's Law, and initiating reforms in the everyday life of the Jews.

III. SURVEY OF EZRA

1. First scan the book, observing such things as the number of

---

10. The references to Ahasuerus (Xerxes) and Artaxerxes in 4:6-7 are part of the parenthesis 4:6-23, inserted out of chronological order with a purpose.

11. There is a brief reference to this interim period in the parenthesis of 4:6-23. (Ahasuerus, 4:6, is probably Xerxes, though some identify him as Cambyses, son of Cyrus.)

12. Isaiah prophesied concerning Cyrus two hundred years before Cyrus was born. Read Isaiah 44:28; 45:1-4.

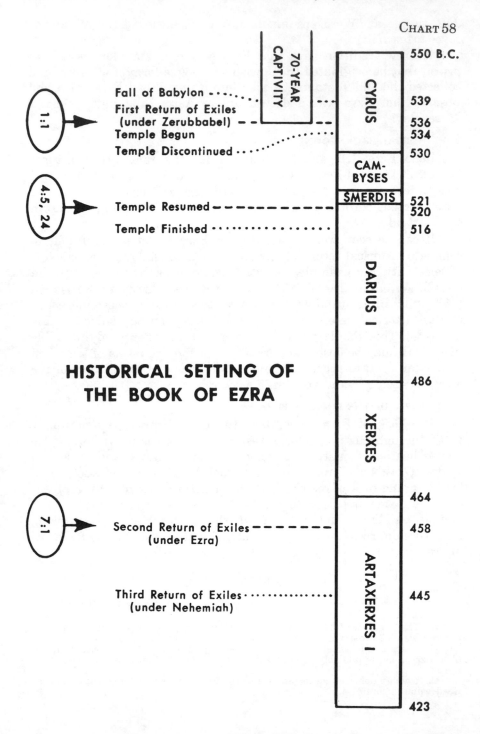

CHART 58

550 B.C.

70-YEAR CAPTIVITY

CYRUS

1:1 → Fall of Babylon · · · · · · · · · · · · · 539
First Return of Exiles
(under Zerubbabel) — — — — 536
Temple Begun · · · · · · · · · · · 534
Temple Discontinued · · · · · · 530

CAM-BYSES

4:5, 24 → Temple Resumed — — — — — — — — ŞMERDIS 521
520
Temple Finished · · · · · · · · · · · · · · · · · 516

DARIUS I

**HISTORICAL SETTING OF
THE BOOK OF EZRA**

486

XERXES

464

7:1 → Second Return of Exiles — — — — — — — 458
(under Ezra)

Third Return of Exiles · · · · · · · · · · · · · · · 445
(under Nehemiah)

ARTAXERXES I

423

chapters, length of chapters, and type of content. Concerning content, how much of the following is found in Ezra: action, conversation, description, listings, letters, prayers? Mark your Bible wherever blocks of the last three types appear. What are some of your first impressions of the book?

2. Next read the book chapter by chapter. As you read, become aware of the reasons for each new chapter division as the book progresses. Assign chapter titles, and record these on paper. (Note: 8:33 replaces 9:1 as the beginning of a new unit of thought.)

3. Where are references made to kings? Mark these places in your Bible, and locate these kings on Chart 57.

4. Mark in your Bible the letters recorded in Ezra.

5. Compare the beginning and ending of the book. Does the beginning introduce, and does the ending conclude?

6. Where is the first appearance of the man Ezra in the book? Who is the leader mentioned in 2:2a? How often does he appear in chapters 1-6? Does he appear in chapters 7-10? (An exhaustive concordance will quickly answer this.)

7. Where is the decree of Cyrus recorded? The first journey to Canaan? The decree of Artaxerxes? The second journey?

8. Try to identify *groupings* of content:
a) the main subjects of the two divisions (chaps. 1-6 and 7-10)
b) the main subjects of the four sections (chaps. 1-2; 3-6; 7-8; 9-10)
Compare your conclusions with the outlines shown on Chart 59.

9. In your own words, what is the main theme of Ezra?

10. Compare your survey studies with the items shown on Chart 59.

11. The ten chapters of Ezra are divided into two main parts, with 7:1 beginning the new section. The first section concerns the first return of exiles under the leadership of Governor Zerubbabel; the second section is about the second return, under the leadership of Ezra the priest. How many years elapsed between the two returns?

12. The main work accomplished on the first return was the rebuilding of the Temple. On the second return, Ezra's main task was to bring his people to a place of repentance, confession of sin, and restitution, so that true worship of God could be restored. The sin of mixed marriages (between Israelites and the heathen) was a major defilement at this time. How did this sin affect the religious life of Israel?

13. Observe, from the dates shown on the chart, the duration of the time between chapters 6 and 7. Consult Chart 57, and note that the book of Esther is located in this period.

14. The names of the three important kings of Persia—Cyrus, Darius, and Artaxerxes—are placed on the chart where they relate to the story.

15. In chapters 4-7, Ezra records much of the official correspondence involving the kings' offices and having to do with the Jews' permission to return to Canaan. Originally these letters were written in Aramaic, which was the official language of diplomatic discourse in those days. Ezra preserved the letters in their original Aramaic form. This is one of the few Aramaic sections in the Hebrew Bible. Identify the sender and addressee in each case: 4:11-16; 4:17-22; 5:7-17; 6:6-12; 7:11-26.

16. Compare the two sections identified on the chart as *The Work*. Why were these activities important in the life of the Jews?

IV. PROMINENT SUBJECTS OF EZRA

A. RESTORATION UNDER ZERUBBABEL (chaps. 1-6)

A simple outline shows the content of this first half of the book.
I. The Journey   (1:1—2:70)
  A. Decree of Cyrus   (1:1-4)
  B. Preparations for the Journey   (1:5-11)
  C. List of Returning Exiles   (2:1-70; scan Neh 7:5-73 for a similar list)
II. The Work   (3:1—6:22)
  A. Work Begun   (3:1-13)   (536 B.C.)
  B. Work Opposed (4:1-24)   (534 B.C.)
  C. Work Resumed   (5:1—6:12)   (520 B.C.)
  D. Work Finished   (6:13-22)   (516 B.C.)
  (Locate the above four dates on Chart 57.)

The last two verses of the above section could be called key verses for Ezra. They summarize the first return of Jewish exiles from captivity in 536 B.C., with the aid of God and through the favor of an Assyrian king (6:21-22). When the core is extracted from these verses, a bright note of gladness is the emphasized concluding message: "The sons of Israel . . . ate . . . with joy, for the LORD had caused them to rejoice."

B. REFORMS UNDER EZRA (chaps. 7-10)

As the survey Chart 59 shows, the subject of these chapters is similar to that of the first half of the book. The two main parts are "The Journey" (7:1—8:32), and "The Work" (8:33—10:44).

1. The journey (7:1—8:32). (Study the section with the following four points in view.)

a) The permission (7:1-26)
b) The psalm (7:27-28)
c) The people (8:1-14)
d) The pilgrimage (8:15-32)

About sixty years transpired between chapters 6 and 7. They were probably years of spiritual decline for Jews in Judah. The coming of Ezra the scribe with a second contingent of returning exiles was very timely, for Ezra was a man of God who had a heavy burden to teach Israel the "statutes and judgments" of God (read 7:10, KJV). So his ministry was bound to touch not only the lives of those making the journey with him, but also the lives of those already in the land.

The story of the book of Esther fits chronologically between chapters 6 and 7 of Ezra. The divine providence shown to the Jews during the reign of Xerxes, predecessor of Artaxerxes, may have influenced Artaxerxes to show favor to the Jews during his reign, such as encouraging them to return to their homeland (7:11-26).

2. The work (8:33—10:44). The building of the Temple had been completed during Zerubbabel's governorship (6:14), so Ezra did not have this responsibility when he arrived in Jerusalem. Yet his work centered about the Temple. Read 7:18-20, 27 to recall what one of his tasks was, of a physical nature. Also read 7:10 again and note the spiritual ministry which Ezra intended to engage in during his stay in Jerusalem. Obviously, everything he accomplished is not recorded in the book of Ezra. But that which is recorded shows how effectively Ezra was used of God to minister to the Jews in Palestine.

Study these chapters with the following outline in view:

I. The Program (8:33-36). In these verses are recorded the two projects which were first given attention when Ezra's group arrived in Jerusalem. What were they? For the Temple beautification project, the Jews had the assistance of the king's presidents and governors on the western side of the Euphrates River, who "supported the people and the house of God" (8:36*b*). The program lasted for about four months (cf. 9:1*a* and 10:9).

II. The Problem (9:1-4). Read Exodus 34:15-16 and Deuteronomy 7:1-3 for the Law which God had given His people and which they were now violating. The guilty ones were not only of Ezra's group of returnees, but also of the Jews already settled in the land. The problem did not originate overnight. Why was Ezra's grief so intense?

III. The Prayer (9:5-15). This is one of the Scripture's prominent examples of a prayer of contrition and confession. Study it carefully.

CHART 59

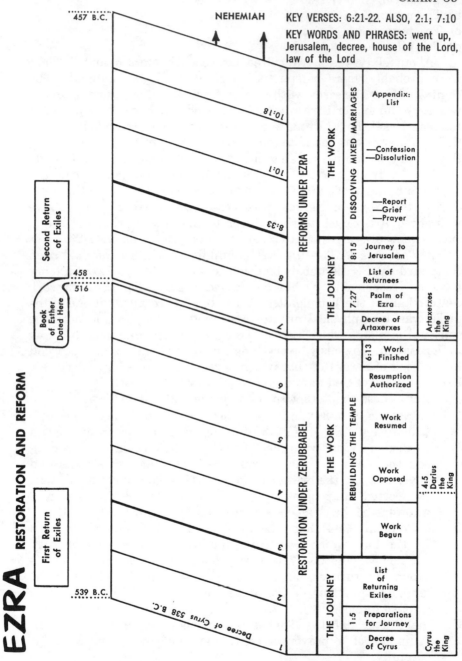

457 B.C.

NEHEMIAH

KEY VERSES: 6:21-22. ALSO, 2:1; 7:10

KEY WORDS AND PHRASES: went up, Jerusalem, decree, house of the Lord, law of the Lord

Second Return of Exiles

458
516

Book of Esther Dated Here

EZRA RESTORATION AND REFORM

First Return of Exiles

539 B.C.

Decree of Cyrus 538 B.C.

REFORMS UNDER EZRA

THE WORK

DISSOLVING MIXED MARRIAGES

10:18 — Appendix: List

10:1 — —Confession —Dissolution

8:33 — —Report —Grief —Prayer

THE JOURNEY

8:15 — Journey to Jerusalem

8 — List of Returnees

7:27 — Psalm of Ezra

7 — Decree of Artaxerxes

Artaxerxes the King

RESTORATION UNDER ZERUBBABEL

THE WORK

REBUILDING THE TEMPLE

6:13 — Work Finished

6 — Resumption Authorized

5 — Work Resumed

4 — Work Opposed

3 — Work Begun

4:5 Darius the King

THE JOURNEY

2 — List of Returning Exiles

1:5 — Preparations for Journey

1 — Decree of Cyrus

Cyrus the King

IV. The Penitence (10:1-4). Ezra's example of contrition was contagious, as these verses indicate. Someone other than Ezra suggested a way of deliverance (vv. 2-4). Could this have been Ezra's strategy of silence concerning hope—to cause the people *themselves* to recognize that they had come to the end of the line, and that they *must* cry out for mercy? Make a study of these important phrases in this paragraph:

"We have been unfaithful to our God."

"Yet now there is hope."

"Let us make a covenant with our God."

"Be courageous and act."

V. The Propitiation (10:5-17). The story of Ezra ends by showing how the sin of mixed marriages was dealt with, and how peace with God was thereby restored. (Recall the words "hope" and "covenant" of 10:2-3.)

The price of restoration was high. This is perhaps the main truth of these closing verses of Ezra. Observe the following in your study:

a) Firm authority of God's spokesman (10:5).

b) Deep remorse (10:6).

c) Thorough investigation (10:7-8, 14).

d) No one excused from examination (10:8).

e) Sense of fear (10:9, 14).

f) Tragic consequences involved in the solution (10:44).

g) Way to restoration (the word "propitiation" in this outline means atonement, or restored fellowship by sacrifice): confession of sin (10:11*a*), offering for sin (10:19), dissolution of marriage (10:11*b*).

V. KEY WORDS AND VERSES OF EZRA

Some key words and phrases of Ezra are: "went up," "Jerusalem," "decree," "house of the LORD," "hand of the LORD upon him," "law of the LORD." The Word of God is prominent throughout the book, under various designations. Look up each verse cited here and jot down the word or phrase used: 1:1; 3:2; 6:14, 18; 7:6, 10, 14; 9:4; 10:3, 5.

VI. APPLICATIONS OF EZRA

1. What are some important spiritual qualifications of God's servants?

2. What lessons about worship and praise can be learned from this book?

3. Satan always tries to oppose God's work. What can Christians do to prevent such opposition, or overcome it when it exists?

4. Does God use unbelievers to fulfill tasks in His work? If so, how and why? Can you cite examples on the contemporary scene?

5. What constitutes a mixed marriage today, in the sense in which it was a sin of Ezra's time? Why is it such a dangerous evil?

VII. BACKGROUND OF NEHEMIAH

A. TITLE AND PLACE IN THE CANON

The book of Nehemiah is named after its main character and its opening words (1:1*a*). In all Old Testament canonical lists it has been classified as a historical book. Both Hebrew and Greek Bibles of the earliest centuries treated Ezra and Nehemiah as one book. The two-book classification of our English Bibles may be traced back to the Latin Vulgate Bibles.

B. DATE AND AUTHORSHIP

Authorship of the book may be attributed to Nehemiah, who probably wrote most of it around 420 B.C. Some parts of the book contain his memoirs (1:1—7:5; 11:1-2; 12:27-43; 13:4-31). The list of Jewish families given in 7:5-73 was from a document already existing (the list is practically identical with that of Ezra 2:1-70). The third-person references to Nehemiah in 8:9; 10:1; 12:26, 47 do not contradict his authorship when the context is recognized.[13]

C. THE MAN NEHEMIAH

Nehemiah was born of Jewish parents in exile, and was given the name *Nehem-Yah*, meaning "the comfort of Jehovah." We may gather from this that Nehemiah's home was a godly one. At a young age he was appointed to the responsible office of being cupbearer to King Artaxerxes. This was the contact that God used later to secure imperial permission for the return to Jerusalem of the third contingent of exiles, namely, Nehemiah and his project crew.

Nehemiah was truly a man of God, filled with the Spirit. He had a sensitive ear to God's voice concerning even the details of the work he was doing (2:12; 7:5). Prayer was a natural and essential part of his life. He knew what work was, and he worked and inspired others to do so. When opposition arose from the enemy, he stood strong and tall. He was alert also to the subversive plots of false brethren within the Jewish commonwealth. And when some of his own people became discouraged, he turned their eyes to the help of God, and found a ready response. Leader, worker, soldier, servant of God—this was Nehemiah.

---

13. See *The Wycliffe Bible Commentary*, p. 435, for an explanation of this.

D. HISTORICAL BACKGROUND

There is a period of twelve years after the book of Ezra closes (457 B.C.) before the book of Nehemiah begins its story (cf. Ezra 7:8; 10:16-17; and Neh 1:1; 2:1). Then Nehemiah records events of the next twenty years (445-425 B.C.).[14]

Refer to Chart 57 and note the following:

1. Artaxerxes I was king of Persia[15] when Nehemiah ministered.
2. 458 B.C.—Second return of Jews to Jerusalem, led by Ezra.
3. 446 B.C.—The enemies force the Jews to cease building the walls, and virtually destroy the parts already built (Ezra 4:23). News of this reaches Nehemiah (Neh 1:3).
4. 445 B.C.—Nehemiah leads a small group of exiles to Jerusalem to organize the Jews already there to rebuild the walls. Nehemiah is appointed by Artaxerxes to be governor of Judah (a province of Persia at this time).
5. 444 B.C.—The walls project is completed (Neh 6:15).
6. 433 B.C.—Nehemiah goes to Babylon on official business (cf. 2:6 and 13:6). The date 433 B.C. is derived from Nehemiah 5:14.
7. 425 B.C.—Nehemiah returns from Babylon (Neh 13:7).

It must have been a heartwarming experience for Ezra when he learned that such a zealous believer as Nehemiah had arrived in Jerusalem with a new contingent of Jewish exiles.

While Nehemiah served as governor of Judah, Ezra was still ministering to the spiritual needs of the Jews there. (Ezra plays an important part in chapters 8 and 12 of Nehemiah.)

Nehemiah also counted on the spiritual services of the prophet Malachi during those last years of Old Testament history. Many of the evils denounced in the book of Malachi are part of the historical record of the book of Nehemiah.

E. PURPOSES

In general, the book of Nehemiah seeks to show how God favored His people, so recently exiled, by strengthening their roots in the homeland of Judah in the face of all kinds of opposition.

Specifically, the book shows how the broken-down walls of Jerusalem and the failing faith of the Jews were restored, through (1) the competent leadership of Nehemiah, a man of prayer and faith; and (2) through a host of Jewish brethren, who responded to the divine challenge to rise and build.

---

14. Some of this material is a review of the historical setting described earlier in the chapter.

15. Persia at this time included the vast territory from India to Ethiopia, Judah being one of its provinces.

VIII. Survey of Nehemiah

1. Scan the book, chapter by chapter, observing such things as organization of a theme, and the prevailing atmosphere.

2. Concerning organization:
Is there an introduction and conclusion to the book?
Is the book mainly narrative? How much, if any, is autobiographical?
Is there a progression?
Is there a turning point?

Observe the places in the book where *lists* appear. (These are of various kinds.)

3. Concerning atmosphere, what is the general tone of the book? Reread the first few verses of each chapter and observe the *intensity* of the tone involved. Note especially these verses: 1:4; 2:1; 4:1; 5:1; 6:1; 8:1; 9:1; 13:1.

4. Observe also the simplicity in which the action is described. There are no embellishments of a litterateur attempting to give color to the drama. The intensity of the action remains even in the simplicity of the reporting. One writer has remarked, "We see throughout the writing of an honest, earnest man,—and through him the history closes with a sublime dignity."[16]

5. What are your first impressions of the book of Nehemiah? Does any passage of the book stand out prominently in your mind? If so, what?

6. Now reread the book of Nehemiah more slowly. Record chapter titles on paper. (Note the divisional points at 6:15; 7:73b; 12:27; and 12:44 shown on Chart 60. Why are divisions made at these places?)

7. Always be on the lookout for key words and phrases as you study.

8. Identify the main characters of the book. Among other things, note when Ezra appears in the story. Also, who are the most frequently mentioned enemies of Nehemiah?

9. Make a note of Nehemiah's prayers in the book's first and last chapters.

10. What is the key project of the story? How is the book organized around this project? Where is the first activity of that project recorded? What verse records the project's completion? How long did the project last? Try making some outlines of the book's story.

---

16. Howard Crosby, "Nehemiah," in Lange's *Commentary on the Holy Scriptures*, p. 1.

11. In your own words, write out a theme for the book. Also, suggest a title.

12. Study carefully the survey Chart 60. Compare its observations and outlines with your own work thus far.

13. Observe that 7:73*b* marks a turning point on Chart 60. Some Bible students locate the main division at 7:1, which would make the passage 7:1-73*a* the opening of the second half of the book. Because of the nonnarrative nature of most of this passage, it may be considered either as the close of the first half or the opening of the second half of the book. The reason for including 7:1-73*a* in the first half of the book is that it more greatly emphasizes the aspect of *physical* security (cf. 7:1-4), whereas at 7:73*b* the narrative begins to focus on building for *spiritual* security (cf. 8:1).

14. The structure of the book of Nehemiah is very simple: two equal main parts, with each chapter adding a new point to the chapters preceding it. Study the various two-part outlines.

15. Relate the outlines on the chart to the suggested title.

16. Scan the book once again with this survey chart in mind. This will bring together in your mind the many unrelated observations which you may have made along the way.

IX. PROMINENT SUBJECTS OF NEHEMIAH

A. PRAYERS

Prayer is prominent throughout the book of Nehemiah. Study especially the prayer of 1·4-11, noting confession, claim, plea, and underlying tone. Then make a comparative study of these references to prayer: 1:4-11; 2:4; 4:4-5, 9; 5:19; 6:9, 14; 13:14, 22, 29, 31.

B. BUILDING PROJECTS (chaps. 1-7)

The historians Ezra and Nehemiah have recorded for us practically all that is known of Jewish history during the restoration period from 538 to 425 B.C. Nehemiah's contribution was the firsthand account of the part he played, especially in the rebuilding of Jerusalem's walls, a project not accomplished during the years covered by the book of Ezra.

It all began for Nehemiah while he was serving as cupbearer in the palace of Artaxerxes, king of Persia. When Nehemiah received news of the affliction and reproach of the Jewish remnant in Judah, and the most recent desolation of Jerusalem's walls and gates, his heart burned with a sense of urgency that something must be done. How God stirred Nehemiah to lead his fellowmen in rebuilding what

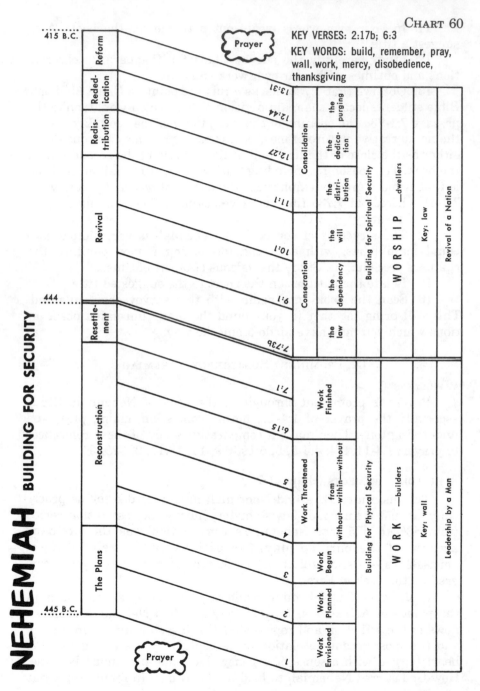

CHART 60

KEY VERSES: 2:17b; 6:3
KEY WORDS: build, remember, pray, wall, work, mercy, disobedience, thanksgiving

had been broken down—the city's walls, but, more important, the city's faith—is told in these chapters. Use the following outline as you study the narrative:

I. Work Begins (3:1-32).
II. Work Continues Despite Opposition (4:1—6:14).
   A. Opposition from Without (4:1-23).
   B. Opposition from Within (5:1-19).
   C. Opposition from Without (6:1-14).
III. Work Is Finished (6:15—7:73a).
   A. Building Program Completed (6:15-19).
   B. Jerusalem Guarded (7:1-4).
   C. Families Resettled (7:5-73a).

The completion of the building project was a blow to the enemies of Israel. Nehemiah reports that they were much cast down, "for they recognized that this work had been accomplished with the help of our God" (6:16). (The two verses of 6:15-16 are Nehemiah's concluding words for the reporting of the building project.)

C. REVIVAL (7:73b—10:39)

A major turn is made in the book of Nehemiah at 7:73b. The shift is from the physical and material rebuilding to building for spiritual security. The reading of God's Word is given no higher honor than in chapter 8; thanksgiving and penitence are blended together in sublime and startling proportions in the prayer of chapter 9; and the people's determination to prove the sincerity of that prayer by action is wonderfully exemplified in chapter 10. The people solemnly covenanted "to walk in God's law," which they were proud to claim as having come to them through "Moses, God's servant" (10:29). Among other things, they said, "We will not neglect the house of our God" (10:39).

The passing of time would tell how faithfully they and their children would keep this covenant.

D. CONSOLIDATION (11:1—13:31)

The last chapters of Nehemiah record important aspects of Israel's life as they entered the phase of consolidation. Those aspects are: the nation's size and distribution; the nation's defense; and the nation's purity. The same subjects appeared earlier in the book, but in a slightly different context. Chart 61 gives a survey of this final section of Nehemiah. Mark the divisions in your Bible, with the outlines, as a guide for your reading.

11:1	12:27	12:44 13:31
REGISTERED LISTS	OFFICIAL DEDICATION	NECESSARY REFORMS
families	walls	laws
The nation's size and distribution	The nation's defense	The nation's purity

X. KEY WORDS AND VERSES OF NEHEMIAH

Some of Nehemiah's key words are: build, remember, pray, wall, work, mercy, disobedience, thanksgiving. Suggested key verses are 2:17*b* and 6:3. Look for others.

XI. APPLICATIONS OF NEHEMIAH

1. Nehemiah is an invigorating and challenging book, showing what God can do through a remnant of believers who rise to God's call through His servant to restore a vital, worshipful relationship with Him. John C. Whitcomb makes this appraisal of the book:

> It must be said . . . that no portion of the Old Testament provides us with a greater incentive to dedicated, discerning zeal for the work of God than the Book of Nehemiah. The example of Nehemiah's passion for the truth of God's Word, whatever the cost or consequences, is an example sorely needed in the present hour.[17]

Problems, pains, prayer, and perseverance are some of the ingredients of the success story of Nehemiah. What other ingredients have you observed in your study of the book? Think back over the chapters and list at least ten spiritual lessons on *service for God* taught by Nehemiah.

2. Follow this pattern of analogy as you apply various parts of the Nehemiah story:

BOOK OF NEHEMIAH	ILLUSTRATIVE OF
the believing Jews	Christians
broken-down walls	aspects of the Christian life in need of restoration (e.g., prayer, worship, service)
rebuilding the walls	revival and restoration

3. The subject of revival is often discussed by Christians, but less

---

17. John C. Whitcomb, "Nehemiah," in *The Wycliffe Bible Commentary*, p. 435.

often experienced. Revival is the renewal of the believer's intimate relationship with God. The price of revival is high, but the way is simple. These three chapters present that way, in the correct order:

Chapter 8: the work of God's Word (exposure to, and understanding of the Word)

Chapter 9: the experience of genuine prayer (confession of sin, and worship of God)

Chapter 10: decision and action (in the spirit of sacrifice)

Reflect on these truths, especially as they apply to Christian living.

XII. BACKGROUND OF ESTHER

Now we return to a time earlier than Nehemiah, for Esther's setting is dated between chapters 6 and 7 of Ezra.[18] The Old Testament history of Israel closes with the last chapter of Nehemiah (c. 425 B.C.). Were it not for the events of the book of Esther, however, there may not have been a story for Nehemiah to record. Esther was included in the biblical account to show how God's chosen people were spared extermination during their exilic years. It is a story that should inspire Christians today to an increased trust in God, who sovereignly controls world history and preserves His own children.

A. TITLE

The title "Esther" is assigned to this book because Esther is the main character. Jews call the book *Megilloth Esther* ("Esther Roll") because it is one of the five rolls assigned for reading at Jewish holidays.[19]

B. AUTHORSHIP AND DATE

Authorship of the book is unknown. The author was probably a Jew living in Persia during the latter half of the fifth century B.C., when the action of the book took place. Some have suggested Ezra or Nehemiah as possible authors, on the basis of similarity of writing style.

C. PLACE IN THE CANON

The book of Esther is listed last in the historical books of the English Bible, and eighth in the "Writings" (*Kethubhim*) section of the Hebrew Bible. Though its canonicity has been challenged by

---

18. See Chart 57. The reason for studying Nehemiah directly after Ezra is to maintain the continuity of the theme of Ezra-Nehemiah.

19. The book of Esther is read at the Jews' Feast of Purim (March 14-15).

some, it has remained firmly in the canon.[20] The Jews have always accepted the book as canonical.

D. THE LADY ESTHER

Esther was a Jewish orphan maiden who lived in Shushan, Persia's principal city. She was reared by a cousin, Mordecai, who was an official in the king's palace (2:5-7, KJV). King Xerxes (Ahasuerus)[21] chose Esther to be the new queen of Persia afer he had divorced his wife. Through Esther's influence, Jews living in Persia were spared extermination.

The name Esther (*'ester*) may have been derived from the Persian word for "star" (*sitareh*). Esther's Hebrew name was Hadassah (2:7), which means "myrtle."

It is interesting to note that only one other book in the Bible is named after a woman: Ruth. One writer has made this comparison: "Ruth was a Gentile woman who married a Jew. Esther was a Jewish woman who married a Gentile."[22]

The story of Esther reveals a woman of very commendable character. Among her traits were genuine piety, faith, courage, patriotism, compassion, maturity, and natural charm. Your study of the book of Esther will show how such a woman was used of God in the interests of His chosen people, the Jews.

E. HISTORICAL BACKGROUND

History always originates in *places,* so it is helpful first to visualize the geography of the book of Esther. Refer to Map O and observe the location of Shushan (Gr., *Susa*) in Persia,[23] where Esther lived and served as queen. (This is the same city where Daniel had received a vision from God about eighty years earlier, Dan 8:2.) Some have estimated that between two and three million Jews were living in Persia and Babylon during the time of the book of Esther. Read Esther 1:1 and note the extensive domain of Xerxes, king of Persia: 127 provinces from India to Ethiopia.

The story of Esther took place between the first return of exiles under Zerubbabel (536 B.C.) and the second return under Ezra (458 B.C.). Chart 62 shows the major points of this historical setting.

---

20. Some Bibles (e.g., Catholic) add "Additions to Esther" (identified as 10:4—16:24) to the canonical book, intended mainly to compensate for the absence of the name of God. The fact that no portion of the book of Esther has yet been discovered in the Qumran area (place of the Dead Sea Scrolls discoveries) indicates that the Essenes of Qumran probably rejected the canonicity of Esther.
21. The term Ahasuerus may have been a Persian title for *king,* rather than a name, similar to the title *pharaoh.* See Esther 1:1-2.
22. John Phillips, *Exploring the Scriptures,* p. 91.
23. The modern name for Persia is Iran.

CHART 62

HISTORICAL SETTING OF ESTHER

423 B.C. ....

ARTAXERXES I

458 .... | Second Return of Exiles Under Ezra | .... EZRA 7:9

464 ....

473 ·· Feast of Purim ....
Esther 9

478 ·················· Esther Crowned Queen
Esther 2:17

483 ·· Feast of Xerxes ····· Queen Vashti Deposed ·········
Esther 1:3   Esther 1:10—2:4

486 ....

| BOOK OF ESTHER (between chaps. 6 and 7 of Ezra) |

XERXES

DARIUS

516 ·· Temple Project Finished ·································· EZRA 6:15

521 ....

SMERDIS

CAMBYSES

530 ....

536 ·· Temple Project Started ······· | First Return of Exiles Under Zerub-babel |

| KINGS of Persia | →

CYRUS

550 B.C. ....

Observe the following:

1. The events of this book cover a period of more than ten years (483-473 B.C.). If one would see in 10:1 an indirect reference to the death of King Xerxes (d. 464 B.C.), then it could be said that the book covers a span of about twenty years.

2. Xerxes was the king of Persia during all of this period.

3. All of the book is dated between chapters 6 and 7 of Ezra.

4. The book opens with a feast (Xerxes) and closes with a feast (Purim). The former was to honor the king and his empire; the latter was to commemorate the Jews' deliverance.

It is interesting to observe that around the time of the book of Esther, three great world battles were fought (Salamis, Thermopylae, and Marathon), and two great world leaders died (Confucius and Buddha).

F. PURPOSE OF THE BOOK

The major purpose of the book of Esther is to show how a host of Jews living in exile were saved from being exterminated by the hand of a Gentile monarch. Though no name for God appears in the book, the divine Providence pervades the narrative.[24] It is the same One who preserved the nation of Israel in the oppressions of Pharaoh, and through such devastating judgments as those of the wilderness journeys, the Assyrian and Babylonian invasions, the destruction of Jerusalem in A.D. 70, and Hitler's mass slaughters.

XIII. SURVEY OF ESTHER

1. Follow the usual procedures of survey study. After you have scanned the book, read the entire story more slowly. Because of its intriguing plot, the book holds one's attention throughout.

2. Four people are the main characters of the narrative: King Ahasuerus, Esther, Mordecai, and Haman. Observe the part played by each, as you read the story.

3. Where is the turning point of the Jews' situation?

4. Try making an outline of the book. In your own words, state the book's theme.

5. Study survey Chart 64. Compare its outlines with your own observations.

6. Observe the elevation of a Jewess, Esther, in chapter 2, and the exaltation of a Jew, Mordecai, in chapter 10.

---

24. Matthew Henry writes, "If the name of God is not here, His finger is." See 4:14 for an example of an implied divine Providence.

7. What were the occasions for the feasts of the book? Note the comparison made of the feasts of chapters 1 and 9.

XIV. PROMINENT SUBJECTS OF ESTHER

A. THE JEWS ARE THREATENED

A key word of the book is "Jew." The singular form appears eight times; the plural form, forty-three times. The term *Jew* is derived from the word *Judah*. Since most of the returning exiles were of the tribe of Judah, the title Jew was applied to them, and extended in later years to all Hebrew people.

The fate of the Jews throughout centuries of unbelief has been one endless tragedy. Wars, famines, broken homes, political upheaval, plagues, and premature death were some of the judgments of the years of judges and kings. Then came the deprivations of the Assyrian and Babylonian captivities; coldness of heart in the four hundred years before Christ; and a worldwide dispersion to the present day for the rejection of the Messiah. The slaughter of millions of Jews by the Hitler regime reveals how much hatred the human race is capable of heaping upon a people.

The story of Esther concerns deliverance for the Jews during *exile* years. The book does not intend to extol the Jew, but to show that the fate of the nation—good or bad—is in the hands of a sovereign God. There have been tragic pogroms in the history of Israel, but there have also been miraculous deliverances, and the book of Esther records one such deliverance.

As of chapter 3, the extermination of all Jews in Xerxes' empire merely awaited the arrival of the day of slaughter, eleven months later, on the thirteenth of Adar (3:13). That date had been determined by lot ("Pur," see 3:7). The decree was distributed in letter form by couriers throughout the empire, ordering the authorities "to destroy, to kill, and to annihilate all the Jews, both young and old, women and children, in one day" (3:13). What made the king sign such a decree? (3:2).

B. THE JEWS ARE SPARED (4:1—10:3)

From time to time God has raised up women to perform a special work for the blessing of His people. Such was the sovereignly determined lot of Queen Esther, who was in a position to appeal to the king to spare the Jews from the planned pogrom. Her foster father, Mordecai, saw the hand of God in this when he exclaimed to her, "Who knows whether you have not attained royalty for such a time as this?" (4:14). Study 4:1—7:10, using the outlines of Chart 63.

ESTHER 4:1—7:10 CHART 63

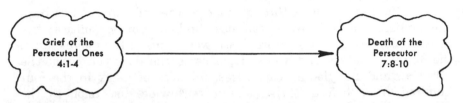

4:1	5:1	6:1	7:1	7:10
Audience with the King Planned	King Favors Esther	King Honors Mordecai	King Hangs Haman	

Esther's First Banquet   Esther's Second Banquet

Grief of the Persecuted Ones 4:1-4 ⟶ Death of the Persecutor 7:8-10

The deliverance of the Jews is the story of chapters 8 and 9. This is followed by the account of Mordecai's exaltation (chap. 10). Use the following outlines when you study these chapters:

8:1	9:17	10:1 10:3
Deliverance of a People	Commemoration of the Deliverance	Exaltation of a Deliverer
Two Decrees	Two Letters	Two Men
Decree to Kill Decree to Defend	Feasting Fasting	Ahasuerus Mordecai

XV. KEY WORDS AND VERSES OF ESTHER

Note the key words and key verse shown on Chart 64. Look for others as you study the book.

XVI. APPLICATIONS OF ESTHER

1. What is divine Providence? What does the book of Esther teach concerning this?

2. What is God's interest in the Jews today, and what is the reason for it?

3. Derive a few spiritual lessons from the key verse, 4:14*b*.

4. God's sovereignty includes the good things He efficiently wills, and the evil things He permits. Show examples of these from the book of Esther.

ESTHER BOOK OF PROVIDENTIAL CARE

473 B.C.

A KEY VERSE: 4:14b

KEY WORDS: Jew (51x), feast

Exaltation of a Jew

Feast of God's Prince Mordecai (chap. 9)

Deliverence of the Jews

Feast of Purim

10:1

Exaltation

Commem-oration

9:17

Influence of a Jewess

Feast of Esther ②

8

The Jews Are Spared

7

Deliverance

Feast of Esther ①

6

5

Threat Against the Jews

474
479

Elevation of a Jewess

Feasts of Ahasuerus

4

480

Honoring the New Queen

3

The Jews Are Threatened

Plot

Gentile Setting

483 B.C.

Honoring the Glorious Kingdom

2

Setting

Feast of the World's Prince Ahasuerus (chap. 1)

1

5. How does the doctrine of divine sovereignty relate to Christian living?

6. When, if ever, is it not evil to refuse to obey civil law? Does Acts 5:29 relate to this question?

XVII. FURTHER STUDY IN EZRA-NEHEMIAH-ESTHER

1. Make biographical studies of the main persons of these books, including Ezra, Nehemiah, Esther, Zerubbabel, Ahasuerus, Mordecai, Haman.

2. In a Bible dictionary, read brief descriptions of the ministries of the prophets during these years. (See Chart 57 for their names.)

3. Study more about the Temple rebuilding project.

4. Study what the New Testament teaches about the Jews' destinies in end times (e.g., Rom 11).

5. As noted earlier, the name of God does not appear in the book of Esther. Also, there are no explicit references to prayer, worship, the Law, Jerusalem, or the Temple. One explanation of the exclusion is that the Jews living in Esther's time had disassociated themselves from the theocratic institution when they refused King Cyrus's permission to return to Palestine (recorded in the early chapters of Ezra). God's name was not at this time linked with them as such, though continued providence and future covenant dealings with the nation were not thereby annulled. Can you think of other possible reasons?

XVIII. SELECTED READING

GENERAL INTRODUCTION

Archer, Gleason L. *A Survey of Old Testament Introduction*, pp. 395-406.
Eason, J. Lawrence. *The New Bible Survey*, pp. 195-208.
Free, Joseph P. *Archaeology and Bible History*, pp. 224-54.
Phillips, John. *Exploring the Scriptures*, pp. 87-94.
Whitcomb, John C., Jr. *Studygraph on Old Testament Kings and Prophets.*
Whitley, C. F. *The Exilic Age.*
Wood, Leon J. *A Survey of Israel's History*, pp. 377-411.

COMMENTARIES AND RELATED STUDIES

Armerding, Carl. *Esther.*
Bruce, F. F. *Israel and the Nations*, pp. 93-119.
Crosby, Howard. "Nehemiah." In Lange's *Commentary on the Holy Scriptures.*
Ironside, H. A. *Notes on the Book of Ezra.*
Luck, G. Coleman. *Ezra and Nehemiah.* Everyman's Bible Commentary.
Morgan, G. Campbell. *Living Messages of the Books of the Bible*, pp. 236-82.
Pfeiffer, Charles F., and Harrison, Everett F. *The Wycliffe Bible Commentary*, pp. 423-57.

Pfeiffer, Charles F., and Vos, Howard F. *The Wycliffe Historical Geography of Bible Lands.*
Redpath, Alan. *Victorious Christian Service.*

Part 3

Reflections and Worship During the Monarchial Years

During the early years of Israel's kingdom, God inspired a few writers to compose for Scripture some poems, songs, and dialogues reflecting the meditations and questions of their hearts and minds. These are the five books which comprise the third section of our English Old Testament, called the "Poetical Books." The books are Job, Psalms, Proverbs, Ecclesiastes, and Song of Solomon.[1] Psalms is the example par excellence of Hebrew poetry. Job, Proverbs, and Ecclesiastes are usually classified contentwise as "Wisdom Literature," because their message represents the wise observations and interpretations of everyday life.

Job

Psalms

Proverbs

Ecclesiastes

Song of Solomon

---

1. There are poetical passages in other parts of the Old Testament as well. (E.g., Exod 15; Deut 32; Judg 5; 2 Sam 22; Hab 3. See *The Zondervan Pictorial Bible Dictionary*, p. 671, for a list of shorter poems.)

15

Job: Knowing God Better Through Adversity

The book of Job answers questions asked by people who believe in God but who are stunned or mystified by the complex problem of pain. Here are some of those questions:

Does justice triumph?

Is God intimately concerned about the lives of His children?

Why are some godly people crushed with tragedy?

What are the enduring values of life?

Is Satan real?

Is there a life beyond the grave?

The very fact that God inspired a book like Job to be written and included in the canon of the Holy Bible is strong evidence of His love for His children. This book records His perfect answers to the many agonizing questions about life. Through those answers, severe trials and testings in life take on a new quality and Peter's words, bringing Christ into the picture, shine forth in all their splendor: "That the proof of your faith, being more precious than gold which is perishable, even though tested by fire, may be found to result in praise and glory and honor at the revelation of Jesus Christ" (1 Pet 1:7).

I. PREPARATION FOR STUDY

Job is the first of the five poetical books.[2] Therefore, it is helpful to become acquainted with the various aspects of poetic literature, so the language and style of these five books will be more intelligible.

---

2. In ancient times the Jews regarded Job, Proverbs, and Psalms as the *major* poetical names. They called them *Books of 'Emeth* ("Truth"), the word *'emeth* representing the first letters of the names of each of the three books *'iov* (Job), *meshallim* (Proverbs), and *tehillim* (Psalms).

A. OLD TESTAMENT POETRY

1. Purposes. The underlying purpose of the poetic books is common to all Scripture, whether the book be didactic or inspirational. Apply 2 Timothy 3:16-17 here. Because the poetic books are charged with feeling, they appeal especially to the human emotions and will, and so are very persuasive in exhorting and reproving.

The poetic writings deal with problems and experiences common to all mankind, which make them timeless and universally attractive. J. Sidlow Baxter writes of this.

> These books portray real human experience, and grapple with profound problems, and express big realities. Especially do they concern themselves with the experiences of the *godly*, in the varying vicissitudes of this changeful life which is ours under the, sun. Moreover, experiences which are here dealt with were permitted to come to men in order that they might be as guides for the godly ever afterward. These experiences are here recorded and interpreted for us by the Spirit of inspiration through "holy men of old" who spoke and wrote "as they were moved" by Him. Thus, in these poetical books we have a most precious treasury of spiritual truth.[3]

2. Main Types. There are three main types of Hebrew poetry: lyric, didactic, and dramatic.

a) lyric. This type is called lyric because the poetry was originally accompanied by music on the lyre. Religious lyric poetry expresses the poet's emotions as they are stirred by and directed toward God. Most of the Psalms are lyric. W. T. Purkiser observes that "while there had been lyric poetry even before Moses, the form grew in beauty and sensitivity until it reached its highest point of perfection in David, the 'sweet singer of Israel.'"[4]

b) didactic. This is sometimes referred to as a gnomic type, because the unit of thought is a gnome, or maxim. The main purpose is to share observations and evaluations of life, not to communicate feeling as such. Proverbs and Ecclesiastes are examples of this type.

c) dramatic. In Hebrew drama, the action is mainly that of dialogue, to get across thoughts and ideas. Job and the Song of Solomon are of this type.

3. Characteristics. Some of the distinguishing characteristics of Hebrew poetry are the following:

a) Hebrew poetry does not depend on rhyme or meter as such, but is built around a thought pattern.[5] This allows the author much liberty

---

3. J. Sidlow Baxter, *Explore the Book*, 3:11.
4. W. T. Purkiser, *Exploring the Old Testament*, pp. 213-14.
5. A few passages reflect something of rhyme in Hebrew (e.g., Job 10:9-18; Psalm 6).

in terms of the structure of a single line, and accounts for the large variety in line lengths, from very short to very long.

b) The unit of Hebrew poetry is the line. A pair of two lines (called *distich*) usually constitutes a verse. But *tristichs* (three lines) are common, and some stanzas include *tetrastichs* (four lines) and *pentastichs* (five lines). (Read Psalm 37 and note the variety of combinations of lines.)

c) Hebrew poetry brings out the color and vitality of the Hebrew language. The language's makeup invites this. For example, the most prominent part of speech in Hebrew is the verb, the action word. The language's grammatical structure is simple and direct. (There is no indirect speech in the Hebrew Old Testament.) Metaphors and antitheses[6] appear often in the text, and repetition is a common device. Whatever is written is the experience, thoughts, and emotions of the author. In choosing words to share such a testimony, the Hebrew author avoids abstract philosophical and theological terms, and uses concrete and pictorial ones.

d) Parallelism is the essential feature of Hebrew poetry. It is the structure of a verse which shows a correspondence between two or more lines of that verse. For example, after a statement has been made in the first line of a verse, that thought is repeated, enlarged, or even contrasted in the remaining line or lines. Basically, there are three types of parallelism in Hebrew poetry:[7]

(1) Synonomous. Here the second line is a repetition of the thought of the first line (Psalm 37:2,6,10,12).

(2) Antithetic. The second line expresses an idea contrasted with that of the first (Psalm 1:6; 30:5; 37:9).

(3) Synthetic. The second and later lines enlarge upon or complete the thought of the first line (Psalm 2:6; 19:7; 24:9; 37:4,5,13; 95:1-3; Prov 16:3,5; Job 19:25).

Other characteristics of Hebrew poetry will be cited from time to time in the course of these next few chapters on the poetical books. For example, in the next section of this chapter (Background) the literary style of the book of Job is discussed.

As you begin your survey of this third section of the Old Testament ("Poetical Books"), it will be helpful to review the prominent themes of the books of the two preceding sections ("Law," and "History"). The following list of words chosen by J. Sidlow Baxter suggests

---

6. A metaphor is a figure of speech in which a word or phrase which ordinarily means one thing is used of another thing in order to suggest a likeness between the two (e.g., "Benjamin is a ravenous wolf." Gen 49:27). An antithesis is a contrast of ideas (e.g., Psalm 1:6).

7. See Purkiser, pp. 211-13, for descriptions of other types of parallelism.

the leading subjects of each of the seventeen books.[8] Go through the list and see if you know why each word was chosen to represent each book. You might want to use different words in some cases. This exercise will be a good review of your surveys thus far.

LAW   HISTORY

Genesis—Destitution   Joshua—Possession
Exodus—Deliverance   Judges, Ruth—Declension
Leviticus—Dedication   1 Samuel—Transition
Numbers—Direction   2 Samuel—Confirmation
Deuteronomy—Destination   1 Kings—Disruption
                                       2 Kings—Dispersion
                                       1, 2 Chronicles—Retrospection
                                       Ezra—Restoration
                                       Nehemiah—Reconstruction
                                       Esther—Preservation

Later, when you have finished surveying each of the five poetical books, you will want to look back and compare the themes of those writings. As a preview to the group, read the following lists, which identify the main subjects of the books.[9]

Job:	The Problem of Pain	Blessing Through Suffering
Psalms:	The Way to Pray	Praise Through Prayer
Proverbs:	The Behavior of the Believer	Providence Through Precept
Ecclesiastes:	The Folly of Forgetting God	Verity Through Vanity
Song of Solomon:	The Art of Adoration	Bliss Through Union

Some Bible students see an overall progression of teaching in the group of five books. Do you observe any progression?

Refer to Chart 3 and observe at the bottom of the chart the period during which the poetical books were written.

---

8. The list is from Baxter, 3:10.
9. The middle list is from John Phillips, *Exploring the Scriptures*, p. 98; the right-hand list is from Baxter, 3:13. Used by permission.

II. Background of Job

A. THE MAN JOB

1. Name. There are two possible literal meanings of the name Job. If the name's origin is in the Arabic language, it means "one who turns back" (i.e., repents). If its origin is Hebrew, it means "the hated (persecuted) one." It is interesting that both of these meanings are reflected in experiences of Job as recorded in the book bearing his name.

2. Biography and descriptions. Job was a real person, not a fictitious character, as some critics contend. Read Ezekiel 14:14-20 and James 5:11 for clear evidence of this. Listed below are a few things known about this man.

a) Job was a native of the land of Uz (1:1). This region was somewhere northeast of Palestine, near desert land (1:19), probably between the city of Damascus and the Euphrates River. This would place the region near the boundary lines of present-day Iraq and Saudi Arabia (see Map Q). Read 1:3 and note that Job was from an area called "the east."

b) Job probably lived before or around the time of Abraham. This is partly indicated by the fact that the book of Job does not mention any Israelite covenant relationship with God, which is the core of Hebrew history from the call of Abraham (Gen 12) onward.[10] Also, there is no reference to Hebrew institutions (e.g., the Law). The family-altar worship of 1:5 was before or outside the Mosaic-type worship, with its priests.[11] Based on the above observations, the man Job lived sometime between the tower of Babel event and the call of Abraham, or shortly thereafter.[12] Read Genesis 11:9—12:1 to fix this chronological setting in your mind. Then read the words of God in Job 39 and note the different kinds of animals, including the horse, with which Job was familiar. Man's habitat has not changed radically during the long course of world history!

c) Some have suggested that Job was as old as sixty when the experiences of the book took place. Whatever his age, we know nothing of his earlier life. Questions which remain unanswered include: Who were his parents? From whom did he first learn about God? How widespread was his witness for God?

---

10. If Job was a contemporary of Abraham, or lived after him, then he was a believer outside the covenant family of Israel (cf. Acts 14:17).

11. The "burnt offerings" of 1:5 are not Levitical offerings, according to this view.

12. References to a Job as early as 2000 B.C. appear in extrabiblical texts. The footnote of the Berkeley Version at 42:16-17 reads, "His many years [140] suggest the period of Abraham."

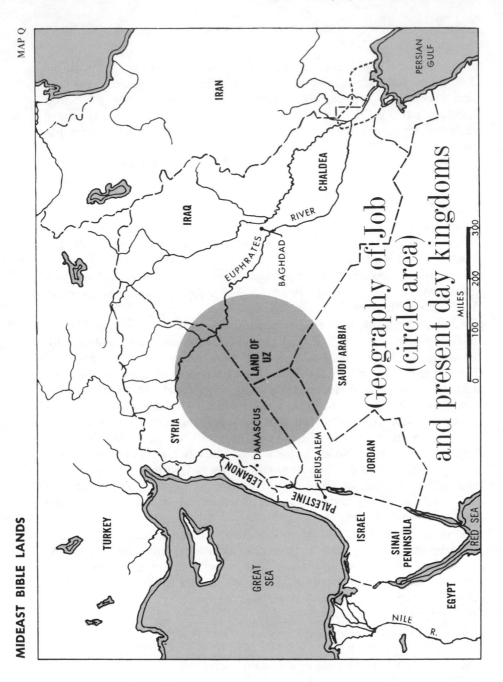

MAP Q

TURKEY

IRAN

PERSIAN
GULF

CHALDEA

IRAQ

EUPHRATES

RIVER

BAGHDAD

LAND OF
UZ

SYRIA

DAMASCUS

SAUDI ARABIA

Geography of Job
(circle area)
and present day kingdoms

LEBANON

JERUSALEM

JORDAN

PALESTINE

ISRAEL

GREAT
SEA

SINAI
PENINSULA

RED SEA

EGYPT

NILE

R.

MILES

0   100   200   300

d) Job was very wealthy (read 1:3,10). He and his sons were homeowners in a large city of the region (cf. 1:4; 29:7). (The ruins of over three hundred ancient cities in the area of Uz have been discovered by archaeologists, indicating a very active civilization in this region in those early days.)

e) He was a respected and popular judge and benefactor of his fellow citizens (29:7-25).

f) He was a righteous man in God's eyes (read 1:1,5,8; cf. also Ezek 14:14-20 and James 5:11). What does the last phrase of Job 1:5 suggest about his relationship to God?

g) He lived to a very old age. If Job was as old as sixty when he was first tested (chap. 1), then he was at least two hundred years old when he died (42:16-17). Compare this with the longevities of the people listed in Genesis 11:10-26 (cf. also Gen 25:7).

As you survey the book of Job and read the Bible text, you will become better acquainted with Job as a person.

B. THE BOOK OF JOB

1. Title. The book is named for its main character, not for its author. The book of Ruth is another example of a writing so named.

2. Author and date. The human author is anonymous, and the date of writing uncertain.[13] Such is the case for many Bible books. Among those suggested as writer are Moses, Solomon, a contemporary of Solomon's (cf. 1 Kings 4:29-34), Isaiah, Jeremiah, Baruch, a prophet of the captivity, and Job. Most scholars are agreed that the author lived at a time later than Abraham and Moses. If he was a contemporary of Solomon, an approximate date of writing would be 950 B.C. One writer supports an early date before the prophets and before exile.

> The grandeur and spontaneity of the book and its deeply empathic re-creation of the sentiments of men standing early in the progress of revelation point to the early pre-Exilic period, before the doctrinal, especially the eschatological, contribution of the prophets.[14]

Chart 65 shows the historical setting of possible dates involving the man Job and the book written about him.

The book's authority and dependability rest not on the human aspect of its authorship, but on divine revelation. Only God could

---

13. This open question of human authorship and date does not limit one's study of this remarkable book of the Old Testament.

14. Meredith G. Kline, "Job," in *The Wycliffe Bible Commentary*, p. 460.

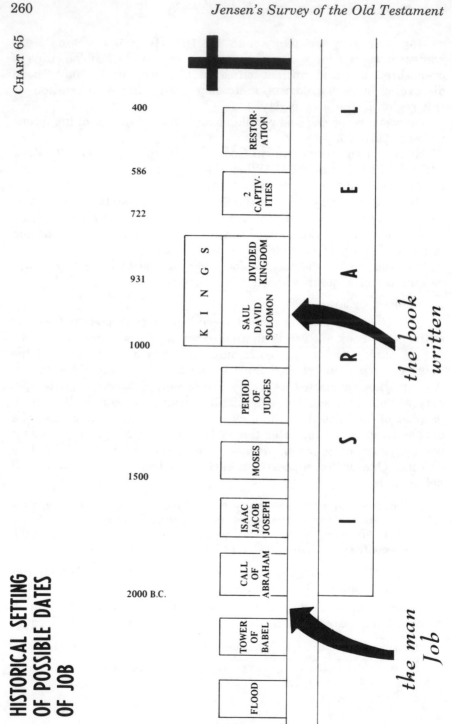

CHART 65

HISTORICAL SETTING
OF POSSIBLE DATES
OF JOB

reveal such things as the conversation between Himself and Satan, recorded in chapters 1-2.

3. Purposes. Job is a book about a physical and spiritual experience of an ancient patriarch whose faith was tested to the uttermost. Its main purposes are not to teach Israelite history, Messianic prophecy, the ABC's of how to be saved, or the mission of the Church. These are the big tasks of other parts of Scripture. The underlying purposes of Job are the following:

a) To reveal who God is.

b) To show the kind of trust He wants His children to have. (For example, trust God even though you cannot fully account for your circumstances.) Approval by God means "tried and found true" (cf. Rom 16:10, Berkeley).

c) To reveal His favor toward His children and His absolute control over Satan.

d) To answer man's questions about why a righteous person may suffer while an evil man may be healthy and prosperous.

The fourth purpose (d) above) is placed last because, although the book's entire story is about this problem of pain, the answer to the problem is found in the areas of the first three statements. Stated simply, *who God is* determines *what He does*; therefore, we must *trust Him without reservation.*

4. Doctrinal content. The book of Job makes reference, directly or indirectly, to most of the key doctrines of the Bible. Subjects for which the book is particularly known are:

a) Doctrine of God.

b) Doctrine of man.

c) Nature. Many references to God's creation appear throughout the book. Included are such astronomical facts as:

names of stars and constellations (38:31-32)

suspension of the earth in space (26:7)

the earth as a sphere (22:14, margin)

(Scan chaps. 38 and 39, which are filled with similar references.)

d) Satan.

e) Sin and righteousness.

f) Affliction, discipline, and blessing.

g) Justice.

h) Faith.

In your survey study you will be observing these and other doctrines. Does it surprise you that such a great variety of truth was revealed to men of God even before the Scriptures began to be recorded?

5. Style. As noted earlier in this chapter, Job is classified as dramatic poetry. The book is recognized even in the secular world of literature as the most magnificent dramatic poem ever written. Thomas Carlyle wrote, "There is nothing written, I think, in the Bible or out of it, of equal literary merit."

Since poetry is the language of the heart, Job reveals the innermost thoughts of men more so than their outward deeds. The poetry section of the book (3:1—42:6) uses the poetic structure of parallelism in its arrangement of lines. Recall the three main kinds of parallelism. Then read each of the examples from Job cited below.

a) synonymous (4:9)

b) antithetic (16:20)

c) synthetic (4:19-21)

In drama, not everything spoken by the actors is necessarily true. This is so in the book of Job, where, for example, Job's three friends, Eliphaz, Bildad, and Zophar, give their own interpretations of Job's afflictions, and are later rebuked by God for not speaking "what is right" (42:7). (The speeches of Job's three friends take up nine chapters of the book.)

6. Relation to other books of the Bible. As noted earlier, all the books before Job, from Genesis to Esther, are for the most part historical in nature. If Job lived before or outside the Abrahamic setting, an interesting comparison may be made between the poetical and historical books. This is shown on Chart 66.

The book of Job is intimately related to the New Testament, even though it is explicitly quoted only once by a New Testament book (1 Cor 3:19, quoting Job 5:13). The problems and questions of the man Job are answered completely and perfectly in Christ. It should be very clear why Christ's ministry is the culmination and interpretation of all Old Testament history. E. Heavenor relates this book to Christ's ministry correctly:

> Like the other books of the Old Testament Job is forward-looking to Christ. Questions are raised, great sobs of agony are heard, which Jesus alone can answer. The book takes its place in the testimony of the ages that there is a blank in the human heart which Jesus alone can fill.[15]

Were it not for the atoning work of Christ neither the faith of Job nor that of any other Old Testament saint would have availed to bring them into the heavenly city, written about in Hebrews.

> These men of faith I have mentioned died without ever receiving all that God had promised them; but they saw it all awaiting them on

---

15. E. Heavenor, "Job," in *The New Bible Commentary*, rev. ed., p. 422.

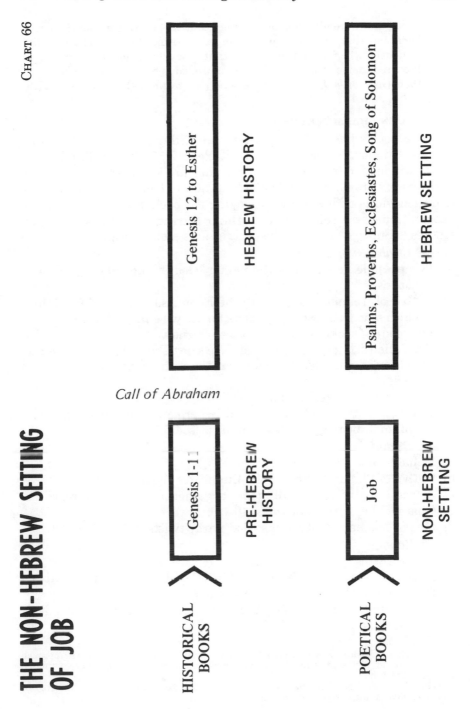

CHART 66

THE NON-HEBREW SETTING OF JOB

HISTORICAL BOOKS

Genesis 1-11 — PRE-HEBREW HISTORY

Call of Abraham

Genesis 12 to Esther — HEBREW HISTORY

POETICAL BOOKS

Job — NON-HEBREW SETTING

Psalms, Proverbs, Ecclesiastes, Song of Solomon — HEBREW SETTING

ahead and were glad, for they agreed that this earth was not their real home but that they were just strangers visiting down here. And quite obviously when they talked like that, they were looking forward to their real home in heaven. . . . And now God is not ashamed to be called their God, for *he has made a heavenly city for them* (Heb 11:13-16, TLB, italics added).

C. THE MAIN CHARACTERS OF JOB

The book's five main characters are Elihu, Job, and Job's three friends: Eliphaz, Bildad, and Zophar. Read 2:11-13 and 32:1-5 for a brief introduction to these men. Since they are key characters in most of the book's drama, it would be helpful now to learn more about them and their views on life before surveying the book. Study the following descriptions and refer back to them during the course of your studies.[16] Enlarge or revise the descriptions along the way.

1. Eliphaz.

a) Two possible meanings of the name: "God is fine gold"; or "God is dispenser."

b) Native of Teman (2:11), a city of Edom, southeast of Palestine, which was traditionally famous for its wise men (Jer 49:7).

c) The leading spokesman of the three friends.

d) The "scientist" of the group; his speeches show clearer reasoning and more considerate criticism than those of the other two friends.

e) Noble, sincere, wise, courtly.

f) Two of his main contentions: God is perfectly pure and righteous; and, man brings trouble on himself (see 5:7).

2. Bildad.

a) Name means "Son of contention."

b) Native of Shuah (Sukhu of the Euphrates region?) (2:11).

c) A traditionalist (cf. 8:8-10); more argumentative than Eliphaz.

d) Charged Job with godlessness (8:13).

e) One of his main contentions: God never twists justice (see 8:3).

3. Zophar.

a) Name means "hairy," or "rough."

b) Native of Naamah, or Naamath (2:11), probably of North Arabia.

c) Possibly the oldest of the three friends.[17]

d) A dogmatist and moralist; blunt; sometimes displayed a holier-than-thou attitude.

---

16. This procedure is deductive in nature. If one followed the inductive approach here, he would arrive at character descriptions of the men *after* he had completed studying the Bible text.

17. Some feel that Eliphaz was the oldest of the three men, for which Oriental courtesy gave him the right to speak first in a group.

e) Charged Job with boasting (11:2-6).
f) One of his main contentions: God knows iniquity when He sees it (see 11:11).
   4. Elihu.
a) Name means "He is my God."
b) Native of Buz (possibly of Arabia or Syria).
c) The youngest of the four men, not an intimate companion of Job's three friends.
d) One of his main contentions: God is good (see 33:24). Of the four men, Elihu gave the best diagnosis of Job's plight, saying that sufferings are often God's way of refining the righteous. He did not go far enough in his diagnosis, however.

III. SURVEY

The book of Job is a good example of the necessity of making an overview of the text in general before analyzing its small parts. For example, we might read one of the speeches of Job's three friends and reach very wrong conclusions if we did not first relate the speech to the total story, which includes how Job's plight originated (chaps. 1-2), and what God thought of the three friends' interpretations (e.g., 42:7).

A. A FIRST SCANNING

1. How many chapters are there in the book?
2. Scan the opening phrases of the chapters. Would you say the book is mainly action, or mainly discourse? Where in the book do the speeches begin, and where do they end?[18]

B. CHAPTER CONTENT

Now scan the book again, and identify more specifically the content of each of the chapters. For the speeches (3:1—42:6) you need now only note who the speakers are. Sometimes a speech covers more than one chapter (e.g., Eliphaz's speech of chaps. 4-5). Only two chapters of the poetry section contain speeches that are shorter than a full chapter (see chaps. 40,42). Record the speakers of each chapter on a work sheet that has four columns under the names of Job, Eliphaz, Bildad, and Zophar.

Read each of the following sections, and record the theme of each on paper:

---

18. The format of such versions as the *New American Standard Bible* is excellent for a study of a book like Job. The prose (narrative) is printed in the usual style, and the speeches, which are dramatic poetry, are printed in stanzas made up of single lines.

CHART 67

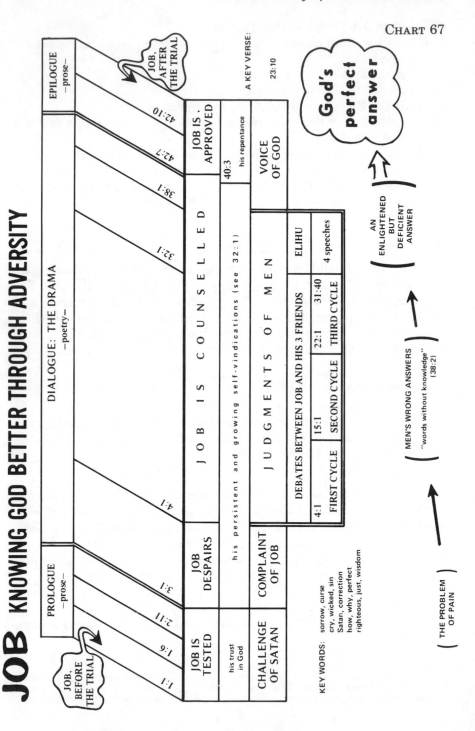

JOB KNOWING GOD BETTER THROUGH ADVERSITY

JOB, BEFORE THE TRIAL

JOB, AFTER THE TRIAL

PROLOGUE —prose—	DIALOGUE: THE DRAMA —poetry—	EPILOGUE —prose—

1:1   1:6   2:11   3:1   4:1   32:1   38:1   42:7   42:10

JOB IS TESTED	JOB DESPAIRS	JOB IS COUNSELLED	JOB IS APPROVED

his trust in God

his persistent and growing self-vindications (see 32:1)

40:3 — his repentance

CHALLENGE OF SATAN	COMPLAINT OF JOB	JUDGMENTS OF MEN	VOICE OF GOD

DEBATES BETWEEN JOB AND HIS 3 FRIENDS

4:1	15:1	22:1 31:40	ELIHU
FIRST CYCLE	SECOND CYCLE	THIRD CYCLE	4 speeches

A KEY VERSE: 23:10

God's perfect answer

AN ENLIGHTENED BUT DEFICIENT ANSWER

MEN'S WRONG ANSWERS "words without knowledge" (38:2)

THE PROBLEM OF PAIN

KEY WORDS: sorrow, curse
cry, wicked, sin
Satan, correction
how, why, perfect
righteous, just, wisdom

1:1—2:13	4:1—14:22	38:1—42:6
	15:1—21:34	
3:1-26	22:1—31:40	42:7-17
	32:1—37:24	

The first three passages of the middle column (above) represent the debates between Job and his three friends. The speeches of Elihu are recorded in 32:1—37:24.

C. SURVEY CHART

Chart 67 is a survey chart of Job, showing the book's organization by various outlines. Refer to this chart as you make the following observations and complete the study suggestions:

1. Note how the book opens ("Job Before the Trial"), and how it closes ("Job After the Trial"). Read the passages involved.

2. Observe the three-part outline of style at the top of the chart.

3. Study the outlines shown below the base line. Check out these outlines with the results of your own survey study. You may need to scan the biblical text at some places to verify an outline. Justify the location of main divisions at 38:1; 40:3; and 42:7.

4. What is the basis for dividing the controversies of chapters 4-31 into three cycles? (Refer back to your work sheet, showing the alternations of speakers in the dialogues.)

5. Observe the progression at the bottom of the chart, beginning with "The Problem of Pain."

6. Read these other choice passages of Job at this time: 1:21; 5:17; 14:14; 16:21; 19:23-27; 26:7-14; 28:12-28; 42:1-6.

7. You may wonder why such a large portion of the book is devoted to the wrong diagnoses and arguments of Job's three friends. If their main charge was that Job's suffering was caused by his personal sins, do you suppose their own security was imperiled by the possibility of the same kind of suffering befalling them? If so, does this partly explain their persistence in dealing with Job?

IV. PROMINENT SUBJECTS

Of the many important subjects of the book of Job, three are especially prominent: Satan, the problem of pain, and genuine trust.

A. SATAN

Much can be learned about Satan from the book of Job. For example, Satan is not a name representing impersonal evil; Satan is the personal enemy of God and His children. The persons and events of the narrative of Job are real persons and actual events. "There was a man. . .. There was a day. . . . Then Satan . . . smote Job" (1:1, 6; 2:7). This is precise, genuine history. And, lest one think that Satan is no longer active in accusing the children of God, the last book of the Bible reveals the sober truth of Satan's continuing work until end times: "The accuser of our brethren has been thrown down, who accuses them before our God day and night" (Rev 12:10; cf. 1 Pet 5:8).

Satan first appears in the story of man in the Garden of Eden. Recall the account of his beguiling Adam and Eve (Gen 3:1-7). The text refers to him as "the serpent." How do you know that this was Satan? (Cf. Rev 12:9.) Why is Satan antihumankind? Note that the name *Satan* literally means "adversary." Of its nineteen appearances in the Old Testament, fourteen are in Job. The name *devil* means "slanderer," and is found only in the New Testament (sixty times).

B. THE PROBLEM OF PAIN

The book of Job is the Bible's fullest treatment of this vexing problem. The summary given below shows how the book opens with the problem and concludes with the solution.
1. The Problem of Pain: Why do the righteous suffer, and the wicked prosper?
2. The Wrong Answer of Job's Three Friends: Suffering is God's judgment for sin.
3. The enlightened answer of Elihu: Suffering is God's way to teach, discipline, and refine.
4. God's perfect answer: Suffering is a test of trusting God for who He is, not for what He does.

C. GENUINE TRUST

The book of Job teaches that the person with genuine trust worships God basically for *who* He is. That person may have unanswered questions as to why God does what He does, but he still worships God wholeheartedly for who He is. Job the combatant became Job the worshiper when he heard God reveal Himself to His smitten child (38:1 ff.). E. Heavenor writes: "The Word came through a fresh vision of God. . . . That Word brought a transformation which the word of man had been totally unable to achieve. . . . The Word convinced Job that he could trust such a God."[19]

---

19. Heavenor, pp. 442-43.

V. Key Words and Verses

Some of the main key words of Job are: sorrow, curse, cry, wicked, sin, Satan, how, why, perfect, righteous, just, and wisdom. Read 23:10 as a key verse of the book. Choose others from the Bible text.

VI. Applications

1. What do you think are God's purposes in permitting Satan to exercise certain powers, limited though these powers may be?

2. If Satan is the Christian's active archenemy, what help does the child of God have in such a daily warfare? Does the book of Job give any answers? Read what the New Testament teaches in Luke 22:31-32 and 1 Peter 5:6-11.

3. Does all suffering of believers originate the way Job's did? What answers to this question do the following passages give: Psalm 66:10; John 9:1-3; Philippians 3:8; Hebrews 2:18; 5:8; 1 Peter 2:21; 3:18; 4:12-14; 5:10?

4. How is a believer's suffering related to Christ's suffering, according to these verses: 2 Corinthians 1:5-7; Philippians 3:10-11; 1 Peter 2:21-23; 4:13; 5:1?

5. How would you answer the following challenge of an unbeliever concerning the problem of pain:

> If God were good, He would wish to make His creatures perfectly happy, and if God were almighty He would be able to do what He wished. But the creatures are not happy. Therefore God lacks either goodness, or power, or both.[20]

6. What is the connection, if any, between physical sickness and sin?

7. Some of Job's words reveal the depths of despondency to which a child of God may sometimes fall. What preventives from this mood of despair does the Christian have today? What antidotes for despair does the believer have?

8. "Neither is there any daysman [umpire, arbiter, mediator] betwixt us, that might lay his hand upon us both" (Job 9:33, KJV). This was Job's cry for firsthand contact with God. In what ways is Jesus, as Mediator between God and man (1 Tim 2:5), the answer to man's needs?

9. The balance of justice will come to rest in eternity. To what extent does retribution for sin fall in this life?

---

20. See C. S. Lewis, *The Problem of Pain*, pp. 14 ff., for answers to this challenge.

10. Some Christians experience trial over such a long period of time that they begin to wonder if God is even aware of their plight. Where can they find help?

11. What does the book of Job teach about the ministry of comforting others?

12. Why must God reveal Himself to man if man is to know truly who He is? (Read John 14:9.) In what sense is Jesus the revelation of God the Father?

13. Read Job 23:14. In what ways is the doctrine of the sovereignty of God encouraging to Christians?

14. Bildad's last words (Job 25) are fatalistic, leaving man without hope. How do God's love and the cross of Calvary shed light on such hopelessness?

15. What are some of the good fruits of God's chastening His children? (Cf. 33:19-30.)

16. Many people deny the truth of 34:12, and accuse God of injustice and coldness for allowing such catastrophes as the drowning of whole villages by a tidal wave. What are your thoughts about this?

17. What is genuine confession of sin? What is the place of such confession in the heart of a Christian?

18. Apply Hebrews 11:6 to the trying experience of suffering. Observe the references to physical suffering in Hebrews 11.

19. Why is revelation from God, such as the Holy Scriptures, a necessary ingredient of Christian counseling?

20. Read James 5:11 and 1:12 in the light of the book of Job. What do the verses teach?

VII. FURTHER STUDY

1. Extend your study of the Bible's teachings about Satan by reading the various passages listed in *Unger's Bible Handbook*, pages 520-21.

2. Read C. S. Lewis, *The Problem of Pain*.

VIII. SELECTED READING

GENERAL INTRODUCTION

Archer, Gleason L. *A Survey of Old Testament Introduction*, pp. 418-23; 438-49.

Manley, G. T. *The New Bible Handbook*, pp. 186-91.

Purkiser, W. T. *Exploring the Old Testament*, pp. 209-14; 238-49.

Schultz, Samuel J. *The Old Testament Speaks*, pp. 279-85.

Young, Edward J. *Introduction to the Old Testament*, pp. 281-86; 309-21.

COMMENTARIES

Delitzsch, F. *The Book of Job*, vols. 1, 2.
Heavenor, E. S. P. "Job." In *The New Bible Commentary*.
Kline, Meredith G. "Job." In *The Wycliffe Bible Commentary*.
Morgan, G. Campbell. "The Book of Job." In *The Analyzed Bible*.
Zoeckler, Otto. "Job." In Lange's *Commentary on the Holy Scriptures*.

OTHER SOURCES

Blair, J. Allen. *Living Patiently*.
Lewis, C. S. *The Problem of Pain*.
Morgan, G. Campbell. *The Answers of Jesus to Job*.
Unger, Merrill F. *Unger's Bible Handbook*.

16

Psalms: "Bless the Lord, O My Soul"

Psalms is one of the most practical books of the Bible, wondrously suited to the human heart. It is especially dear to every child of God, perhaps because there is no experience of the believer which does not find its counterpart in the Psalms. Someone, in speaking of the whole Bible as "the Temple of Truth" and the different books as different rooms of that temple, has called Psalms "The Music Room." It is filled with heavenly music suited to man's every experience. Here the Holy Spirit sweeps every chord of human nature: from the low, wailing note of Psalm 51, to the high, exultant note of Psalm 24. That Psalms was a favorite book of the first-century believers is shown by the fact that of the New Testament's 283 direct quotations from the Old Testament, 116 are from Psalms.

I. PREPARATION FOR STUDY

1. Be acquainted with the various literary devices used by the authors of poetic writing. Some of the main ones are:

a) Simile: comparison of two things, usually employing the words *as* or *like* (e.g., "He will be like a tree," Psalm 1:3).

b) Metaphor: comparison of two things without using the words *as* or *like* (e.g., "The LORD is a sun and shield," Psalm 84:11).

c) Hyperbole: exaggeration for effect (e.g., "Every night I make my bed swim, I dissolve my couch with my tears," Psalm 6:6).

d) Personification: applying personality traits to inanimate objects (e.g., "All my bones will say, 'Lord, who is like Thee,'" Psalm 35:10).

272

e) Apostrophe: addressing inanimate things (e.g., "What ails you, O sea, that you flee?" Psalm 114:5).

f) Synecdoche: representing the whole by a part, or a part by the whole (e.g., "the arrow that flies by day," Psalm 91:5).

2. Praise and prayer are keynotes of the psalms. Before surveying the book, think much about what is genuine praise and what is genuine prayer.

II. BACKGROUND

A. NAME

When the individual lyrics of David and the other authors were brought together as one anthology, possibly as early as 500 B.C., the Hebrew title given to the anthology was *Tehillim,* meaning "praise songs." The Greek Septuagint translators gave the title *Psalmoi,* meaning "songs to the accompaniment of a stringed instrument," and this was the Greek title used in the days of Jesus (read Acts 1:20). Thus, our English title *Psalms* is really an ancient title, even in pronunciation. The term *Psalter,* by which this book is sometimes called, is derived almost letter for letter from the Greek word for "stringed instrument."

B. PLACE IN THE BIBLE

In the Hebrew Scriptures the scroll of Psalms appeared at the beginning of the third division called "Writings." (Recall the three divisions of the Hebrew Bible as Law, Prophets, and Writings; cf. Luke 24:44.) As such, this collection of sacred songs was the inspired prayer and praise book of the nation of Israel. In the fourfold grouping of books in our English Bibles (Law, history, poetry, prophets), the book of Psalms is the second book of the third division.

C. AUTHORS

The book of Psalms is commonly spoken of as David's because he wrote the larger number of individual psalms (seventy-three are ascribed to him in their titles).[1] He was known as "the sweet psalmist

---

1. The following is a classification of the psalms by authorship as designated by the superscriptions:
David: Psalms 3-9; 11-32; 34-41; 51-65; 68-70; 86; 101; 103; 108-10; 122; 124; 131; 133; 138-45
Descendants of Korah: Psalms 42; 44-49; 84-85; 87
Asaph: Psalms 50; 73-83
Solomon: Psalms 72; 127
Ethan: Psalm 89
Heman: Psalm 88
Moses: Psalm 90
Anonymous: all other psalms

of Israel" (2 Sam 23:1), and had an extraordinary combination of talents. On one occasion he was referred to as being "a skillful musician, a mighty man of valor, a warrior, one prudent in speech, and a handsome man; and the LORD is with him" (1 Sam 16:18; cf. 2 Sam 6:5, 15; 1 Chron 16:4-5; 2 Chron 7:6; 29:25; Amos 6:5).

Twenty-seven psalms are ascribed to authors other than David. They are descendants of Korah, ten; Asaph, twelve; Solomon, two; Ethan, one; Heman, one; and Moses, one.

Fifty psalms are anonymous. However, there is reason to believe that some of these were written by David. For example, Psalm 2 is ascribed to David in Acts 4:25. And Psalm 1 seems to be by the same author. Also compare 1 Chronicles 16:7-22 with Psalm 105 and 1 Chronicles 16:23-36 with Psalm 96.

David also arranged the Temple service of song (1 Chron 25), probably writing much of its music.

See Chart 70 for the general identification of authors of each group of psalms.

D. DATES

On the basis of authorship and historical references of some of the psalms, we may conclude that most of the psalms were written over a period of about five hundred years, between 1000 and 500 B.C., as shown by Chart 68.

DATES OF THE PSALMS   CHART 68

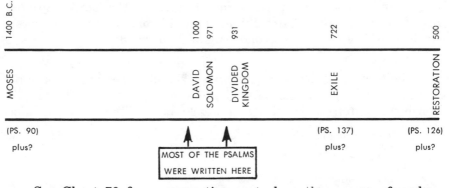

See Chart 70 for a suggestion as to how the groups of psalms were collected into one unit during Old Testament times. Actually, very little is known about the facts (who, when, why, and so forth) of this collection process.[2]

---

2. See W. Graham Scroggie, *The Psalms*, 1:15-18.

E. TYPES

Because many subjects are treated by the psalms, they have a wide application. The psalmist may be reviewing the past (history)[3]; envisioning the future (prophecy); or reflecting the present (experience). In all of the psalms the writer is responding to the very real fact of a living God and His relation to men. Thus, it is not surprising to find that the outstanding subjects of the psalms have to do with God: the person of God, the Son of God, the Word of God, the works of God, and the people of God.

When classified more specifically as to subject matter and attitude of writing, many types emerge. These are the major types:[4]

1. Didactic. (E.g., Psalms 1,5,7,15,17,50,73,94,101.) Such psalms might be called psalms of formal instruction.

2. History. (E.g., Psalms 78,105,106,136.) These psalms are almost wholly composed of references to historical events of the nation of Israel. A summary of the highlights of practically all of Israel's history is given in the historical psalms. References to historical events appear frequently throughout the book of Psalms.

3. Hallelujah. (E.g., Psalms 106,111-13, 115-17, 135, 146-50.) The theme of praise in these psalms is obvious.

4. Penitential. (E.g., Psalms 6,32,38,51,102,130,143.) Confession of sin occupies the greater part of each of these. Psalm 51 is the classic example of this type of psalm.

5. Supplication. (E.g., Psalm 86.) The psalmist cries to God in his own need, or he intercedes for another's need.

6. Thanksgiving. (E.g., Psalms 16,18.) The note of praise and thanksgiving pervades the whole book of Psalms, but some individual psalms are particularly thanksgiving psalms.

7. Messianic. (E.g., Psalms 2, 20-24, 41,68,118.) There is a strong prophetic character of the Psalms. Many of the hymns prophesy the suffering and sorrows of God's people, Israel, and their coming deliverance, restoration, and blessing in a future glorious Kingdom. But, most of all, they prophesy of Christ in His two advents: His first advent in humiliation, and His second advent in glory. Such psalms are called Messianic psalms. Some of the Old Testament's most minute prophecies of Christ are found here. They are about His person (God and man); His character (righteous and holy); His work (death and resurrection); and His offices (priest, judge, and king).

---

3. Scroggie says that "without the Psalter our knowledge of the religious history of Israel, as that may be derived from the Historical Books, would be not only imperfect but misleading" (Ibid., 1:27). See this cited work, pp. 28-29, for a comprehensive list of historical facts appearing in the Psalms.

4. One way to study the psalms systematically is to study them group by group, according to the classifications cited here.

8. *Nature.* (E.g., Psalms 8,19,29,33,65,104.) God's handiwork is an inspiring subject for any poetical writing.

9. *Pilgrim.* (E.g., Psalms 120-34.) This group of psalms, each bearing the title "Song of Degrees," was probably a hymnbook used by the Jews on their pilgrimage up to the Temple on the occasions of the national feasts.

10. *Imprecatory.* (E.g., Psalms 35,52,58,59,69,83,109,137,140.) The imprecatory (cursing) passages of these psalms are generally looked upon with a great deal of perplexity. Many cannot understand how such utterances could be acceptable to God. The problem is answered when one recognizes the age and the setting of their writing. Gleason L. Archer writes:

> It is important to realize that prior to the first advent of Christ, the only tangible way in which the truth of the Scripture could be demonstrated to human observers was by the pragmatic test of disaster befalling those who were in error and deliverance being granted to those who held to the truth. As long as the wicked continued to triumph, their prosperity seemed to refute the holiness and sovereignty of the God of Israel. A Hebrew believer in the Old Testament age could only chafe in deep affliction of soul as long as such a state of affairs continued. Identifying himself completely with God's cause, he could only regard God's enemies as his own, and implore God to uphold His own honor and justify His own righteousness by inflicting a crushing destruction upon those who either in theory or in practice denied His sovereignty and His law.[5]

III. Survey

1. Study the survey Chart 70, and observe that the 150 psalms are divided into five groups. These divisions date back to ancient times. We do not know the original reasons for identifying groups as such. Some think that each group was compared with each book of the Pentateuch. (See those comparisons on the chart.) The old rabbis are known to have called Psalms the "Pentateuch of David." There is no clear-cut topical outline of these five parts of the book of Psalms.[6]

2. Note on the chart that each of the five groups of Psalms ends with a doxology. Read and compare the doxologies. G. Campbell Morgan sees these as the clue to the content of each of the five divisions. He says that an examination of the doxologies "will reveal a certain conception of God, and an attitude of the soul in worship

---

5. Gleason L. Archer, *A Survey of Old Testament Introduction*, p. 437.

6. Scroggie says, "The Psalter is the hymn book of the Hebrews, and a hymn book does not lend itself to formal analysis" (W. Graham Scroggie, *Know Your Bible*, 1:107).

resulting from such conception."[7] His outline centered on "worship" is shown on the chart.

3. Scan the book of Psalms and observe that most of the psalms have superscriptions—sometimes referred to as titles.[8] (Note: Do not confuse the ancient superscription with titles assigned by the publisher. For example, the superscription of Psalm 14 is "For the choir director. A *Psalm* of David." The title assigned by the NASB editors is "Folly and Wickedness of Men.") These were not part of the original psalms, but were added later, probably at least before 200 B.C. In the superscription are words indicating such things as (1) occasion of the psalm[9]; (2) type of psalm (e.g., *tepillah*, "prayer"); and (3) musical instructions (e.g., *lammenasseah*, "to the choir leader"). The superscriptions do not have the weight of dependability as does the inspired biblical text itself, but the best rule of thumb is to accept them as they stand.[10]

4. Scan each psalm individually, reading the first line of each stanza of each psalm. This can be done in a short time if you are using a version (such as NASB) which clearly shows the stanza divisions. Such an exercise will help you get the overall *feel* of the book of Psalms. It will also help you identify whether the psalm is a meditation, a prayer, a hymn of praise, or a prophecy.

5. Read the *New American Standard Bible* titles printed at the top of the psalms. List these on paper. Then study the list from the standpoint of subject matter (content). Among other things, look for groups of psalms, contentwise. Compare your studies with the two outlines on Chart 70 about "Worship" and "Topical Likeness to Pentateuch." Try making your own five-point outline of the Psalms, identifying content at least in a general way.

6. Compare the first and last psalms. How does each serve as the book's introduction and conclusion, respectively?

IV. PROMINENT SUBJECTS

A. DAVID

David, who wrote so many of the psalms, has given the reader an insight into the rich and varied experiences of his life with God, to the

---

7. G. Campbell Morgan, *Notes on the Psalms*, p. 9.
8. One hundred sixteen psalms have superscriptions.
9. When studying a particular psalm, use the historical superscription to advantage. For example, the superscription of Psalm 3 states that it is a psalm of David when he fled from Absalom, his son. By reading the historical account of this in 2 Samuel 15, the psalm becomes clearer. Most Bibles show such cross-references (e.g., 2 Sam 15) in the marginal notes (or footnotes).
10. See Archer, pp. 428-30, for a discussion of superscriptions.

extent that no other writer has done. Anyone familiar with David's life cannot fail to be struck with this fact. He was, at different times in his life, a humble shepherd boy, a servant in the king's palace, a successful warrior, a fugitive, a great king, an exile, an old man. He was sometimes poor and sometimes rich, sometimes hated and sometimes beloved, sometimes persecuted and sometimes honored, sometimes obscure and sometimes prominent, sometimes profligate and sometimes penitent, sometimes sad and sometimes joyful. But in all these varied experiences, and under all these changing circumstances, David talked to God, pouring forth his heart, his thoughts, his feelings to his Maker. David's utterances to God at these times are recorded in the psalms, and, as the psalms are inspired by the Holy Spirit, they show us what kind of talking to God and what kind of heart attitude is acceptable to Him when we, too, pass through similar experiences.

B. NAMES OF GOD

God Himself is the key Person of the Psalms, for without Him there could be no song at all. In studying the different psalms, it is always interesting to observe how God is identified, whether by name, attribute, or action ascribed to Him.

Four names of God are prominent in Psalms: *El, Adonai, Jehovah,* and *Shaddai.* The meanings of the names, and the frequency of each in the five books of the Psalms, are tabulated in Chart 69.[11]

NAMES OF GOD IN THE PSALMS   CHART 69

HEBREW NAME[12]	KING JAMES TRANSLATION	MEANING	BOOK I 1-41	BOOK II 42-72	BOOK III 73-89	BOOK IV 90-106	BOOK V 107-50
El	God	Almighty One	67	207	85	32	41
[13] Adonai	Lord	Sovereign Lord	13	19	15	2	12
Jehovah	Lord	Covenant Maker and Fulfiller	277	31	43	101	226
Shaddai	Almighty	Provider; Blesser		1	1	1	

11. From Scroggie, *The Psalms*, 1:36.

12. Associated forms of the name words are included (e.g., *Elohim* is included under *El*). For an enlightening study on the names of God, see Nathan J. Stone, *Names of God in the Old Testament.*

13. The King James text does not distinguish between *Adonai* ("Lord") and *Jehovah* ("LORD"). (Use Strong's *Exhaustive Concordance* for identifying which Hebrew word is being translated.)

C. WORSHIP AND PRAISE

Many of the psalms are about Mount Zion, its sanctuary, and worship by God's people. Beginning at Psalm 90, most of the hymns are of a liturgical nature, associated with public worship. It is not difficult to see why Psalms is sometimes called the hymnbook of Scripture. Praise is the dominant note of these psalms. The last five psalms (Psalms 146-50) are the climactic group, and are appropriately called "The Great Hallel," or "The Hallelujah Chorus." This is what C. H. Spurgeon writes of Psalm 150:

> We have now reached the last summit of the mountain chain of Psalms. It rises high into the clear azure, and its brow is bathed in the sunlight of the eternal world of worship. It is a rapture. The poet-prophet is full of inspiration and enthusiasm. He stays not to argue, to teach, to explain; but cries with burning words, "Praise him, Praise him, Praise ye the Lord."[14]

D. SIN AND RIGHTEOUSNESS

Since man's worship of God is a prominent theme in the Psalms, the spiritual conditions for such access to a holy God are referred to throughout the book. Psalm 1, which in many ways introduces the whole book of Psalms, clearly distinguishes between the righteous man and the wicked man. The righteous man fellowships with God; sin is a wall that separates sinful man from God. Scroggie compares this subject with just one part of the New Testament when he says, "Scarcely less distinct in the Psalms than in the Johannine Writings is the clean-cut distinction between sin and righteousness, the wicked and the righteous."[15] The prominence of this subject in Psalms is supported by the repetition of such words as these:
"righteous" and "righteousness"—over 130 times
"sin" and "iniquity"—at least 65 times[16]
"good" and "evil"—about 40 times each
"judgment" and its cognates—more than 100 times

E. PROPHECIES OF CHRIST

As noted earlier, the Messianic psalms prophesy about the person and work of Christ. In many ways the prophecies supplement what the New Testament records about Christ. For example, we read in

---

14. C. H. Spurgeon, *The Treasury of David*, 7:449.
15. Scroggie, *The Psalms*, 1:30.
16. John Sampey says, "Seven of the best known poems in the collection are so charged with a sense of sin and of its deadly fruits that they have been known for centuries as the Penitential Pss (6, 32, 38, 51, 102, 130, 143)" ("Psalms," in *The International Standard Bible Encyclopedia*, 4:2493).

PSALMS BLESS THE LORD, O MY SOUL

DATE WRITTEN: mainly between 1000 and 500 B.C.

TYPES OF PSALMS
1. didactic
2. history
3. hallelujah
4. penitential
5. supplication
6. thanksgiving
7. messianic
8. nature
9. pilgrim
10. imprecatory

	BOOK I	BOOK II	BOOK III	BOOK IV	BOOK V
(psalm range)	1 — 41 psalms — 42	42 — 31 psalms — 73	73 — 17 psalms — 90	90 — 17 psalms — 107	107 — 44 psalms — 150
DOXOLOGY AT	41:13	72:18-19	89:52	106:48	150:6
	ADORING WORSHIP	WONDERING WORSHIP	CEASELESS WORSHIP	SUBMISSIVE WORSHIP	PERFECTED WORSHIP
TOPICAL LIKENESS TO PENTATEUCH	GENESIS —man—	EXODUS —Israel—	LEVITICUS —sanctuary—	NUMBERS —Moses and wilderness—	DEUTERONOMY —Law and land—
AUTHORS	mainly (or all) DAVID	mainly DAVID and KORAH	mainly ASAPH	mainly ANONYMOUS	mainly DAVID
POSSIBLE STAGES OF COLLECTION	ORIGINAL GROUP BY DAVID	BOOKS II AND III ADDED DURING THE REIGNS OF HEZEKIAH AND JOSIAH		MISCELLANEOUS COLLECTIONS COMPILED IN TIMES OF EZRA AND NEHEMIAH	

Matthew 27:35-36 that men nailed Jesus to the cross; that they parted His garments among them and cast lots over His vesture; that they sat around the cross and watched His sufferings. The gospels also record a few words which Jesus spoke at this time. But they do not reveal much of the thoughts and feelings of Jesus. It is Psalm 22 that affords us the experience of listening to Jesus communing with His Father in that dread hour. Notice that Matthew 27:35 states that Psalm 22 is a prophecy of Christ. We recognize the agonized cry of the opening verse of the psalm, and such verses as 16 and 18 show that the prophecy goes far beyond any of David's experiences.

The Messianic psalms speak of Christ as the royal Messiah (Psalms 2, 18, 20, 21, 45, 61, 72, 89, 110, 132); the suffering Messiah (Psalms 22, 35, 41, 55, 69, 109); and the Son of man (Psalms 16, 40). Other Messianic psalms are: Psalms 23, 24, 31, 50, 68, 96-98, 102, 118.

V. Applications

The psalms are unsurpassed for devotional reading. Every reader can identify with them because their authors write as those totally dependent on God's grace and mercy, which He gives to undeserving sinners. Only eternity will reveal how many souls in desperation have fled to a psalm for help and strength.

The ministry of the psalms in public services is also immeasurable. For example, what psalms especially come to mind when you think of a funeral service?

VI. Further Study

Make extended studies of the following subjects:
1. prophecy in the Psalms
2. applying the imprecatory psalms in the Christian setting
3. the Word of God in Psalms, especially in Psalm 119

VII. Selected Reading

GENERAL INTRODUCTION

Manley, G. T. *The New Bible Handbook*, pp. 191-98.
Purkiser, W. T. *Exploring the Old Testament*, pp. 209-37.
Scroggie, W. Graham. *Psalms*, 1:9-44.
Wyngaarden, Martin J. "Psalms." In *The International Standard Bible Encyclopedia*, 4:2487-94B.
Young, Edward J. *An Introduction to the Old Testament*, pp. 281-300.

COMMENTARIES AND OTHER AIDS

Alexander, Joseph A. *The Psalms Translated and Explained.*

Armerding, Carl. *Psalms in a Minor Key.*

Delitzsch, Franz. *Biblical Commentary on the Psalms.*

Gaebelein, A. C. *The Book of Psalms.*

Jensen, Irving L. *Psalms.* Self-Study Guide.

Kirkpatrick, A. F. *The Book of Psalms.*

Leslie, E. A. *The Psalms.*

Leupold, Herbert C. *Exposition of the Psalms.*

Maclaren, Alexander. *The Psalms.*

Morgan, G. Campbell. *Notes on the Psalms.*

Perowne, J. J. Stewart. *The Book of Psalms.*

Rhodes, Arnold B. *The Book of Psalms.*

Scroggie, W. Graham. *The Psalms.*

Spurgeon, C. H. *The Treasury of David.*

Yates, Kyle M. "Psalms." In *The Wycliffe Bible Commentary.*

17

Proverbs: Walking in the Fear of the Lord

Proverbs is the second of three Bible books designated as "Wisdom Literature," the other two being Job and Ecclesiastes. Wilbur M. Smith identifies the "wisdom" theme of Proverbs as a message about the fear of God.

> The book of Proverbs contains the distilled essence of wisdom which is based upon a fear of God, setting forth in remarkable figures of speech, with innumerable contrasting clauses, what is right and what is wrong, in the sight of God, pertaining to man's conduct. . . . The basic truth constantly affirmed in Proverbs is expressed in the famous statement, "The fear of the Lord is the beginning of wisdom" (1:7 and 15:33).[1]

I. PREPARATION FOR STUDY

1. Review what you have already studied about poetic literature.
2. What different things does the word *wisdom* suggest to you? With the help of a concordance, study what the New Testament teaches about true wisdom. Compare your findings with the following description of the Old Testament concept of wisdom:

> [In the Old Testament there are] six different Hebrew words setting forth various aspects of wisdom, as discernment, knowledge, meditation, prudence, etc. Wisdom among the Hebrews differs from wisdom among other Oriental peoples in that it rested firmly on the conviction of a personal and holy God. It assumes that the universe is regulated by reason and law. It is practical and not speculative as it was with the Greeks. Its exhortations have a universal application—it is interesting to note that neither the word Israel nor Jerusalem is even referred to in

---

1. Wilbur M. Smith, *The Incomparable Book*, pp. 36-37.

Proverbs, Ecclesiastes or Job. Wisdom is derived from experience and is often expressed in similitudes and parables taken from nature, rarely by historical events. The wise man, according to the Old Testament, is one who walks in the way of the Lord, which is a way of truth and righteousness, whose life is consequently blessed by God, and is a benediction to those within his family and circle of influence, and brings contentment to his own heart.[2]

II. BACKGROUND

God inspired the writing of Proverbs partly as an antidote to the spiritual apostasy of His people, Israel. Like all Scripture, the book of Proverbs arose out of an immediate, local setting, involving people and their relationships to each other and to God. An understanding of the setting and characteristics of this twentieth book of the Bible greatly enhances one's study of its text.

A. TITLE

The common title of the book is "Proverbs," from the opening phrase "The proverbs of Solomon" in 1:1. The Hebrew word for "proverb," *mashal,* comes from a root meaning "to be like," or "to represent." This is very appropriate, since most proverbs use *comparison* to teach their truths. (An example: "He that hath no rule over his own spirit is like a city that is broken down, and without walls" 25:28, KJV.) Proverbs are terse maxims about conduct and character, primarily in the realms of the spiritual, moral, and social. Read the following verses of other books where the word "proverb(s)" appears:
Numbers 21:27—first appearance of the word in the Bible
1 Samuel 10:12—first citation of a proverb
2 Peter 2:22—a New Testament citation of a biblical proverb

B. AUTHORS

Most of the biblical proverbs originated with Solomon, son of David. (Read 1:1; 10:1; and 25:1, which are the opening verses of the three largest sections of the book.) Chapters 30 and 31 are assigned to Agur and Lemuel, respectively, whose identities are unknown.[3] The section 22:17—24:34 is attributed to "the wise men" (see 22:17; cf. 24:23). Read 1 Kings 4:31 for a reference to such a class of men. If the wise men of Proverbs 22:17 lived before Solomon's time, Solomon may have been the one to assemble their

---

2. Ibid.
3. Some hold that these two names may be poetic references to Solomon himself.

writings and add them to his own. The proverbs of chapters 25-29 were written by Solomon and edited about two hundred years later by a committee appointed by King Hezekiah (c. 700 B.C.). Some think that this group called "men of Hezekiah" (25:1) may have included Isaiah and Micah, who were contemporaries of Hezekiah.

Solomon is the author of three books of the Bible. One commentator has suggested this possibility of the books being written at different stages of his career:[4]

Song of Solomon—written when he was young, and in love

Proverbs—written during middle age, when his intellectual powers were at their peak

Ecclesiastes—written in old age, when he was disappointed and disillusioned with the carnality of much of his life

C. DATE

As noted above, most of Proverbs was written by Solomon. This would date his work around 950-900 B.C.[5] See Chart 71. Hezekiah's collection was formed around 700 B.C. It is reasonable to conclude that the various groups of proverbs were brought together as one book around that date, namely 700 B.C..[6]

Refer to Chart 71 again, and note how close Proverbs and Psalms are as to time of writing. David's psalms give us a vivid view of the *worship* by God's people before the kingdom's decline, and the book of Proverbs reflects the zealous concern of believers for a righteous *walk*. The prophets came later, during the years of Israel's apostasy and idolatry, to call the people to a saving knowledge of God.

D. PURPOSE

Read 1:2-4 and note the book's own statement of its purpose: to impart wisdom. This wisdom is not mere head knowledge, but divinely enlightened understanding of what is good and what is evil (1 Kings 3:9), and a personal experiential knowledge of the Lord.

Solomon also wrote about the purpose of his proverbs in Ecclesiastes 12:9-14. Compare this passage with the phrase "instruction in righteousness" of 2 Timothy 3:16 (KJV).

---

4. John Phillips, *Exploring the Scriptures*, p. 108.

5. The historical background of chapters 1-29, though sparse, corresponds very closely to the conditions of Solomon's reign. See G. T. Manley, *The New Bible Handbook*, p. 199. Read 29:18; 15:8; and 21:3, 27 for references to the Law and sacrifices of Israel.

6. This assumes that Agur, Lemuel, and "the wise men," noted earlier, lived no later than Hezekiah.

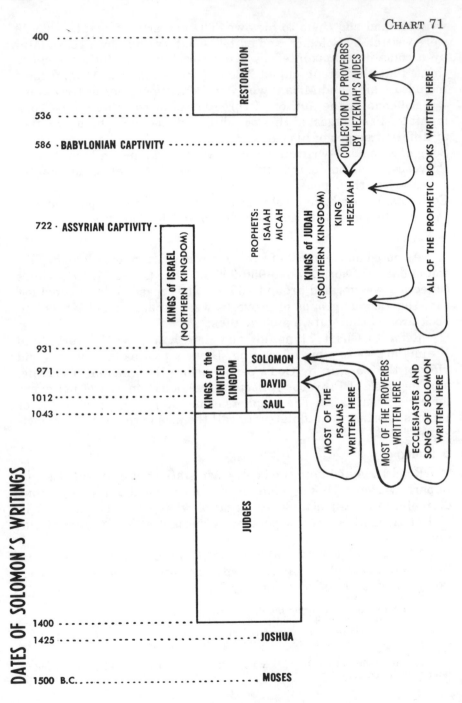

CHART 71

DATES OF SOLOMON'S WRITINGS

400

RESTORATION

536

586 · BABYLONIAN CAPTIVITY

722 · ASSYRIAN CAPTIVITY ·

KINGS of ISRAEL (NORTHERN KINGDOM)

PROPHETS: ISAIAH MICAH

KINGS of JUDAH (SOUTHERN KINGDOM)

KING HEZEKIAH

COLLECTION OF PROVERBS BY HEZEKIAH'S AIDES

ALL OF THE PROPHETIC BOOKS WRITTEN HERE

931

971

1012

1043

KINGS of the UNITED KINGDOM

SOLOMON

DAVID

SAUL

MOST OF THE PSALMS WRITTEN HERE

MOST OF THE PROVERBS WRITTEN HERE

ECCLESIASTES AND SONG OF SOLOMON WRITTEN HERE

JUDGES

1400

1425 · · · · · · · JOSHUA

1500 B.C. · · · · · · · · MOSES

One cannot help but be impressed after reading Proverbs that God is so vitally interested in the smallest details of the daily walk of His children.

E. PLACE IN THE BIBLE

In the English canon, Proverbs is the third of the five poetical books. In the Hebrew canon, it is the second of eleven books in the final section called "Writings." In both canons it follows Psalms. John Genung says that it holds this leading position, after Psalms, "probably because it would be most natural to begin this section with standard collections nearest at hand, which of course would be psalms and proverbs."[7]

Chart 72 shows comparisons of Proverb's message with that of other Old Testament books.

CHART 72

PROVERBS COMPARED WITH OTHER OLD TESTAMENT BOOKS

BOOKS	KEYNOTES	USES
Books of the Law	revelation and guidance	manual of history and legislation
Books of the Prophets	authority	message for today and tomorrow
Job	questionings and reasonings	answers from God and man
Psalms	worship	handbook of devotion
Proverbs	observation and reflection	guide to practical living

The New Testament writers quote and allude to Proverbs several times. Read the references listed below.

PROVERBS	N.T. QUOTE OR ALLUSION
3:7	Romans 12:16
25:21-22	Romans 12:20
3:34	James 4:6
24:21	1 Peter 2:17
16:7	1 Peter 3:13

---

7. John Franklin Genung, "Book of Proverbs," in *The International Standard Bible Encyclopedia*, 4:2471.

11:31	1 Peter 4:18
26:11	2 Peter 2:22
3:11-12	Hebrews 12:5-6
4:26	Hebrews 12:13
10:12	1 Peter 4:8
22:9	2 Corinthians 9:7
25:6-7	Luke 14:10

The epistle of James is one book of the New Testament which concentrates on the conduct of believers, just as Proverbs does in the Old Testament. In fact, James is sometimes referred to as Proverbs of the New Testament.

The relation of Proverbs to Christ is deeper than appears on the surface. Some see Christ foreshadowed in such explicit passages as 8:22-31; 23:11; and 30:4. A foundational connection is that the wisdom spoken of in Proverbs is found completely in Christ (1 Cor 1:30). "The aspiration in Proverbs is for wisdom to become incarnate (Prov. 8), as indeed it did when 'all the treasures of wisdom and knowledge' became flesh in Christ (Col. 2:3)."[8] The "wise" man of Proverbs is the righteous man. And no man is righteous except as he is clothed with the righteousness of Christ. So the truly wise man today is the born-again Christian.

III. Literary Characteristics

Any reader of Proverbs quickly observes that its style and content are different from other parts of the Bible, such as the book of Genesis, or Matthew. An understanding of such literary characteristics helps one's study of the book's text.

A. TYPE

As noted earlier, the book of Proverbs is classified as "Wisdom Literature." In Old Testament times Israel was ruled by judges and kings, and ministered to by such groups as priests, prophets, scribes, historians, singers, and "wise men," or philosophers. King David was both king and singer. His son Solomon was both king and philosopher. Hebrew "wise men" were usually elders associated with schools of wisdom, who shared their practical views of life and the world with their Jewish brethren.

---

8. Norman L. Geisler, *Christ: The Theme of the Bible*, p. 96.

B. STYLE

The following descriptions show the variety of styles and forms in which the proverbs appear:

1. Various forms. Poetry, brief parables, sharp questions, minute stories. For two examples of poems, read the following:

1:20-33 "Wisdom's Cry of Warning" (a dramatic monologue)

3:1-10 "The Commandment and Reward" (a sonnet)

2. Common devices.

Antithesis—comparing opposite things (16:22)

Comparison—comparing similar things (17:10)

Imagery—using picture language (26:27)

Personification—assigning personality to an inanimate thing (9:1)

3. Prominent teaching method. Contrast. Scan chapters 10-15 and note the repeated word "but." Gleason Archer writes,

> The constant preoccupation of the book is with the elemental antagonisms of obedience versus rebellion, industry versus laziness, prudence versus presumption, and so on. These are so presented as to put before the reader a clear-cut choice, leaving him no ground for wretched compromise or vacillating indecision.[9]

4. Length. Unit proverbs (one to four verses); and clusters (group of unit proverbs). In the early chapters the common unit proverb is one verse. An example of a cluster is the passage about fools in 26:1-12.

5. Symmetry. Most of the proverbs are symmetrical (e g , the antithetical maxims of two lines connected by the word "but"). But Hebrew writers were not bound by symmetry. "Modern hands itch to smooth away irregularities—often overlooking the fact that an asymmetrical proverb can be richer than a symmetrical."[10]

Note that Proverb-type writings were not exclusively Israel's. Archaeologists have uncovered proverbs of other nations as well.[11] The main difference is not in style, but in content. Compare the following two proverbs. What is the notable difference?

"Do not lean on the scales, nor falsify the weights, nor damage the fractions of the measure" (proverb of Amen-em-ope, of Eygpt).

"Differing weights and differing measures, both of them are abominable to the LORD" (proverb of Solomon, 20:10).

---

9. Gleason L. Archer, *A Survey of Old Testament Introduction*, p. 452.
10. Derek Kidner, *The Proverbs*, p. 28.
11. There is strong evidence that heathen writers even borrowed from the canonical Proverbs for their own purposes. See W. Jones and Andrew Walls, "The Proverbs," in *The New Bible Commentary*, p. 516.

IV. SURVEY

1. Read the first verse of each chapter of Proverbs. What headings (or titles) appear at these points: 1:1; 10:1; 25:1; 30:1; 31:1? (Also, read 22:17.) Do these verses suggest any organization of the book?

2. Most books of the Bible have an introduction and a conclusion. Look for these in Proverbs. For the introduction, begin reading the first chapter. How many verses would you identify as an introduction?

3. The identification of a conclusion is more difficult. The last segment is about a virtuous woman (31:10-31). If this is not the conclusion, then the previous segment should be included (31:1-9). But if 31:1 is a part of the conclusion, then the similar heading of 30:1 should also be included. Therefore, one might say that Proverbs concludes with an *epilogue* of two supplements (chaps. 30-31). The introduction, then, could be called a *prologue*. Using 1:1-6 as the extent of that introduction, the basic structure of the book would be this:

1:1	1:7	30:1 31:31
PROLOGUE	M A X I M S	EPILOGUE

4. Chart 73 shows the various divisions of Proverbs which we have observed thus far, and includes outlines of content. Answer the following questions on the basis of the chart:

a) Where in the book is the purpose of Proverbs stated?

b) What group of chapters develops the primary theme of the book?

c) Where is there a concentration of one-verse proverbs?

d) What part of the book is addressed especially to young people? Confirm your answer by these verses: 1:8; 2:1; 3:1; 4:1; 5:1; 6:1; and so forth.

e) What groups of chapters are specifically assigned to Solomon?

5. Make a final scanning of the book of Proverbs with survey Chart 73 in mind.

V. PROMINENT SUBJECTS

A. KING SOLOMON

The book of Proverbs is not a narrative about Solomon, but its pages reveal much about this wise man. (Consult a Bible dictionary or encyclopedia for a sketch of his colorful career.[12]) Solomon was a

---

12. D. A. Hubbard describes Solomon as the "Master Sage," the "Iron Ruler," the "Enterprising Merchant," and the "Peaceful Emperor" (*The New Bible Dictionary*, pp. 1202-4).

unique character in many ways; he was musician, poet, botanist, zoologist, businessman, administrator, and king. From 1 Kings 3:12 and 4:29 we learn that his wisdom was a direct gift from God. This was in answer to Solomon's petition (1 Kings 3:5-9). He was the author of 3,000 proverbs and 1,005 songs (1 Kings 4:32). Read 1 Kings 3:16-28; 4:29-34; and 10:1-9, noting other things said about Solomon.

B. PERSONAL ETHICS

The proverbs are God's detailed instructions and exhortations to His people concerning their thought-and-deed life. Much of the book is addressed especially to young people (e.g., 1:4, 8). The proverbs are mainly about personal ethics, not as the sinner's way to God, but as the believer's walk with God on this earth. Although the book is not intended to elaborate on the way of salvation, such key phrases as "the fear of the LORD" (1:7) tell basically how a sinner is brought into fellowship with God. The counsel of Proverbs is profitable for all people—saved and unsaved—but the unsaved do not gain salvation by attempting to perform its good deeds (cf. Eph 2:8-9).

C. VARIETY OF ILLUSTRATIONS AND APPLICATIONS

The list of different subjects written about in Proverbs seems endless. Here are some examples:[13]

Topics: wisdom, sin, tongue, wealth, pride, idleness, love, pleasure, success, temperance, morals

Contrasting subjects: God and man; time and eternity; truth and falsehood; wealth and poverty; purity and impurity; justice and injustice; pleasure and misery

Evil people: prating fool; talebearer; whisperer; backbiter; false boaster; speculator

Social relations: master and servant; rich and poor; husband and wife; parents and children

VI. KEY WORDS AND VERSES

Study the list of key words shown on Chart 73. Also read the key verses in the Bible text. There are other verses which could serve as key verses.

VII. APPLICATIONS

The book of Proverbs is filled with commands and exhortations about daily conduct. The reader has hardly begun reading the book when he is confronted with such words as "If sinners entice you, do not consent" (1:10). God knew that His people would need to be

---

13. See W. Graham Scroggie, *Know Your Bible*, 1:140-41.

reminded again and again about how to think, speak, and act, so He inspired the writing and collection of Proverbs.

Here are some suggestions for interpreting the maxims of Proverbs, leading to application:

1. Recognize that the proverbs are instructions from the Lord, not mere secular maxims. It is very significant that the name "LORD" (Jehovah) appears eighty-six times in the book.

2. Interpret "wisdom" in the book as representing *righteousness,* or *holiness,* which describes the heart of that person who truly knows God. Likewise, interpret such words as "fool" and "folly" as representing *wickedness* of the unsaved man.

3. Recognize the device of personification whenever it appears in the book. For example, the foolish woman of 9:13-15 is not primarily an individual person as such, but *spiritual folly,* or *wickedness* (the opposite of *spiritual wisdom,* or *righteousness*).

4. Let the surrounding verses shed light on a proverb when its meaning is unclear. However, because of the miscellaneous character of the listings of many proverbs, it may be necessary to refer to more distant verses (e.g., in another chapter or even in another book) where a similar phrase appears, for its clarification. (For example, the phrase "strange woman" in 20:16 KJV, is partly explained by 2:16.) An exhaustive concordance is a valuable help here.

5. When the most obvious interpretation of a proverb seems to contradict another Scripture, seek its deeper meaning. (Cf. Prov 10:27 and Gen 4:8; and Prov 16:7 and Acts 14:19.)

6. If a proverb is unclear or ambiguous in the Bible version you are using, compare the reading of a modern paraphrase.[14]

7. Let the key verse 1:7 be the controller of all your interpretations of the many proverbs of this book of God.

The book of Proverbs is very practical because it concerns the believer's daily walk. It does not include much doctrine, but it does emphasize practice. One writer describes its Christian purpose thus:

> While other parts of Scripture show us the glory of our high calling, this may instruct in all minuteness of detail how to "walk worthy of it." Elsewhere we learn our completeness in Christ (Col ii.10); and most justly we glory in our high exaltation as "joint heirs with Christ," etc. (Rom. viii.17; Eph. ii.6). We look into this book, and, as by the aid of the

---

14. Modern paraphrases are the interpretations of the authors writing the paraphrases. They are not intended to be a word-for-word translation of the Bible text. One of the main purposes of a paraphrase is to clarify an ambiguous word or phrase of the Bible text.

CHART 73

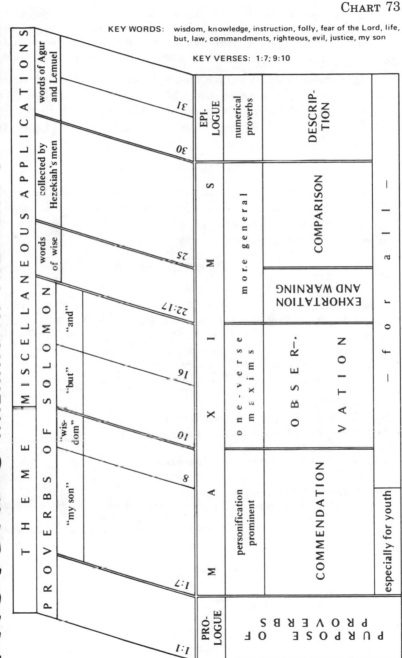

PROVERBS WALKING IN THE FEAR OF THE LORD

KEY WORDS: wisdom, knowledge, instruction, folly, fear of the Lord, life, but, law, commandments, righteous, evil, justice, my son

KEY VERSES: 1:7; 9:10

THEME: MISCELLANEOUS APPLICATIONS / PROVERBS OF SOLOMON

PROVERBS OF SOLOMON — "my son" — "wis-dom" — "but" — "and"

words of wise

collected by Hezekiah's men

words of Agur and Lemuel

1:1 | 1:7 | 8 | 10 | 16 | 22:17 | 25 | 30 | 31

PRO-LOGUE | M A X I M S | EPI-LOGUE

PURPOSE OF PROVERBS

personification prominent — one-verse maxims — more general — numerical proverbs

COMMENDATION — OBSER-VATION — EXHORTATION AND WARNING — COMPARISON — DESCRIP-TION

especially for youth — for all

microscope, we see the minuteness of our Christian obligations; that there is not a temper, a look, a word, a movement, the most important action of the day, the smallest relative duty, in which we do not either deface or adorn the image of our Lord, and the profession of His name.[15]

Proverbs truly shows how the believer "may adorn the doctrine of God our Saviour in all things" (Titus 2:10, KJV). Even unbelievers recognize the value of Proverbs as a manual for conduct. How much more should it apply to Christians, who have the indwelling Spirit to help them live the life it describes.

VIII. FURTHER STUDY

Read the book of Proverbs verse by verse, identifying what area of life (e.g., home, business, worship) is referred to in each verse. Then compare the various proverbs under each area, and see how much is taught about each area by the book.

IX. SELECTED READING

GENERAL INTRODUCTION

Archer, Gleason L. *A Survey of Old Testament Introduction*, pp. 449-58.
Baxter, J. Sidlow. *Explore the Book*, 3:130-40.
Genung, John Franklin. "Proverb," and "Book of Proverbs." In *The International Standard Bible Encyclopedia*, 4:2469-76.
Phillips, John. *Exploring the Scriptures*, pp. 108-11.
Scroggie, W. Graham. *Know Your Bible*, 1:137-42.

COMMENTARIES

Delitzsch, F. *Proverbs of Solomon*, vols. 1, 2.
Harris, R. Laird. "Proverbs." In *The Wycliffe Bible Commentary*.
Ironside, H. A. *Notes on the Book of Proverbs*.
Jones, W., and Walls, Andrew. "The Proverbs." In *The New Bible Commentary*.
Kidner, Derek. *The Proverbs*.
Zoeckler, Otto. "Proverbs." In Lange's *Commentary on the Holy Scriptures*.

---

15. Otto Zoeckler, "Proverbs," in Lange's *Commentary on the Holy Scriptures*, p. 3.

18

Ecclesiastes: Vanity Under the Sun, But Hope Is in God

Ecclesiastes is a book that investigates life and tells what kind of life is worth living. It is the quest of a soul who sees only vanity all about him until his eyes are opened to the hope offered by God. The book has been described as a confession of failure and pessimism when God is excluded.

Ecclesiastes is a perplexing book to many, partly because its perspectives and purposes are not understood. The background and survey studies that follow will help to throw light on these important concerns.

I. PREPARATION FOR STUDY

The dictionary defines philosophy as the investigation of causes and laws underlying reality. Stated simply, philosophy is man's search for truth. Are you acquainted with people who are sincerely and seriously looking for truthful answers to their painful questions about life?

Generally speaking, there are two main schools of thought in philosophy: empiricism and rationalism. Empiricism says that human experience, especially of the senses, is the only source of knowledge. That is, man can know only what he experiences. Rationalism says that human reason is the prime source of knowledge and of spiritual truth. That is, man can know only what he can mentally grasp. A study of Ecclesiastes shows truth vainly being sought for in both ways:

"I made"; "I got"; and so forth (2:4,7, KJV)—empiricism
"I set my mind to know" (1:17)—rationalism

The conclusion in both quests is stated over and over again: "All is vanity." Such a frustration serves to show that if truth is to be known, it must come by *revelation from God*. (See Chart 74.) The God-centered life view which Solomon teaches in the book came from divine revelation.

TRUTH BY DIVINE REVELATION   CHART 74

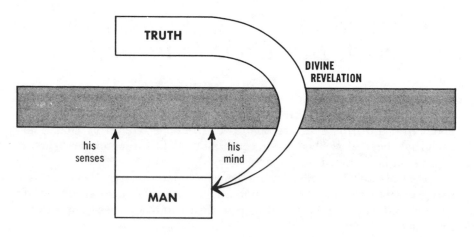

Throughout the book of Ecclesiastes, Solomon presents the position of one who is searching for truth and reality and meaning. From this standpoint, then, it would be correct to say that Ecclesiastes is a book of philosophy. The student about to read the book should keep this in mind, to avoid misinterpretation and to reap maximum instruction.

II. Background

Not many details are known about the immediate setting of Ecclesiastes. This lack only serves to let the book shine forth in its essential quality, as a timeless and contemporary message to all generations since its writing. The things that *are* known about the book's setting are both interesting and important.

A. TITLE

The title for this book comes from the opening phrase, "The words of the Preacher" (1:1). The word "Preacher" is traced back to the original Hebrew text as follows:

Hebrew—*qoholeth*[1]—from *qahal*, "to assemble"
Greek version—*ecclesiastes*—from *ek*, "out of", and *klesis*, "a calling"
English—*Preacher* (1:1)—one who speaks to an assembly of people
　　Ecclesiastes (title)—one who speaks to an assembly of people
In Old Testament days a *qoholeth* was an official speaker to an assembly of people. Other appearances of the word "Preacher" in Ecclesiastes are at 1:1, 2, 12: 7:27; 12:8, 9, 10. The word is not found in any other Old Testament book.

B. AUTHOR

The author is not named in the Bible text. In 1:1 he is identified as "the son of David, king of Jerusalem." Internal evidences favor the traditional view that Solomon is meant by this phrase.[2] The following descriptions in the text coincide with what is known about Solomon from the historical record (e.g., 1 Kings).
1. the author's unrivaled wisdom (1:16)
2. his wealth (2:8)
3. his extensive building projects (2:4-6)
4. his collection of proverbs (12:9)

Refer to Chart 71 and observe when Ecclesiastes was written, if Solomon was the author. Note among other things that the preaching ministries of the Bible prophets did not begin until after Solomon's time.

C. PLACE IN THE BIBLE

Ecclesiastes is the fourth of five poetical books in our English Bible: Job, Psalms, Proverbs, Ecclesiastes, Song of Solomon.[3] In the Hebrew Bible it is the fourth of five *Megilloth* writings ("Five Rolls"): Song of Solomon, Ruth, Lamentations, Ecclesiastes, Esther.[4] Chart 75 shows comparisons of the poetical books, as to some of their major subjects. (Lamentations is included because it is written in poetical style also.)

---

1. In the Hebrew Old Testament, as well as the Greek New Testament, the first letter of a proper noun is not distinguished from the other letters, like the capitalizations in the English language (e.g., Preacher).

2. Many commentators feel that the author lived a few hundred years after Solomon's time. See Gleason L. Archer, *A Survey of Old Testament Introduction*, pp. 462-72, for a defense of Solomonic authorship. Some hold the view that the author was an impersonator of Solomon in the book, and that he lived a few hundred years after Solomon.

3. It is interesting to observe that the historical, poetical, and prophetical sections of the Old Testament are of approximately equal length, chapterwise: historical books, 249 chapters; poetical books, 243 chapters; prophetical books, 250 chapters.

4. Each of the five "rolls" was read at an annual Jewish feast. Ecclesiastes was read at the Feast of Tabernacles, which was the most joyous of the festivals.

POETICAL BOOKS COMPARED

CHART 75

		KEY THOUGHTS	KEY SUBJECTS
3 DIDACTIC BOOKS	*PROVERBS*	WISDOM	*DESCRIPTIONS AND FRUITS OF THE RIGHTEOUS MAN*
	ECCLESIASTES	FUTILITY	*THE WAY TO GOD*
	JOB	TRIAL	*CRUCIBLE OF TESTING*

3 DEVOTIONAL BOOKS	*PSALMS*	WORSHIP	*MEDITATIONS AND WORSHIP OF THE RIGHTEOUS MAN*
	SONG OF SOLOMON	LOVE	*THE WAY OF GOD*
	LAMENTATIONS	DESTRUCTION	*CRUCIBLE OF JUDGMENT*

D. STYLE

As noted in earlier chapters, Proverbs, Job, Ecclesiastes, and parts of other Old Testament books are classified as "Wisdom Literature." The style of these books is that of the philosopher, who shares his observations, reflections, reasonings, and conclusions in terse and brief lines, often in poetical form. Here is one writer's evaluation of Ecclesiastes' composition: "Whether prose or verse, I know nothing grander in its impassioned survey of mortal pain and pleasure, its estimate of failure and success."[5]

III. SURVEY

A. FIRST READINGS

Scan Ecclesiastes once or twice to catch its tone and large emphases. What are your impressions after this first reading? (Do not tarry over details in this scanning stage, or you might lose sight of the broad panorama.)

B. FURTHER READINGS

Your next readings should be in shorter portions at a slower pace. But keep in mind that you are in the *survey* stage of study. (The *analysis* stage tarries over details.) Here are some suggestions for study:

1. Ecclesiastes may be divided into eleven sections of varying lengths. These begin at the following verses: 1:1, 12; 2:24; 3:16; 5:1; 6:1; 7:1; 8:14; 10:1; 12:8, 9. Mark these divisions in your Bible.

2. What repeated words and phrases have you already observed in the text of Ecclesiastes? Keep looking for others during the remainder of your survey. Three key examples are: "vanity," "under the sun," and "God." Read through the book and underline or circle these words every time they appear. Look for *groupings* of each of the phrases. (Such groupings or concentrations are clues to emphasis.) The importance of these phrases is indicated by their many appearances in the book:

"vanity"—thirty-nine times
"under the sun"—twenty-nine times
"God"—forty times[6]

3. Read 1:14 and note the close relation between "under the sun" and "vanity." The phrase "under the sun" refers to the earthbound, temporal outlook and experience of the natural man, and this is vanity, or futility. So, in Ecclesiastes the phrases "under the sun" and

---

5. E. C. Stedman, quoted by W. Graham Scroggie, *Know Your Bible*, 1:144.
6. The familiar Old Testament name of "LORD" does not appear in Ecclesiastes.

"vanity" refer to the same thought. The opposite outlook, the hopeful one, is that which looks toward God, who is *above* the sun. With this in mind, scan your marked Bible, with its markings of the key phrases noted above. Observe which sections are about *God* more than they are about *vanity*, and which are about vanity more than about God. Record your findings on paper. Do you observe any pattern?

4. Compare 1:2 and 12:8. Since these similar verses appear at the beginning and end of the book, what do they suggest as a prominent theme of the chapters in between?

5. Read 1:1-11. How does the section serve as an introduction to the book?

6. Read 12:9-14. How do these verses conclude the book?

C. SURVEY CHART

Chart 76 is a survey chart of Ecclesiastes, showing how the book is organized, thoughtwise.[7] Refer to it as you follow each of these suggestions:

1. Note how the introduction (1:1-11) is identified. The premise, or proposition, that "all is futility" (1:2, margin) is restated in the conclusion, at 12:8.

2. The main body of the book is 1:12—12:7. Observe on the chart that this is divided into four sermons. These sermons of the Preacher could also be called discourses of the Teacher. Each sermon expounds on two subjects: (1) futility (vanity); and (2) hope. In other words, in each sermon Solomon first shows the hopelessness of life where the outlook is earthbound ("under the sun"); and then he shows that real hope is founded only on God, whose dwelling place is beyond the heavens.

3. Observe what is recorded in the oblique spaces on Chart 76. The first part of each sermon is mainly *observation,* where the preacher tells what he, as a natural man, saw. Hence, the repeated phrase in these sections, "I saw" (e.g., 4:7). The second part of each sermon also includes observation, but it is mainly *instruction* and *counsel* about things of God.

4. Note how the conclusion (12:8-14) is a condensed summary of the four sermons:

Part One: Observation: "All is vanity" (12:8).

Part Two: Instruction and Counsel: "Fear God" (12:9-14).

---

7. Various outlines have been made of Ecclesiastes. Some expositors feel there is no organization of thought, that the book is "disjointed in construction" (G. S. Hendry, "Ecclesiastes," in *The New Bible Commentary,* p. 538). The position of this book is that there is a discernible pattern of thought, developed in four "sermons," shown on Chart 76.

5. Groups of proverbs appear at a few places in the book. Chapter 10 is an example. Note how this is identified on Chart 76.

IV. Prominent Subjects

A. TWO LIFE VIEWS

Throughout the book of Ecclesiastes the author shows two opposite life views. First, he views things around him as the natural man would do, without the light of divine revelation. His conclusion is "All is vanity." (Read 1 Cor 2:14.) (He went through this searching experience himself some time earlier in his career; read 1:13-14.) But then the author writes as one to whom God has revealed Himself, and now his observations and conclusions have the ring of surety and hope. For example: "Everything God does will remain forever" (3:14). This pattern of alternating perspectives continues throughout the book, as was observed in the survey study.

It should be noted that when the author of Ecclesiastes writes from the second perspective noted above, it is not as one who knows God from *full* revelation. He views life as a man does who knows and worships God *primarily* as Creator. This is confirmed by the fact that every time he names Him he uses the word *Elohim,* which is the name especially associated with the work of creation (cf. Gen 1:1). The name "Lord" *(Jehovah),* which is the Old Testament equivalent of *Redeemer-Saviour,* does not appear once in the book.[8] Today when the reader of Ecclesiastes reaches the last command of the book, "Fear God and keep His commandments" (12:13), he is ready to be introduced to Christ the Redeemer. "As the law was designed to lead men to Christ, so this book was written to lead those 'under the sun' to the Son (cf. Heb 1:1)."[9]

The purposes of Ecclesiastes, then, are to show the futility of pursuing materialistic, earthly goals as an end in themselves, and to point to God as the source of all that is truly good.[10] The theme of the book is determined by these purposes, and may be stated in this twofold way:

---

8. Read Exodus 5:22—6:9 for the significance of this covenant-name *Jehovah* ("Lord," KJV). Solomon refers to Jehovah often in the book of Proverbs, so it isn't that he himself did not know God as "Lord." If Ecclesiastes was composed after Proverbs, Solomon is recalling his search for meaning in life before he came to know God as his Redeemer (cf. 1:13). Some maintain that he wrote from a backslidden spiritual condition.

9. Wick Broomall, "Ecclesiastes," in *The Zondervan Pictorial Bible Dictionary*, p. 232.

10. A marginal note of NASB suggests the word "futility" as a translation of "vanity" (1:2). The use of this word helps one's understanding of the message of Ecclesiastes.

1. Every pursuit of man is futile if God is excluded.
2. Only God's work endures, so that only He can impart true value to man's life and service.

B. VANITY

Read the following selected verses as an introduction to the subject of vanity (futility) in this book.[11]

THE TEN VANITIES

Human wisdom—2:15-16	Human fame—4:16
Human labor—2:19-21	Human insatiateness—5:10
Human purpose—2:26	Human coveting—6:9
Human rivalry—4:4	Human frivolity—7:4
Human avarice—4:8	Human awards—8:10, 14

V. KEY WORDS AND VERSES

Observe the key words listed on Chart 76. Read in the Bible the two key verses, which are also cited. How are these reflected in the title assigned to the book?

VI. APPLICATIONS

1. What are your thoughts about the statement, "There is nothing new under the sun" (1:9)? Read 2 Peter 3:3-7.

2. What is lacking in the heart of a person who is never satisfied (1:8)? Is human *desire* normal or abnormal?

3. "Thou hast made me for Thyself, and my heart will not rest until it rests in Thee." Compare this statement by Augustine with Ecclesiastes 2:25b, "Who can have enjoyment without Him?"

4. "Life is not worth living, apart from redemption." This is how Oswald Chambers identifies the theme of Ecclesiastes.[12] What does Ecclesiastes reveal about man's salvation from the predicament of hopelessness? Compare Chamber's statement with 1 Corinthians 15:19.

5. What are some conditions for genuine enjoyment in the experience of a Christian? Compare Ecclesiastes 11:8a and Philippians 4:4.

6. Do the scales of divine justice always settle and balance quickly? If not, why the delays?

7. "Fear God and keep His commandments" (12:13). Relate this command to the doctrine of salvation.

---

11. The list is from J. Sidlow Baxter, *Explore the Book*, 3:163. (Used by permission.)

12. Oswald Chambers, Preface, *Shade of His Hand.*

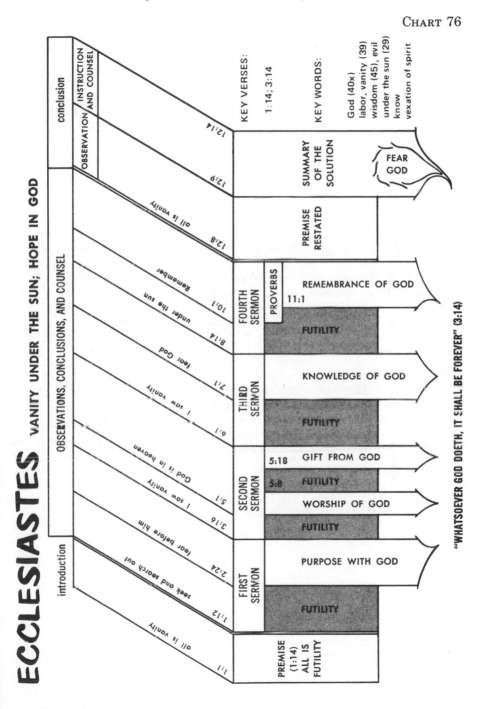

ECCLESIASTES — VANITY UNDER THE SUN; HOPE IN GOD

introduction

OBSERVATIONS, CONCLUSIONS, AND COUNSEL

conclusion

OBSERVATION / INSTRUCTION AND COUNSEL

KEY VERSES:
1:14; 3:14

KEY WORDS:
God (40x)
labor, vanity (39)
wisdom (45), evil
under the sun (29)
know
vexation of spirit

SUMMARY OF THE SOLUTION — FEAR GOD

PREMISE RESTATED

all is vanity 12:8

FOURTH SERMON

PROVERBS 11:1 — REMEMBRANCE OF GOD

FUTILITY

Remember 10:1
under the sun 8:14

THIRD SERMON

KNOWLEDGE OF GOD

FUTILITY

fear God 7:1
I saw vanity 6:1

SECOND SERMON

5:18 GIFT FROM GOD

5:8 FUTILITY

WORSHIP OF GOD

FUTILITY

God is in heaven 5:1
I saw vanity 3:16

FIRST SERMON

PURPOSE WITH GOD

FUTILITY

fear before him 2:24
seek and search out 1:12

PREMISE (1:14) ALL IS FUTILITY

all is vanity 1:1

"WHATSOEVER GOD DOETH, IT SHALL BE FOREVER" (3:14)

VII. Further Study

1. Make an extensive study of the subject "vanity" in Ecclesiastes.

2. Study the Bible's descriptions of the Jews' Feast of Tabernacles.

This was the Jews' most joyous feast of the year. Why do you suppose they chose to read Ecclesiastes, with its many pessimistic portions, at that feast?

VIII. Selected Reading

GENERAL INTRODUCTION

Archer, Gleason L. *A Survey of Old Testament Introduction*, pp. 459-72.

Beecher, Willis J. "Ecclesiastes." In *The International Standard Bible Encyclopedia* 2:894-97.

Delitzsch, Franz. *Commentary on the Song of Songs and Ecclesiastes*, pp. 179-217.

Hendry, G. S. "Ecclesiastes." In *The New Bible Commentary*, pp. 570-71.

McNeile, A. H. *An Introduction to Ecclesiastes.*

Morgan, G. Campbell. *Living Messages of the Books of the Bible*, pp. 56-70.

Oesterley, W. O. E. *The Wisdom of Egypt and the Old Testament.*

Williams, A. Lukyn. *Ecclesiastes*, pp. v-lv.

Young, Edward J. *An Introduction to the Old Testament*, pp. 339-44.

COMMENTARIES

Chambers, Oswald. *Shade of His Hand.*

Delitzsch, Franz. *Commentary on the Song of Songs and Ecclesiastes.*

Laurin, Robert. "Ecclesiastes." In *The Wycliffe Bible Commentary.*

Leupold, H. C. *Exposition of Ecclesiastes.*

Rankin, O. S. "The Book of Ecclesiastes." In *The Interpreter's Bible.*

19

Song of Solomon: Union and Communion

A healthy balance in Bible study is maintained when the Song of Solomon is studied along with Ecclesiastes. Ecclesiastes focuses on the *intellect* of man—his mental outlook on life. The Song of Solomon is a book about the *emotions* of man—in particular, the emotion of love.

It is a recognized fact that man's total experience is directed by these three responses: intellect, emotions, and will. Actually, all three responses are involved in a full experience of genuine love, just as this is true of genuine faith. To say that the Song of Solomon is a book about the emotion of life is not to rule out intellect and will.[1] It is just that the emotion aspect is prominent in the story.

But the Song of Solomon is more than a human love story. It is a picture of the love between the Lord God and His people. If your study of the Song of Solomon will arouse in you a more genuine love for your Lord, as well as a deeper gratitude for His love to you, then it will not surprise you that God chose to include such a love story in His Holy Scriptures.

I. PREPARATION FOR STUDY

Read the New Testament book of Ephesians to learn of the intimate relation between Christ, the Bridegroom, and His Bride, the Church (e.g., Eph 5:25-32). What does the picture of the marriage relationship teach about the believer's salvation?

---

1. For example, a person in love exercises his will in choosing whom to love.

II. Background

A. TITLE

The opening verse gives the title "The Song of Songs." This is the Hebrew way of expressing the superlative. Of Solomon's 1,005 songs (1 Kings 4:32), this one was his best or most important. The more common title assigned to the book is "Song of Solomon," also based on 1:1. Sometimes the book is referred to as Canticles ("series of songs").

B. AUTHOR

The traditional view is that Solomon was the author. This is strongly supported by internal characteristics of the book. (Refer to outside sources for a discussion of this.) The name Solomon appears at these places in the book: 1:1,5; 3:7,9,11; 8:11,12. The reference at 1:1 may be translated either "of Solomon" or "about Solomon."

C. DATE WRITTEN

Solomon probably wrote this book while he was still young, before being drawn away from Jehovah by his seven hundred wives (1 Kings 11:3-4). A suggested date is 965 B.C.

D. RELATION TO OTHER BOOKS OF THE BIBLE

In our English Bibles the Song of Solomon is the fifth of the poetical books: Job, Psalms, Proverbs, Ecclesiastes, Song of Solomon. In the Hebrew Bible it is the first of the "Five Rolls" *(Megilloth):* Song of Solomon, Ruth, Lamentations, Ecclesiastes, Esther. Portions of it were sung on the eighth day of the Passover feast, which was the Jews' first and greatest of the annual feasts. In ancient times the Jews revered Canticles as uniquely sublime. They likened Proverbs to the outer court of the Temple; Ecclesiastes to the holy place; and Song of Solomon to the most holy place. The New Testament book that has the same type of purpose as the Song of Solomon—reflection about a Bridegroom and His Bride—is the epistle to the Ephesians.

E. FORM

The book is a unified lyrical poem. It is a series of stanzas or songs of varied lengths.[2] Our later survey study will reveal that there is a topical unity of the various songs, even though there is no defined

---

2. Franz Delitzsch identifies six acts of the melodrama:
a. The mutual affection of the lovers 1:2—2:7
b. The mutual seeking and finding of the lovers 2:8—3:5
c. The home-bringing of the bride, and the marriage 3:6—5:1
d. Love disdained, but won again 5:2—6:9
e. Shulamith, the attractively fair but humble Princess 6:10—8:4
f. The ratification of the covenant of love in Shulamith's native home 8:5-14
   (Franz Delitzch, *Commentary on the Song of Songs and Ecclesiastes,* pp. ix-x).

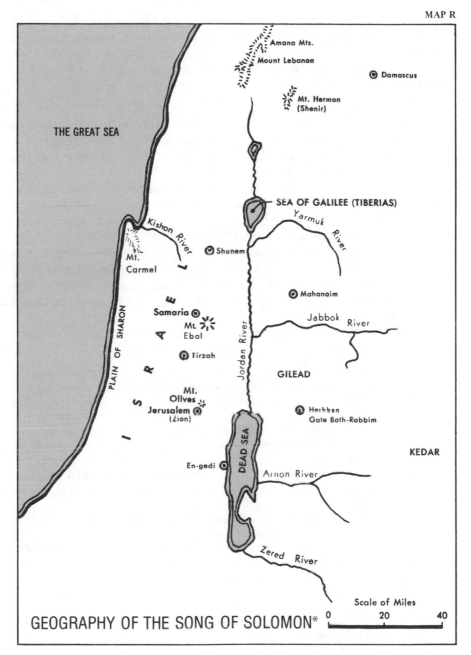

GEOGRAPHY OF THE SONG OF SOLOMON*

*The locations of *Baal-hamon* (8:11) and *Bether* (2:17) are unknown.
Bether may not be a proper name (see Berkeley Version).

dramatical progression, as in the book of Job. Because of its poetical form, we may expect to find the usual figures of speech found in poetry (e.g., simile: "Thy hair is as a flock of goats," 4:1, KJV). Also, the phraseology of the poetry is strictly Oriental, and must be read in that light (e.g., chap. 4).

F. SETTING OF STORY

The main characters of the Song of Solomon are Solomon, a Shulamite woman, and a group called "daughters of Jerusalem":

1. Solomon. The king of Israel (1 Kings 1:32-37), Solomon was the son of David and Bathsheba (2 Sam 12:24).

2. A Shulamite woman. The name "Shulamite" appears only at 6:13 (KJV). It is probably derived from the place called Shunem, located a short distance north of Jezreel near the plain of Megiddo (cf. Josh 19:18; 1 Sam 28:4; 1 Kings 1:3; 2 Kings 4:8). See Map R.

3. Daughters of Jerusalem. The identity of these women is not disclosed. They may have been companions of the bride, attendants of the king's palace, or interested onlookers. Some commentators assign a few verses of the text to other speakers (e.g., an officer of the king's guard, 3:7-10).

H. A. Ironside's description of the setting of this story, as summarized by Merrill Unger, is quoted here at length:

> King Solomon had a vineyard in the hill country of Ephraim, about 50 miles N of Jerusalem, 8:11. He let it out to keepers, 8:11, consisting of a mother, two sons, 1:6, and two daughters—the Shulamite, 6:13, and a little sister, 8:8. The Shulamite was "the Cinderella" of the family, 1:5, naturally beautiful but unnoticed. Her brothers were likely half brothers, 1:6. They made her work very hard tending the vineyards, so that she had little opportunity to care for her personal appearance, 1:6. She pruned the vines and set traps for the little foxes, 2:15. She also kept the flocks, 1:8. Being out in the open so much, she became sunburned, 1:5.
>
> One day a handsome stranger came to the vineyard. It was Solomon disguised. He showed an interest in her, and she became embarrassed concerning her personal appearance, 1:6. She took him for a shepherd and asked about his flocks, 1:7. He answered evasively, 1:8, but also spoke loving words to her, 1:8-10, and promised rich gifts for the future, 1:11. He won her heart and left with the promise that some day he would return. She dreamed of him at night and sometimes thought he was near, 3:1. Finally he did return in all his kingly splendor to make her his bride, 3:6-7.[3]

---

3. H. A. Ironside, *Addresses on the Song of Solomon,* pp. 17-21, summarized by Merrill Unger, *Unger's Bible Handbook,* pp. 299-300.

The above description will help you catch something of the tone of the book as you begin your survey study.

G. SCHOOLS OF INTERPRETATION

The Song of Solomon has been interpreted in three different ways:

1. Naturalistic. It is a human love story, of literary merit, with no typical or figurative meaning intended.

2. Allegorical. It is purely figurative, not based on historical fact.

3. Typical. It is teaching by (1) example, from historical facts; and (2) type, from viewing these historical facts as figurative representations. In the words of Scroggie, "As in Jonah, we have allegory emerging from history."[4] G. Campbell Morgan describes this methodology of interpretation.

> The songs should be treated then, first as simple and yet sublime songs of human affection. When they are thus understood, reverently the thoughts may be lifted into the higher value of setting forth the joys of the communion between the spirit of man and the Spirit of God, and ultimately between the Church and Christ.[5]

This survey guide follows the typical view.

H. TYPICAL TEACHING

As indicated earlier, the characters of the dialogue of Canticles are Solomon, the Shulamite woman, and the daughters of Jerusalem. In the story, Solomon is the bridegroom, and the Shulamite woman is the bride.[6] Two applications of typical teaching may be intended.

1. Israel is the bride, and God the Bridegroom. Read these other Old Testament passages where this bride and groom relationship is clearly taught: Isaiah 54:5-6; Jeremiah 2:2; Ezekiel 16:8-14[7]; Hosea 2:16,[8] 18-20. Jewish believers of Old Testament times clearly saw this typical intent of Canticles, which helped to impress them regarding the book's canonicity.

2. The Church is the Bride, and Christ the Bridegroom. Read Ephesians 5:23-25; 2 Corinthians 11:1-2; Revelation 19:7-9; 21:9.

A third application is derived from the second, in the sense that an *individual* believer (of the whole believing Church) is the particu-

---

4. W. Graham Scroggie, *Know Your Bible,* 1:118.
5. G. Campbell Morgan, *The Analyzed Bible,* p. 197.
6. A figurative interpretation of the daughters of Jerusalem, if intended, might be that these are not saved ones, though they are near the Kingdom of God.
7. Ezekiel 16:20-21, 32, 38 reveals the unfaithfulness of Israel to her Husband, God.
8. In the King James Version, "Ishi" means "my husband," and "Baali" means "my master."

lar object of Christ's love. From a practical standpoint this is the most intimate application which a Christian can make of the book's typical teaching for his own Christian life.

Some Bible students see another character involved in the story of Canticles: a shepherd-lover (1:7), from whose affection Solomon tries to lure the Shulamite woman away:

> Solomon uses all the dazzle and splendor of his court to woo the girl away from her true love, seeking to get her to become one of his wives instead. In like manner the world is ever seeking to attract away from Christ those who are "espoused" to Him. Solomon is unable to accomplish his goal, however, for the Shulamite resists all his overtures and remains true to her beloved shepherd to whom, at last, she is reunited.[9]

The reason why there are different views as to the "plot" of Canticles is that the speakers are not identified by name in the Bible text. For example, the two-speaker view (Solomon, Shulamite woman) says that Solomon speaks all of 4:1-15; whereas the three-speaker view says that Solomon is the speaker of 4:1-6, while 4:7-15 are the words of the shepherd-lover. But, as John Phillips points out, "The abiding value of the Song of Solomon is clear whichever view is taken. As human life finds its highest fulfillment in the love of man and woman, so spiritual life finds its highest fulfillment in the love of Christ and His Church."[10]

An interesting comparison has been made between Ecclesiastes and the Song of Solomon involving their pointing to Christ:

> In Ecclesiastes we learn that without Christ we cannot be satisfied, even if we possess the whole world—the heart is too large for the object. In the Song of Solomon we learn that if we turn from the world and set our affections on Christ, we cannot fathom the infinite preciousness of His love—the Object is too large for the heart.[11]

I. PURPOSES

The purposes of the Song of Solomon are:
1. literal: to honor pure human love and marriage
2. figurative: to show the Lord's love for Israel, and Christ's love for His Church and for each individual Christian; how the Bride in each case should return that love

---

9. See John Phillips, *Exploring the Scriptures,* p. 116. One commentary which follows this view is Arthur E. Cundall, *Proverbs to Isaiah 39,* pp. 50 ff.
10. Phillips, p. 116.
11. Quoted by Robert Lee in *The Outlined Bible,* p. 21.

The literal purpose of the book has often been twisted by those not prepared to read frank and intimate expressions of love. Asceticism and lust—two perversions of the holiness of marriage—are slain by the message of this book. If the reader is licentiously excited when he reads the Song of Solomon, he is out of tune with its purpose. The book's literal message is perverted only by those who do not see the purity and true beauty of all of God's creative acts.

III. SURVEY

Keep in mind that the purpose of survey study is to view the book in a general way, and thus discover its main theme and related subjects.

A. A FIRST READING

Because the parts of the dialogue of these poems are not identified in the Bible text as to who is speaking, it is important to mark your Bible, showing who the speakers are, if your Bible does not already show this in its headings.[12] The speakers shown below *begin* each new part at the verses cited. Mark these in your Bible.[13]

The Shulamite woman: 1:2, 4*a*, 5, 12, 16; 2:3; 4:16; 5:2, 10; 6:2; 7:9*b;* 8:10, 14

Solomon: 1:8, 15; 2:2; 4:1; 5:1*a;* 6:4, 13*h;* 8:5*b*, 13

Daughters of Jerusalem: 1:4*b*, 11; 3:6; 5:9; 6:1, 13*a;* 8:5*a;* 8

Read through the Song of Solomon in one sitting, aloud if possible. What are your first impressions? What one word clearly expresses the main subject of this book?

B. SURVEY CHART

Read through the book a second time, and observe other things which you did not see in the first reading.

The Song of Solomon is difficult to outline in detail because a progressing plot is not detectable, except in a general way. Chart 77 will help you see the main parts of this book, on which you may base your later studies.

1. Note on the chart that Canticles has a title verse (1:1), but no formal conclusion, such as we are accustomed to find in a Bible book. Read 1:1; then read the last few verses of chapter 8.

---

12. Versions which identify the speakers include: *New Scofield Reference Bible* (King James Version); *New American Standard Bible; Berkeley Version;* and *The Living Bible* (paraphrase).

13. For a few of the parts it is difficult to determine who the speaker is (e.g., 6:11). This accounts for differences shown in the headings of commentaries and versions. The identifications shown here are for the most part those of the *New American Standard Bible.*

2. Observe the six main segments shown on the chart, beginning at 1:2. Mark these major divisions in your Bible.

3. Study the outline shown directly under the main base line (beginning with "Bride muses"). The heading "The wedding" is based partly on 3:11*b:* "the day of his wedding." Read 3:6-11. Scan the Bible text of the whole book again, segment by segment, and see if this outline represents the contents of each.

4. The top of the survey chart divides the Song of Solomon into three main parts. What are they?

5. What outline on the chart divides the book into two main parts?

6. Note the progression from *quest* to *conquest,* involving bride and groom. Read the verses in your Bible. (In fact, underline the verses in your Bible as strong verses.)

7. Try constructing outlines of your own to represent the contents of this book.

IV. Unique Characteristics

The Song of Solomon is unique among the books of the Bible in many ways. Some of these are described below.

1. It is one of the most misunderstood books of the Bible. Its Oriental expressions of intimate love partly account for this.

2. It is the only book of the Bible where love between humans is the main plot and theme. (Other similar passages of love are to be found in Psalm 45 and the book of Ruth.)

3. There is only one direct reference to God in the book ("the Lord," 8:6). (In the King James Version there is no such reference. Instead, at 8:6 the Hebrew word *Yah* is translated "vehement." The book of Esther records no name of God.)

4. There is no specific or direct reference to sin.

5. There is no specific or direct reference to the religious realm as such.

6. No other Old Testament book is alluded to here.

7. The book is not alluded to by Christ, nor is it quoted elsewhere in the New Testament.[14]

V. Key Words and Verses

Read the key words which are listed on Chart 77. Add others to the list. Do the same for the key verses.

---

14. The historicity of the book's action is clear. One support of this is its geographical setting—there are over fifteen geographical references. (See Map R.)

VI. Applications

This book was written especially to stir up the *feelings* of God's people. Ecclesiastes stresses *thinking;* the Song of Solomon stresses *feeling,* of the meditative type. Andrew Miller wrote long ago, "There is nothing which the men of this world dread more than solitude and reflection. They would rather be overpressed with engagements than have leisure for thought."[15] Has human nature changed since then?

The Christological purpose of Canticles is to inspire Christians to take time to meditate on Jesus Christ. "The calm, reflective quiet of the soul in communion with the Person of the exalted Lord, is what characterises its sweetest moments while here on earth."[16]

Canticles' teachings about love should be applied in two ways: typical and literal.

A. TYPICAL

The key to the full meaning and purpose of the Song of Solomon is Jesus Christ. The book as a love story is unexcelled only if Christ is the Lover in its pages—for no one can surpass His love: "Christ lives in me; and the life which I now live in the flesh I live by faith in the *Son of God, who loved me, and delivered Himself up for me*" (Gal 2:20, italics added). In the Song of Solomon it is the *person* of Christ, not His *work,* which is the prominent characteristic ("He is wholly desirable," 5:16). The Christian reader who involves himself in the book is overwhelmed by the beautiful and reassuring truth of his union and communion with such a Saviour.

B. LITERAL

No other book of the Bible gives such an extended description of the beauties of a love relationship between a man and a woman. The inclusion of this human love story in God's Book demonstrates the sacred honor which He has given to the union of husband and wife. Study the Song of Solomon to learn its literal teachings about the kind of human love that honors God. Below is a partial list of aspects of *love* which are referred to in the book.

physical: beauty, purity, body, sexual instincts, desire, attraction, satisfaction, giving and receiving, presence and separation, physical wedlock

non-physical (social, mental, and spiritual): attraction, companionship, union and communion, hope, pleasure, giving and receiv-

---

15. Andrew Miller, *Meditations on the Song of Solomon,* p. 1.
16. Ibid.

CHART 77

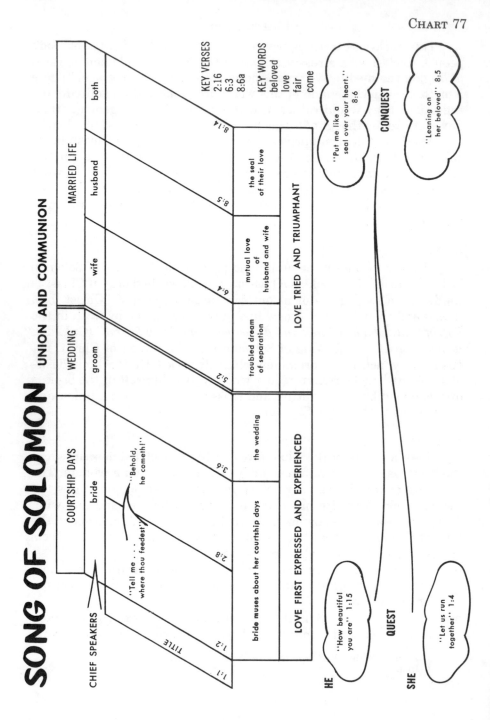

ing, presence and separation, tenderness, sacrifice, faithfulness, praise, beauty, love, purity, wholesomeness, humility

VII. FURTHER STUDY

For a concluding study, read the following New Testament passages for their teaching about the physical body and marriage:

physical body: Romans 6:12-13, 19; 1 Corinthians 6:18-20; 1 Thessalonians 5:23

marriage: Matthew 19:5-6; 1 Corinthians 7; Ephesians 5:22-33; 1 Timothy 4:1-5; 5:14; Hebrews 13:4

VIII. SELECTED READING

GENERAL INTRODUCTION

Baxter, J. Sidlow. *Explore the Book,* 3:169-95.
Delitzsch, Franz. *Commentary on the Song of Songs and Ecclesiastes,* pp. 1-15.
Harper, Andrew. *The Song of Solomon,* pp. ix-li.
Young, Edward J. *An Introduction to the Old Testament,* pp. 323-28.
Zoeckler, Otto. "The Song of Solomon." In Lange's *Commentary on the Holy Scriptures,* pp. 1-47.

COMMENTARIES

Adeney, Walter F. *The Song of Solomon.*
LaBotz, Paul. *The Romance of the Ages.*
Cameron, W. J. "Song of Solomon." In *The New Bible Commentary.*
Ironside, H. A. *Addresses on the Song of Solomon.*
Miller, Andrew. *Meditations on the Song of Solomon.*
Taylor, J. Hudson. *Union and Communion.*
Woudstra, Sierd. "Song of Solomon." In *The Wycliffe Bible Commentary.*

Part 4

Ministries of the Prophets

Seventeen books of prophecy are in our English Bible. These were written by sixteen different prophets, if Jeremiah wrote Lamentations as well as the book bearing his name. The books are classified as either "major" or "minor," the classification assigned primarily for their relative length. The prophecies were written over a period of more than four centuries, from about 840 B.C. (Obadiah) to 420 B.C. (Malachi). Below are the names of the writers, listed in the order of their books appearing in the Old Testament canon.

Writers of the Major Prophetical Books	Writers of the Minor Prophetical Books		
Isaiah	Hosea	Jonah	Zephaniah
Jeremiah	Joel	Micah	Haggai
Ezekiel	Amos	Nahum	Zechariah
Daniel	Obadiah	Habakkuk	Malachi

Why the seventeen prophetic books were placed at the end of the Old Testament Scriptures is not known. George Adam Smith says that perhaps "it was held fitting that prophecy should occupy the last outposts of the Old Testament towards the New."[1]

---

1. George Adam Smith, *The Book of the Twelve,* 1:3.

20

Isaiah: The Glorious Throne of Jehovah the Holy One

Of all the writing prophets, Isaiah is justly accounted the greatest. His prophecy is one of the longest, is quoted more frequently than any other in the New Testament, and he more often than any other prophet tells of the coming Messiah. Isaiah prophesied for about fifty years (see Chart 80) during very critical times of both kingdoms, Israel and Judah. He was greatly responsible for the sweeping reforms introduced by Hezekiah, who was one of Judah's righteous kings.[1] Merrill Unger says this of Isaiah: "Isaiah . . . is the great messianic prophet and prince of OT seers. For splendor of diction, brilliance of imagery, versatility and beauty of style, profundity and breadth of prophetic vision, he is without peer."[2]

I. THE OLD TESTAMENT PROPHETS

Without question the ministry of the prophet, along with that of priest, judge, and king, was crucial in the life of the Jews in Old Testament times. The word "prophet," in its various forms, appears over six hundred sixty times in the Bible, two-thirds of which are in the Old Testament. One cannot spend too much time studying the prophetic books.

Since this is the opening chapter of the section on the prophets, attention should first be fixed on the general subject of Old Testament prophecy.

A. THE AUDIENCE OF THE PROPHETS

Most messages of the Old Testament prophetic books were addressed to the generations of God's people who lived approximately

---

2. Merrill F. Unger, *Unger's Bible Handbook*, p. 306.

between the years 840 and 420 B.C. (see Chart 45). The ten tribes,
known specifically as the kingdom of Israel,[3] lived in north Canaan
(New Testament areas of Samaria and Galilee) before they were
deported by the Assyrians in 722 B.C. The other two tribes, known as
the kingdom of Judah, lived in south Canaan before they were taken
captive by the Babylonians in 586 B.C. This is shown on Map S.

AUDIENCE OF THE PROPHETS   MAP S

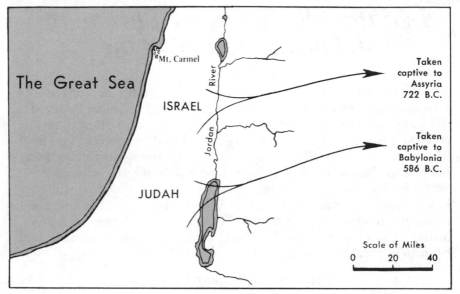

The people of God were not always divided into two camps. The
split of the kingdom came at the end of Solomon's reign, Jeroboam I
being the first king of the north, and Rehoboam the first king of the
south. This story is recorded in 1 Kings 12-16. Recall your earlier
studies of these tragic years of the people's history.

Recall from your studies of chapter 12 that the history of the
Jews during Old Testament times generally falls into four periods,
called Camp, Commonwealth, Crown, and Captivity (with restoration). (See Chart 38.) The audience of the writing prophets was the
people living during the last two periods.

B. THE TERM "PROPHESY"

The primary task of the Old Testament prophets was not to
foretell future events but to *forthtell* the will of God which He had

---

3. The name Israel in the Old Testament sometimes refers to the entire nation;
otherwise it refers to just the northern tribes. In this book the name is used in the
former sense (general) unless otherwise stated.

revealed to His prophets. Concerning the verb "prophesy," Gleason Archer writes:

> The Hebrew word is *nibba'* . . . a word whose etymology is much disputed. The best founded explanation, however, seems to relate this root to the Akkadian verb *nabu,* which means "to summon, announce, call . . . ." Thus the verb *nibba'* would doubtless signify one who has been called or appointed to proclaim as a herald the message of God Himself. From this verb comes the characteristic word for prophet, *nabi',* one who has been called. On this interpretation the prophet was . . . one called by God to proclaim as a herald from the court of heaven the message to be transmitted from God to man.[4]

C. OTHER TITLES APPLIED TO THE PROPHETS

The prophets of the Old Testament were sometimes designated by other titles. Of these, the three most frequently used were:
1. "man of God"—suggesting an intimate spiritual relationship
2. "seer"—suggesting perception of the true, and insight into the invisible things of God (cf. 1 Sam 9:9)
3. "servant" of Jehovah
The prophets were also known as messengers of Jehovah, men of the Spirit (cf. Hos 9:7), interpreters and spokesmen for God.

D. QUALIFICATIONS OF THE PROPHET

Listed below are some of the qualifications of the high office of the prophet. Considering the nature of the prophet's work, it is not surprising that the qualifications were so strict:

   1. Sovereign calling. God's sovereign will determined who were His prophets (cf. Isa 6; Jer 1).

   2. Special abilities. These were given by God's Spirit, enabling the prophet to perceive the truth (as "seer"), and equipping him with the gift of communicating the revelation of God to people.

   3. Spiritual qualities. These were not a few. Included were unselfishness, obedience to the voice of God, love, faith, courage, and long-suffering.

E. THE ORAL AND WRITING PROPHETS

All of God's prophets shared the same purpose for which they were divinely called. Their primary ministry was to deliver a message from God to an unbelieving and apostate Israel (cf. Deut 18:18-19). Some of these, now referred to as the writing (or literary) prophets, were chosen of God not only to a public-speaking ministry, but also to be the authors of the inspired canonical books of prophecy. The

---

4. Gleason L. Archer, *A Survey of Old Testament Introduction,* p. 284.

others, now referred to as the oral prophets, ministered mostly by the spoken word.

1. Oral prophets. The Bible records the names of only a few of the oral prophets. And most of these names are not commonly known. Refer to Chart 45 and locate the following oral prophets: Ahijah, Iddo, Jehu, Elijah, Elisha, Oded, Shemaiah, Azariah, Hanani, Jahaziel, and Huldah. To this list might be added Nathan of Gad, of David's generation; Micaiah; and Eliezer. Which of these names do you recognize? You may want to look up the unfamiliar names in a Bible dictionary for a brief description of their part in Bible history. Note from Chart 45 that most of these prophets ministered before the appearance of the writing prophets.

The office of prophet probably originated around the time of Samuel, who founded and presided over various schools of young prophets ("company of the prophets," 1 Sam 19:20). These prophets are also classified as oral prophets. Concerning these schools, Fred E. Young writes:

THREE PERIODS OF THE PROPHETS   CHART 78

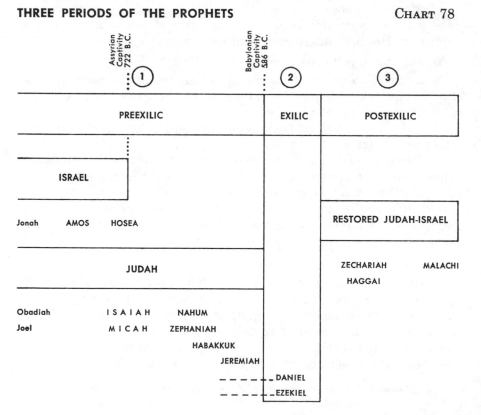

The origin and history of these schools are obscure. According to [1 Sam] 3:1, before the call of Samuel as a prophet, the prophetic word was rare in Israel, and prophecy was not widespread. There is little doubt that these unions of prophets arose in the time of Samuel, and were called into existence by him . . . . These unions may have grown until the time of Elijah and Elisha. They arose only in Israel, not in Judah.[5]

2. *Writing prophets.* As noted earlier, sixteen writing prophets authored the seventeen books of prophecy in our English Bible. Study Chart 78, which shows the three main periods during which the prophets ministered.

a) Preexilic. Eleven prophets ministered during the years leading up to the Assyrian Captivity (722 B.C.) and the Babylonian Captivity (586 B.C.). Notice the two big clusters of four prophets each:

> TO ASSYRIAN CAPTIVITY: *Amos* and *Hosea,* prophets mainly to Israel; *Isaiah* and *Micah,* prophets mainly to Judah

> TO BABYLONIAN CAPTIVITY: *Nahum, Zephaniah, Jeremiah,* and *Habakkuk* (Judah)

> THREE EARLIER PROPHETS: *Jonah* (Israel), *Obadiah,* and *Joel* (Judah)

b) Exilic. Two of the four major prophets were prophets of the Exile. They were *Ezekiel* and *Daniel.*

c) Postexilic. The three postexilic prophets were *Zechariah, Haggai,* and *Malachi.* The first two ministered in the early years of Israel's return to their land, and Malachi ministered at the close of this restoration period.

The writing prophets, in addition to composing their prophecies in written form, also had a wide ministry of speaking at public gatherings in the Temple or on the streets. For future generations of God's people, however, their major work was in their writing.

F. MESSAGE OF THE PROPHET

Whether the prophet was called to preach or to write or to do both, his message was the same. All the prophetic words of the Old Testament could probably be compiled under the following four large areas of truth about which the prophet engaged himself:

1. *Instruction of the great truths about God and man.* The prophets devoted much time telling the people about God—His character, His domain, His purposes, and His Law. They also gave a true diagnosis of the spiritual health of the nation as a whole and of individual souls.

---

5. Fred E. Young, "First and Second Samuel," in *The Wycliffe Bible Commentary,* pp. 287-88.

2. Warning and appeal to those living in sin. It cannot be said that God brings judgment upon men without forewarning. Over and over again the prophets warned of judgment to come for sin, and exhorted the people to repent and turn to God.

3. Comfort and exhortation to those trusting and obeying God. These are the warm and bright portions of the prophets' messages. The last part of Isaiah abounds in such notes of hope and consolation.

4. Prediction of events to come. Prophetic predictions were of two major subjects: (1) national and international events, of both near and far-distant future; and (2) the comings of Jesus the Messiah—His first and second comings.

When you read a book of prophecy, various things should be kept in mind. Some of these are briefly described below.

a) The immediate setting. Be acquainted with the political and religious conditions which prevailed at the time any given prophet was speaking. For most of the prophetic books this can be ascertained by reading in the books of Kings and Chronicles the history of the kings who were ruling at any particular period. For example, the first verse of Isaiah gives the names of the four kings who were reigning while Isaiah was prophesying. By turning back to the historical books and reading the accounts of these reigns, one can realize the evils which existed and against which Isaiah was thundering.

The setting of foreign powers also throws light on the prophetic books. For each book you will want to know something of the surrounding nations, especially those vying for world suzerainty. The three reigning world powers during the years of the prophets were:

Assyrian—up to 612 B.C. (fall of Nineveh)
Neo-Babylonian—up to 539 B.C. (fall of Babylon)
Persian—up to Malachi (and beyond)

b) The God of history. You will appreciate and understand more of the historical movements of the prophets' days if you always keep in mind that human history is in the sovereign hands of an omniscient, omnipotent God. Everything transpires either by His permissive or directive will. He foreknows every event before it becomes history, and on many occasions He gave such prophetic revelation to His prophets to share with the nations.

c) The chosen nation. Israel was God's elect nation, called into being by His sovereign decree, and preserved through the ages (sometimes in a very small remnant) in fulfillment of His covenant originally made with Abraham.

d) The four prophetic points. The utterances of the prophets, for the most part, centered around four points in history: (1) their own time;

(2) the threatening captivities (Assyrian and Babylonian), and subsequent restoration; (3) the coming of their Messiah; and (4) the Millennium. This is illustrated by Chart 79.

It was as though the prophet were on some high eminence (see A on Chart 79) looking off into the distance and speaking of what he saw. Most often he saw the sins which prevailed in his own day, and spoke of them (see one on the chart). Then he would look off to the day when the nation would be taken out of their land into captivity. He also saw an eventual regathering of the Jews from the captivities (see two). At times the Spirit enabled him to look further into the future and foretell of the coming Messiah (see three). Occasionally he saw still further into the future, and spoke of a glorious time of restoration and peace coming to God's people in the Millennium (see four).

In order to get the true meaning of the words of a prophet, one must determine in each individual utterance which of these four events is his subject.[6] The very language of the prophet and the context in which he speaks the words usually indicate this. For example, read Isaiah 53 and determine to which of these four points in history (as indicated on Chart 79) the prophet is referring.

e). Two Messianic themes. When a prophet speaks of Christ, he refers

FOUR PROPHETIC POINTS   CHART 79

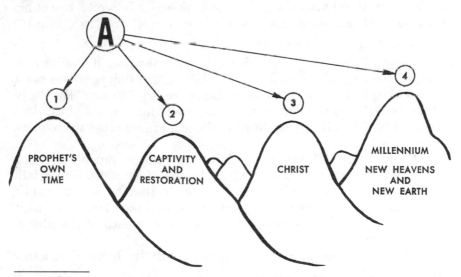

PROPHET'S OWN TIME

CAPTIVITY AND RESTORATION

CHRIST

MILLENNIUM NEW HEAVENS AND NEW EARTH

---

6. Sometimes a prophecy may have a multiple intention of fulfillment. E.g., a prophecy of restoration of the Jews may concern (1) return from Babylonian captivity, and (2) regathering of Israel from all parts of the world in the end times.

to Him in either of His two comings—either in the first coming, as the suffering Messiah (e.g., Isa 53), or in the second coming, as the reigning Messiah (e.g., Isa 11). The prophets were apparently not aware that a long interval of time would transpire between Christ's manifestation in suffering (first advent) and Christ's revelation in glory (second advent). His suffering and His reigning appeared to them to be very close in time. The student of prophecy must keep this in mind when he studies the predictive sections of the prophetic books.

II. The Man Isaiah

Isaiah is the first of four prophets known as the major prophets (Isaiah, Jeremiah, Ezekiel, and Daniel). See Chart 94, which compares the lives and ministries of these men of God.

A. HIS NAME

The name Isaiah translates a short form of the prophet's Hebrew name, *Yeshaiah*. The long form, which is how his name appears in his book and in all other Old Testament references, is *Yeshayahu*. This is a compound name having such meanings as "Jehovah saves," "Jehovah is salvation," and "salvation of Jehovah."

Surely the prophet was given this name by divine design. Whenever people mentioned his name, they were audibly reiterating the great theme of his message. In the book which he wrote, two of his favorite words are those translated "he shall save" and "salvation."

B. THE TIMES IN WHICH HE LIVED

Dates of Isaiah's birth and death are unknown. If the date of Isaiah 7:3 is around 734 B.C., and if Isaiah's son at that time was not a mere child, Isaiah may have been born around 760 B.C. "His early years were therefore spent in the prosperous, luxurious and careless days of king Uzziah, the conditions of which are reflected in chapters ii., iii."[7]

From Isaiah 1:1 we learn that most of the prophet's public ministry took place during the reigns of these kings of Judah: Uzziah, Jotham, Ahaz, and Hezekiah. It is possible that he did no public preaching after Manasseh succeeded Hezekiah on the throne. Consult a Bible dictionary for a review of the careers of each of the above-named kings.

Study carefully Chart 80, and compare it with the larger Chart 45.

---

7. G. T. Manley, *The New Bible Handbook*, p. 214.

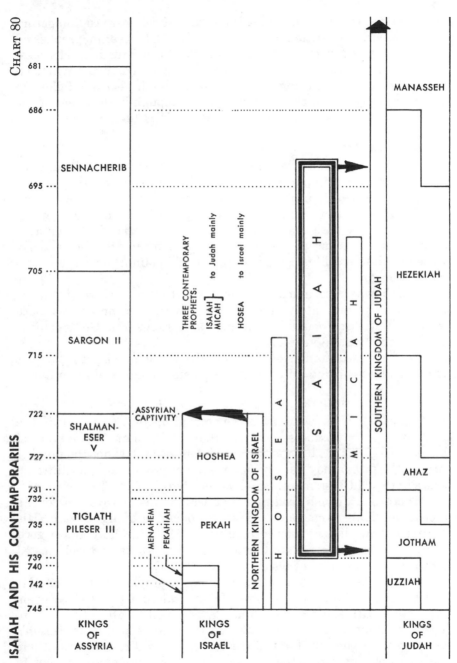

CHART 80

ISAIAH AND HIS CONTEMPORARIES

KINGS OF ASSYRIA

KINGS OF ISRAEL

KINGS OF JUDAH

681

686

695

705

715

722

727

731
732

735

739
740

742

745

SENNACHERIB

SARGON II

SHALMAN-
ESER
V

TIGLATH
PILESER III

MENAHEM

PEKAHIAH

ASSYRIAN
CAPTIVITY

HOSHEA

PEKAH

NORTHERN KINGDOM OF ISRAEL

HOSEA

ISAIAH

MICAH

SOUTHERN KINGDOM OF JUDAH

MANASSEH

HEZEKIAH

AHAZ

JOTHAM

UZZIAH

THREE CONTEMPORARY
PROPHETS:

ISAIAH]
MICAH] to Judah mainly

HOSEA   to Israel mainly

Observe from the chart that Hosea and Micah were contemporary prophets with Isaiah (cf. Hos 1:1 and Mic 1:1). Isaiah prophesied during the last seventeen years of the Northern Kingdom. His message, however, was primarily to the Southern Kingdom. When Israel's throne was tottering because of sin, Judah also was following her sister kingdom in the downward path, though with slower steps. For the historical setting of Isaiah, read 2 Kings 14-21.

C. HIS CHARACTER

Isaiah was bold, fearless, and absolutely sincere. He talked to his fellow countrymen in plain language, showing them how they looked in God's sight. No class of society escaped his scathing denunciations.

Isaiah was stern and uncompromising when the occasion demanded, but he also had a tender heart. He warned of judgment because he loved his people, and like a loving mother he tenderly wooed them to heed his counsel so they could claim the prospects of a glorious future.

Isaiah was also a man of great spirituality and strong faith. Associating so intimately and constantly with God, he had no place for worldliness and doubt. He saw men and things from God's point of view, in the light of eternity.

Isaiah was a many-sided genius. His ministry of prophecy was enhanced by his being gifted as a poet, a statesman, and an orator.

D. HIS LIFE AND MINISTRY

Very little is known of Isaiah's personal history. Emphasis in the Bible is given to the message rather than to the man. All we know of his parentage is that he was the son of Amoz (Isa 1:1; not the prophet Amos). His father may have been a person of prominence, for thirteen times in the Old Testament, Isaiah is referred to as the "son of Amoz."

There is a Jewish tradition that Isaiah was of royal descent, a brother of King Amaziah, and so a cousin of King Uzziah. His writings show that he was blessed with a fine intellect and a good education. He was very familiar with the Scriptures and well posted on the political affairs of his day.

Isaiah was married, and his wife was a prophetess (Isa 8:3). He had two sons whose names were Maher-shalal-hash-baz ("speedy is the prey," 8:3) and Shear-jashub ("a remnant shall return," 7:3). These peculiar names illustrated the two great points in Isaiah's message to the nation. First, if the nation refused to turn from their idolatry and sin, God would punish them by allowing a nation to conquer them and carry them out of their land to remain captives in another country for many years. The picture is that of a ferocious wolf pouncing upon a lamb and taking it away to his den. The second name symbolically prophesied that after God had punished the nation by this captivity He would allow them to return to their own land, but that only a remnant would avail themselves of this opportunity.

The time and circumstances of Isaiah's death are not known. According to tradition (Talmud), he was sawed in half by the wicked King Manasseh (cf. 2 Kings 21:16; Heb 11:37).

III. THE BOOK OF ISAIAH

A. STYLE

The book of Isaiah is basically a series of discourses by the prophet delivered at different times and on different occasions. The arrangement of these discourses is generally chronological whenever history is involved.[8] The topical arrangement will be studied later when a survey is made of the book.

Isaiah's style is lofty and strongly rhetorical. He excelled as an orator, and designed his discourses to attract and stir his audiences. Though his writing is not poetry, he uses many of the devices of the poet, especially figures of speech. He excels in variety of vocabulary, and in the use of words to convey powerful truths. Perhaps the most biting and stinging method he employs is that of satire. (Satire is the use of sarcasm or irony to expose or rebuke actions and attitudes. E.g., 40:19-20; 41:6-7; 44:13-20.)

B. SIMILARITY OF OUTLINE

In character and broad outline, many of Isaiah's discourses are very similar. The following four points can usually be seen in such discourses: (1) indictment or accusation; (2) threat; (3) exhortation or entreaty; (4) promise of purification or blessing.

The first discourse, chapter 1, is an illustration of this:

1. The Indictment or Accusation (vv. 1-9)
2. The Threat (vv. 10-15)
3. The Exhortation or Entreaty (vv. 16-20)
4. The Promise of Purification and Blessing (vv. 21-31)

C. SONGS IN ISAIAH

Although Isaiah is not a book of poetry, various songs and refrains appear throughout the book. Some of the more prominent ones are:

---

8. The datelines (specific references to dates) of Isaiah are 1:1; 6:1; 7:1; 14:28; 20:1; 36:1.

1. Song of the Vineyard (chap. 5)
2. Song of the Redeemed (chap. 12)
3. Song of the Blossoming Desert (chap. 35)
4. Song of the Restored Wife (chap. 54)

IV. SURVEY

Follow the procedures of survey study established in the earlier chapters of this book. This includes scanning the entire book of Isaiah and assigning a chapter title to each of the sixty-six chapters. Compare the opening and closing chapters. Look for groupings of subject matter. Be alert to key repeated words and phrases. Determine a théme and title of the book.

Study carefully the survey Chart 81. Observe that there are two main parts in the book of Isaiah, the division coming between chapters 39 and 40. Does this observation agree with the overall patterns of your chapter titles? On the survey chart the two main divisions are identified as (1) Judgment of God and (2) Comfort of God. Think more about these two subjects as they are discussed below.

A. JUDGMENT OF GOD (chaps. 1-39)

Judgment is the prominent thought of the first division of Isaiah—judgment on Judah and Jerusalem for their sins, and judgment on the nations which are hostile to the chosen people. But although judgment is the keynote of this first division, scattered here and there are promises for Judah, and hopes for both Jew and Gentile, in the predictions of the Messiah. Amid the darkness there are frequent flashes of the "great light" mentioned in 9:2; glimpses of the "bright morning star" (see Rev 22:16), and the coming Redeemer, of whom Isaiah speaks so fully in the later chapters.

Looking more closely at the chapters, it is convenient for study to subdivide this first division. For example, the chart shows that the first twelve chapters are discourses addressed chiefly to Judah and Jerusalem; chapters 13-27 are discourses regarding the nations which were hostile to Judah; chapters 28-35, various warnings and promises; and the last four chapters of the section are purely historical, being a review of Hezekiah's reign, given in 2 Kings 18-20. (Recall from Chart 80 when Hezekiah reigned as king.) Read in the Bible text each of the sections just cited, and try to justify the outlines shown on the chart.

B. COMFORT OF GOD (chaps. 40-66)

In this second division of the book, *comfort* is the predominant note, although there are repeated warnings to the wicked.

The discourses in this division are chiefly predictive. They fall into three groups of nine chapters each. Read 48:22 and observe the common utterance, "'no peace for the wicked,' says the LORD" which concludes each of the first two groups (cf. 57:21).

The first of the three groups (chaps. 40-48) compares Jehovah, the true God, with idols, the false gods. The second group (chaps. 49-57) speaks almost entirely concerning the Messiah. The third group (chaps. 58-66) describes the final restoration of God's people, with God on the throne (66:1) acknowledged as Lord over all (66:23).

Note also the following outline on the chart:
Redemption Promised
Redemption Provided
Redemption Realized

In your survey reading of Isaiah, try to observe how the above outlines represent the various sections. Study the other parts of Chart 81 for what they contribute to an understanding of the overall message of Isaiah.

An easy way to remember the broad organization of Isaiah by chapters is to note these coincidental likenesses to the entire Bible:

a) Isaiah has sixty-six chapters. The Bible has sixty-six books.

b) Isaiah has two main divisions: the first, of thirty-nine chapters; and the second, of twenty-seven chapters. The Bible has two main parts: the Old Testament, of thirty-nine books; and the New Testament, of twenty-seven books.

c) The prevailing note in the first division of Isaiah is *judgment;* in the second division, *comfort.* The prevailing note of the Old Testament is *Law;* of the New Testament, *grace.*

d) In the first section of Isaiah, there are frequent allusions to and predictions of the Messiah; but He is described with great fullness in the second. In the Old Testament there are frequent allusions to Christ in types and prophecies; but in the New Testament He is presented in all His fullness.[9]

V. PROMINENT SUBJECTS

A. ISAIAH'S CALL TO THE PROPHETIC OFFICE

Isaiah must have received his call to the prophetic office at an early age. He describes the circumstances vividly in chapter 6. Recall the similar experiences of Moses (Exod 3) and Saul of Tarsus (Acts 9). When God showed Himself in a vision to these men, they recognized

---

9. The likenesses between Isaiah and the Bible which are cited here are the reasons for the book being called "The Miniature Bible."

themselves as vile, worthless creatures, with no power or wisdom of their own. They surrendered to God, and wholly committed themselves to do His bidding, whatever it might be. Isaiah's words of consecration have been an inspiration and challenge to multitudes of God's servants: "Here am I. Send me!" (6:8).

B. WARNING AND COMFORT

Isaiah, like most of the prophets, preached a twofold message, as discussed earlier in this chapter: warning of judgment for sin, and comfort of salvation for righteousness. In his book the two themes stand out in bright contrast. John Phillips writes, "One moment his book is black with the thunder and the darkness of the storm. The next, the rainbow shines through, and he sweeps his readers on to the Golden Age that still lies ahead for the world."[10] Isaiah spoke mainly to the chosen people of God, but his message was also directed to foreign nations, prophesying judgment but also proclaiming the evangel to them (read 11:10; 42:6; 45:22).

C. MESSIANIC PROPHECIES

Isaiah is known mostly for his Messianic prophecies. Some of these, such as chapter 53, are classic examples of literature at its finest. There are more Messianic prophecies in Isaiah than in any other prophetic book. Unger says, "Every glory of our Lord and every aspect of His life on the earth are set forth in this great evangelical prophecy."[11] Read the following passages and note what each prophecy of Christ contributes to the topics listed:
salvation: 12:1-2; 40:10; 52:7; 61:1
pardon: 6:7; 40:2; 53:5; 55:7
cleansing: 1:18, 25; 27:9; 52:15
peace: 9:6; 26:12; 32:17; 53:5
Continue this exercise by reading the following passages, noting what each says about Christ: 7:14-15; 8:8; 9:1-2, 7; 11:1-2; 35:5-6; 40:12-18; 42:1-3; 50:5-6; 51:13; 52:13-14; 53:1-12; 59:20; 61:2; 63:1-6; 66:15-19.

One can easily see why Isaiah is called the evangelical prophet. He speaks of Christ and of His redemption with almost the same clearness and fullness as any of the New Testament writers. The way of salvation is plainly and simply set forth. In the passages you have just studied you have seen prophecies concerning such things as His virgin birth, human and divine names, twofold nature, humiliation, sacrifice, and exaltation.

---

10. John Phillips, *Exploring the Scriptures*, p. 131.
11. Unger, p. 307

D. PROPHETIC PROSPECTIVE

Isaiah, like many of the prophets, was given divine revelation concerning four prophetic points: (1) the prophet's own time, (2) coming captivity, (3) coming of Christ, (4) new heavens and new earth. (See Chart 79.) How these are distributed throughout the book is summarized below.

1. The prophet's own time. Messages concerning this appear throughout the book. Forthtelling was Isaiah's major role.

2. Captivity. Isaiah foresaw Judah taken captive by the Babylonians. God alone knew when the captivity would come (586 B.C.). The first mention of Babylon (Shinar) as the captor is in 11:11. In the days of King Hezekiah the prophecy was made very clear (cf. 39:6).

3. Coming of Christ. These prophecies abound in the "Book of Consolation" (chaps. 40-66). They concern both the first and second comings of Christ.

4. New heavens and new earth. Isaiah prophesies of end times, especially with reference to the Millennium, with Christ as the Prince of peace (9:6), and the elect nation of Israel gathered together after their worldwide dispersion (27:12-13; 43:5-7; 65:8-10). On the most distant horizon he sees the new heavens and new earth (65:17).

VI. KEY WORDS AND VERSES

One of the key phrases of Isaiah is "Holy One of Israel." It is the prophet's favorite reference to God, appearing more than twenty-five times in the book (first appearance at 1:4).

Isaiah is a book about "The Glorious Throne of Jehovah, the Holy One." An appropriate key verse is "Holy, Holy Holy, is the LORD of hosts, the whole earth is full of His glory" (6:3).

VII. APPLICATIONS

The spiritual applications of the book of Isaiah are legion. They involve such areas of life as the divine call to Christian service; living in light of who God is; confession of sin; hardened hearts; judgment for sin; and the redemptive ministry of Christ for man.

VIII. FURTHER STUDY

1. Study the New Testament passages where Isaiah is quoted or referred to. Some are listed below. (Note: In the King James Version the prophet's name is Esaias, after the Greek spelling of the name.)

CHART 81

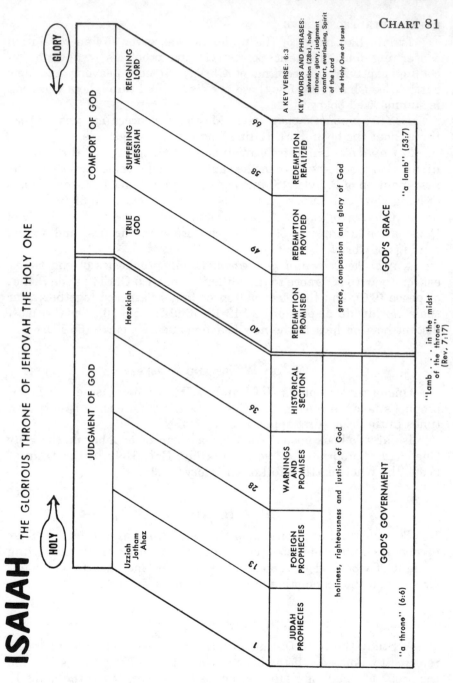

ISAIAH   THE GLORIOUS THRONE OF JEHOVAH THE HOLY ONE

HOLY →

← GLORY

JUDGMENT OF GOD

COMFORT OF GOD

Uzziah
Jotham
Ahaz

Hezekiah

| JUDAH PROPHECIES | FOREIGN PROPHECIES | WARNINGS AND PROMISES | HISTORICAL SECTION | REDEMPTION PROMISED | TRUE GOD | REDEMPTION PROVIDED | SUFFERING MESSIAH | REDEMPTION REALIZED | REIGNING LORD |

1   13   28   36   40   49   58   66

holiness, righteousness and justice of God

grace, compassion and glory of God

GOD'S GOVERNMENT

GOD'S GRACE

"a throne" (6:6)

"a lamb" (53:7)

"Lamb . . . in the midst of the throne" (Rev. 7:17)

A KEY VERSE: 6:3

KEY WORDS AND PHRASES: salvation (28x), holy throne, glory, judgment comfort, everlasting, Spirit of the Lord the Holy One of Israel

Cited by	Passages	Isaiah Passages Quoted
Matthew	Matthew 4:14-16; 8:17; 12:17-21	9:1-2; 53:4; 42:1-4
John the Baptist	John 1:23	40:3
Jesus	Luke 4:16-21	61:1-2
Apostle John	John 12:38-41	53:1; 6:9-10
Ethiopian treasurer	Acts 8:28-33	53:7-8
Paul	Acts 28:25-27	6:9-10; 10:22-23
	Romans 9:27,29; 10:16,20; 15:12	1:9; 53:1; 65:1; 11:10

2. The authorship of Isaiah has been the subject of much controversy. Many feel that more than one author wrote the book. Read the various arguments advanced for and against the one-author view.[12]

IX. SELECTED READING

GENERAL INTRODUCTION

Allis, Oswald T. *The Unity of Isaiah.*

Culver, Robert D. *The Suffering and the Glory of the Lord's Righteous Servant.*

Fitch, W. "Isaiah." In *The New Bible Commentary,* pp. 556-62.

Freeman, Hobart E. *An Introduction to the Old Testament Prophets,* pp. 11-132; 191-214.

Payne, J. Barton. *Encyclopedia of Biblical Prophecy,* pp. 278-320.

Robinson, George L. "Isaiah." In *The International Standard Bible Encyclopedia,* 3: 1495-1508.

Schultz, Samuel J. *The Old Testament Speaks,* pp. 299-321.

Young, Edward J. *Introduction to the Old Testament,* pp. 197-222.

―――. *Isaiah Fifty-Three.*

―――. *Studies in Isaiah.*

―――. *Who Wrote Isaiah?*

COMMENTARIES

Alexander, J. A. *Commentary on Isaiah.*

Archer, Gleason L. "Isaiah." In *The Wycliffe Bible Commentary.*

Delitzsch, Franz. *Commentary on Isaiah.*

Jennings, F. C. *Studies in Isaiah.*

Kissane, E. J. *The Book of Isaiah.*

Skinner, J. *The Book of the Prophet Isaiah.*

Young, Edward J. *The Book of Isaiah.*

---

12. For example, consult Edward J. Young, *Who Wrote Isaiah?*

21

Jeremiah: Book of Judgment

About sixty years after Isaiah's death, God called Jeremiah, a young man of about twenty-one, to the difficult but urgent task of proclaiming His word to Judah on the eve of national disaster.

I. Preparation for Study

1. Review your studies of chapter 20 concerning Old Testament prophecy in general. Refer to Chart 78 and observe when Jeremiah prophesied as compared with Isaiah and other prophets.

2. Read 2 Kings 24:1—25:30. This passage reports the fall of Jerusalem, which is the tragic event of Jeremiah's prophecy.

II. The Man Jeremiah

A. HIS NAME

The name Jeremiah translates the Hebrew word *yirmeyahu,* to which has been assigned the literal meaning "Jehovah throws." On the basis of this, various translations have been made, such as "Jehovah establishes," "Jehovah exalts," "Jehovah is high," and "whom Jehovah appoints." Any of these names would have been appropriate for the prophet called to such a ministry as his.

B. HIS RANK AMONG THE PROPHETS

Someone has said of Jeremiah, "Amid all the bright stars of Old Testament history there is not a name that shines brighter than that of Jeremiah." By divine design it was Jeremiah who was called to prophesy in the darkest hours of Judah, when Judah as a nation died. He is known as the "weeping prophet" and "the prophet of the broken heart." But he wept not for his own trials, grievous as they were. It was the sins of his nation and the fearful destruction these sins were bringing upon them that broke Jeremiah's heart. Jeremiah lived in a day when tragic events were unfolding, and he, as perhaps no one else at the time, comprehended their full significance. He knew that within a short time the proud, beautiful city of Jerusalem with its magnificent Temple would be in ruins, and that his beloved people would be in captivity. He also knew that the nation which had been God's own peculiar treasure would be set aside for a time because of incorrigibility, and that supremacy would be given to the Gentiles. No wonder Jeremiah wept.

Of all the writing prophets, Jeremiah and Isaiah stand out preeminently. To place one above the other is perhaps arbitrary, for in many ways their ministries were different, and therefore difficult to compare. Their personalities differed, Isaiah being the bold and fearless type, Jeremiah the gentle and compassionate type. Isaiah lived more than one hundred years before the captivity of Judah; Jeremiah ministered just before and during the final catastrophe. (See Chart 45.) Isaiah had *foretold* the judgments which were coming unless the nation turned to God; Jeremiah's particular mission to Judah, toward the end of his career, was to notify the nation that their judgment *was at hand,* that God had rejected them (at least for the present), and that nothing now could save them from the punishment they so fairly deserved.

Chart 82 shows other prophets who ministered during Jeremiah's time. You may want to refer to a Bible dictionary for a brief description of each of these as background to your study of Jeremiah. The prophets are: Nahum, Zephaniah, Habakkuk, Daniel, and Ezekiel. They were all faithful spokesmen for God; Jeremiah was prince among them.

C. TIMES IN WHICH HE LIVED

When one reads the history of the times in which Jeremiah lived (2 Kings 22-25), he does not wonder that God would no longer bear with His people. Through Isaiah, God had said all He could say to keep them back from ruin, but they would not hearken. So when Isaiah's voice was still, there was virtual silence on God's part for about sixty years. Look at Chart 45 and observe the absence of a prophet during the reign of King Manasseh.

Scarcely had Isaiah and good King Hezekiah died when idolatry and numberless heathen abominations began to flourish in the land under the reign of Manasseh, one of the worst of Judah's kings. One of Manasseh's gravest sins was to desecrate the court of the Temple by building altars to Baal, and to set up a graven image in the holy house where God had set His name (read 2 Kings 21).

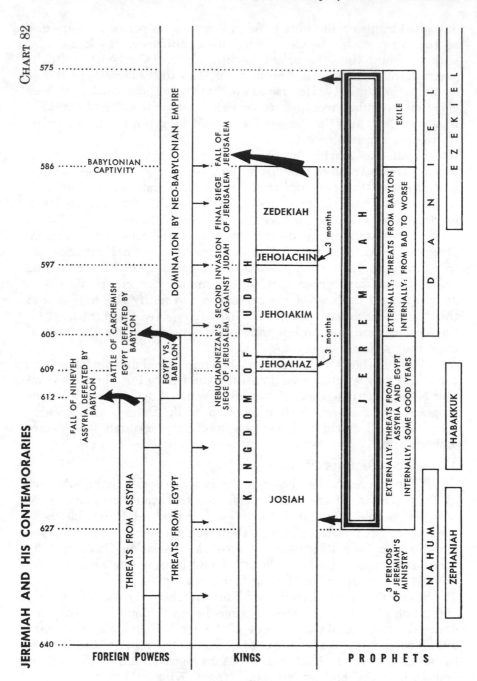

CHART 82

JEREMIAH AND HIS CONTEMPORARIES

FOREIGN POWERS   KINGS   PROPHETS

The moral condition of Judah in the days of Jeremiah is pungently described by the prophet in 5:31: "The prophets prophesy falsely, and the priests rule on their own authority; and My people love it so!" For fifty years blasphemous insults to God were heaped up by king, priest, and people, until the climax was reached, and Judah's doom was irrevocably sealed. Although the judgment was postponed for a while because of the tender heart and righteous life of King Josiah, twenty-five years after his death the kingdom of Judah was a thing of the past.

Into this political and moral turmoil, God sent Jeremiah to be His spokesman. Much of Jeremiah's ministry concerned the international situation in which Judah was intimately and precariously involved. Look at Map T and observe that Canaan was the geographical link between Egypt in the southwest and Syria, Assyria, Babylon, and other nations in the north. Each nation sought to be *the* world power. Control of Canaan was a must for such a claim.

D. HIS CONTEMPORARIES

Study Chart 82 for orientation to the historical setting of Jeremiah. Observe the three groups of contemporaries:

1. Contemporary prophets. These have been referred to above.

2. Contemporary kings. These are the kings who were reigning over Judah while Jeremiah prophesied. Only Josiah was a good king. Jehoahaz and Jehoiachin reigned for only a brief time. Josiah, Jehoiakim, and Zedekiah are the kings who played a major role in Jeremiah's career. Sections of the book of Jeremiah referring to these reigns are:

Josiah: 2:1—12:17
Jehoiakim: 13:1—20:18; 25:1—27:11
Zedekiah: 21:1—24:10; 27:12—39:18

3. Contemporary foreign powers. Observe that in the early part of Jeremiah's ministry, Judah was threatened mainly by Egypt and Assyria. Judah was continually tempted to make alliance with one power so as to be protected from the other. Jeremiah's consistent message was to get right with God and trust *Him* for protection from any nation.

In the latter part of Jeremiah's career, the threats were from Babylon. Two events had brought about the change of threat: (1) the Assyrians were defeated by the Babylonians in 612 B.C. with the fall of Nineveh; (2) the Egyptians were defeated by the Babylonians in 605 B.C. at the Battle of Carchemish. Judah resisted Babylon; but Jeremiah, by direction from God, urged Judah to give in to Babylon

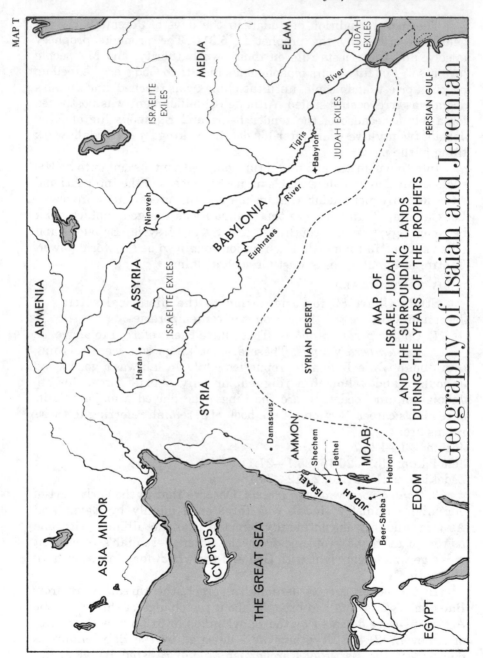

Geography of Isaiah and Jeremiah

MAP OF
ISRAEL, JUDAH,
AND THE SURROUNDING LANDS
DURING THE YEARS OF THE PROPHETS

so as to avoid *utter destruction,* since the divine judgment of captivity was inevitable.

The various prophecies of Jeremiah, spoken at different times in his ministry, are more understandable when this international setting is kept in mind.

E. HIS CHARACTER

Jeremiah's personality did not seem to match the severe task for which he was commissioned. Jeremiah, in the words of one writer, was

> afraid of people's "faces," one whom we should consider singularly unfitted for the work placed upon him. That he tenaciously clung to his assigned task through the succeeding years of rejection and persecution is a tribute both to the mettle of the man and to the grace of God, without which his personality surely would have gone to pieces.[1]

Though Jeremiah was timid by nature, he was given a bold message to proclaim—and he proclaimed it. Though he was very sensitive, his task was to pronounce drastic and extreme judgment. He was sympathetic and loyal to his fellowmen, but these qualities did not surpass his loyalty to God and his love for God's righteousness.

Jeremiah had a keen awareness that God was real; his faith was dauntless; he believed in prayer; he was willing to suffer for God's sake. The prophet was by nature gentle and meek, patient and brave, candid and passionate. His honesty would not let him be bribed; his deep emotions would not give place to a stony resignation to judgment. He was utterly devoted to one task, that of preaching the message of God. As someone has put it, he was the "bravest, grandest man of Old Testament history."

F. HIS LIFE AND MINISTRY

Jeremiah was born when the very wicked King Manasseh was still ruling Judah. He was raised in a small town called Anathoth, located just a few miles north of Jerusalem. His father was a priest, Hilkiah by name. Following in the footsteps of his father, Jeremiah entered the priesthood at an early age. When he was still a young man, probably around twenty-one, God made known to him that he had been divinely ordained to be a prophet, and that his duties as priest were terminated (Jer 1).

---

1. John Graybill, "Jeremiah," in *The Wycliffe Bible Commentary,* p. 656.

Jeremiah immediately embarked on his new course and for about fifty years stood as the representative and spokesman for God. Kings, rulers, priests, and politicians, as well as the false prophets, vehemently opposed the policy which he recommended to the nation.

Jeremiah has recorded some of the trying experiences he endured when he was ridiculed, ignored, beaten, misrepresented, starved, mocked, threatened, and cursed by all classes of people, even by those whom he had considered to be his friends. (Read 11:18-23; 12:6; 18:11-18; 26:1-15; 32:1-3; 38:6-13, 28.)

Jeremiah's life as a prophet was one long, sad, stormy day. Often he grew discouraged and was almost ready to give up the battle, but the fire of the Spirit in his bones kept him true to God (read 20:9). James Gray describes the fiery trials:

> God placed him between two "cannots" or, if you please, between two fires. There was the fire of persecution without, and that of the Holy Spirit within, the latter being the hotter of the two. To avoid being consumed by the one, he was more than willing to walk through the other. "I cannot speak any more in God's name," he says at one time, and follows it by adding, "I cannot refrain from speaking."[2]

Jeremiah's personal life was very lonely. As noted above, even his friends and relatives plotted to kill him. He was instructed of God not to marry and raise a family (16:1-4). But he had one companion at his side throughout most of his career: Baruch. Baruch served as Jeremiah's secretary, playing an important part in the story of the scrolls of the prophet's messages (36:4-8). Chapter 45 is devoted wholly to a message from God to him. Baruch remained close to Jeremiah throughout all the stormy years, and the two went into exile together.

Part of Jeremiah's task was to convince the people and rulers of Judah that Babylon, the nation from the "north" (4:6), was the divinely destined master of Judah for the near future, and that Judah's flirting relations with other nations would add to the horror of the doom to come. But his appeals were rejected. In 588 B.C., the Babylonian conqueror, Nebuchadnezzar, did come, the siege of Jerusalem began, and about thirty months later (586 B.C.) the city and its Temple were utterly destroyed.

The Bible gives no details of Jeremiah's death. One tradition says that he was stoned to death in Egypt by the very Jews he tried so hard to save.

---

2. James M. Gray, *Synthetic Bible Studies*, p. 148.

III. THE BOOK OF JEREMIAH

Jeremiah did not write this book overnight, nor even over a short period of time. Many years and many experiences were the setting of its composition.

Though the theme of divine judgment for sin runs throughout the book of Jeremiah, the organization of the book's materials is not always clear. From the record itself we learn that Jeremiah wrote the different parts, including biography, history, doctrine, and prediction, at various times and under diverse circumstances. When all the parts were brought together on one scroll as one book, a general pattern of composition was followed, placing the discourses in the first half of the book and reserving the latter half mainly for narrative. Jeremiah appropriately used the story of his call and commission as the introduction of the book, and supplements were added at the end of the book. Here is the general pattern of the entire book:

1	2	21	34	45	52
INTRO. CALL	DISCOURSES	SPECIAL PROPHECIES	NARRATIVE	SUPPLEMENTS	

By its very nature, such a pattern does not call for a strict chronological sequence. It is very clear that Jeremiah's approach was primarily topical, not chronological.[3] At the same time, it may also be said that there is a *general* chronological progression in the order of Jeremiah's discourses. Refer to Chart 84 and note the order of kings: Josiah, Jehoiakim, Zedekiah.

There is an underlying topical progression in the book of Jeremiah. The climax is the fall of Jerusalem, which is recorded at two places toward the end of the book. All that goes before, which includes mainly Jeremiah's discourses and personal experiences, points to that hour of tragedy.

The prophecy of Jeremiah is basically composed of discourses (or oracles), with narrative portions interspersed throughout. They appear in the pattern of the following sequence: chapters 1 through 20, mainly prophetic oracles; 21 through 33, an interweaving of discourse and narrative; 34 through 45, mainly narrative; 46 through 52,

---

3. That historical chronology is not observed in the book can be seen by the references to the kings. The order of the kings of this period is, as we know, Josiah, Jehoahaz, Jehoiakim, Jehoiachin, and Zedekiah. (See 1:1-3. Also refer to Chart 82.) For example, observe that 21:1 sets the time of that discourse when Zedekiah was reigning; 25:1 goes back to the fourth year of Jehoiakim; 26:1 and 27:1 to the beginning of the reign of this king; 28:1 refers again to the time of Zedekiah. One must keep this in mind when reading this book.

mainly oracles. The oracles spoken to men or nations are usually introduced with the authoritative "Thus saith the LORD" or its equiva-lent, and are composed in a style that reflects Hebrew poetry.[4]

IV. SURVEY

1. The first thing to do for this "skyscraper view" is to make a brief scanning of the entire book, chapter by chapter, observing what the general contents of each chapter are. Record a list of chapter titles on paper.

2. Do you see any *groupings* of chapters with similar content? Compare your findings with these groups:

Chapters	*Content*
2-20:	Series of prophecies of doom
21-29:	Nebuchadnezzar appears throughout this section
30-33:	The bright prophecies concerning the new covenant
34-39:	Account of the siege and fall of Jerusalem
40-44:	After the fall of Jerusalem
46-51:	Prophecies concerning the foreign nations

Note that most of the book of Jeremiah is represented by the above groups. You will want to go back to some of the chapters and look at them more closely.

3. Study the survey Chart 84. Refer to it as you continue the studies suggested below.

4. The main body of the prophecy is made up of chapters 1-44. Chapters 45-52 comprise three supplements.

5. The main body is divided into two parts: Book 1 and Book 2. The division is made at chapter 21, because (1) at this point historical narrative begins to play an important part in the prophecy; and (2) these chapters refer mostly to the time of King Zedekiah, whereas the previous chapters referred to the reigns of Josiah and Jehoiakim.

6. There are three groupings of discourses in which Jeremiah denounced sin, urged repentance, and warned of judgment to come:
Public Sermons (chaps. 2-10)
Personal Experiences (chaps. 11-20)
Certainty of Captivity (chaps. 21-29)
Read these chapters again to justify the outline.

7. The brightest section of the book is that of chapters 30-33, known as the "Book of Consolation." (Read the chapters.) Here

---

4. E.g., see the poetic format in *The Westminster Study Edition of the Holy Bible;* in Harold Lindsell, ed., *Harper Study Bible;* and in Edward Naegelsbach, "Jeremiah," in Lange's *Commentary on the Holy Scriptures.*

Jeremiah looks beyond the years of captivity and sees a restoration; and he looks beyond the age of the old covenant and sees the new (cf. 31:31). It is noteworthy that this bright prophecy appears in the text just before Jeremiah narrates the siege and fall of Jerusalem. Compare this with the location of *songs* throughout the book of Revelation just before the descriptions of judgments.

8. Chapters 34-44 are mainly narrative, recording the key event of the book—the fall of Jerusalem—and the events preceding and following it. (Read the chapters.) In chapters 40-44, two interesting observations may be made: (1) Jeremiah was just as faithful to God and to the Jews after the judgment fell as he was before; and (2) the Jews remained just as stubborn and impenitent as ever.

9. Observe the contents of each of the three supplements. Why would each of these be placed at the end of the book? Concerning the oracles against the foreign nations, it should be observed that God judges all nations alike on the issue of sin. For example, though God used Babylon as His agent of punishment against the Jews, Babylon was not spared judgment for its own sin (read 50:14).

V. Prominent Subjects

A. JEREMIAH'S CALL (1:4-19)

Jeremiah must have received his call to the prophetic office when he was a mere youth. His call was much more commonplace than that of Isaiah (cf. Isa 6). Jeremiah saw no dazzling vision, no throne or seraphim. Quietly the Lord spoke to his heart, setting before him his difficult task, and promising to be with him through every experience.

Read Jeremiah 1:4-10, and notice the following points regarding his call:
1. It was prenatal (vv. 4-5).
2. He shrank from the work because of his youth and inexperience (v.6).
3. He was not excused from service (v.7).
4. God assured him of divine guardianship (v.8).
5. He received the personal touch of God and His divine message (v.9).

Jeremiah's call clearly teaches that the main task of a prophet was to *speak for God*. It was God who would bring down judgment upon the people of Judah for their sin; and it was God who would spare a remnant. But God wanted a man to warn Judah of those judgments, and to console the faithful few for their faith.

God did not search in vain for such a man. He was on hand, by predetermined design, serving among the priests of Anathoth. Now the hour for his call had arrived, and God sent the word that moved him to the office of prophet. When Jeremiah accepted the commission, he was thrust forth with an indelible impression of sovereign appointment, sovereign message, and sovereign protection.

B. TWOFOLD MESSAGE

Jeremiah's message was twofold: destruction and construction. (Note the words "destroy" and "build" in 1:10.) When identified more specifically, there are four parts to his message, as shown on Chart 83.

JEREMIAH'S MESSAGE   CHART 83

	Four Themes	Emphasis	Time element
DESTRUCTION	1. Rebuke	People's sin	Present condition (cf. 2:1-37)
	2. Warning	God's righteousness	Future predicted (cf. 20:4; chaps. 23—26, 31)
CONSTRUCTION	3. Invitation	God's grace	Present offer (cf. 3:1—4:4)
	4. Consolation	People's hope	Future predicted (cf. 23:1-40; 30:4-11; 32:37-41; 33:14-26)

Jeremiah's ministry concentrated on the first two themes noted on the chart. However, the prophet did not only preach judgment. Often he voiced God's invitation to return to Him: "'Return, faithless Israel,' declares the LORD; 'I will not look upon you in anger'" (3:12). That was his message of conditional, immediate restoration. He also spoke of the more distant future, prophesying preservation of a remnant, the initiating of a new covenant, and the coming of a Saviour. Though he did not prophesy as much as Isaiah did on this subject, his prophecies were just as strong and clear. (Read such passages as 23:5-6; 31:31-34; 32:37-41.)

C. CONFESSIONS

The book of Jeremiah contains much that is autobiographical and confessional. This is unlike the book of Isaiah, which contains comparatively little of the life of its author. Read Jeremiah's confession of sin in 10:23-24; 11:18—12:6; 15:10-18; 17:9-11, 14-18; 18:18-23; 20:7-18.

D. SYMBOLS

Many symbols appear in the book of Jeremiah. The main ones involve actual experiences of Jeremiah, where God was teaching him, and thus Judah, some vital spiritual truths. Here are some of the prominent ones. (Read the passages.)
1. the linen girdle (waistband) (13:1-11)
2. the potter and the clay (18:1-8)
3. the shattered vessel (19:1-13)
4. celibacy of Jeremiah (16:1-9)
5. field of Anathoth (32:6-44)

E. END TIMES

Jeremiah, like his predecessor Isaiah, foretold the sure restoration of God's people to their land. But passages like Jeremiah 30:3; 31:8-30, 31-37; 32:36-44; 33:6-18 indicate that the return from Babylon at the end of the seventy years was not considered as a complete fulfillment of these prophecies. (Read the passages cited.) The prophet had a greater restoration in view, a fuller and more complete fulfillment of the prophecies. In the above passages, both Israel and Judah are mentioned as returning. The gathering is spoken of as being not only from Babylon, but from all nations of the earth. Also, references to the new covenant, great prosperity and blessing, and deep penitence and obedience of the people, speak of a still future time.

What is the basis for such a bright hope for God's people in the end times? The question is answered in various Scriptures, one of them being the words of God Himself recorded in the book of Jeremiah:

> I have loved you with an everlasting love;
> Therefore I have drawn you with lovingkindness.
> Again I will build you, and you shall be rebuilt,
> O virgin of Israel! (31:3-4)

Israel has a future, spoken of by Paul in Romans 11, only because of the unchangeable, unfathomable, eternal love of God.

VI. KEY WORDS AND VERSES

A very prominent key word of Jeremiah is "return," appearing forty-seven times in the book. See Chart 84 for other key words and suggested key verses.

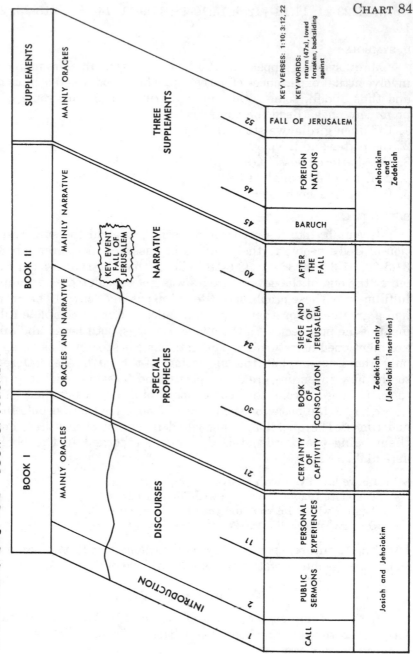

CHART 84

KEY VERSES: 1:10; 3:12, 22

KEY WORDS: return (47x), loved forsaken, backsliding against

JEREMIAH BOOK OF JUDGMENT

BOOK I		BOOK II		SUPPLEMENTS
MAINLY ORACLES	ORACLES AND NARRATIVE	MAINLY NARRATIVE		MAINLY ORACLES

DISCOURSES	SPECIAL PROPHECIES	NARRATIVE	THREE SUPPLEMENTS

KEY EVENT FALL OF JERUSALEM

INTRODUCTION		CERTAINTY OF CAPTIVITY	BOOK OF CONSOLATION	SIEGE AND FALL OF JERUSALEM	AFTER THE FALL	BARUCH	FOREIGN NATIONS	FALL OF JERUSALEM
CALL	PUBLIC SERMONS	PERSONAL EXPERIENCES						

1   2   11   21   30   34   40   45   46   52

Josiah and Jehoiakim	Zedekiah mainly (Jehoiakim insertions)	Jehoiakim and Zedekiah

VII. Applications

The sixth-century B.C. book of Jeremiah is important for the twentieth-century world because the similarities between Jeremiah's day and today could hardly be stronger. As in Jeremiah's day, this is a time of deep sin; apostasy and hypocrisy abound; the balance of power among nations totters precariously, and alliances change with apparent recklessness from decade to decade; God's heralds are in a lonely minority; and the rumblings of doomsday, like an approaching avalanche, get louder by the minute. Very evident in Jeremiah's message is the fact that the destinies of peoples and nations are not fulfilled outside the hand of God. During these last days of the Church on earth, the Christian will find in this ancient book a timely message and many answers to questions about God's ways in the world today and tomorrow. After you have finished your survey of the book, write a list of present-day applications.

VIII. Further Study

Use outside sources for help in these two suggested projects:

1. Make biographical studies of these kings whose reigns involved the ministry of Jeremiah: Josiah, Jehoahaz (Shallum), Jehoiakim, Jehoiachin (Jeconiah or Coniah), and Zedekiah.[5] (Read 2 Kings 22-25; 2 Chron 34-36.)

2. Study the chronological structure of the book of Jeremiah.[6]

IX. Selected Reading

GENERAL INTRODUCTION

Cawley, F. "Jeremiah." In *The New Bible Commentary.*

Freeman, Hobart E. *An Introduction to the Old Testament Prophets,* pp. 237-50.

Jensen, Irving L. *Jeremiah and Lamentations.* Everyman's Bible Commentary, pp. 5-15; 117-25.

Payne, J. Barton. *Encyclopedia of Biblical Prophecy,* pp. 320-47.

Schultz, Samuel J. *The Old Testament Speaks,* pp. 322-43.

Young, Edward J. *Introduction to the Old Testament,* pp. 223-33.

COMMENTARIES

Ball, C. J., and Bennett, W. H. *The Book of Jeremiah.*

Graybill, John F. "Jeremiah." In *The Wycliffe Bible Commentary.*

Hyatt, J. Philip. *Jeremiah, Prophet of Courage and Hope.*

---

5. See Irving L. Jensen, *Jeremiah and Lamentations,* in Everyman's Bible Commentary, p. 122.

6. Ibid., pp. 117-19.

Jensen, Irving L. *Jeremiah and Lamentations.* Everyman's Bible Commentary.
Latsch, Theodore. *Jeremiah.*
Leslie, Elmer A. *Jeremiah.*
Morgan, G. Campbell, *Studies in the Prophecy of Jeremiah.*
Peake, A. S. *Jeremiah and Lamentations.*
Smith, George Adam. *Jeremiah.*

22

Lamentations: Mourning over Affliction

The fall of Jerusalem in 586 B.C. is the historical event common to the books of Jeremiah and Lamentations. Jeremiah prophesies and anticipates the fall, and Lamentations looks back at the holocaust in utter distress.

Knowing from his prophecies how Jeremiah wept over his people before judgment fell, it is not difficult for us to imagine the depths to which his soul sank in utter grief as he watched the holy city burning and his people being ravished. Lamentations reveals something of the pathos of that experience.

I. PREPARATION FOR STUDY

Read the two passages of Jeremiah concerning the fall of Jerusalem: chapters 34-39 and 52. Recall your survey of those chapters in their context.

351

II. Background

A. TITLE

Two of the most common titles assigned to this book in Hebrew Bibles are:

1. Ekhah. Translated "Ah, how," or "Alas," this is the opening word of chapters 1, 2, and 4. Note how the word is translated in your English Bible at these places.

2. Qinoth. Translated "Lamentations," or "Elegies," this is a title representing the content of the book and the melancholy meter of its five poems. The *Qinoth* title was retained in the Greek Bibles, with the Greek translation *Threnoi* ("lamentations," from *threomai,* "to cry aloud"). This was carried over into the Latin Bibles as *Liber Threnorum* ("Book of Lamentations"), and thence into the English Bibles as *Lamentations.*

B. PLACE IN THE BIBLE

In the threefold Hebrew Bible (Law, Prophets, Writings), Lamentations appears in the last part, in a section called *Megilloth.* Recall that the *Megilloth* is a group of five Old Testament books which the Jews read publicly on national holidays. Lamentations is read on the ninth day of Ab (about mid-July), the anniversary of the destructions of Jerusalem in 586 B.C. and A.D. 70.

In some ancient versions of the Bible, Lamentations appeared as an appendix to Jeremiah, and often was not included in the listing of the Old Testament books.

In our English Bible, Lamentations very appropriately follows the book of Jeremiah. The translators of the Greek Septuagint (100 B.C.), recognizing its Jeremianic authorship, also placed it here.

C. AUTHOR AND DATE

Lamentations was very likely written soon after 586 B.C., while memories of the appalling siege of Jerusalem were still fresh. Some think that the author wrote chapter 5 a little later than the first four chapters, "when the intense anguish of the catastrophe had given way to the prolonged ache of captivity."[1]

As to authorship, the evidence points strongly, though not conclusively, to Jeremiah.[2] Such evidence includes the following:

---

1. D. A. Hubbard, "Book of Lamentations," in *The New Bible Dictionary,* p. 707. If Jeremiah was the author, it would be better to describe his experience as "exile" (in Egypt), rather than "captivity." (Cf. Jer 43.)

2. Such people as Baruch are suggested as the author. Arguments for and against Jeremianic authorship are extensively developed in Lange's commentary on Lamentations, pp. 6-16 and 19-35.

1. The Septuagint introduction to the book: "Jeremiah sat weeping and lamented with this lamentation over Jerusalem, and said."
2. Hebrew and Gentile tradition.
3. Similarities between Lamentations and poetical portions of Jeremiah (cf. also 2 Chron 35:25).[3]
4. The writer was an eyewitness of Jerusalem's destruction, with a sensitivity of soul (cf. Jer 9:1; 14:17-22), and ability to write.

D. COMPOSITION AND STYLE

Lamentations is a set of five elegies (melancholy poems), the first four of which follow an acrostic pattern (first letter of lines, or groups of lines, representing each of the twenty-two letters of the Hebrew alphabet).

The poetic meter is described as a limping meter, with three beats in the first line trailing away in a mourning two-beat line. When publicly read, the chanting of the Hebrew text gave support to the mood of the words.

Many poetic styles and devices appear in these poems. Vivid imagery is perhaps the most prominent one.

One of the distinctive features of the book is the acrostic format of chapters 1-4.[4] In chapters 1, 2, and 4, each verse begins with a word whose first letter is successively one of the twenty-two letters of the Hebrew alphabet. Chapter 3 has sixty-six verses, each successive letter of the alphabet having three verses allotted to it instead of one.

Various views are held as to why the author used this acrostic device. Among them are: (1) as an aid to memorization; (2) as a symbol of the *fullness* of the people's grief (i.e., from A to Z); (3) to confine the expression of boundless grief by the limiting device of acrostic.

E. MESSAGE

The message of Lamentations is threefold:

1. Mourning over Jerusalem's judgment for sin. Most of the book presents this. Compare Jesus' mourning over Jerusalem in Luke 13:34-35 and 19:41-44.

2. Confession of sin (e.g., 1:8; 3:59; 5:16).

3. Ray of hope (e.g., 3:21-32; 5:21). Only one who saw into the far-distant future could speak of hope. Babylon was the conqueror now, and Jerusalem the vanquished; in that future day, it would be glory for Jerusalem and desolation for Babylon. With such a hope, the author could exclaim, "Great is Thy faithfulness" (3:23*b*).

---

3. See Edward J. Young, *Introduction to the Old Testament,* pp. 333-36.
4. Psalm 119 is a classic example of acrostic writing.

III. SURVEY

Scan the book of Lamentations, chapter by chapter. Check your own observations with the following:

1. The book has five chapters, each of which is a separate poem.

2. Sometimes Jeremiah speaks for himself ("I"); sometimes the Jewish captives (including Jeremiah) speak ("We"); and sometimes Jeremiah writes about his brethren ("They").

3. The prevailing tone is utter grief and resignation. At a few places a ray of hope shines through. Such hope is brightest in the middle of chapter 3.

4. There is much imagery in the book. (E.g., "From on high He sent fire into my bones," 1:13.)

5. Short prayers to God appear from time to time. The entire last chapter is a prayer.

6. Jeremiah continually acknowledges God's holiness, justice, and sovereignty in the judgments which He has sent upon Judah.

7. References to the people's sins appear from time to time in the book.

8. The book ends on a note of hope (5:19-22).[5]

9. Study carefully the survey Chart 85. Relate it to the survey you have already made of the book. Note the following on the chart, rereading the Bible text to justify any outlines which do not seem clear:

a) The first four chapters are dirges, written in acrostic style. Chapter 5 is basically a prayer; and it is nonacrostic.

b) The middle chapter (3) is the brightest. Various references to the Lord's mercies are made here.

c) There is a natural progression of thought throughout the chapters. In chapter 1, the prophet and people are weeping over Jerusalem's destruction; in chapter 2, God's judgments, as the cause of the grief, are described; chapter 3 shows where hope is to be found; in chapter 4, sin is acknowledged as the cause of divine judgment; and in chapter 5, the prophet prays in behalf of his brethren as he pleads for God's deliverance.

d) Each of chapters 1-3 ends with a prayer. Although this is not so of chapter 4, all of the succeeding chapter (5) is a prayer.

---

5. Though the last verse reads despairingly, an alternate reading supports the optimism of verse 21. The *Revised Standard Version,* along with other translations, prefers to read the text as a question: "Or hast thou utterly rejected us? Art thou exceedingly angry with us?" (5:22). It is interesting to note that today, when Jews read publicly the text of Lamentations, they read verse 22 before verse 21, so that the concluding note is not despairing. They do the same for the last verse of Malachi.

IV. KEY WORDS AND VERSES

Note the key words on Chart 85. Also read the Bible text of the key verses cited.

V. APPLICATIONS

Ross Price comments on how contemporary the book of Lamentatins is:

> In these days of personal, national, and international crises (and disaster) the message of this book is a challenge to repent of sins personal, national, and international, and to commit ourselves afresh to God's steadfast love. Though this love is everpresent and outgoing, a holy and just God must surely judge unrepentant sinners.[6]

When Christ is seen in the book of Lamentations, the Christian can apply its truths in different ways. The many references to the Lord ("Jehovah") in the book of Lamentations may be applied today to the ministry of Jesus Christ. This is because the works of God the Father are one with the works of His Son. For example, when we read, "It is of the LORD's mercies [loving-kindnesses] that we are not consumed" (3:22, KJV), we may rightly say, "It is of Christ's mercies that we are not consumed" (cf. Jude 21).

There are some descriptions of Israel in Lamentations which, while not intended to be predictive of Christ's ministry, do represent, picturewise, different aspects of that ministry.[7] Among these are Christ as

1. the afflicted of the Lord (1:12)
2. despised of His enemies (2:15-16)
3. derision to all the people (3:14)
4. the smitten and insulted One (3:30)
5. the weeping Prophet (cf. Matt 23:37-38).

The applications of such illustrations are clear.

VI. SELECTED READING

GENERAL INTRODUCTION

Baxter, J. Sidlow. *Explore the Book,* 3:277-87.

---

6. Ross Price, "Lamentations," in *The Wycliffe Bible Commentary,* p. 696. The religious calendars of the Jewish and Catholic faiths assign the reading of the book once a year. For the latter, it is read on the last three days of Holy Week.

7. Care should be exercised in this area of application. In the words of Norman Geisler, "Any Old Testament passage may be appropriately applied to Christ, even though the New Testament writers did not apply it, providing that it exemplifies something from the life of the Messianic people which finds an actual correspondence with the truth about Christ presented somewhere in the Bible" *(Christ: The Theme of the Bible,* p. 65).

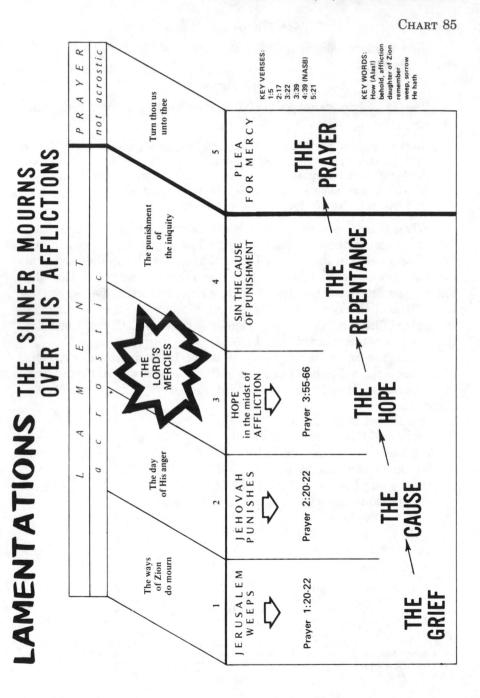

LAMENTATIONS THE SINNER MOURNS OVER HIS AFFLICTIONS

	L A M E N T				*P R A Y E R*
	a c r o s t i c				*not acrostic*
	The ways of Zion do mourn	The day of His anger	HOPE in the midst of AFFLICTION	The punishment of the iniquity	Turn thou us unto thee
	1	2	3	4	5
	JERUSALEM WEEPS	JEHOVAH PUNISHES		SIN THE CAUSE OF PUNISHMENT	PLEA FOR MERCY
	Prayer 1:20-22	Prayer 2:20-22	Prayer 3:55-66		
	THE GRIEF	THE CAUSE	THE HOPE	THE REPENTANCE	THE PRAYER

THE LORD'S MERCIES

KEY VERSES:
1:5
2:17
3:22
3:39
4:39 (NASB)
5:21

KEY WORDS:
How (Alas!)
behold, affliction
daughter of Zion
remember
weep, sorrow
He hath

Harrison, Roland K. "Lamentations." In *The Zondervan Pictorial Bible Dictionary,* pp. 474-75.
Morgan, G. Campbell. *The Analyzed Bible,* pp. 234-41.
Unger, Merrill F. *Introductory Guide to the Old Testament,* pp. 386-89.

COMMENTARIES

Hillers, Delbert R. *Lamentations.*
Naegelsbach, C. W. Edward. "Lamentations." In Lange's *Commentary on the Holy Scriptures.*
Price, Ross. "Lamentations." In *The Wycliffe Bible Commentary.*
Stephens-Hodge, L. E. H. "Lamentations." In *The New Bible Commentary.*

23

Ezekiel: The Glory of the Lord

When God sent His people into exile as punishment for their sin, He still continued to speak to them. For if He was to purge the nation of their corrupt idolatry, they needed to hear more of the very word which they had so stubbornly resisted. Among the Jews taken captive by King Nebuchadnezzar of Babylon in his second invasion of Judah in 597 B.C. was a man named Ezekiel. This was the one whom God chose to be His prophet to the exiles, while Daniel served as God's ambassador to the court of the captor king.

It was during the captivity years that some of the Jews returned to God. This was the beginning of the religion of Judaism, and because Ezekiel was the prominent prophet at this time, he has been called "the father of Judaism."

I. PREPARATION FOR STUDY

1. Keep in the back of your mind the highlights of the message and ministry of Jeremiah. Much of what Ezekiel preached was very similar to Jeremiah's preaching, which the former prophet must have listened to often in Jerusalem, up until his exile at age twenty-five.[1] But the differences were many and marked, as your survey of Ezekiel will show.

2. Study Chart 86 to familiarize yourself with the contemporaries of Ezekiel and the times in which he lived.

---

1. Jeremiah may have been as much as twenty years older than Ezekiel. Ezekiel and Daniel were about the same age. Concerning Ezekiel's familiarity with Jeremiah's message, it has been said that Ezekiel was "the prolongation of the voice of Jeremiah." The two prophets were brought into juxtaposition, especially in connection with Jeremiah's letter to the exiles, to whom Ezekiel was ministering. (Read Jer 29.)

EZEKIEL AND HIS CONTEMPORARIES

CHART 86

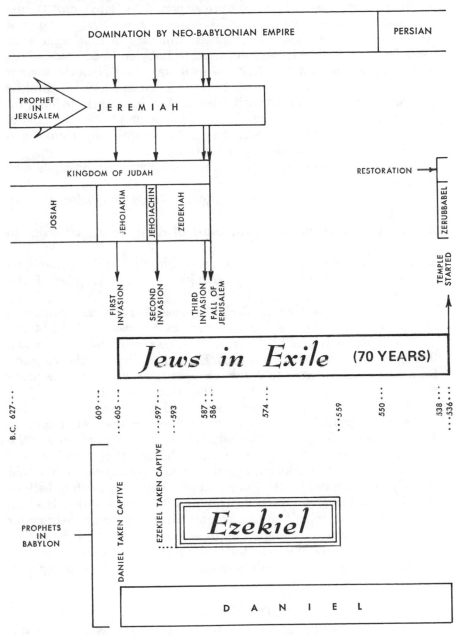

Observe on the chart that neither Daniel nor Ezekiel began their prophetic ministries until they were deported to Babylonia. Daniel was taken captive in 605 B.C., in Nebuchadnezzar's first invasion of Jerusalem, and he began his prophetic ministry in that same year (read Dan 1:1-7). Ezekiel was deported to Babylon in 597 B.C., along with King Jehoiachin and hosts of citizens, when Nebuchadnezzar invaded Jerusalem the second time (read 2 Kings 24:10-16). Ezekiel was not called to prophesy until after he had been in Babylonia for about five years. Thus, Jeremiah was the lone prophet in the land of Judah for the last twenty years before Jerusalem's fall; Daniel and Ezekiel served as prophets only in captivity.

The different ministries of the three contemporary prophets may be identified thus:

1. Jeremiah: prophet mainly to the Jews in Jerusalem, before the city fell.
2. Daniel: prophet mainly to the court of King Nebuchadnezzar, in Babylonia.
3. Ezekiel: prophet mainly to the exiles in Babylonia, before and after the fall of Jerusalem. Ezekiel was *the* prophet of the captivity.

It is interesting that in Ezekiel's book there is no mention of Jeremiah, whereas Daniel is mentioned three times (Ezek 14:14, 20; 28:3). Daniel, because of his favor at the king's court, was well known throughout Babylonia by the time Ezekiel arrived in the country. Daniel's prophecy refers to Jeremiah once (Dan 9:2), and the name Ezekiel does not appear in either of the other two books.

The idolatry which Ezekiel saw as Judah's blight before he left Jerusalem was the same condition he faced in the settlements of Jewish exiles in Babylonia. The judgment of captivity did not stir the first contingents of exiles to repentance. In fact, they found it very hard to believe, as Ezekiel was prophesying, that Jerusalem would actually be destroyed by the Babylonians. They were loath to believe that Jehovah had given world dominion to Babylon, and that His will was for Judah to submit to this enemy. Hence, it was necessary for Ezekiel in Babylon—and Jeremiah in Jerusalem—to show the people how unfounded were any expectations of immediate deliverance.

3. Acquaint yourself with Map U, which shows the geography of Ezekiel and Daniel.

II. THE MAN EZEKIEL

Very little is known of the personal history of Ezekiel. But

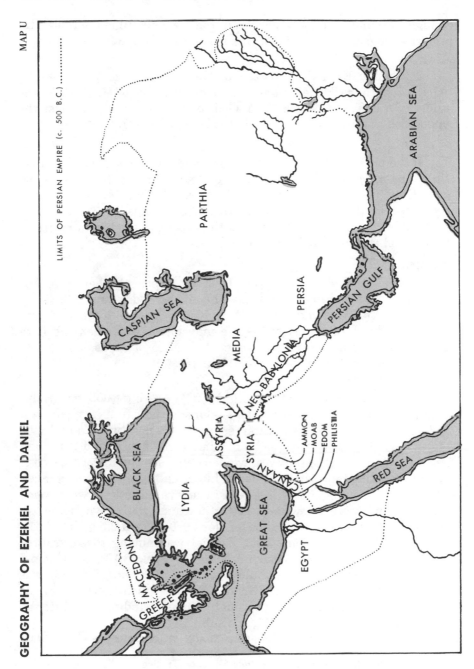

MAP U

GEOGRAPHY OF EZEKIEL AND DANIEL

LIMITS OF PERSIAN EMPIRE (c. 500 B.C.)

enough information may be garnered from various Bible references to project a biographical profile of this fascinating prophet.

A. NAME

The name Ezekiel is written in Hebrew as *Yehezqe'l,* meaning "God strengthens." The prophet was truly a tower of strength in the midst of a defeated people. Also, God made him strong to resist the opposition of hardhearted and rebellious Israelites (read 3:8-9).

B. BIRTH

If the phrase "thirtieth year" of 1:1 refers to Ezekiel's age at that time (593 B.C.), then he was born in 623 B.C., during the reign of the good King Josiah. Ezekiel was a child when the book of the Law was recovered in the course of renovating the Temple in 621 B.C. The years of his boyhood and youth were thus spent in the bright reformation period that followed that recovery.

C. FAMILY

Ezekiel, like Jeremiah, was born of a priestly heritage. His father's name was Buzi, a priest possibly of the Zadok line (1:3; 40:46; 44:15). Ezekiel was married, but it is not known if he had any children. The darkest day of his life may have been when the Lord announced to him two tragic events: the siege of Jerusalem (24:2), and the death of his beloved wife (24:15-18).

D. IN EXILE

When Ezekiel was about eighteen years old (605 B.C.), the Babylonians (also known as Chaldeans) made their first invasion into Judea, carrying away some captives, among whom was Daniel (see Map U). Eight years later (597 B.C.) they came again, and this time Ezekiel was among the captives, which comprised the upper classes of Judah. Read 2 Kings 24:10-17 for the historical record of this (cf. Ezek 1:2; 33:21). Some of the exiles were incarcerated; others were made slaves; many were allowed to settle down in their own homes in various settlements of the exiles (cf. Jer 29:1-7; Ezra 2:59; Neh 7:61). It was of divine providence that Ezekiel was among those granted such liberties. His home was in Tel-abib (Ezek 3:15), a principal colony of exiles near the fabulous city of Babylon. Tel-abib was located by the canal Chebar ("Grand Canal") which flowed from the Euphrates fork above Babylon through Nippur, winding back into the Euphrates near Erech.[2] (Cf. 1:1, 3; Psalm 137:1.)

Ezekiel's home was a meeting place where the Jewish elders

---

2. See Merrill F. Unger, *Unger's Bible Handbook,* p. 364.

often came to consult with him (8:1; 14:1; 20:1). It may be that his home was open to any of the exiles who wanted spiritual help.

E. CALL AND COMMISSION

Five years after his arrival in the strange land of Babylon, Ezekiel received his call to the prophetic office, to minister to the exiles in Babylonia.[3] What he experienced and heard in this call is recorded in the first three chapters of his book.

Twenty-two years later (see 29:17), when Ezekiel was around fifty-two years old, he was still prophesying to the exiles. It is not known how much longer his ministry continued.

F. CHARACTER

Ezekiel the prophet was strong and fearless. This is what God made him (3:8-9), and this was his dominant characteristic. He had boundless energy, and a love for the simple, clear and direct. Though his disposition was firm, he had a shepherd's heart for his countrymen. "Ezekiel is the one who, in the first place, breaking in pieces the hard hearts with the hammer of the law, represents the strict inexorable judge, but therefore, pouring soothing balm into the open wounds, approves himself as the healing physician."[4]

Ezekiel's book reveals that he was methodical, artistic, and mystic. With a deeply introspective nature, he must have studied the message of God a great deal as it applied to himself and his brethren. He was truly a practical theologian, and for this he has been called "the first dogmatist of the Old Testament" and "the prophet of personal responsibility."

G. MESSAGE

Ezekiel stressed three points in his preaching.

1. It was sin which brought the people's judgment of exile. The people must repent and return to God.

2. The exile would last for seventy years, even though false prophets were preaching an early return. The people had a letter from Jeremiah (Jer 29) which concurred with Ezekiel's preaching. The seventy-year captivity began in 605 B.C., with the first deportation of Jews (Jer 25:11-12; Zech 7:5). Before the Jews could return to Jerusalem, they must return to the Lord.

---

3. Ezekiel's activities during this five-year period are not chronicled for us, but we may assume that he ministered to his people's spiritual needs, and did much studying of the Law and other Scriptures. God was preparing the priest to be the prophet during these years.

4. The quote is from *Calwer Handbuch*, as cited by F. W. J. Schroder, "Ezekiel" in Lange's *Commentary on the Holy Scriptures*, p.2.

3. There would be a future restoration of Israel, for a believing remnant. The general impression of these consolatory messages was that this restoration was in the far-distant future. Most of the adults of Ezekiel's audience had no other hope than this, for seventy years of captivity precluded their returning to Jerusalem in their lifetime.

The tone of Ezekiel's preaching was austere and impressive, for the prophet constantly stressed the Lord's sovereignty and glory. The phrase "glory of the LORD" or its equivalent appears eleven times in the first eleven chapters of his book. The statement of God, "They shall know that I am the LORD," or its equivalent, appears about seventy times in the book.

A comparison of the main themes of the four "greater prophets" is shown here:
Isaiah: salvation of the Lord
Jeremiah: judgment of the Lord
Daniel: kingdom of the Lord
Ezekiel: sovereignty and glory of the Lord

III. THE BOOK OF EZEKIEL

A. STYLE

While it is true that most of the book of Ezekiel consists of the direct addresses of the Lord,[5] the form and style in which those words were recorded is attributable to the writer Ezekiel. Ezekiel's style is very lofty. He has brought prose and poetry together in one masterpiece. The book abounds with visions, parables, allegories, apocalyptic imagery, and various symbolic acts. Jerome called the book "an ocean and labyrinth of the mysteries of God." Although the interpretations of some of its symbols are difficult, it is a singularly fascinating and interesting book.

Ezekiel apparently had very methodical habits of recording events and dates. This is seen especially in connection with the messages he received from God. There are twelve such dated messages in his book.[6] Read each one, and note particularly the year of captivity cited: 1:1-2; 8:1; 20:1; 24:1; 26:1; 29:1; 30:20; 31:1; 32:1;

---

5. Scan through the book and note the frequency of the phrase, "And the word of the LORD came unto me, saying."
6. There are other datelines besides these dated messages in the book (cf. 33:21).

32:17; 40:1. The methodical style of Ezekiel is also seen in the orderly organization of his book, which will be evident in the survey stage of study.

B. VISIONS

Ezekiel is known as "The Prophet of Visions." The very first verse of his book reads, "The heavens were opened and I saw visions of God." A vision in Bible days was a miraculous experience of a man of God on a special occasion, whereby God revealed truth to him in some pictorial and audible form. Visions were of all kinds, differing in such things as length, intensity, number of symbols, and whether the vision was perceived in the spirit (as in a dream) or by the conscious physical senses.

These are the visions recorded in Ezekiel:
1. Vision of the Cherubim (vision of God): Ezekiel's inaugural vision   1:4-28
2. Vision of the Roll or Scroll   2:9—3:3
3. Vision of the Plain   3:22-23
4. Visions of Jerusalem
   a) Four abominations in the Temple   8:1-18
   b) Inhabitants slain   9:1-11
   c) City destroyed by fire   10:1-22
   d) The Lord departs from the city   11:1-25
5. Vision of Dry Bones   37:1-10
6. Visions of the New Temple and Associated Scenes   40:1—48:05

C. SYMBOLIC ACTIONS

Ezekiel, perhaps more than any other prophet, taught by symbolic *actions*—those strange things which God asked His prophets to do in order that His messages might impress the people vividly and intensely. God told Ezekiel, "I have set you as a sign to the house of Israel" (12:6). So his symbolic actions were revelatory signs. Some of the things he was commanded to do must have been extremely hard and trying. He was continually exposing himself to the jeers and scorn of the skeptical.

But the symbolic acts produced the desired effect, at least upon the hearts of the serious-minded, causing them to ask what these things meant (see 12:9; 24:19; 37:18). This was the prophet's opportunity to explain their significance and drive home the application.

Following is a list of the main symbolic actions of Ezekiel:

SIGN	TEACHING	PASSAGE
1. Sign of the Brick	Jerusalem's siege and fall	4:1-3
2. Sign of the Prophet's Posture	Discomforts of captivity	4:4-8
3. Sign of Famine	Deprivations of captivity	4:9-17
4. Sign of the Knife and Razor	Utter destruction of the city	5:1-17
5. Sign of House Moving	Removal to another land	12:1-7,17-20
6. Sign of the Sharpened Sword	Judgment imminent	21:1-17
7. Sign of Nebuchadnezzar's Sword	Babylon the captor	21:18-23
8. Sign of the Smelting Furnace	Judgment and purging	22:17-31
9. Sign of Ezekiel's Wife's Death	Blessings forfeited	24:15-27
10. Sign of the Two Sticks	Reunion of Israel and Judah	37:15-17

D. ALLEGORIES

Allegories in the Bible are stories intended to teach spiritual lessons. John Bunyan's *The Pilgrim's Progress* is a classic example of an allegory. In Ezekiel the allegories have the same purpose as the symbolic actions. They differ in that the allegories teach by words; the symbolic actions teach by actual events. Below are listed the main allegories of Ezekiel. Read each allegory, and try to determine the spiritual lesson it teaches.

1. The Vine   15:1-8
2. The Faithless Wife   16:1-63
3. The Two Eagles[7]   17:1-21
4. The Cedar   17:22-24
5. The Two Women   23:1-49
6. The Boiling Caldron   24:1-14

E. APOCALYPTIC IMAGERY

Apocalyptic writing prophesies of things to come by means of much symbol and imagery. Daniel and Revelation are the two books of the Bible usually classified as apocalyptic. Ezekiel contains many apocalyptic passages. Identify the contents of each of the following:

6:1-14	28:25-26	38:1-23
7:5-12	34:25-31	39:1-29
20:33-44	36:8-15, 33-36	47:1-12

There are many resemblances between Ezekiel and Revelation. This is clearly seen when passages like the following are compared:

---

7. This story, along with that of the boiling caldron (24:1-14), may be classified as a parable, as 17:1-2 and 24:3 identify them.

Ezekiel	Revelation	Ezekiel	Revelation
1:1	19:11	14:21	6:8
1:5	4:6	26:13	18:22
1:10	4:7	27:28-30	18:17-19
1:22	4:6	37:10	11:11
1:24	1:15	37:27	21:3
1:28	4:3	38:2-3	20:8
2:9	5:1	40:2	21:10
3:1, 3	10:10	40:3	11:1
7:2	7:1	43:2	1:15
9:4	7:3	43:16	21:16
9:11	1:13	47:1, 12	22:1-2
10:2	8:5	48:31	21:12

F. POEMS

The poems of Ezekiel are lamentations, or elegies. They are found at 19:1-14 and 27:1-36.

IV. SURVEY

1. Scan the entire book in one sitting. This should only be a cursory reading, for main impressions and observations of atmosphere. What things stand out to you?

2. Secure a chapter title for each of Ezekiel's forty-eight chapters. Record these on paper.

3. Now begin to look for groupings of chapters, according to similar content.

4. Is there any turning point in the book?

5. Be on the lookout for words and phrases which are repeated throughout the book. Such words and phrases, if they are strong, are clues to the theme of the book.

6. From this introductory study of the text, what does the book teach about God? About the prophet Ezekiel? About the people?

7. Study carefully survey Chart 87, comparing the outlines with the survey you have made thus far. The observations and suggestions which follow concern this survey chart.

8. Observe that basically the book of Ezekiel is made up of three main parts:

Fate of Judah (desolation)

Foes of Judah (destruction)

Future of Judah and Israel (restoration)

Actually, the first three chapters could be considered a separate introductory division in the book, recording the call and commission of Ezekiel. But since the commission of Ezekiel involved pronouncing the judgment of captivity, these three chapters may rightly be placed in the large division called "Fate of Judah."

9. There is a turning point in the book, made up of two parts. (See bottom of the chart.) At 24:2, Ezekiel is informed by God that the king of Babylon has begun the siege against Jerusalem. At 33:21, the actual turning point, Ezekiel learns from a messenger that the city has fallen. Up to 24:2, Ezekiel's message is mainly "The city shall be destroyed." After 33:21, Ezekiel looks to the next prophetic peak, and prophesies, "The city shall be restored." It is at chapter 24 that the prophet learns that when Jerusalem falls, his tongue will be loosed to speak a new message of hope; and people, sobered by the reality of Jerusalem's destruction, will begin to give him a hearing. (Read 24:25-27.)

10. The middle section (chaps. 25-32) concerns the foreign nations. At first glance this may appear to be out of place in the outline of the book. Considering the broad context noted above, show how this section is very appropriately located here. Is restoration promised any of these Gentile nations?

11. If the book of Ezekiel were divided into two main parts, the division would then be at chapter 33. Note the outline "Jehovah Not There"; "Jehovah There." In the first division, God is represented as leaving the city (chaps. 10-11); in the last division, He is shown as returning (43:1-5), and remaining (48:35). Note how chapters 10 and 11 depict God as withdrawing *gradually* and *reluctantly*. At 10:4, He is standing over the threshold of His house. At 10:18, He moves and stands over the cherubim; at 10:19, He is at the door of the east gate. Finally, at 11:22-23, He pauses again upon the Mount of Olives east of Jerusalem, as though bidding a last farewell to the city where He had set His name.

12. Study the outline which breaks down the large divisions into smaller sections (Call and Commission; Judgment Foretold; and so. forth). Compare these groupings with those which you observed in your earlier study. Make a note of these sections in your Bible.

13. A few comments may be made here concerning the last division of the book "Restoration to Come" (chaps. 33-48). This division has two distinct sections: the first consists of seven chapters, dealing principally with prophecies anticipating the final restoration of Israel; the second consists of nine chapters, dealing with Israel in the land, especially with reference to the Temple.

14. Notice especially the shepherd chapter (chap. 34), and compare it with the shepherd psalm (Psalm 23) and the shepherd chapter in John (chap. 10). Read carefully 36:16-23 and observe that Ezekiel agrees with all the prophets, from Moses onward, that Israel's resto-

ration is not to be because of anything in themselves but for the glory of God's great name, and to convince all mankind of the same thing, that His judgments shall make manifest that "I am the LORD."

15. The last vision which Ezekiel sees is of the restored Temple (chaps. 40-48). The chief point of this vision is that the glory of the Lord, which Ezekiel had seen departing from the first Temple, is now seen to return and abide in this Temple.

16. For a concluding survey exercise, read the book of Ezekiel more slowly than before, referring to Chart 87 as you read. This will help bring together the various items of the book as you make one final overview of the Bible text.

V. PROMINENT SUBJECTS

Some prominent subjects have already been identified in this chapter. Here are others.

A. EZEKIEL'S CALL AND COMMISSION (2:1—3:27)

Like the other prophets, Ezekiel received a vision of God which put him on his face in the dust before his Maker (1:26-28). Compare Isaiah's vision (Isa 6) and John's vision (Rev 1:10-18). Observe that in each instance it was the Lord who was seen, and that each vision produced the same humbling effect upon the beholder. Compare the three visions and observe the different ways in which the Lord manifested Himself. To Isaiah, His *holiness* was emphasized; to Ezekiel, His *power, majesty,* and *government;* and to John, His *love.*

B. THE GLORY AND MAJESTY OF THE LORD

The book of Ezekiel underscores the truths about the Lord's glory and majesty. Key verses which reflect these are: 1:1*b*, 28*b;* 2:3; and 3:23.

C. MESSIANIC PROPHECIES

The chief Messianic passages of Ezekiel, as listed by Anton T. Pearson in *The Wycliffe Bible Commentary,* are:[8]

1. The Lord, the sanctuary	11:16-20
2. The wonderful cedar sprig	17:22-24
3. The rightful King	21:26-27
4. The faithful Shepherd	34:11-31
5. The great purification	36:25-35
6. The great resurrection	37:1-14
7. The great reunion	37:21-28
8. The overthrow of Gog	38:1—39:29
9. The life-giving stream	47:1-12

8. Anton T. Pearson, "Ezekiel," in *The Wycliffe Bible Commentary,* p. 705.

D. FUTURE RESURRECTION OF ISRAEL (37:1—48:35)

At the commencement of his prophetic ministry, Ezekiel was given a vision of the glorious Lord reigning in heaven. The people of Israel had once known the blessings of such a glory shining in their midst, but now the glory had departed because of Israel's sin. It was Ezekiel's task to announce to his fellow exiles the coming judgment of desolation of the holy city and captivity of its inhabitants. When the city fell in 586 B.C., God loosed the prophet's tongue to speak the new message of restoration to come, for those who would turn to the Lord. For fifteen years it was his happy privilege to quote the Lord as saying,

> Now I shall restore the fortunes of Jacob, and have mercy on the whole house of Israel. Then they will know that I am the LORD their God. . . I . . . gathered them again to their own land. . . . And I will not hide My face from them any longer, for I shall have poured out My Spirit on the house of Israel (39:25, 28-29).

This bright message did not contradict Ezekiel's earlier minatory oracles. The seventy-year captivity must first be fulfilled, and then there would be a return to the land on the part of a believing remnant of a new generation. The Temple would be rebuilt, and the glory of the Lord would come down to Israel again. But Ezekiel's prophecy, like most of the Old Testament consolatory prophecies, referred mainly to a latter-day Messianic fulfillment, when Israel would be reestablished in the millennial Kingdom, and Christ would sit on David's throne. All the bright promises given to the nation could be fulfilled only in Christ, Israel's Messiah.

E. OTHER SUBJECTS

The following list identifies more of the prominent subjects of Ezekiel:

Attributes of God: His glory, sovereignty, name, holiness, justice, mercy

Man: individual responsibility, corrupt heart

Israel: idolatry, judgment, elect nation, hope

Gentile nations: accountability, judgment

Last days: restored kingdom

VI. KEY WORDS AND VERSES

Here are some of the outstanding phrases of Ezekiel:

"Son of man" appears over ninety times in Ezekiel. The prophet is the one so designated. The title was symbolic of Ezekiel's identity with the people to whom he was sent, even as Jesus, the Son of man, was so identified. This title was Jesus' favorite title of Himself. (It appears almost ninety times in the gospels.) Ezekiel has been called "The other Son of man."

"The word of the LORD came unto me" appears forty-nine times.

"Glory of the God of Israel" or "glory of the LORD" appears eleven times in the first eleven chapters.

"LORD God" appears over two hundred times.

"I shall be sanctified through you" (or equivalent phrases) appears six times. Read 20:41; 28:22, 25; 36:23; 38:16; 39:27.

"The hand of the LORD was upon me" (or similar phrases) appears seven times: 1:3; 3:14, 22; 8:1; 33:22; 37:1; 40:1.

VII. APPLICATIONS

1. What does the book of Ezekiel teach about God, glory, righteousness, sin, judgment, mercy, restoration?

2. What spiritual lessons can be learned from the life and ministry of the prophet Ezekiel?

3. What should prophecies of Israel's future restoration do for Christians today? Will Israel's restoration take place before or after the rapture of the Church?

4. Underlying the prophecies of Israel's restoration are the general grand truths about God and His ways with all His children. Anton T. Pearson suggests how these general principles apply to the Church. Evaluate his words:

> The Christian Church, all through her history, draws from these chapters, not minute allegorical or typological details of her life, but the broad general principle of God's presence with his people and the fructifying power of his Holy Spirit. They point the Church, especially in their adaptation in Rev 21:22, to the consummation awaiting God's people at the *parousia* (second coming) of his Son, who has prepared abiding places for his own in the Father's house. They remind the Church of her pilgrim character in this world, that she looks for "new heavens and a new earth wherein dwelleth righteousness" (II Pet 3:13).[9]

VIII. FURTHER STUDY

1. Other men of God saw visions of God (theophanies), but Ezekiel's vision of 1:4-28 is the most detailed one. For comparative study, read the theophanies of Moses (Exod 24:9-12); Isaiah (Isa 6); Jeremiah (Jer 1:4-10); Daniel (Dan 7:9-14); John (Rev 4:2-11).

2. Consult outside sources for extended discussions of the following subjects:

---

9. Ibid., p. 759.

CHART 87

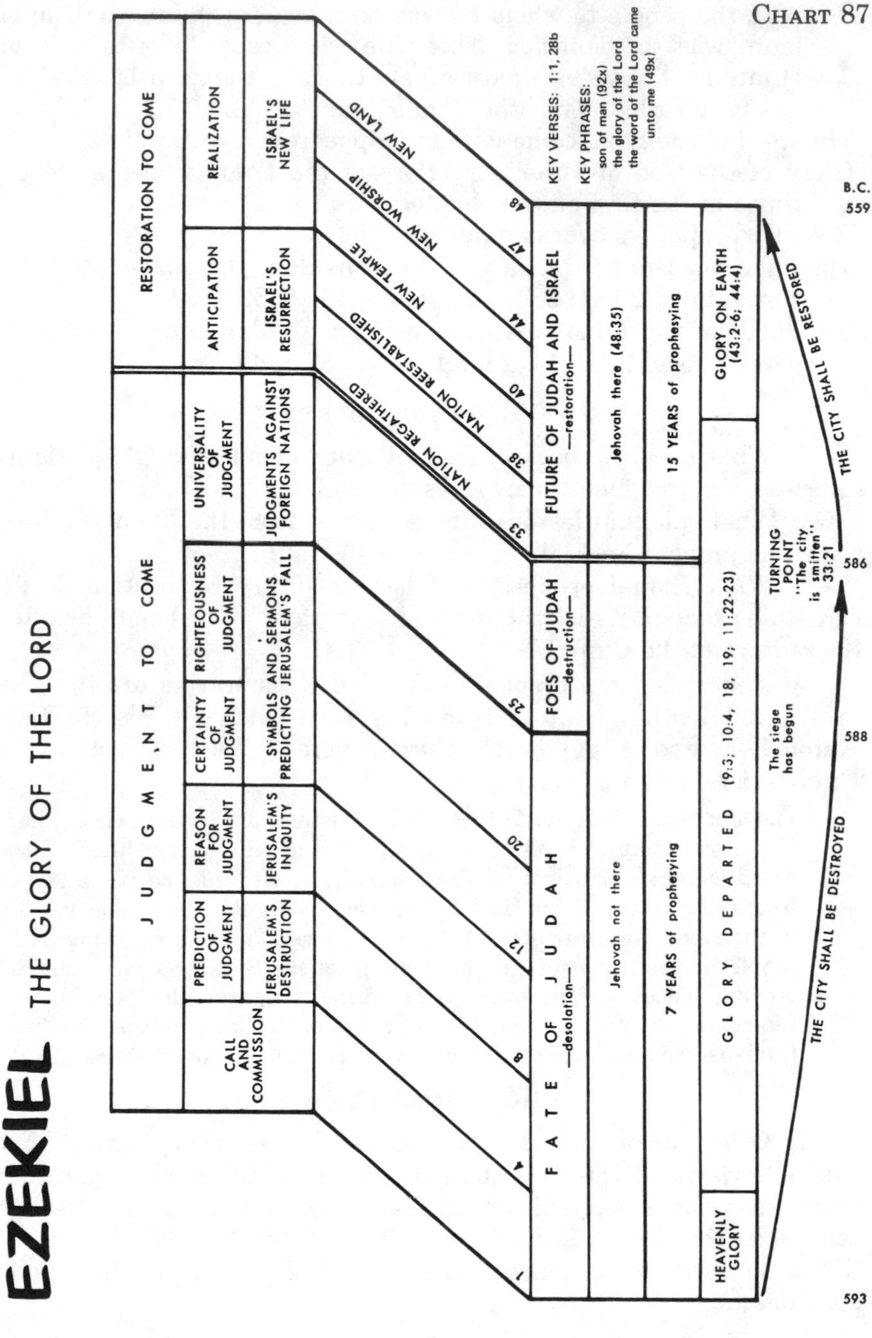

EZEKIEL

THE GLORY OF THE LORD

	JUDGMENT TO COME				RESTORATION TO COME	
CALL AND COMMISSION	PREDICTION OF JUDGMENT	REASON FOR JUDGMENT	CERTAINTY OF JUDGMENT	RIGHTEOUSNESS OF JUDGMENT	UNIVERSALITY OF JUDGMENT	ANTICIPATION	REALIZATION
	JERUSALEM'S DESTRUCTION	JERUSALEM'S INIQUITY	SYMBOLS AND SERMONS PREDICTING JERUSALEM'S FALL		JUDGMENTS AGAINST FOREIGN NATIONS	ISRAEL'S RESURRECTION	ISRAEL'S NEW LIFE

NEW LAND

NEW WORSHIP

NEW TEMPLE

NATION REESTABLISHED

NATION REGATHERED

1   4   8   12   20   25   33   38   40   44   47   48

FATE OF JUDAH
—desolation—

FOES OF JUDAH
—destruction—

FUTURE OF JUDAH AND ISRAEL
—restoration—

Jehovah not there

Jehovah there (48:35)

7 YEARS of prophesying

15 YEARS of prophesying

GLORY DEPARTED (9:3; 10:4, 18, 19; 11:22-23)

GLORY ON EARTH (43:2-6; 44:4)

HEAVENLY GLORY

The siege has begun

TURNING POINT "...the city is smitten". 33:21

THE CITY SHALL BE DESTROYED

THE CITY SHALL BE RESTORED

KEY VERSES: 1:1, 28b

KEY PHRASES:
son of man (92x)
the glory of the Lord
the word of the Lord came unto me (49x)

B.C. 559

586

588

593

a) types and symbols in the Bible[10]
b) Israel's title deed to Palestine[11]
c) literal Israel and spiritual Israel[12]

IX. SELECTED READING

PROPHETIC THEMES

Hengstenberg, E. W. *Christology of the Old Testament.*
Payne, J. Barton. *Encyclopedia of Biblical Prophecy,* pp. 349-69.
Pentecost, J. Dwight. *Israel in Prophecy.*
―――. *Prophecy for Today,* pp. 51-60; 102-13.
Sauer, Erich. *From Eternity to Eternity,* pp. 157-61; 179-84.
Tan, Paul Lee. *The Interpretation of Prophecy,* pp. 64-67; 82-85; 152-74; 293-98; 318-22.

GENERAL INTRODUCTION

Archer, Gleason L. *A Survey of Old Testament Introduction,* pp. 356-64.
Baxter, J. Sidlow. *Explore the Book,* 4:8-46.
Freeman, Hobart E. *Introduction to the Old Testament Prophets,* pp. 295-325.
Moller, Wilhelm, "Ezekiel." In *The International Standard Bible Encyclopedia,* 2:1071-81.
Scroggie, W. Graham. *Know Your Bible,* 1:202-6.

COMMENTARIES

Beasley-Murray, G. R. "Ezekiel." In *The New Bible Commentary.*
Ellison, H. L. *Ezekiel: The Man and His Message.*
Feinberg, Charles L. *The Prophecy of Ezekiel.*
Pearson, Anton T. "Ezekiel." In *The Wycliffe Bible Commentary.*
Schroder, F. W. J. "Ezekiel." In *Lango's Commentary on the Holy Scriptures.*

---

10. E.g., see Paul Lee Tan, *The Interpretation of Prophecy,* pp. 152-74.
11. E.g., see J. Dwight Pentecost, *Prophecy for Today,* pp. 61-68.
12. Some Bible students do not see the literal nation of Israel in end-time prophecies. See Erich Sauer, *From Eternity to Eternity,* pp. 157-61, for a defense of the view that literal Israel is intended by such prophecies. Also see Tan, pp. 318-22, for a discussion of the millennial temple, prophesied in Ezekiel 40-49.

24

Daniel: God Rules the World

The book of Daniel has been described as "the greatest book in the Bible on godless kingdoms and the kingdom of God."[1] The godless kingdoms referred to here are the Gentile nations, and the Kingdom of God is the millennial reign centered about Israel. The grand truth which applies to all kingdoms is summed up in four words: God rules the world.

Daniel is a relatively short book, but compacted into its pages are multitudes of fascinating prophecies and basic doctrines which challenge the Bible student to tarry long in its study.

The importance of the book of Daniel is underscored in this comprehensive evaluation by John Walvoord:

> Among the great prophetic books of Scripture, none provides a more comprehensive and chronological prophetic view of the broad movement of history than the book of Daniel. Of the three prophetic programs revealed in Scripture, outlining the course of the nations, Israel, and the church, Daniel alone reveals the details of God's plan for both the nations and Israel. Although other prophets like Jeremiah had much to say to the nations and Israel, Daniel brings together and interrelates these great themes of prophecy as does no other portion of Scripture. For this reason, the book of Daniel is essential to the structure of prophecy and is the key to the entire Old Testament prophetic revelation. A study of this book is, therefore, not only important from the standpoint of determining the revelation of one of the great books of the Old Testament but is an indispensable preliminary investigation to any complete eschatological system.[2]

---

1. W. Graham Scroggie, *Know Your Bible,* 1:199.
2. John F. Walvoord, *Daniel: The Key to Prophetic Revelation,* p. 7.

I. Preparation for Study

Read Luke 21:20-28. Note especially the phrase "the times of the Gentiles" (21:24). Daniel lived and prophesied at the beginning of this notable epoch in the world's history. Concerning the epoch, note these two things:

1. Its distinctive character: During this time, by divine design Gentiles, not Jews, have political power and supremacy in the world.

2. Its duration: The "times of the Gentiles" began with the Babylonian Captivity of Judah under Nebachadnezzar, and it will end with the second coming of Christ in glory (Luke 21:20-28).

God had offered world supremacy to the Jews (Deut 28) on the condition of obedience to Him, but the Jews would not comply with that condition. So, beginning in 605 B.C., God withdrew the offer and gave the supremacy to the Gentiles, at that time represented by the nation of Babylon. Nebuchadnezzar, as absolute monarch of Babylon, was thus made "master" of the world.

In Babylonian captivity, Daniel was prophet to both Gentile and Jew. He prophesied to the Gentiles concerning the events which would take place among the Gentile nations during the times of the Gentiles (when political dominion of the earth would be vested in Gentile nations). His mission to Israel mainly concerned the unborn generations of Jews. He prophesied of an eventual Messianic Kingdom, which God would set up when the times of the Gentiles had been fulfilled. (See Chart 88.)

PROPHECY OF MESSIANIC KINGDOM   CHART 88

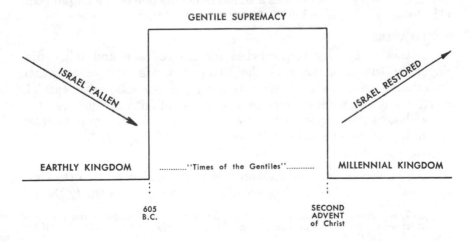

II. DANIEL AND HIS CONTEMPORARIES

Study carefully Chart 89. Observe the following:

1. Daniel's ministry in Babylon lasted for at least seventy years (605-536 B.C.). He was among the Jewish captives of the first deportation (605 B.C.; Dan 1:1-6), and he lived in Babylon throughout the entire seventy-year captivity period (536 B.C. is the date referred to in 10:1).

2. Babylon, the land of Jewish exile, came under three powers during Daniel's career: Neo-Babylonian, Median, and Persian. The rulers that played an important part in the book of Daniel are:

Nebuchadnezzar; Belshazzar   (Neo-Babylonian)
Darius the Mede[3]   (Median)
Cyrus   (Persian)

3. In 539 B.C., when Belshazzar was coregent with Nabonidus, Babylon fell to the Persian King Cyrus. This began the Persian period of supremacy.

4. The return of Jewish exiles to Jerusalem and the beginning of construction on the new Temple began at the end of Daniel's career.

5. What prophets and kings of Judah were contemporaries of Daniel? Recall your earlier studies of these men.

III. THE MAN DANIEL

A. NAME

The name Daniel translates the Hebrew word *Daniyye'l,* meaning "God is Judge [Prince]" or "God is my Judge [Prince]." The name given Daniel by Nebuchadnezzar's officer (1:7) was Belteshazzar, meaning "Bel's prince." It was a name honoring one of the pagan gods of Babylon (cf. 4:8; also Isa 46:1; Jer 50:2; 51:44).

B. CHARACTER

Daniel is usually remembered for his courage and faith, displayed in the experience in the lions' den. He had many other outstanding traits as well. He was strong of purpose, wise, tactful, courteous, brave, modest, humble, and a man of faith and prayer. It is not without significance that three times heavenly messengers refer to him in visions as a man of "high esteem" (9:23; 10:11, 19).

C. BIOGRAPHY

Daniel was born into a Judean family of nobility, around the time of the reformation under King Josiah (621 B.C.). Some identify Daniel

---

3. This Darius has been identified as Gubaru, general under Cyrus, king of Persia, whom Cyrus made governor, or sub-king, over the region of Chaldea (Babylonia). (Cf. 5:31; 6:1; 9:1.)

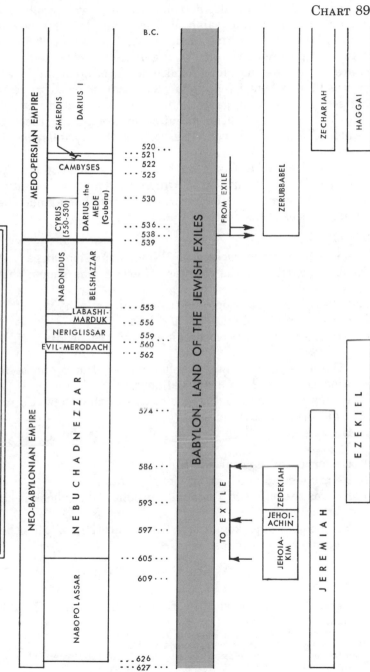

DANIEL AND HIS CONTEMPORARIES

Daniel

B.C.

MEDO-PERSIAN EMPIRE

SMERDIS

DARIUS I

520 ...
... 521
... 522
... 525

CAMBYSES

... 530

CYRUS (550-530)

DARIUS the MEDE (Gubaru)

... 536 ...
538 ...
539

NABONIDUS

BELSHAZZAR

LABASHI-MARDUK ... 553

NERIGLISSAR ... 556

EVIL-MERODACH
559 ...
560
562

574 ...

NEO-BABYLONIAN EMPIRE

N E B U C H A D N E Z Z A R

586 ...

593 ...

597 ...

... 605 ...

609 ...

NABOPOLASSAR

... 626
... 627 ...

BABYLON, LAND OF THE JEWISH EXILES

FROM EXILE

TO EXILE

ZEDEKIAH

JEHOI-ACHIN

JEHOIA-KIM

ZERUBBABEL

ZECHARIAH

HAGGAI

EZEKIEL

J E R E M I A H

as one of King Hezekiah's descendants, who was prophesied about in 2 Kings 20:17-18 and Isaiah 39:7 (cf. Dan 1:3). He was in his late teens when taken captive in the first deportation of 605 B.C. In the same group were three other young men no less noble than himself in character. These were four handsome, intelligent, and well-educated youths (1:4), whom King Nebuchadnezzar selected to be trained for his service. The king gave them names associated with the gods of Babylon, but they had no intention of worshiping those gods. They remained true to Jehovah. The book of Daniel tells the story of the years that followed.

Daniel served as God's prophet at least until 536 B.C. (10:1).[4] Soon after this he wrote his book, which no doubt was brought back to Jerusalem when the exiles returned to their homeland. The date and circumstances of his death are unknown.

D. MISSION

The prominent aspects of Daniel's mission already have been discussed earlier in the chapter. There it was shown that Daniel's mission was:

1. to Gentiles of Babylon, and to Jews in exile
2. concerning Gentile nations and Israel
3. with respect to the succeeding centuries, leading up to the end times

Daniel was a unique prophet among the prophets for various reasons, some of which are listed here:

1. He may not have had a special call to the prophetic ministry, as did Isaiah and Jeremiah.
2. He was given the prophetic gift, but not the prophetic office as such.
3. He served in the courts of kings.
4. He prophesied much about Gentile nations.
5. He was the only Old Testament prophet whose book is classified as apocalyptic.
6. His book is the key to the interpretation of all other biblical prophecies of the last days.

IV. THE BOOK OF DANIEL

A. AUTHENTICITY

The Daniel referred to by Ezekiel (Ezek 14:14, 20; 28:3) and by

---

4. This dateline in 10:1 probably refers to the third year of Cyrus's rule over Babylon, or 536 B.C. The phrase "the first year of Cyrus the king" (1:21) probably has reference to the first year of the Jews' permission to return to Jerusalem. See Robert D. Culver, "Daniel," in *The Wycliffe Bible Commentary*, p. 776.

Jesus (Matt 24:15; Mark 13:14) is the author of this book. From 7:2 onward, the book uses the autobiographical first person; and, considering the unity of the book, God's words to Daniel in 12:4 imply authorship of the entire book by Daniel. Liberal critics have denied its genuineness, mainly because of (1) its fantastic miracles (e.g., Daniel's deliverance from the lions); (2) its explicit prophecies (many of which were fulfilled in the centuries before Christ); and (3) *alleged* historical inaccuracies. Despite such objections, the book's authenticity has endured through the centuries.

B. PLACE IN THE CANON

In our English Bibles, Daniel appears as the last of the five major prophetical books (Isaiah, Jeremiah, Lamentations, Ezekiel, Daniel). In the Hebrew Bibles, Daniel is not grouped with the prophetical books, but appears as a historical book in the Hebrew section called Writings. That it was not included among the prophetical books is explained by the fact that while Daniel had the gift and function of prophet (cf. Matt 24:15), his position was that of a government official. That his book was placed in the Writings as a historical book can be explained by its content, with its apocalyptic visions of world history.

C. DATE WRITTEN

Daniel probably wrote his book soon after the last dated event occurred (10:1; 536 B.C.). An approximate date would be 530 B.C., or when the prophet was around ninety years of age.

D. TYPE OF LITERATURE

Daniel is an apocalyptic book, the only Old Testament book so classified.[5] Revelation is the one New Testament Apocalypse.[6] The word *apocalypse* in its Greek form is translated as "revelation" in Revelation 1:1. Apocalypse is a revelation, an unveiling of secret purposes of God not known before that unveiling. Those purposes concern particularly world events leading up to the Messianic Kingdom and the consummation of things in the end of the world. The manner in which these events are unveiled is mainly by visions, where imagery and symbolism appear throughout. In Daniel the word "vision" appears twenty-two times; and "visions," ten times.

Usually apocalyptic literature is written as prose, but because so

---

5. Parts of other books (e.g., Ezekiel and Zechariah) are apocalyptic.

6. Revelation and Daniel are very closely related to each other, treating the same great subjects, and using many of the same symbols. Studying one helps in studying the other. One author has written, "The writer of the Apocalypse [Revelation] and Daniel have all things in common, as though they have been let together into the very arena of God."

much picture language is involved, the prose at places looks very much like poetry. In the *Westminster Study Edition of the Bible*[7] the following portions are printed in poetic verse form: 2:20-23; 4:3, 10-12, 14-17, 34*b*-35; 6:26*b*-27; 7:9-10, 13-14.

One unique feature of Daniel is that the book is written in two languages, Hebrew and Aramaic. The reasons for this language structure appear later in the survey study.

V. SURVEY

1. First scan the book in one sitting, aloud if possible. Record at least five of your impressions of this book, coming from this reading. Did any words or phrases stand out?

2. Now read through the book a second time, chapter by chapter, seeking a title for each chapter. Record these titles on paper.

3. Look at the first verses of each chapter, noting the references to the kings. These date the events and visions of Daniel. (Review the reigns of the kings as shown on Chart 89.)

4. What chapters mainly record narrative? What chapters mainly record visions?

5. How is chapter 1 an introductory chapter to the whole book? Does the last chapter seem to be a unit by itself, or does it continue the vision of chapter 11? How is the last verse of Daniel a concluding verse to the entire book?

6. Who is the interpreter of the dreams in chapters 1-6? Who is the interpreter of the dreams in chapters 7-12?

7. Compare Nebuchadnezzar's dream of chapter 2 with Daniel's vision of chapter 7.

8. Observe how most of the visions of the book of Daniel concern Gentile nations. Read chapter 9 again and observe whether this vision is about Gentiles or about Israel.

9. Continue this survey study, noting such things as relations, emphases, progression, and turning point. Does there seem to be a unity about the book? Compose a title for the book that represents its main theme. Compare your studies up to this point with the overview of Chart 95. The following observations relate to that chart. Study the chart carefully.

10. The top of Chart 95 shows how the book may be divided into two equal parts. Also shown here is the chronological progression of kings, in two sequences:

Nebuchadnezzar-----Belshazzar-----Darius
         Belshazzar-----Darius-----Cyrus

---

7. *Westminster Study Edition of the Bible.*

This "backtracking" on the part of the book's writer is for topical purposes. Note how it fits in with the two-division outline shown above.

11. The bottom of the chart shows an outline suggested by the two languages used in the original text. Such an outline is not apparent to the reader of the English Bible.[8] (The one reference at 2:4a to "in [Syriac] Aramaic" is not enough information for the English reader concerning this outline.)

Here is what is involved in this structure:

a) From 1:1 to 2:4a, Daniel wrote in Hebrew, the language of the Jews.[9]

b) From 2:4b to 7:28, Daniel wrote in Aramaic, the official language of diplomatic discourse of that day.

c) From 8:1 to the end of the book, Daniel wrote in Hebrew again. The vital question is Why did Daniel compose his book this way? The best explanation is that in the two Hebrew sections the Jews are prominent, and so the message is in their language; in the Aramaic section the Gentile nations are prominent, and so the prophetic decrees are delivered to them, as it were, in the official diplomatic language of the world. The survey chart shows the two main sections thus:[10]

Chapters 2-7: Gentile Nations
Chapters 8-12: Hebrew Nation

The introductory chapter 1 involves the Gentile setting, but the spotlight is on the four Jewish boys in that setting. Gentile nations appear much in chapters 8-12, but only as the setting for the experiences of Israel up to the end times.

12. On the basis of your study thus far, what appears to be the book's main theme? Can you think of any supporting themes as well?

13. What do the prophecies reveal concerning the relations between Gentile nations and Israel?

14. How is God shown in this book to be the God of all history?

15. Your survey of Daniel has not answered all questions that arise out of such a difficult book. The purpose of the survey, as with

---

8. This linguistic structure of Daniel is fully described by Culver in "Daniel," in *The Wycliffe Bible Commentary* and in his book *Daniel and the Latter Days.*

9. It may be observed here that Hebrew as the Jews' vernacular began to disappear during the exile years, though it has always remained as the language of the Jews' religion. (Now, since the establishment of the State of Israel in 1948, Hebrew is once again the official native tongue of the people.)

10. The Gentile section here is made to begin at 2:1. Actually, Daniel began writing in Aramaic at 2:4b, to emphasize the change at the natural point. The spirit of 2:1-4a brings those verses into this Gentile section.

all survey study, is to see the highlights and main themes, which in turn open doors to ever increasing understanding of the book.

VI. PROMINENT SUBJECTS

Each of the subjects discussed below is not expounded in detail. Helpful suggestions are given for any later studies made on the subjects.

A. PROPHECY OF END-TIME WORLD HISTORY

Daniel's unique contribution to the canon of Scripture is that it gives detailed descriptions of the destinies of Gentile nations under the directive sovereign hand of God. Other prophets of Israel spoke of this, but more sparingly, for their main message concerned their own people. The Holy Spirit inspired Daniel to write more about "world" history.

Some Bible scholars see all of Daniel's Gentile and Israel prophecies fulfilled by the second century B.C. or, at the latest, during Christ's earthly ministry. The opposite view, which is reflected in this book, is that the fulfillments of the prophecies culminate in the end times.[11] This long-range scope of interpretation is concisely summarized by John Walvoord.

> In many respects, the book of Daniel is the most comprehensive prophetic revelation of the Old Testament, giving the only total view of world history from Babylon to the second advent of Christ and interrelating Gentile history and prophecy with that which concerns Israel. Daniel provides the key to the overall interpretation of prophecy, is a major element in premillennialism, and is essential to the interpretation of the book of Revelation. Its revelation of the sovereignty and power of God has brought assurance to Jew and Gentile alike that God will fulfill His sovereign purposes in time and eternity.[12]

B. NEBUCHADNEZZAR'S DREAM AND DANIEL'S VISION (chaps. 2 and 7)

Nebuchadnezzar, who had so recently been raised to the position of "world" ruler, was anxiously thinking about his newly acquired possessions when God revealed to him in a dream a prophetic outline of the future history of the world powers (2:1-30). About fifty years later Daniel had a vision (also called a dream, 7:1) concerning the same world powers (chap. 7). Chart 90 shows some of the major similarities of the two dreams.

The Fulfillment column is a widely accepted conservative system of interpretation of these chapters. Note how much of the prophecies

---

11. See Culver, *Daniel and the Latter Days,* pp. 14-15.
12. Walvoord, p. 27.

DREAMS OF THE IMAGE AND FOUR BEASTS
Daniel 2 and 7

	NEBUCHADNEZZAR'S DREAM OF THE IMAGE		FULFILLMENT	DANIEL'S VISION OF THE FOUR BEASTS	
	PROPHECY		WORLD POWERS	PROPHECY	
	DREAM 2:31-35	INTERPRETATION 2:36-45		INTERPRETATION 7:15-28	DREAM 7:1-14
① HEAD			NEO-BABYLONIAN 612-539 B.C.		LION ①
② BREASTS AND ARMS			MEDO-PERSIAN 539-331 B.C.		BEAR ②
③ BELLY AND THIGHS			GRECIAN 331-63 B.C.		LEOPARD ③
④ LEGS FEET			ROMAN —3 PERIODS ① Supremacy of Ancient Rome 63 B.C.—A.D. 476 ② Rome-derived governments ③ Antichrist		DIVERSE BEAST ④ 10 HORNS LITTLE HORN
			C O N S U M M A T I O N		
STONE	GOD'S INDESTRUCTIBLE KINGDOM 2:44		MESSIANIC KINGDOM		ANCIENT OF DAYS (God) on the throne
			CHRIST		SON OF MAN (Christ) given dominion

were fulfilled before Christ's first coming. The identification of Antichrist as the little horn is based on New Testament passages referring to these last times. (Read 2 Thess 2:3-10; Rev 11:2; 13:2, 5-10, 15-17; 19:20.)[13] Chart 91 shows the premillennial, pretribulational view of end times, which is the setting for such an interpretation of the two dreams. (The most intense activity of Antichrist is during the Great Tribulation.)

C. VISION OF THE SEVENTY WEEKS (9:1-27)

Among Evangelicals there are two main schools of interpretation of this vision. Both are agreed that the "weeks" of the vision are heptads ("sevens") of years, one week being seven years. One view, referred to by Edward J. Young as the "traditional messianic interpretation,"[14] sees the seventieth week as fulfilled in the first century A.D., without a hiatus of a Church age. According to this view, the prince of 9:26 is Titus, destroyer of the Temple and Jerusalem in A.D. 70; and the "he" of 9:27 is Christ, whose death removed the need for further sacrifices under the old covenant.

The other view, recognizing a gap between the sixty-ninth and seventieth weeks, sees the vision as an outline of Israel's history up to the Great Tribulation of the end times. This is diagramed on Chart 92.

Study Chart 92 in connection with the text of Daniel 9:24-27. Robert D. Culver gives the following reasons for holding to a time gap in this vision:

> 1. Jesus placed· the culminating week with its "abomination" in the times of the final Antichrist, just before His second advent (Mt 24:15).
> 2. Daniel 7:25, parallel to 9:27, is a prophecy of the times of the final Antichrist.
> 3. The period of three and one-half times or years is always mentioned in Scripture in an eschatological (end times) setting (Rev 11:2-3; 12:6, 14).
> 4. The six things to be accomplished in the seventy weeks (Dan 9:24) require the second advent of Christ, and the restoration and conversion of Israel.[15]

You will want to come to your own conclusions as to whether a time gap is intended by the vision. Refer to the commentaries already cited for further help on the two main views outlined here.

---

13. Read Culver, "Daniel," in *The Wycliffe Bible Commentary,* pp. 790-91, for further light on this subject.
14. This is the view held by Edward J. Young, *The Prophecy of Daniel.*
15. Culver, "Daniel," in *The Wycliffe Bible Commentary,* p. 795.

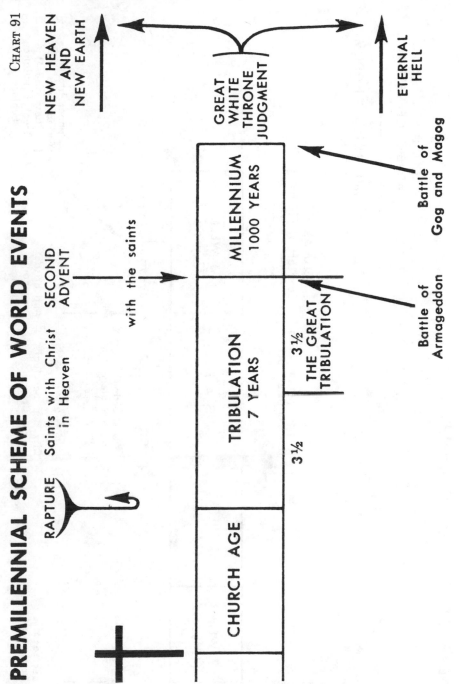

CHART 91

PREMILLENNIAL SCHEME OF WORLD EVENTS

RAPTURE   Saints with Christ   SECOND
                  in Heaven   ADVENT

with the saints

NEW HEAVEN
AND
NEW EARTH

GREAT
WHITE
THRONE
JUDGMENT

ETERNAL
HELL

CHURCH AGE

TRIBULATION
7 YEARS

MILLENNIUM
1000 YEARS

3½

3½
THE GREAT
TRIBULATION

Battle of
Armageddon

Battle of
Gog and Magog

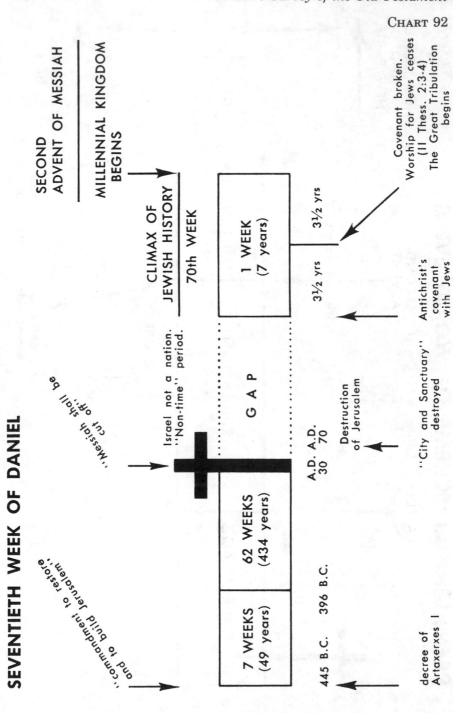

SEVENTIETH WEEK OF DANIEL

SECOND ADVENT OF MESSIAH

MILLENNIAL KINGDOM BEGINS

CLIMAX OF JEWISH HISTORY

70th WEEK

1 WEEK (7 years)

3½ yrs

3½ yrs

Covenant broken. Worship for Jews ceases (II Thess. 2:3-4) The Great Tribulation begins

Antichrist's covenant with Jews

"Messiah shall be cut off."

Israel not a nation. "Non-time" period.

G A P

Destruction of Jerusalem

"City and Sanctuary" destroyed

A.D. A.D.
30   70

"...commandment to restore and to build Jerusalem..."

62 WEEKS (434 years)

7 WEEKS (49 years)

396 B.C.

445 B.C.

decree of Artaxerxes I

D. COMPARISONS OF DANIEL'S VISIONS

A survey of the book of Daniel cannot get into all the details of the visions. In order to help the reader see the large elements of the visions (without dwelling on the details), Chart 93 compares the visions in summary form.

VII. KEY WORDS AND VERSES

Two key words of Daniel are "dream" and "vision." What others are key words? Read 4:17 as a key verse of the book.

VIII. APPLICATIONS

1. What lessons can be learned from the stories of Daniel and his friends? What light is thrown on what it means to be "in the world" but not "of the world" (John 17:11, 16)?

2. What does the book teach about effective prayer?

3. God is the sovereign Lord of all history. In what different ways is this taught by the book of Daniel?

IX. FURTHER STUDY

1. Now that you have finished your survey of Daniel, compare all four major prophets as to such things as experiences and messages. Chart 94 brings some of these observations together.

2. The many differences of interpretation of Daniel's prophecies indicate something of the difficulty of studying this book. Refer to various commentaries for their help in this stage of Bible study. Highly recommended for the premillennial viewpoint is John F. Walvoord, *Daniel: The Key to Prophetic Revelation.*

X. SELECTED READING

GENERAL INTRODUCTION

Archer, Gleason L. *A Survey of Old Testament Introduction*, pp. 365-88.
Culver, Robert D. *Daniel and the Latter Days.*
Freeman, Hobart E. *Introduction to the Old Testament Prophets*, pp. 261-94.
Payne, J. Barton. *Encyclopedia of Biblical Prophecy*, pp. 369-92.
Saggs, H. W. F. *The Greatness That Was Babylon.*
Walvoord, John F. *Daniel: The Key to Prophetic Revelation*, pp. 11-27.
Young, Edward J. "Daniel." In *The New Bible Commentary*. (Amillennial viewpoint.)

COMMENTARIES

Culver, Robert D. "Daniel." In *The Wycliffe Bible Commentary.*
DeHaan, M. R. *Daniel the Prophet.*
Ironside, H. A. *Lectures on Daniel the Prophet.*

COMPARISONS OF DANIEL'S VISIONS   CHART 93

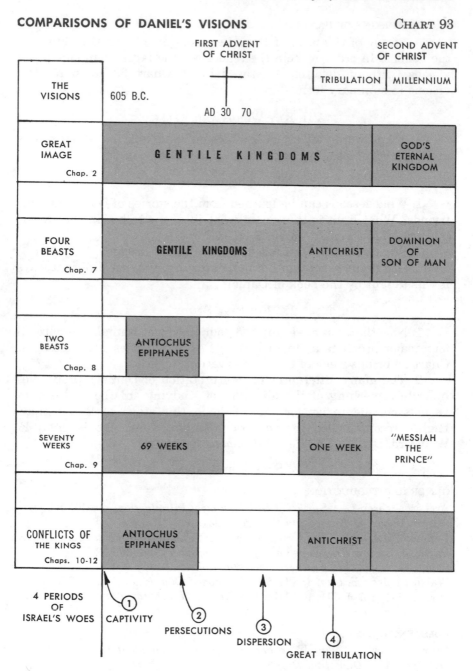

		FIRST ADVENT OF CHRIST		SECOND ADVENT OF CHRIST	

			TRIBULATION	MILLENNIUM

THE VISIONS — 605 B.C.   ✝   AD 30 70

GREAT IMAGE — Chap. 2 — GENTILE KINGDOMS — GOD'S ETERNAL KINGDOM

FOUR BEASTS — Chap. 7 — GENTILE KINGDOMS — ANTICHRIST — DOMINION OF SON OF MAN

TWO BEASTS — Chap. 8 — ANTIOCHUS EPIPHANES

SEVENTY WEEKS — Chap. 9 — 69 WEEKS — ONE WEEK — "MESSIAH THE PRINCE"

CONFLICTS OF THE KINGS — Chaps. 10-12 — ANTIOCHUS EPIPHANES — ANTICHRIST

4 PERIODS OF ISRAEL'S WOES — CAPTIVITY ① PERSECUTIONS ② DISPERSION ③ GREAT TRIBULATION ④

COMPARISONS OF THE FOUR MAJOR PROPHETS   CHART 94

	ISAIAH	JEREMIAH	EZEKIEL	DANIEL
KNOWN AS:	The Royal Prophet Evangelical Prophet Messianic Prophet	The Weeping Prophet The Prophet of Judgment	The Prophet of Visions The Prophet of the Exile The Other Son of Man	The Prophet of Gentile Times
PROPHESIED TO:	Jews in Judea	Jews in Judea and in Captivity	Captive Jews in Babylon	Gentile Kings and Captive Jews
CONCERNING:	Judah and Jerusalem, Isa. 1:1; 2:1	Judah and Nations, Jer. 1:5, 9-10; 2:1-2	The Whole House of Israel, Ezek. 2:3-6; 3:4-10, 17	Gentile Nations, Dan. 2:36 ff., and Israel, Dan. 9
DURING REIGNS OF:	Uzziah, Jotham, Ahaz and Hezekiah, Kings of Judah, Isa. 1:1	Josiah, Jehoahaz, Jehoiakim, Jehoiachin, Zedekiah, Kings of Judah, Jer. 1:2-3	Zedekiah, King of Judah and Nebuchadnezzar, King of Babylon	Jehoiakim, Jehoiachin and Zedekiah (Kings of Judah), Nebuchadnezzar, Darius and Cyrus (Gentile Kings)
DATES B.C.:	From 739 to 692	From 627 to 574	From 593 to 559	From 605 to 536
NUMBER OF YEARS HE PROPHESIED:	47	53	34	69
PROPHET'S CALL:	Isa. 6	Jer. 1:4-19	Ezek. 1—3	———
POLITICAL CONDITION:	Judah Menaced by Syria and Israel Alliance with Assyria Assyria Repulsed	Hostilities with Egypt and Babylon Deportation of Captives	Some Jews Captive in Babylon Other Jews Still in Judea Threatened with Captivity	Jews in Babylonian Captivity
RELIGIOUS CONDITION:	Backslidden Hypocritical	Revival Under Josiah Much Sin and Idolatry After Josiah's Death	National Unbelief, Disobedience and Rebellion	As a Nation out of Communion with God A Small Believing Remnant
HISTORICAL SETTING:	II Kings 15—20 II Chron. 26—30	II Kings 24—25	Dan. 1—6	Dan. 1—6

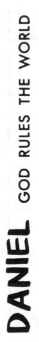

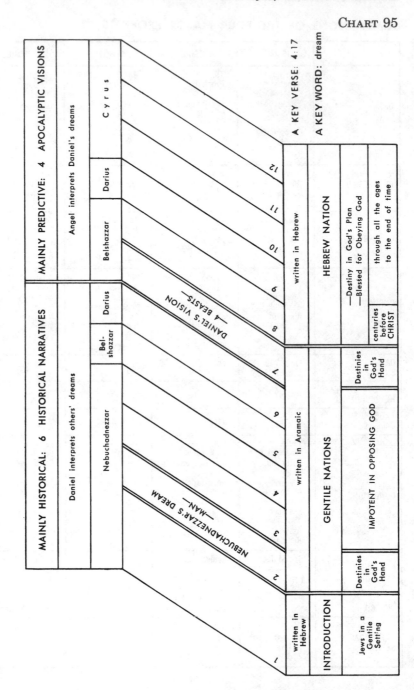

DANIEL GOD RULES THE WORLD

MAINLY HISTORICAL: 6 HISTORICAL NARRATIVES	MAINLY PREDICTIVE: 4 APOCALYPTIC VISIONS
Daniel interprets others' dreams	Angel interprets Daniel's dreams

Nebuchadnezzar	Bel-shazzar	Darius	Belshazzar	Darius	C y r u s

NEBUCHADNEZZAR'S DREAM —MAN—

DANIEL'S VISION —4 BEASTS—

A KEY VERSE: 4:17

A KEY WORD: dream

written in Hebrew	written in Aramaic	written in Hebrew
INTRODUCTION	GENTILE NATIONS	HEBREW NATION
Jews in a Gentile Setting	IMPOTENT IN OPPOSING GOD	—Destiny in God's Plan— —Blessed for Obeying God—
Destinies in God's Hand	Destinies in God's Hand	centuries before CHRIST
		through all the ages to the end of time

Johnson, Philip C. *The Book of Daniel.*
Leupold, H. C. *Exposition of Daniel.* (Amillennial viewpoint)
Luck, G. Coleman. *Daniel.* Everyman's Bible Commentary.
McClain, Alva J. *Daniel's Prophecy of the Seventy Weeks.*
Newell, Philip R. *Daniel.*
Pentecost, J. Dwight. *Prophecy for Today,* pp. 69-79.
Walvoord, John F. *Daniel: The Key to Prophetic Revelation.*
Wood, Leon J. *A Commentary on Daniel.*

25

The Twelve Minor Prophets

The last twelve books of our Old Testament are commonly referred to as the minor prophets. These books will receive our attention for the remainder of this study guide.

I. Titles

The common title for these books is "minor prophets." This title originated in Augustine's time (late fourth-century A.D.). The books are "minor" only in the sense of being much shorter than such prophecies as Isaiah and Jeremiah (called "major prophets"). Their message is surely not less important today, nor was it when first delivered in Old Testament times. They were minor prophets preaching a major message.

The Hebrew Bible regards these writings as one book, and calls them simply "The Twelve." It was because of the books' brevity that the Jews in Old Testament times joined the twelve writings together into one scroll, so that the combined length was about the same as that of Isaiah or Jeremiah. Hence, it was very natural to consider them as one book, *The Twelve.*[1] At least the title is not misleading, as "minor prophets" can be.

II. Canon

The twelve minor prophets have never been strongly challenged as being part of the inspired canon of Scripture. Their messages are just as lofty and unique as those of the major prophets, and have been recognized as such.

As noted earlier, in the Hebrew Bible (Law, Prophets, Writings) *The Twelve* is listed as just one book of the Prophets section. This partly explains why the Hebrew Bible has a total of only twenty-four books, although those twenty-four are the exact equivalent of our

---

1. The following second-century B.C. nonbiblical reference shows that the books were so designated before the time of Christ: "And of the Twelve Prophets may the bones flourish again from their place, for they comforted Jacob and redeemed them by assurance of hope" (Ecclesiasticus 49:10).

thirty-nine. In the English Bible, the minor prophets comprise twelve of the seventeen prophetic books.

III. Order of the Minor Prophets in the English Bible

This is the order of the list of minor prophets in our English Bible:

1. Hosea	7. Nahum
2. Joel	8. Habakkuk
3. Amos	9. Zephaniah
4. Obadiah	10. Haggai
5. Jonah	11. Zechariah
6. Micah	12. Malachi

It is not fully known what originally determined the order of this list. There is a general chronological pattern if, as suggested by this study guide, the first six books were written before the last six.[2] (See Chart 96.)

As far as ministry is concerned, the twelve minor prophets may be identified as three groups: prophets of Israel; prophets of Judah; and postexilic prophets (see Chart 96).

When the books of the minor prophets are listed within each group in the chronological order of their writing, this is the order:

THREE GROUPS OF THE TWELVE MINOR PROPHETS

GROUP	BOOK	NUMBER OF CHAPTERS	TOTAL
1—PROPHETS OF ISRAEL	Jonah Amos Hosea	4 9 14	27
2—PROPHETS OF JUDAH	Obadiah Joel Micah Nahum Habakkuk Zephaniah	1 3 7 3 3 3	20
3—POSTEXILIC PROPHETS	Haggai Zechariah Malachi	2 14 4	20

---

2. The dates assigned to the prophets by this study guide are essentially those of John C. Whitcomb's chart, *Old Testament Kings and Prophets*. George Adam Smith lists the prophets in this chronological order: Amos, Hosea, Micah, Zephaniah, Nahum, Habakkuk, Obadiah, Haggai, Zechariah, Malachi, Joel, Jonah. (*The Book of the Twelve Prophets*, 2 vols.)

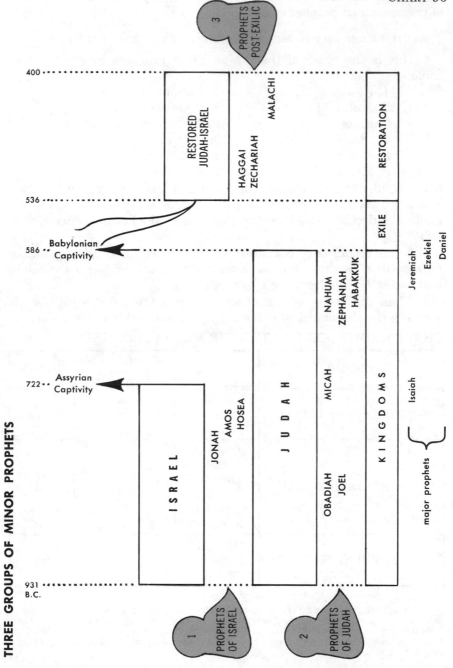

THREE GROUPS OF MINOR PROPHETS

3 PROPHETS POST-EXILIC

400 ·········

MALACHI

RESTORED JUDAH-ISRAEL

RESTORATION

HAGGAI ZECHARIAH

536 ·········

Babylonian Captivity

586 ·········

EXILE

Jeremiah
Ezekiel
Daniel

NAHUM ZEPHANIAH HABAKKUK

JUDAH

MICAH

KINGDOMS

Assyrian Captivity

722 ··

JONAH AMOS HOSEA

ISRAEL

Isaiah

OBADIAH JOEL

major prophets

931 ·········
B.C.

1 PROPHETS OF ISRAEL

2 PROPHETS OF JUDAH

The order listed above is the order in which the books are surveyed in this book.

IV. CONTEMPORARIES OF JONAH, AMOS, AND HOSEA

Chart 97 shows which kings were reigning in Israel during the public ministries of each of the three prophets. In a few instances there were coregencies (e.g., both Jehoash and Jeroboam II ruled between 793 and 782 B.C.) How many kings reigned during Hosea's ministry? Note that the Assyrians took Israel captive toward the close of Hosea's ministry. Since the captivity was God's judgment for sin, what does this reveal about the spiritual burden on Hosea's shoulders? Consult the Appendixes for a listing of the kings of Israel and related data and descriptions.

KINGS CONTEMPORARY   CHART 97
WITH THE
MINOR PROPHETS OF ISRAEL

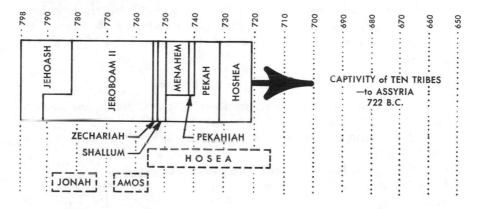

Below are listed the approximate dates of the reigns of Israel's kings and ministries of its prophets, between 798 and 713 B.C.

REIGNS OF THE KINGS		MINISTRIES OF THE PROPHETS	
Jehoash	798-782		
Jeroboam II	793-753	Jonah	784-772
Zechariah	753-752		
Shallum	752	Amos	765-755
Menahem	752-742		
Pekahiah	742-740	Hosea	755-713
Pekah	752-732		
Hoshea	732-722		

V. MAIN SUBJECTS OF THE MINOR PROPHETS

The messages of the minor prophets are generally the same as that of the major prophets, since their ministries were similar as to time, place, and people.

A. INSTRUCTION AND EXHORTATION (FORTHTELLING)

Many chapters deal with sin, warning, and judgment, but they do so because that is the very setting of God's Good News of redemption. There is a positive, bright evangel in every book of *"The Twelve:"*

> the irrepressible love of God to sinful men; the perseverance and pursuits of His grace; His mercies that follow the exiled and the outcast; His truth that goes forth richly upon the heathen; the hope of the Saviour of mankind; the outpouring of the Spirit; counsels of patience; impulses of tenderness and of healing.[3]

B. PREDICTION AND EXHORTATION (FORETELLING)

The utterances of the prophets, for the most part, centered around four points in history: (1) their own times; (2) the threatening captivities (Assyrian and Babylonian) and eventual restoration; (3) the coming of their Messiah[4]; and (4) the reign of the Messiah as King.

VI. SOME REVIEW QUESTIONS

1. Name the twelve minor prophets in the order given in our English Bible.

2. Name the minor prophets according to the three groupings identified in this chapter.

3. What does the title "minor prophets" signify?

4. What group name does the Hebrew Bible assign to these books?

5. Who was the reigning world power during the ministries of Jonah, Amos, and Hosea? (See Chart 4.)

6. Distinguish between forthtelling and foretelling, as far as the prophets were concerned.

---

3. Smith, 1:9.
4. The name "Messiah" (literally, "anointed one") appears only twice in the Old Testament: Daniel 9:25-26. The idea of an anointed person or thing, however, is common in the Old Testament. In 2 Samuel 7 the concept of a Davidic Messiah originates, without using either the word "Messiah" or "anointed." In the prophets, Christ is referred to by various names (e.g., "ruler," Mic 5:2).

26

The Minor Prophets of Israel
(Jonah, Amos, Hosea)

Jonah, Amos, and Hosea are the three minor prophets who ministered to the Northern Kingdom of Israel. The messages of their books are extremely contemporary. In fact, someone has said concerning Amos that "he proclaimed a message so far ahead of his time that most of the human race, and a large part of all Christendom have not yet caught up with it."

The three prophets of Israel have been compared this way:
Jonah: prophet of a broken ministry
Amos: prophet of the broken Law
Hosea: prophet of a broken heart
These comparisons suggest in a limited way something of the paths which you will follow as you move from book to book in the survey studies of this chapter.

JONAH: GO YE INTO ALL THE WORLD

The story of Jonah is one of the clearest demonstrations of God's love and mercy for *all* mankind. This universal love is a foundational truth of the whole Bible, taught by the most quoted verse, John 3:16. By studying Jonah before studying the other minor prophets, we will see the full view first—God's love for Gentile *and* Jew—and this will put the later studies about Israel and Judah in proper perspective.

I. BACKGROUND

A. THE MAN JONAH

1. Name and family. The name Jonah (Heb., *Yonah)* means "dove." According to 2 Kings 14:25, he was the son of Amittai,[1] and

---

1. There is a Jewish tradition that Jonah's mother was the widow of the town of Zarephath and that Elijah raised Jonah from the dead (1 Kings 17:8-24).

his hometown was Gath-hepher. This village was located about three miles northeast of Nazareth, Jesus' hometown.[2] Recall that the great prophet Jeremiah was also from a small, little-known town, Anathoth (Jer 1:1).

2. *Ministry as a prophet.* Jonah probably had the same general qualifications for the office of prophet as the other prophets had. Most of his character traits, revealed in the narrative of his book, are not commendable (e.g., disobedience and pouting). The story of Jonah's service to God underscores God's patience and willingness to work through men despite their frailties.

The main purpose of the book of Jonah is to show God's gracious

JONAH AND HIS CONTEMPORARIES   CHART 98

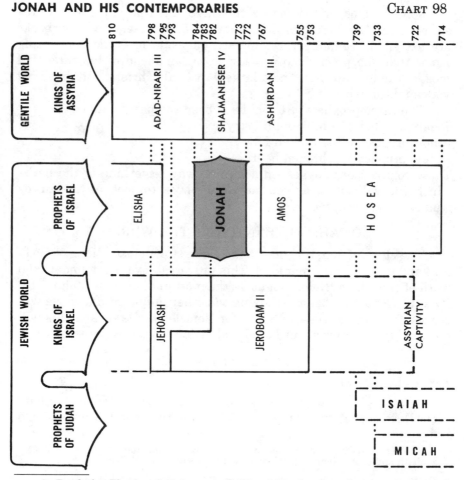

_____
    2. Read the Pharisees' statement of John 7:52 about prophets coming out of Galilee. Were the Pharisees correct?

dealings with the heathen Gentile city of Nineveh. God chose Jonah to be His channel of communication to them.

3. *Jonah's contemporaries.* Chart 98 shows Jonah and some of his contemporaries. Note the following on the chart:

a) Elisha was Jonah's predecessor. In fact, Jonah may have been one of Elisha's disciples, learning much from this "man of God." Read 2 Kings 13:14-20 for the account of Elisha's death. Amos and Hosea were Jonah's successors.

b) Even though the book of Jonah is about the prophet's ministry to the foreign city of Nineveh, Jonah was primarily a prophet of Israel to Israel. However, God did not choose to record in Scripture any details of his homeland ministry beyond what we learn from a passage in 2 Kings (see below).

c) Jeroboam II, the most powerful king of Israel, reigned during all of Jonah's public ministry. Read 2 Kings 14:23-29 for a summary of Jeroboam's evil reign. Note the reference to Jonah's prophecy that Jeroboam would regain Israel's northern boundaries from Syria. "God gave Israel a last chance of repentance [14:26-27], seeing whether prosperity would accomplish what affliction had not."[3] When we study Amos and Hosea we will see that Israel chose not to return to God.

d) In a way, Jonah was an intermediary between the Jewish world and the Gentile world. Assyria was Israel's main military threat during Jonah's ministry, although the worst threat was yet to come (fifty years later). Spiritually, Assyria was as idolatrous as Israel. In light of this information, why would Jonah not want to preach the message of repentance to the Assyrian Ninevites?

e) Only God knows what the relationship between Assyria and Israel would have been after Jonah's preaching to Nineveh (chap. 3) if Israel herself were right with God.

f) Note that Israel fell to Assyria only about fifty years after the close of Jonah's ministry. Do you think Jonah might have had foreknowledge of this imminent captivity?

B. THE BOOK OF JONAH

1. *Author.* The traditional view is that Jonah wrote this book about himself. The fact that the narrative does not use the first-person pronoun does not preclude this. Hebrew authors (e.g., Moses) often wrote autobiography in the style of third-person biography.

2. *Date.* The book was written toward the end of Jonah's career, around 770 B.C.

---

3. H. L. Ellison, "I and II Kings," in *The New Bible Commentary,* p. 325.

GEOGRAPHY OF JONAH   MAP V

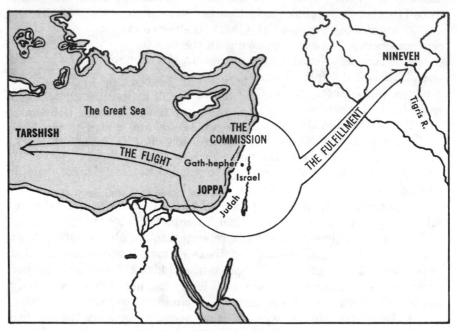

3. Type of writing. The style of Jonah is biographical narrative, similar to the stories of Elijah and Elisha (1,2 Kings), whom Jonah succeeded as prophet.[4] Hidden in the historical account is a predictive, typical purpose. The main type concerns Jonah and the whale, which prefigured Christ's burial and resurrection (read Matt 12:39-41). Jonah's deliverance from the belly of the whale was also a sign to the Ninevites. What did it signify, according to Jesus (Luke 11:29-30)?

4. Purposes. Three main purposes of the book of Jonah are:

a) To teach God's people their responsibility to deliver the message of salvation to all people—Jew and Gentile.[5]

b) To demonstrate that God honors repentance for sin, whoever the person (cf. Jer 18:7-10). Read Romans 1:16; 2:9-10; 3:29; 2 Peter 3:9; Mark 16:15.

---

4. In the Hebrew Bible, 1 and 2 Kings are classified among the Former Prophets, and Jonah among the Latter Prophets.

5. Acts 10-11 and Romans 9-11 show the application of this in New Testament times, when the early Jewish Christians hesitated accepting Gentile believers into their fellowship.

c) To show to people of the Christian era that Christ's death and resurrection, prefigured in Jonah's experience, were in the divine plan before Christ ever walked this earth.

5. *The geography of Jonah.* Map V shows the three key geographical points in the story of Jonah: Jonah's homeland, Tarshish, and Nineveh.

a) The homeland—the place where God commissioned Jonah to go to Nineveh. This was Israel, north of Judah. Exactly where Jonah was when the call of 1:2 came, is not known. Shown on the map are Gath-Hepher, Jonah's hometown, and Joppa, where he boarded a ship to go to Tarshish.

b) Tarshish—the city where Jonah wanted to flee to, to hide from the Lord's presence. It may have been the city of Tartessus, of southwestern Spain.

c) Nineveh—The earliest reference to Nineveh in the Bible is at Genesis 10:11-12. Read these verses and observe the references to Rehoboth, Calah, and Resen. It appears that these three adjoining cities were part of the Nineveh district of city-state, and that the whole area, by virtue of its size, was referred to as a "great city." Nineveh was five hundred miles northeast of the Sea of Galilee, located on the banks of the Tigris River.

II. SURVEY OF JONAH

The book of Jonah is one of the easiest and most interesting books to read in the Bible. One author says it is the most beautiful story ever written in so small a compass.

A. A SURVEY READING

1. First scan the four chapters, for overall impressions. Does the book have a natural opening? What about a conclusion?

2. Is there a progression in the plot of the story? Who is the main person in the action? Are any other individuals involved?

B. SURVEY CHART

Study carefully the survey Chart 99. Observe the following in connection with the chart:

1. The book is of two main parts. What three outlines on the chart show this?

2. Study carefully the bottom of the chart, which compares the

narratives of the two halves of the book. Note the similarities and differences. Refer to the Bible text to support parts of the outlines which are not clear.

3. At some time during your study you may want to make your own outlines of the book.

4. Read the key verses shown. Note also the key words. Add to this list your own choices.

III. Applications of Jonah

What does this book teach about
1. the universal message of salvation
2. the divine commission of service
3. fleeing from God
4. recompense for disobedience
5. repentance
6. forgiveness of sin
7. complaining
8. prayer
9. miracles
10. God's supernatural control of nature

How did Jesus apply the story of Jonah, according to these verses: Matthew 16:4 (cf. Matt 12:39-41); Luke 11:30?

IV. Selected Reading

GENERAL INTRODUCTION

Archer, Gleason L. *A Survey of Old Testament Introduction,* pp. 295-303.
Ellison, H. L. *The Prophets of Israel,* pp. 55-61.
Freeman, Hobart E. *An Introduction to the Old Testament Prophets,* pp. 160-71.
Gaebelein, Frank E. *Four Minor Prophets,* pp. 57-138.
Sampey, John Richard. "Jonah." In *The International Standard Bible Encyclopedia, 3:1727-29.*

COMMENTARIES

Banks, William L. *Jonah.* Everyman's Bible Commentary.
Deane, W. J. *Jonah.* Pulpit Commentary.
Keil, C. F. "Jonah." In *Biblical Commentary on the Old Testament Minor Prophets,* vol. 1.
Kennedy, James H. *Studies in the Book of Jonah.*
Kleinert, Paul. "Jonah." In Lange's *Commentary on the Holy Scriptures.*

AMOS: PREPARE TO MEET GOD

Amos was God's prophet to prosperous Israel, steeped in religios-

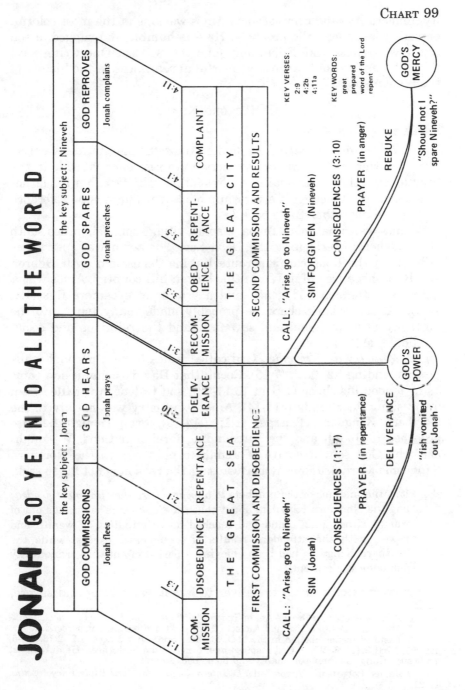

JONAH GO YE INTO ALL THE WORLD

the key subject: Jonah		the key subject: Nineveh	
GOD COMMISSIONS	GOD HEARS	GOD SPARES	GOD REPROVES
Jonah flees	Jonah prays	Jonah preaches	Jonah complains
1:3	2:1	2:10	3:1	3:3	3:5	4:1	4:11
1:1 COM-MISSION	DISOBEDIENCE	REPENTANCE	DELIV-ERANCE	RECOM-MISSION	OBED-IENCE	REPENT-ANCE	COMPLAINT
THE GREAT SEA			THE GREAT CITY		
FIRST COMMISSION AND DISOBEDIENCE			SECOND COMMISSION AND RESULTS		

CALL: "Arise, go to Nineveh"

CALL: "Arise, go to Nineveh"

SIN (Jonah)

SIN FORGIVEN (Nineveh)

CONSEQUENCES (1:17)

CONSEQUENCES (3:10)

PRAYER (in repentance)

PRAYER (in anger)

DELIVERANCE

REBUKE

"fish vomited out Jonah"

GOD'S POWER

GOD'S MERCY

"Should not I spare Nineveh?"

KEY VERSES:
2:9
4:2b
4:11a

KEY WORDS:
great
prepared
word of the Lord
repent

ity, immorality, and complacency. Amos was one of the most colorful personalities among the prophets. He was humble and rugged, a son of the wilderness, like Elijah and John the Baptist. One writer says that his was "one of the most wonderful appearances in the history of the human spirit."[6]

I. BACKGROUND

A. THE MAN AMOS

1. Name and family. The name Amos means "burden-bearer" (from the Hebrew root *amas*, "to carry"). No reference is made in the book to any relative, including Amos's father. The fact that his father is not named may suggest a very humble birth. There is no reference to Amos in any other Bible book.[7]

Amos was a native of Tekoa, a small village some six miles south of Bethlehem, overlooking the Dead Sea. The town was just a few miles from the busy caravan route linking Jerusalem with Hebron and Beer-sheba (see Map W). In this barren hill country, Amos was a herdsman of sheep and goats, and a grower of sycamore figs (1:1; 7:14).[8] As a wool merchant he probably made many trips into the northern cities of Israel and saw firsthand the religious and social corruption of its people.

2. Ministry as a prophet. God called Amos to be a prophet while he was tending his flock (7:15). Recall that David's commission came as he tended his sheep (1 Sam 16:11-13); and Gideon was called from a threshing floor (Judg 6:11-14). Amos's ministry was mainly to the Northern Kingdom of Israel (1:1; 7:14-15), even though he also preached to Judah and the surrounding foreign nations. We might ask why God sent a native of Judah to prophesy to the Northern Kingdom of Israel. James Robertson says the reason is not far to seek.

> It is the manner of the prophets *to appear where they are most needed;* and the Northern Kingdom about that time had come victorious out of war [2 Kings 14:25], and had reached its culmination of wealth and power, with the attendant results of luxury and excess, while the Southern Kingdom had been enjoying a period of outward tranquillity and domestic content.[9]

The message God wanted to deliver to Israel was strong and severe,

---

6. Cornill, quoted by George Adam Smith, *The Book of the Twelve Prophets,* 1:71.
7. The Amos of Luke 3:25 and Amoz of 2 Kings 20:1 are different persons.
8. Pastoral scenes abound in the book at these and other places: 1:2; 2:13; 3:4-5; 4:7; 6:12; 7:1; 8:1; 9:6. When God inspired men to write the Scriptures, He did not set aside such things as their personality and home background.
9. James Robertson, "Amos," in *The International Standard Bible Encyclopedia,* 1:121.

so God chose for His messenger a man who had withstood the rigors of a disciplined life, and who knew what hardness was. In the howling wildernesses around Tekoa, life was full of poverty and danger—it was an empty and silent world. Amos knew God, and he knew the Scriptures, even though he was not trained in the school of the prophets (7:14). Living in Tekoa was ideal preparation for his task and was just as much of God as was his call. His prophetic ministry lasted about ten years (765-755 B.C.).

B. THE BOOK OF AMOS

1. Author and date. Amos wrote this book toward the end of Jeroboam's reign, around 760 B.C. Most of the nine chapters are "the words" (i.e., messages, or sermons) of Amos (1:1). One narrative section appears at 7:10-17.

Chart 100 shows Amos among his contemporaries. Study this carefully, to fix in your mind the book's historical setting. What prophets of Israel ministered before and after Amos? What kings reigned over Israel and Judah during Amos's ministry? Compare 1:1.

2. Audience. Amos's main audience was Israel, which politically and economically was at a zenith of power. The threat of war was eased, and business was booming. A spirit of self-sufficiency and smug complacency thrived on material prosperity. The rich were getting richer, and the poor were getting poorer. Idolatry, hypocrisy, moral corruption, and social injustices were everywhere. The nation was truly on the brink of disaster. In fact, on God's timetable, destruction was due in about three decades (722 B.C.). Such was the soul and destiny of the audience of Amos the prophet.

3. Message. Amos's preaching was so sharp and vigorous that he was accused of sedition by Amaziah, the idolatrous high priest of Bethel (7:10-17).

Like most prophets, Amos underscored these key truths:
a) the people's sin
b) the coming of judgment
c) the righteousness and holiness of God
d) the mercy of God in offering deliverance

The book has often been criticized as a "dark book." But Amos's main purpose in stirring conviction of sin and repentance in the hearts of the people was not to alleviate his own grief over their evil ways. Rather, he yearned that the people, as individuals and as a nation, would come to a personal knowledge of God as their Lord. A key statement of his book is the Lord's gracious invitation, "Seek Me that you may live" (5:4).

GEOGRAPHY OF AMOS

II. Survey of Amos

A. FIRST READINGS

Scan the book once or twice for overall impressions. Here are some things to look for in such a survey:

1. Overall tone (e.g., Is the book severe, mellow, meditative, philosophical, practical?)

2. Tone of the opening chapters as compared with that of the closing verses (9:11-15).

3. Groupings of Amos's messages (e.g., beginning at 7:1 is a group of visions).

4. Repeated words and phrases.

5. Verses which strike you, for whatever reason.

B. SURVEY CHART

Chart 101 is a survey of the book of Amos, showing its structure and highlights. Observe the following on the chart, reading the Bible passages which are cited:

1. The book has a short introduction (1:1-2), but no formal conclusion.

2. There are three types of writing:

a) Lyric prophecy (oracles)—chapters 1-2.

Key repeated phrase: "Thus says the LORD" (e.g., 1:3).

b) Teaching discourse (sermons)—chapters 3-6.

Key repeated phrase: "Hear this word" (e.g., 3:1)

c) Dramatic revelation (visions)—chapters 7-9.

Key repeated phrase: "The Lord GOD showed me" (e.g., 7:1)

3. Most of the book is about judgment. What is the last section (9:11-15) about? What other two-point outline represents the book?

4. Four sections are clearly discernible in the book. Mark these in your Bible. Check the Bible text to see the identifying phrases which mark the sections.

Judgments against the nations—chapters 1-2

Judgments against Israel—chapters 3-6

Visions of judgment—7:1—9:10

Messianic promise—9:11-15

5. Study the two outlines at the top of the chart which identify the people whom Amos's messages are about. Read in your Bible the verses which support the identifications listed on top of page 409.

6. Complete the listing of the five visions, beginning with locusts.

7. As you proceed with your study, look for other references to deliverance and salvation which may appear in the text (e.g., 5:4).

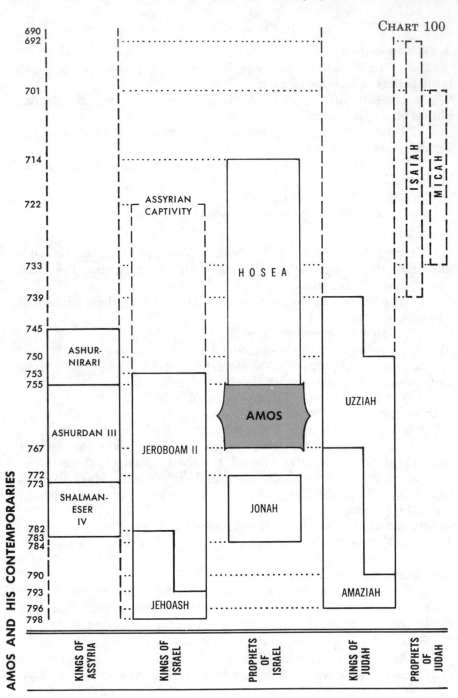

CHART 100

AMOS AND HIS CONTEMPORARIES

690
692

701

714

722 — ASSYRIAN CAPTIVITY

733 — HOSEA

739

745 — ASHUR-NIRARI

750

753
755

ASHURDAN III — JEROBOAM II — AMOS — UZZIAH

767

772
773 — SHALMAN-ESER IV

782
783
784

790

793

796 — JEHOASH — AMAZIAH

798

ISAIAH   MICAH

JONAH

KINGS OF ASSYRIA   KINGS OF ISRAEL   PROPHETS OF ISRAEL   KINGS OF JUDAH   PROPHETS OF JUDAH

(The high point of this redemptive theme is the last section, 9:11-15.)

8. Note the key words and key verses. Add to these lists along the way.

GENTILE and JEW	{ Gentile Nations (1:3—2:3). Judah (2:4-5). Israel (2:6-16).	See 1:3,6,9,11,13; 2:1. See 2:4. See 2:6.
ISRAEL (Northern Kingdom)	Israel (mainly) (3:1—9:10).	See 7:10-17 for a distinction between Israel and Judah.[10]
JEW and GENTILE	{ Israel and Judah (9:11-15). Gentiles	See 9:11-14 for references to the chosen people of God. See 9:12 (KJV) ("heathen").

III. APPLICATIONS

1. How did James apply the message of Amos, according to Acts 15:16-17? (Cf. Amos 9:11-12.)

2. Why is fire often a part of God's judgment?

3. Two basic attributes of God are love and holiness. Are both of these manifested in Old Testament history? What references to God's grace did you read in the book of Amos? How is God's love related to His holiness?

4. People of Judah "rejected the law of the LORD" (Amos 2:4). Is this sin committed today by unbelievers? Can it be committed by backslidden Christians? If so, in what ways?

5. Someone has written, "A man does not choose to be a prophet; he is chosen." How does this truth apply to Amos? See 1:1; 3:8; 7:14-15. Does it apply to Christian workers today?

6. Is there hope for a people when their religious leader is a false shepherd? Recall the story of Amaziah, the priest of Bethel (7:10-17).

7. Evaluate this statement: "Every prophecy of judgment is an invitation to repentance."[11] What do you think is meant by the words, "Prepare to meet your God, O Israel" (4:12b)? Are they a warning; a call to repentance; or both?

8. Write a list of various spiritual lessons taught by 3:1—9:10.

---

10. At some places (e.g., 3:1) in this long section, Amos is speaking about both kingdoms—Israel and Judah. For the most part, however, his message concerns Israel, with its capital at Bethel.

11. Arnold Schultz, "Amos," in *The Wycliffe Bible Commentary, p. 834.*

AMOS PREPARE TO MEET GOD

GENTILE AND JEW		ISRAEL (northern kingdom).			JEW AND GENTILE	
GENTILE NATIONS	2:4 JUDAH	I S R A E L			ISRAEL JUDAH	
	2:6 ISRAEL					GENTILES
lyric prophecy ORACLES		discourse SERMONS		dramatic revelation VISIONS		

1:3 — 2:1 — 3 — 4 — 5 — 9 — 7:1 — 7:10 (parenthesis) — 8:1 — 9:11 — 9:15

JUDGMENTS VS. NATIONS	JUDGMENTS VS. ISRAEL	FIVE VISIONS OF JUDGMENT	MESSIANIC PROMISE
J U D G M E N T			H O P E

THE RIGHTEOUSNESS OF GOD'S LAW | THE LONG-SUFFER-ING OF GOD'S GRACE

"Hear this word"   "The Lord showed unto me"

1. Syria
2. Philistia
3. Phoenicia
4. Edom
5. Ammon
6. Moab
7. Judah
8. Israel

1. locusts
2.
3.
4.
5.

PREPARE TO MEET THY GOD, O ISRAEL 4:12

KEY VERSES:
1:2
4:12
5:4

KEY WORDS:
saith the Lord
transgressions
I will
seek

1:1 introduction

IV. Selected Reading

GENERAL INTRODUCTION

Archer, Gleason L. *A Survey of Old Testament Introduction,* pp. 304-8.
Ellison, H. L. *The Prophets of Israel,* pp. 62-69.
Freeman, Hobart E. *An Introduction to the Old Testament Prophets,* pp. 184-90.
Gaebelein, Frank E. *Four Minor Prophets.*
Howard, J. K. *Amos Among the Prophets,* pp. 1-38.
Motyer, J. A. "Amos." In *The New Bible Commentary,* pp. 726-41.
Scroggie, W. Graham. *Know Your Bible,* 1:162-65.

COMMENTARIES

Driver, S. R. *The Books of Joel and Amos.* Cambridge Bible for Schools and Colleges.
Schultz, Arnold C. "Amos." In *The Wycliffe Bible Commentary.*
Watts, John D. W. *Vision and Prophecy in Amos.*
Wolfe, Rolland E. *Meet Amos and Hosea.*

HOSEA: GOD'S LOVE FOR BACKSLIDERS

Hosea was the last writing prophet to minister to Israel before they fell to the Assyrians in 722 B.C. He has been called the prophet of "Israel's zero hour," because "the nation had sunk to a point of such corruption that a major stroke of divine judgment could no longer be staved off."[12] But even though judgment is a main subject of Hosea's message, the book is remembered mostly for its vivid pictures of God's love and grace. Someone has well remarked, "There is nothing of divine grace that is not found in the book of Hosea." Your study of this inspired Scripture should lead you into a deeper knowledge of who God is and how He deals with sinners.

I. Background

A. THE MAN HOSEA

1. Name. The name Hosea (Heb., *Hoshea)* means "salvation." It is interesting to observe that the names Joshua (Num 13:16) and Jesus (Matt 1:21) are derived from the same Hebrew root as Hosea.

2. Family and home. Hosea's father was named Beeri (1:1). We do not know what Beeri's occupation was. He may have been a middle-class merchant, or a farmer or cattleman. Hosea used many illustrations of agricultural settings when he wrote, which suggests that

---

12. J. Sidlow Baxter, *Explore the Book,* 4:89.

the prophet lived close to the soil in his young life (cf. 4:16; 6:4; 10:12). His home may have been in a town of Ephraim or Manasseh (see Map X), though this also is only speculation.

3. Ministry. Hosea probably had no formal training in a school of the prophets, but his writings show him to be a very knowledgeable man. We do not know precisely when God originally called him to be a prophet. The messages recorded in the book were given to him probably between 754 and 714 B.C. Chart 102 shows who his contemporaries were. Note the following:

a) During Hosea's ministry seven kings reigned over Israel, while four kings reigned on Judah's throne.[13]

b) In a sense Hosea was a successor to the prophet Amos. Recall that Amos was a native of Judah. This makes Hosea the only writing prophet *of* Israel *to* Israel. As one writer has said, "His book is the prophetic voice wrung from the bosom of the kingdom itself."[14]

c) Hosea was ministering at the time the Assyrian invaders conquered Israel (722 B.C.).[15] Refer to Chart 102 and note that Jeremiah was ministering to Judah when the Babylonian Captivity began (586 B.C.). Hosea and Jeremiah both preached the same kind of message; both were "weeping prophets."

d) Isaiah and Micah were prophets of Judah, while Hosea was prophesying to Israel. (As is shown later, a few of Hosea's messages were directed to the Southern Kingdom.)

Hosea was one of the tenderest of the prophets in his contacts with Israel. He has been called "the prophet of the broken heart." His divine commission was to plead with the people of Israel to return to God. They did not respond, and so captivity came (read 2 Kings 17). Although his message went unheeded, he did not fail as a prophet. He was obedient to God who called him, delivering God's message to the people.

B. THE BOOK OF HOSEA

1. Date. The messages of the book of Hosea, delivered sometime between 754 and 714 B.C., were probably compiled by Hosea into one book toward the end of that period. Gleason Archer suggests 725 B.C. as a possible date.[16] If that is so, Hosea completed the book before the

---

13. Only Jeroboam's name is mentioned in 1:1. The omissions have been explained in various ways. (Consult commentaries.)

14. Ewald, quoted by James Robertson, "Hosea," in *The International Standard Bible Encyclopedia*, 3:1425.

15. Some think that Hosea moved to Judah at the time of the conquest.

16. Gleason L. Archer, *A Survey of Old Testament Introduction*, p. 310.

GEOGRAPHY OF HOSEA

MAP X

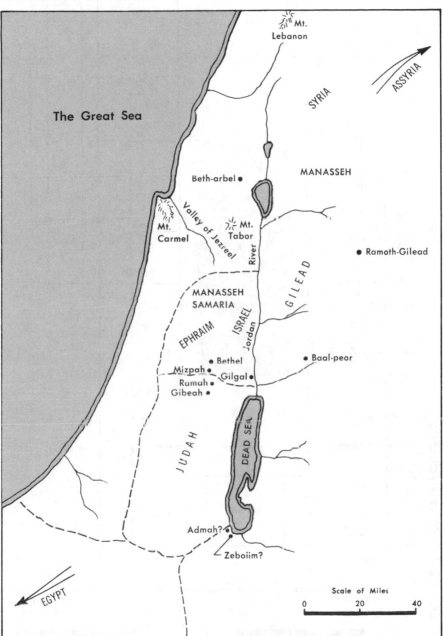

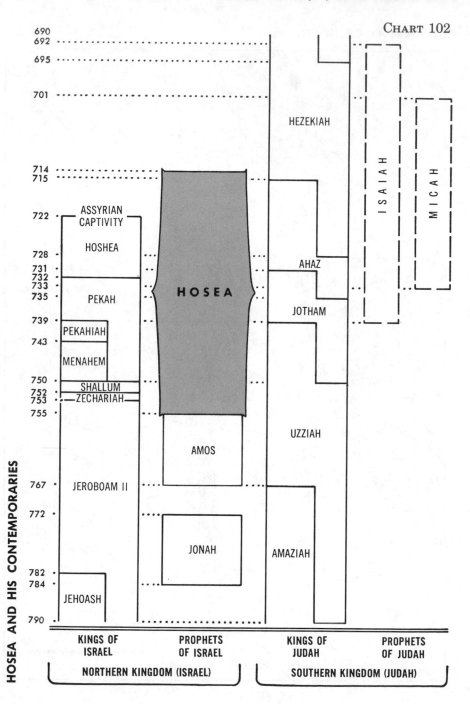

CHART 102

Assyrian Captivity (722 B.C.). That judgment was foretold in the book; it was not reported as having already taken place.

2. Setting. In the days of Hosea, the Northern Kingdom of Israel was politically plagued by anarchy, unrest, and confusion. The quick succession of kings (Chart 102) suggests such an instability. One political faction favored alliance with Egypt; another, with Assyria. One writer comments on 7:11 thus, "Israel was like a silly dove. . . fluttering everywhere but to God."[17]

Economically, the nation was prosperous. Spiritually, it was the darkest hour of Israel. Idolatry, immorality, and haughty rejection of God's love spelled disaster. Israel was a backslidden people when Hosea preached to them (14:4). Read 2 Kings 15-17 to feel how black the darkness was.

3. Theme. The theme of Hosea is this: the tender-loving God offers one last chance of restoration to hardhearted, adulterous Israel. Israel is the unfaithful wife who has deserted her husband and gone after other lovers. God through the prophet Hosea invites her back: "Return, O Israel, to the LORD your God" (14:1). Read these passages about God's love: 2:14,15,19,20; chapter 3; 11:3,4,8; chapter 14; compare Romans 11:22. John has been called the apostle of love in the New Testament; Hosea could be called the prophet of love in the Old Testament.

4. Language and style. Hosea's style is abrupt, short, and sharp ("he flashes forth brilliant sentences"). But tenderness is the book's prevailing tone. Scroggie says, "His message is one of the most profound and spiritual in the Old Testament."[18] The authoritarian tone is heard throughout the book, even though the familiar declaration "thus saith the LORD" appears only four times. Symbols and metaphors abound throughout the book, the prominent one being that of marriage (chap. 1-3). The messages of chapters 4 to 14 were apparently not compiled with an outline in mind. Transitions are hard to detect because they are submerged in the emotional makeup of the book. As one writer observes, "The sentences fall from him like the sobs of a broken heart."[19]

II. SURVEY

1. Scan chapters 1-3. Who are some of the main characters of this narrative? At this point, don't ponder over questions that come to your mind concerning the Lord's instructions to Hosea.

---

17. E. Heavenor, "Hosea," in *The New Bible Dictionary*, p. 539.
18. W. Graham Scroggie, *Know Your Bible*, 1:166.
19. Robertson, 3:1426.

2. Study the survey Chart 103. Observe that there are two main divisions in the book. How do chapters 4-14 differ from 1-3 as to content? Scan chapters 4-14 to verify this.

3. Spend the next hour or so making a casual reading of chapters 4-14. When a verse describes sin or guilt of God's people, mark *S* in the margin of your Bible. Keep scanning until the subject changes to judgment *(J)*, invitation *(I)*, restoration *(R)*, or grace *(G)*. When there is a change of subject, record the new letter at that point. When you have done this for all the chapters, you will note that all the subjects mentioned above appear scattered throughout the whole section. In other words, a clear outline is not evident. However, observe on Chart 103 what subjects seem prominent in chapters 4-8; 9-10; and 11-14. Compare this outline with the markings you have just made. For example, is judgment more prominent than sin in chapters 9-10?

4. How do chapters 4-14 reflect Hosea's experiences in chapters 1-3, according to Chart 103?

5. The last chapter of Hosea (chap. 14) is a key Bible passage on the cure for spiritual backsliding. How does the chapter serve as a conclusion to Hosea's book? Who is the prominent person of the last sentence of the book?

6. Note the list of key words on the chart. Note also the key verses which are cited. Read the verses in your Bible. Relate them to the theme of the book.

III. APPLICATIONS

1. See how the following passages of Hosea are applied in the New Testament:

Hosea 1:9-10; 2:23	—	Romans 9:25; 1 Peter 2:10
6:6	—	Matthew 9:13 (12:7)
13:14	—	1 Corinthians 15:55

2. How is marriage a figurative representation of the Christian's relation to Christ? (Cf. Eph 5:30-32; John 14:3; Rev 19:7-9.) What can mar this intimate relationship, bringing on spiritual adultery? (Cf. James 4:4.)

3. Can a backslidden Christian be restored to fellowship with Christ? If so, how is such a restoration brought about? (Cf. Rev 2:4-5).

4. Relate Hosea 1:4 to these verses about the vengeance of God: Romans 3:5; 12:19; Hebrews 10:30.

5. What is temporary about the pleasures and allurements of the world? See 2:7a. Also, read Hebrews 11:24-26.

6. Why is it important for Christians to continually acknowledge

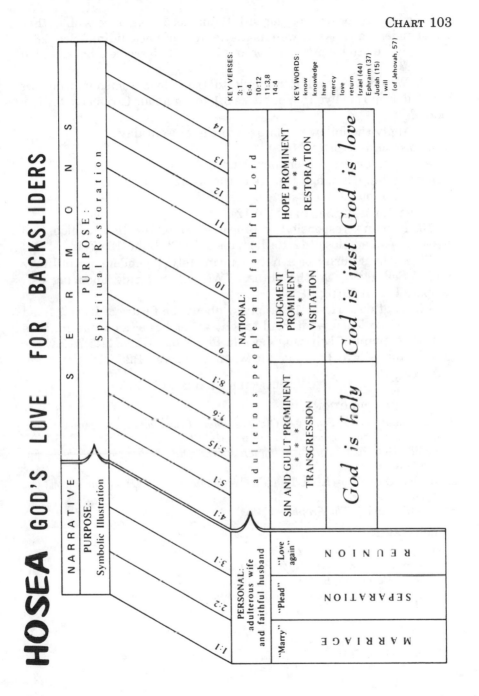

HOSEA GOD'S LOVE FOR BACKSLIDERS

NARRATIVE	SERMONS
PURPOSE: Symbolic Illustration	PURPOSE: Spiritual Restoration

PERSONAL: adulterous wife and faithful husband

NATIONAL: adulterous people and faithful Lord

"Marry"	"Plead"	"Love again"		
1:1	2:2	3:1		
MARRIAGE	SEPARATION	REUNION		

4:1	5:1	5:15	7:16	8:8	9	10	11	12	13	14
SIN AND GUILT PROMINENT * * * TRANSGRESSION			JUDGMENT PROMINENT * * * VISITATION				HOPE PROMINENT * * * RESTORATION			
God is holy			*God is just*				*God is love*			

KEY VERSES:
3:1
6:4
10:12
11:3,8
14:4

KEY WORDS:
know
knowledge
hear
mercy
love
return
Israel (44)
Ephraim (37)
Judah (15)
I will (of Jehovah, 57)

God's gracious provisions for all their needs? Is it possible that ingratitude is a cause as well as a symptom of backsliding? See 2:8.

7. How do the words "she forgot Me" (2:13) describe a backslidden believer?

8. Would you find it difficult to truly love someone who has deserted or harmed you? What does 3:1 teach about God's love for His people?

9. Apply the following phrases to the present day:

"Like people, like priest" (4:9).

"I delight in loyalty rather than sacrifice" (6:6).

"They sow the wind, and they reap the whirlwind" (8:7).

"The days of punishment have come" (9:7).

"It is time to seek the LORD" (10:12).

10. Is man's responsibility proportional to the light which God gives him? Read Hosea 12:10; Romans 1:19-23; Luke 12:47-48.

11. Is the security of a nation ultimately dependent on military might? See 14:3*a*. On the phrase, "We will not ride upon horses," compare Isaiah 30:16; 31:1.

12. What does Hosea 14 prophesy about the future of Israel? Read Romans 11 to learn what Paul taught about Israel as a nation. Was there a remnant of believing Jews in Paul's day (Rom 11:5)? How far into the future was Paul looking when he wrote 11:25-26?

IV. SELECTED READING

GENERAL INTRODUCTION

Archer, Gleason L. *A Survey of Old Testament Introduction,* pp. 308-11.

Ellison, H. L. *The Prophets of Israel,* pp. 95-110.

Freeman, Hobart E. *An Introduction to the Old Testament Prophets,* pp. 172-83.

Schmoller, Otto. "Hosea." In Lange's *Commentary on the Holy Scriptures,* pp. 1-20.

Schultz, Samuel J. *The Prophets Speak.*

COMMENTARIES

Cheyne, T. K. *The Book of Hosea.*

Gaebelein, Frank E. *Four Minor Prophets.*

Morgan, G. Campbell, *Hosea.*

Pfeiffer, Charles F. "Hosea." In *The Wycliffe Bible Commentary.*

27

The Minor Prophets of Judah
(Obadiah, Joel, Micah, Nahum, Zephaniah, Habakkuk)

Six of the twelve minor prophets ministered to the Southern Kingdom of Judah prior to the Babylonian Captivity (see Chart 96). The chronological order in which the prophets ministered is the order followed in the six surveys of this chapter. Chart 104 shows which kings were reigning over Judah during the times of those prophets.[1] The shaded areas indicate the evil reigns; the unshaded areas, the righteous reigns. What seems to have brought on the appearance of prophets: good, or evil reigns? Or is such a pattern not clear? Also keep in mind the larger setting of Old Testament history, as represented on Chart 3.

When you begin to study each book, refer to Chart 104 to help you visualize the setting.

History always involves places, and since the books of the minor prophets have a historical setting, we may expect to see geographical references in the books. Map Y shows the geography of the minor prophets of Judah. Try to fix these places in your mind before you begin to survey the Bible text.

OBADIAH: A ROCK THAT FAILS AND A
KINGDOM THAT ENDURES

Some of God's prophets were commissioned to preach to foreign nations closely involved with Judah's history. Obadiah was His messenger to Edom, hostile kingdom southeast of Judah (see Map Y). The Gentile Edomites felt militarily secure in the fortresses of their steep mountains, and wanted nothing to do with Israel's God.

---

1. Most of the dates are from John C. Whitcomb's *Chart of Kings and Prophets*. See the Appendixes for the listing of all the kings of Judah.

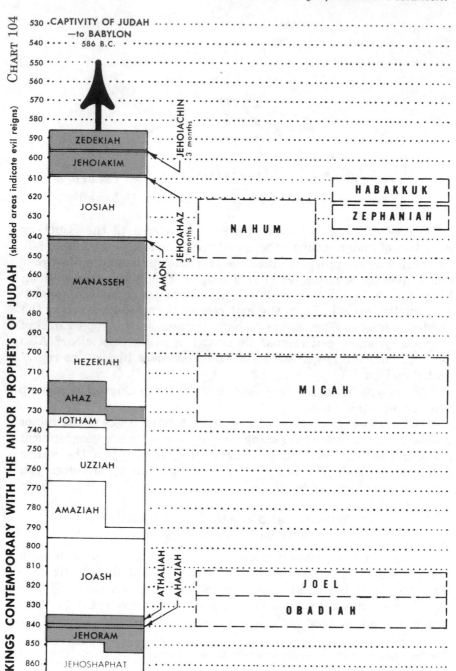

CHART 104

KINGS CONTEMPORARY WITH THE MINOR PROPHETS OF JUDAH (shaded areas indicate evil reigns)

530 ·CAPTIVITY OF JUDAH
   —to BABYLON
540 · · · · 586 B.C.
550
560
570
580

590 ZEDEKIAH
600 JEHOIAKIM
610
620 JOSIAH
630
640
650
660 MANASSEH
670
680
690
700
710 HEZEKIAH
720 AHAZ
730 JOTHAM
740
750 UZZIAH
760
770 AMAZIAH
780
790
800
810 JOASH
820
830
840 JEHORAM
850
860 JEHOSHAPHAT

JEHOIACHIN 3 months

JEHOAHAZ 3 months

AMON

ATHALIAH
AHAZIAH

NAHUM

HABAKKUK

ZEPHANIAH

MICAH

JOEL

OBADIAH

If any city of Edom was a symbol of arrogant self-confidence, it was Petra (Heb., *Sela,* 2 Kings 14:7). This now famous tourist attraction of the red-rock canyons was located about fifty miles south of the Dead Sea. Obadiah may have had Petra in mind when he wrote, "The pride of thine heart hath deceived thee, thou that dwellest in the clefts of the *rock* [Heb., *sela;* Gr., *petra*]"[2] (v. 3, KJV, italics added).

I. Background

A. THE MAN OBADIAH

The name Obadiah appears twenty times in the Bible, representing thirteen different persons. The only reference to the writing prophet is in verse 1 of his book. His home was in Judah, and he lived probably during the reigns of Jehoram, Ahaziah, Athaliah, and Joash (Chart 104).[3] The name Obadiah means "servant of the Lord" or "worshiper of the Lord."

B. THE BOOK OF OBADIAH

1. Date written. There are a few possible dates. If we knew which plundering of Jerusalem Obadiah was referring back to in verses 11-14, we could be more certain of the book's date. (The book was written later than the plundering.) Read verses 11-14. Four invasions of Jerusalem are recorded in Old Testament history:

a) by Shishak, king of Egypt, (925 B.C.); (1 Kings 14:25-26; 2 Chron 12)

b) by Philistines and Arabians (during reign of Jehoram; see Chart 104.); (2 Chron 21:16-17, cf. 2 Chron 21:8-10; Amos 1:6, 11-12)

c) by Jehoash, king of Israel (c. 790 B.C.); (2 Kings 14; 2 Chron 25)

d) by Nebuchadnezzar, king of Babylon (586 B.C.); (2 Kings 24-25; cf. Psalm 137:7)

Read the four groups of passages cited above. This book takes the position that Obadiah, in verses 11-14, was referring to the plundering by Philistines and Arabians (second invasion cited above).[4] Based on this, his book was written between 840 and 825 B.C.

2. Content and style. Obadiah is the shortest book of the Old Testament, but the familiar slogan *multum in parvo* ("much in

---

2. An alternate reading of this phrase is, "Thou that dwellest in the clefts of Sela" (ASV).

3. This is based on the view of an early date of the book, discussed later in the chapter.

4. Read Hobart E. Freeman, *An Introduction to the Old Testament Prophets,* pp. 140-41, for reasons supporting this view. Many Bible students prefer the fourth view, which places Obadiah as the last of the minor prophets of Judah and a contemporary of Jeremiah. Consult various commentaries about this.

GEOGRAPHY OF THE MINOR PROPHETS OF JUDAH   MAP Y

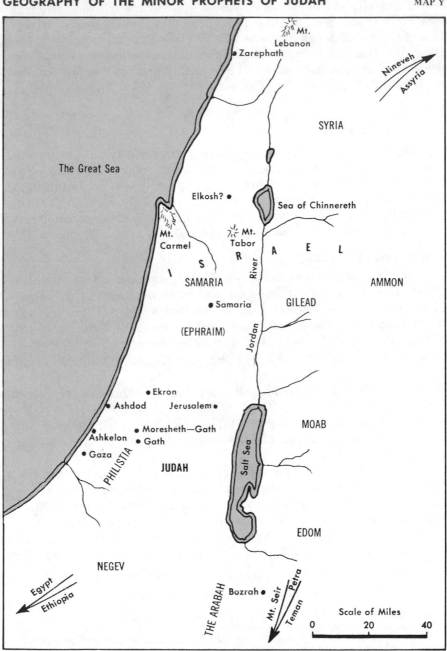

little") certainly applies to it. The style of the book is vigorous and colorful, using many striking comparisons. It is a compact version of the typical prophetic book, where the opening chapters deal with sin and judgment, and bright Messianic prophecies appear toward the end. The tragic aspect of the book is that Edom as a nation has come to a spiritual "point of no return," that is, she is not offered any hope of salvation. One writer says, "She is the only neighbor of the Israelites who was not given any promise of mercy from God."[5] This is not because God was unmerciful. Edom had already spurned the mercies of God.

3. Historical background. Since the destiny of Edom is a key subject of this book, some highlights of that nation's history are listed below, to furnish setting for the prophecy. (Read all the Bible passages.)

a) Nation was descended from Esau (Gen 25:19-34).
b) Nation settled in the regions of Mount Seir, between the Dead Sea and Gulf of Akaba, to the east of the Arabah (Gen 36). (See Map Y.)
c) Nation rejected the Israelites' request to travel through Edom on the journey from Egypt (Num 20:14-21).
d) Antagonism originating with the twin brothers, Jacob and Esau (Gen 27), persisted through the centuries involving Israel (Jacob) and Edom (Esau). Recall the passages cited earlier in this chapter about the plundering of Jerusalem. Also read 2 Samuel 8:14; 2 Kings 14:1-7; 2 Chronicles 28:17.
e) Nation was continually subject to foreign kingdoms, losing its identity as a nation before the time of Christ, and finally disappearing from history in A.D. 70 (Romans' destruction of Jerusalem).

II. SURVEY

Read the twenty-one verses of Obadiah in one sitting, aloud if possible. What are your first impressions? In your own words, what is the book mainly about?

Chart 105 shows the structural organization of the text of Obadiah. Note the following on the chart, referring to the Bible text as you study the chart:

1. The book is of three main sections: verses 1-9; 10-14; and 15-21. Note the three different verb tenses shown at the top of the

5. Clyde E. Harrington, "Edom," in *The Zondervan Pictorial Bible Dictionary*, p. 234.

chart. Read the Bible text to see if these are the prevailing ones of each section. (Note that the past tense of such verses as 2 and 7 in the first paragraph are more correctly represented as future tense.[6]

2. What part does Edom play in the book, according to the outlines shown? Check this out with the Bible text.

3. What part does Judah play in the book? (The reference to "Israel" in verse 20 is not to the Northern Kingdom exclusively, but to the chosen nation as a whole. This also is how the name Israel is used on the chart.)

4. Where is the bright section of the book?

5. Compare the beginning (v. 3) and the end (v. 21) of Obadiah. Relate to this the title shown at the top of the chart.

6. Note the outline of words beginning with the letter *s*. Read the verses in the Bible text.

7. Note the key verses and key words. Add to the list of key words as you study the Bible text further.

III. APPLICATIONS

1. In what ways do people today practice the sin of arrogant independence of God?

2. What does the Bible teach about the consequences which fall upon the nation which oppresses His chosen people? Does Genesis 12:3 apply to today, and to end times?

3. Does justice triumph? This question has been asked by people throughout the ages. Does the book of Obadiah give any answers?

4. God's "mercy endureth for ever" (Psalm 106:1, KJV). Why do some people see a conflict between this truth and the fact of eternal judgment?

5. Compare these verses which state the eternal law of returns:

"As you have done, it will be done to you" (Obad 15).

"By your standard of measure, it shall be measured to you" (Matt 7:2b).

"Whatever a man sows, this will he also reap" (Gal 6:7).

IV. SELECTED READING

GENERAL INTRODUCTION

Archer, Gleason L. *A Survey of Old Testament Introduction,* pp. 287-91.

Ellison, H. L. *The Old Testament Prophets,* pp. 95-97.

Freeman, Hobart E. *An Introduction to the Old Testament Prophets,* pp. 139-44.

---

6. Often a prophet worded a prediction in the past tense, to give the emphasis of *sureness* of fulfillment.

CHART 105

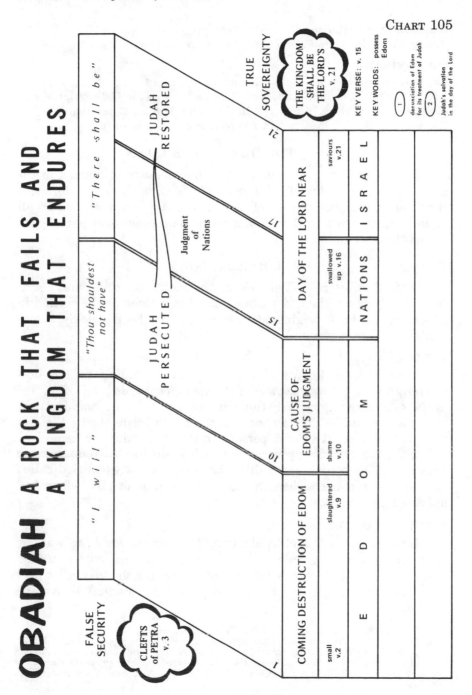

OBADIAH A ROCK THAT FAILS AND A KINGDOM THAT ENDURES

FALSE SECURITY

CLEFTS of PETRA v. 3

"I will"

"Thou shouldest not have"

"There shall be"

JUDAH PERSECUTED

JUDAH RESTORED

Judgment of Nations

TRUE SOVEREIGNTY

THE KINGDOM SHALL BE THE LORD'S v. 21

KEY VERSE: v. 15

KEY WORDS: possess Edom

1 denunciation of Edom for its treatment of Judah

2 Judah's salvation in the day of the Lord

COMING DESTRUCTION OF EDOM		CAUSE OF EDOM'S JUDGMENT	DAY OF THE LORD NEAR	
small v.2	slaughtered v.9	shame v.10	swallowed up v.16	saviours v.21
E	D	O	M	NATIONS	ISRAEL

1   10   15   17   21

Gaebelein, Frank E. *Four Minor Prophets,* pp. 11-53.
Young, Edward J. *Introduction to the Old Testament,* pp. 252-53.

COMMENTARIES
Exell, Joseph S. *Obadiah.* Pulpit Commentary, vol. 14.
Kleinert, Paul. "Obadiah." In Lange's *Commentary on the Holy Scriptures.*
Livingston, G. Herbert. "Obadiah." In *The Wycliffe Bible Commentary.*
Robinson, D. W. B. "Obadiah." In *The New Bible Commentary.*

JOEL: THE DAY OF THE LORD

Joel was the prophet who focused his message primarily on the great and terrible "day of the LORD." His book of three chapters is a clear and strong presentation of the world-history view which sees all history culminating in Christ, and Israel as a prominent participant in end-time events.

I. BACKGROUND

R. A. Stewart calls Joel "one of the most disturbing and heart-searching books of the Old Testament."[7] Let us look at the setting in which such a book originated. (First scan the book quickly before studying the background.)

A. THE MAN JOEL

Very little is known of this prophet. According to 1:1, Joel ("Jehovah is God") was the son of Pethuel ("persuaded of God"). This is the only appearance of Pethuel in the Bible. The name Joel was very common in Old Testament times. This is borne out by the fact that there are about a dozen persons in the Bible with the name.

Joel lived in Judah, possibly Jerusalem, during the reign of King Joash (see Chart 104). Some think he was a priest when God called him to be a prophet.[8] Obadiah was Judah's prophet just before Joel appeared on the scene.

B. THE BOOK OF JOEL

1. Date written. If Joel lived during the reign of Joash, he was one of the earliest writing prophets. The book, then, was written around 820 B.C. (Chart 104). Some Bible students prefer the view that Joel lived after the Babylonian Exile (586 B.C.).[9] This manual follows the view of the early date.

---

7. R. A. Stewart, "Joel," in *The New Bible Dictionary,* p. 639.
8. Recall that Jeremiah was a priest when he received the prophet's call (Jer 1:1).
9. Refer to a commentary for a discussion of the different views on date. Among the authors favoring the early date are Gleason L. Archer, *A Survey of Old Testament Introduction,* pp. 292-95; and J. T. Carson, "Joel," in *The New Bible Commentary,* pp. 690-91.

2. Setting.

a) Political and religious. Joash[10] was king of Judah when Joel ministered as the nation's prophet. He began his forty-year reign when he was only seven years old, and his guardian-instructor in the early years was the godly high priest Jehoiada.[11] Up until Jehoiada's death, Joash's reign was mainly a righteous one (2 Kings 12:2). When Jehoiada died, Joash defected to idolatrous ways, even slaying Jehoiada's godly son (read 2 Chron 24:15-25). Joel probably wrote his book while Joash was still a minor under Jehoiada's tutelage. This may partly account for the absence in Joel of long descriptions of national sin, usually found in the messages of the prophets.

During Joash's reign Judah was not free from the threat of invasion by foreigners. Read 2 Kings 12:17-19 and 2 Chronicles 24:23-25, which describe the Syrian invasion toward the end of Joash's life.

b) Economic. Severe plagues of locusts and drought had recently devastated the land of Judah when Joel penned his prophecy. In the opening lines of the book he asks the elders, "Has anything like this happened in your days or in your fathers' days?" (1:2). He is referring to the locust plagues, described in the next verse:

> What the gnawing locust has left, the swarming locust has eaten;
> And what the swarming locust has left, the creeping locust has
> eaten;
> And what the creeping locust has left, the stripping locust has
> eaten (1:3).

Only those who have witnessed a locust plague can fully appreciate why it is so dreaded. Joel could not have used a better symbol than this to prefigure the coming "terrible day of the LORD."

3. Style. The smooth and vivid style of Joel has contributed to his book being called one of the literary gems of the Old Testament.

4. Purposes. Three main purposes of Joel's prophecy are (1) to foretell coming judgments upon Judah for their sin; (2) to exhort Judah to turn their hearts to the Lord; and (3) to impress upon all people that this world's history will culminate in the events of the Day of the Lord, when the scales of justice will finally rest.

5. The Day of the Lord. Five times in Joel the phrase "the day of the LORD" appears. Joel uses the phrase to refer to end times. Even

---

10. Joash is the shortened form of Jehoash. Both names appear in the Bible, referring to the same king.

11. This story of Joash and Jehoiada is reported in 2 Kings 11-12. Read these chapters to get a feel of the times in which Joel lived.

when the New Testament writers referred to that day, it was still future. For example, read 2 Thessalonians 2:2 and 2 Peter 3:10. In the Old Testament the phrase occurs over thirty times, in such verses as Isaiah 2:12; 13:6, 9; Joel 1:15; Amos 5:18; Ezekiel 13:5; 30:3; Zephaniah 1:7, 14. Read these passages, observing that the descriptions of this "day" are usually about judgment and war against sinners, a necessary purge before righteousness can reign. Saints are involved in this day in the sense that when the Lord brings judgment upon unbelievers, the saints are associated with their Lord in the victory. (For example, the Millennium, issuing out of the Battle of Armageddon, may be considered a part of this "day of the LORD." In this connection it should be observed that it will be during the Millennium that the many Old Testament promises to Israel will be fulfilled. Thus, the Millennium is especially Israel-oriented.) It is the view of this book that Joel's prophecies of "the day of the LORD" are about the Messianic Kingdom at the end of the world, which will begin when God's final judgments will fall upon unbelieving nations, and when believing Israel will be delivered from their enemies.

There are various views as to when the Day of the Lord will begin. Three of the more common views are:

a) at the rapture when the Tribulation period begins

b) shortly after the rapture, during the Tribulation

c) at the revelation (Christ's return to this earth after the Tribulation) when Christ defeats His foes at the Battle of Armageddon (cf. Rev 16:16)

You will want to come to your own conclusions concerning this identification. Refer to commentaries for help.

II. SURVEY

Spend the first ten minutes of your survey in reading the three chapters in one sitting. What are your first impressions? What words and phrases especially stand out as prominent ones?

Study Chart 106 very carefully. As you survey the Bible text, try to justify the inclusion of all the entries and outlines shown on the chart.

1. The first verse is the book's introduction. Is there a similar concluding verse?

2. The book is of two main parts (1:2—2:11 and 2:28—3:21), with a bright section of exhortation sandwiched in between (2:12-27). At what point in the book does Joel look beyond the time of Christ (A.D.)?

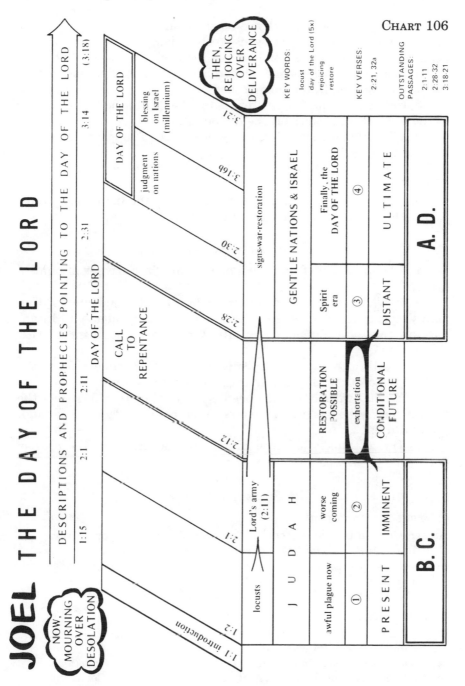

CHART 106

JOEL THE DAY OF THE LORD

DESCRIPTIONS AND PROPHECIES POINTING TO THE DAY OF THE LORD

| 1:15 | 2:1 | 2:11 | 2:31 | 3:14 | (3:18) |

NOW, MOURNING OVER DESOLATION

THEN, REJOICING OVER DELIVERANCE

1:1 introduction	JUDAH	CALL TO REPENTANCE	DAY OF THE LORD
1:2	2:1	2:12	2:28	2:30	3:16b	3:21

DAY OF THE LORD

judgment on nations | blessing on Israel (millennium)

locusts

Lord's army (2:11)

signs-war-restoration

awful plague now	worse coming	RESTORATION POSSIBLE	Spirit era	GENTILE NATIONS & ISRAEL Finally, the DAY OF THE LORD
①	②	exhortation	③	④
PRESENT	IMMINENT	CONDITIONAL FUTURE	DISTANT	ULTIMATE

B. C.   A. D.

KEY WORDS:
locust
day of the Lord (5x)
rejoicing
restore

KEY VERSES:
2:21, 32a

OUTSTANDING PASSAGES:
2:1-11
2:28-32
3:18-21

3. Notice the sequence shown on the chart:
locusts—Lord's army—signs—war—restoration.
Scan the passages in your Bible to see the basis for this outline.

4. Study the other outlines shown below the base line. Is there an overall progression in the theme?

5. Note where the five references to "the day of the LORD" appear in the book. Read each reference in your Bible.

6. What two aspects of "the day of the LORD" appear in the two parts of 2:30—3:21?

7. Compare the beginning of the book ("Now") with the ending ("Then").

8. Read the key verses in your Bible. Note the list of key words. Add to this list as you continue your study of the book.

III. APPLICATIONS

1. Are any or all of God's judgments only for purposes of punishment?

2. In what sense is God sovereign in all of His judgments? Can man's repentance change God's pronouncement of judgment? In answering this, see Jeremiah 18:7-10. When is a judgment of God irreversible?

3. "I will restore to you" (2:25, KJV). Does God still engage in the work of restoration? Support and illustrate your answer.

4. In what ways has Israel been persecuted by Gentiles since the days of Joel? Who has preserved a remnant of believing Jews through the centuries?

5. Try to think of other spiritual lessons taught by the book of Joel.

IV. SELECTED READING

GENERAL INTRODUCTION

Archer, Gleason L. *A Survey of Old Testament Introduction,* pp. 291-95.
Cole, R. A. "Joel." In *The New Bible Commentary,* pp. 716-17.
Freeman, Hobart E. *An Introduction to the Old Testament Prophets,* pp. 145-56.
Graybill, John B. "Joel." In *The Zondervan Pictorial Bible Dictionary.*

COMMENTARIES

Deere, Derward "Joel." In *The Wycliffe Bible Commentary.*
Gaebelein, A. C. *The Prophet Joel.*
Schmoller, Otto. "Joel." In Lange's *Commentary on the Holy Scriptures.*
Smith, Ward, and Smith, Bewer. *Joel.* International Critical Commentary.

MICAH: WHO IS LIKE JEHOVAH?

The book of Micah is especially noted for its predictive messages. For example, Micah predicted the exact location of Jesus' birthplace, Bethlehem (Mic 5:2; cf. Matt 2:5). Hobart E. Freeman observes that no Old Testament prophet exceeds Micah in the proportion of predictions concerning Israel's future and the Messiah's advent and Kingdom.[12]

I. BACKGROUND

A. THE MAN MICAH

1. Name. The name Micah means "Who is Jehovah like?" or "Who is like unto Jehovah?" Read the first words of 7:18. Do you think the prophet may have been thinking of his own name when he penned those words?

2. Home. Micah's hometown was Moresheth-gath (1:1, 14), located about twenty miles southwest of Jerusalem (see Map Y). The name Moresheth-gath means "possession of Gath," which suggests that the town was an annex of nearby Gath. The busy highway from Egypt to Jerusalem went through this area, so the "country boy" Micah was not too far removed from the city ways of his contemporary, Isaiah.

3. Time. Study Chart 80, which shows the contemporaries (kings and prophets) of Micah. Answer the following on the basis of the chart:

a) Between what years did Micah minister as a prophet?
b) What two other prophets ministered during Micah's time?
c) Who were Judah's kings when Micah was prophesying?
d) What calamity befell the Northern Kingdom of Israel in the middle of Micah's ministry?
e) Read Micah 1:5-7. (Samaria was the capital of Israel, just as Jerusalem was the capital of Judah.) Did Micah write these verses before or after the Assyrian Captivity of 722 B.C.?

4. Ministry. Micah was a prophet mainly to Judah, though his messages did involve Israel (cf. 1:1; 3:8). He had a clear conviction as to his prophetic calling (3:8). His messages were directed to various evils: moral corruption, idolatry (1:7; 6:16), formal religion, corrupt leadership by false prophets (3:5-7) and by priests (3:11). There was social decay, with the rulers and wealthy people oppressing the poor (2:2; 3:1-3). There was a haunting political unrest, especially over fear of invasion by foreign powers (see Isa 7-12).

---

12. Freeman, p. 217.

5. Political setting. To learn about the political setting of Micah, read 2 Kings 15:17—20:21 and 2 Chronicles 26-30. (Chronicles reports mainly about the Southern Kingdom.) Refer to Chart 80 as you read these historical sections, to see when each king reigned.

King Uzziah's reign was a successful one, but toward the end of his life he strayed far from God (2 Chron 26:16-23). His son Jotham, who succeeded him, "did right in the sight of the LORD" (2 Chron 27:2). Although he was not able to lead the people out of their corrupt ways, Jotham apparently supported Micah's spiritual program. But when, at his death, his son Ahaz mounted the throne, affairs took a different turn.

During Jotham's reign, clouds had begun to gather on the political horizon in the shape of a military coalition of Syria and Israel against Judah (2 Kings 15:37). When Ahaz became king of Judah, instead of searching out and dealing with the national sins for which God was allowing this chastisement, he formed an alliance with Tiglath-pileser, king of Assyria, an alliance which in the days of his son Hezekiah would prove almost fatal to the kingdom. He also introduced idolatry, with all its attendant evils, and even caused God's holy altar to be set aside, and one of heathen design put in its place (2 Chron 28:22-25).

King Hezekiah, who succeeded Ahaz, honored Jehovah in his administration of the kingdom. But such leadership and example brought only a measure of obedience on the part of the people. Though the outward form and ceremony of Temple worship was kept up, all manner of sins were being committed by the people—sins of idolatry, covetousness, impurity, injustice, and oppression. Against all this, the prophet's voice needed to be lifted. Micah and Isaiah were God's spokesmen for such a time as this.

B. THE BOOK OF MICAH

The content and style of Micah's book reveal that he was a very gifted and knowledgeable servant of God. Let us look at some of the book's characteristics.

1. Date written. A probable date of writing is after the Assyrian conquest of Damascus (734-32 B.C., 2 Kings 16:5-9; Isa 7-10), and before the fall of Samaria (722 B.C., 2 Kings 17).

2. Main theme. The main theme which runs through the book of Micah is that God will send judgment for Judah's sin, but pardon is still offered. The message underscores the two divine attributes cited in Romans 11:22a; "Behold then the kindness and severity of God."

3. Prophecies now fulfilled. Six specific prophecies of Micah have become events of history.
a) fall of Samaria (722 B.C., 1:6-7)
b) invasion of Judah by Sennacherib (702-701 B.C., 1:9-16)
c) fall of Jerusalem, (586 B.C., 3:12; 7:13)
d) exile in Babylon, (586 B.C., 4:10)
e) return from captivity (c. 520 B.C., 4:1-8,13; 7:11,14-17)
f) birth of Jesus in Bethlehem (5:2)

4. Literary forms. Word pictures abound in the book of Micah. Contrasts are prominent (e.g., 3:9-12 and 4:1-5), and questions appear often (1:5; 2:7; 4:9; 6:3,7,10,11; 7:10,18). Compare the first question (1:5) and the last (7:18).

5. Quoted in the Bible. Micah is quoted three times in the Bible. Each occasion is significant. Read the passages:
a) elders of Judah, quoting Micah 3:12 in Jeremiah 26:18
b) magi, quoting Micah 5:2 in Matthew 2:5-6
c) Jesus, quoting Micah 7:6 in Matthew 10:35-36

II. SURVEY

1. Read the book first for overall impressions.

2. Read the Bible text again, watching for key words and phrases. For example, do you observe any repeated words and phrases? What word is common to these three verses: 1:2; 3:1; 6:1? Who is addressed in each verse?

3. Study the opening verse of the book. What is meant by "The word . . . which he saw"? What was the subject of Micah's "visions," according to this verse?

4. Compare the opening and closing verses of the book. For example, compare 1:2 and 6:2.

5. Read each chapter, and record on paper the main content of each. Which chapters refer much to judgment, and which contain promises?

6. Read 6:8 and 7:18. Why may these be regarded as key verses for the book?

7. Study the survey Chart 107. Note that the book of Micah is shown to be organized around three main collections of messages.[13] Note the opening word of each, "Hear."

8. What three-part outlines appear on the chart? According to these, how does Micah's theme progress throughout the book? Com-

---

13. Many Bible students see a main division beginning at 4:1 instead of 3:1. Also, some see a two-fold structure: Denunciation, chaps. 1-3; Consolation, chaps. 4-7. This is similar to Isaiah's twofold makeup, and for this reason Micah has been referred to as "Isaiah in shorthand."

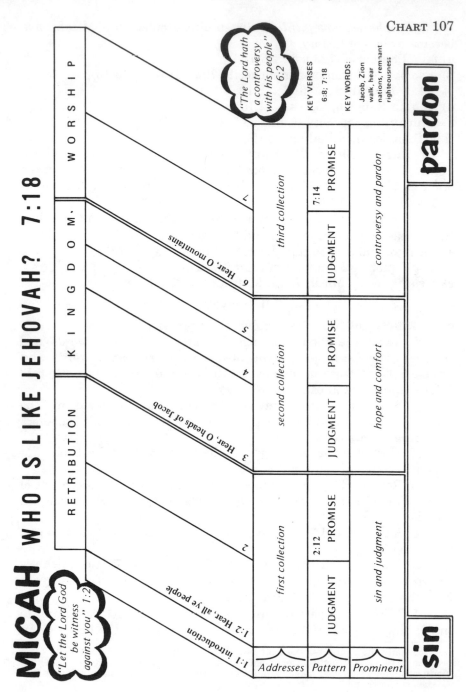

MICAH   WHO IS LIKE JEHOVAH?   7:18

"Let the Lord God be witness against you" 1:2

"The Lord hath a controversy with his people" 6:2

KEY VERSES
6:8; 7:18

KEY WORDS:
Jacob, Zion
walk, hear
nations, remnant
righteousness

	RETRIBUTION	KINGDOM	WORSHIP

1:1 introduction   1:2 Hear, all ye people   2   3 Hear, O heads of Jacob   4   5   6 Hear, O mountains   7

Addresses	first collection	second collection	third collection
Pattern	JUDGMENT 2:12 PROMISE	JUDGMENT PROMISE	JUDGMENT 7:14 PROMISE
Prominent	sin and judgment	hope and comfort	controversy and pardon

sin   **pardon**

pare the outlines with your own observations of the book's organization.

9. What pattern repeats itself in each of the three parts? Mark this in your Bible, scanning the text to justify such an outline.

10. Note the list of key words. Add to the list the words you have observed.

III. APPLICATIONS

1. Leaders of Israel were "supposed to know right from wrong" (3:1, TLB). Are today's Christian leaders accountable for the lives of other people? If so, in what ways?

2. What evil motives can ruin the ministry of Christian workers today? (Cf. 3:11.)

3. What is intended by these words in the Lord's prayer: "Thy kingdom come" (Matt 6:10)? Compare Micah 4:8.

4. Why did God choose a small, insignificant city, Bethlehem, as the place of Jesus' birth? Was God trying to say something about true Messiahship, as well as about His own ways of performing?

5. Why will Jerusalem be a key city in the last times? What is its status now?

6. Does God have a rightful claim on the lives of all people (6:8)?

7. What is genuine repentance? What part does it play in the conversion of a sinner?

8. Does the effectiveness of prayer depend on your believing that God hears your praying (7:7)?

9. In what ways has the Lord been a "light" to you personally since you became a Christian (7:8)? Have you had opportunities to share such a testimony with others?

10. What do these words mean to you: "Thou wilt cast all their sins into the depths of the sea" (7:19)? Do you think the intent is that God overlooks sin, or that no judgment or penalty is involved? Why did Christ die? Whose sins did He bear on the cross?

11. Compare Micah 6:8 with what the New Testament teaches about how a person is saved (e.g., Rom 3:21—5:21).

IV. SELECTED READING

GENERAL INTRODUCTION

Baxter, J. Sidlow. *Explore the Book,* 4:187-94.
Ellison, H. L. *The Old Testament Prophets,* pp. 63-66.
Freeman, Hobart E. *An Introduction to the Old Testament Prophets,* pp. 215-24.
Kelso, James L. *Archaeology and the Ancient Testament,* pp. 169-73.

COMMENTARIES

Archer, Gleason L. "Micah." In *The New Bible Commentary.*
Carlson, E. Leslie. "Micah." In *The Wycliffe Bible Commentary.*
Kleinert, Paul. "Micah". In Lange's *Commentary on the Holy Scriptures.*
Smith, George Adam. *The Book of the Twelve Prophets,* vol. 1.

NAHUM: WOE TO NINEVEH!

Over a hundred years after Jonah preached to Nineveh, God sent another prophet, Nahum, to pronounce its doom. The book of Nahum demonstrates how false is the view that "might makes right." The great Assyrian Empire, of which Nineveh was the capital, boasted its might and wealth, but it did not acknowledge its sin, nor would it listen to God. The fall of such a haughty nation was inevitable, as the text of Nahum reveals.

I. BACKGROUND

A. THE MAN NAHUM

Very little is known of the personal life of Nahum. His name does not appear at any other place in the Bible (unless he is the Naum of Luke 3:25, KJV).

1. Name. The name Nahum, which is a shortened form of Nehemiah, means "consolation" or "comforter."

2. Home. According to 1:1, Nahum was from a town called Elkosh. Four possible locations of Elkosh have been suggested: (1) in Assyria, north of Nineveh; (2) southwest of Jerusalem; (3) somewhere in Galilee; (4) the site of Capernaum (Caper-naum). Wherever Nahum's home was, we should keep in mind that when he was born[14] the Assyrian armies had already invaded Palestine twice:

722 B.C.—conquest of the Northern Kingdom (Israel) by Sargon II (2 Kings 17:6)

701 B.C.—invasions against Judah by Sennacherib (2 Kings 18:13-18)

3. Time. Chart 108 shows the contemporary leaders of Nahum's day. Refer to it as you answer the questions below.

a) During Nahum's ministry, three kings ruled over Judah. Who were they? Whose was the righteous reign? (See Chart 104.)

b) Which was the ruling world empire of Nahum's time?

c) Which Assyrian king was reigning during the earliest years of Nahum's ministry?

d) When did Nineveh fall? What empire succeeded Assyria as the world power?

e) What other prophets were ministering around the time of Nahum?

---

14. The year of Nahum's birth is unknown, but he was probably younger than fifty when he began his prophetic ministry.

CHART 108

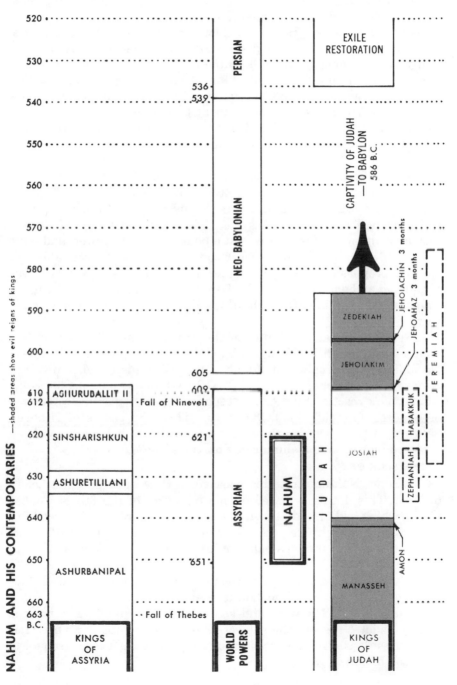

NAHUM AND HIS CONTEMPORARIES —shaded areas show evil reigns of kings

520	
530	
536	PERSIAN
539	
540	
550	NEO-BABYLONIAN
560	
570	
580	
590	
600	
605	

EXILE
RESTORATION

CAPTIVITY OF JUDAH
—TO BABYLON
586 B.C.

ZEDEKIAH

JEHOIAKIM

JEHOIACHIN 3 months
JEHOAHAZ 3 months

JEREMIAH

610	ASHURUBALLIT II
612	Fall of Nineveh
620	SINSHARISHKUN
621	
630	ASHURETILILANI
640	
650	
651	
660	ASHURBANIPAL
663 B.C.	Fall of Thebes

609

ASSYRIAN

NAHUM

JUDAH

JOSIAH

HABAKKUK

ZEPHANIAH

AMON

MANASSEH

KINGS
OF
ASSYRIA

WORLD
POWERS

KINGS
OF
JUDAH

4. Kings and cities. A few things should be noted concerning some rulers and cities directly related to the book of Nahum.

a) King Ashurbanipal. He was the last of the famous kings of Assyria. After his death (633 B.C.) the power of Assyria faded away. Ashurbanipal was exceptionally cruel. Skinning captives alive, forcing a prince to wear the bloody head of his king around his neck, and feasting with the head of a Chaldean monarch hanging above him, are examples of the gruesome stories about this tyrant.

b) King Josiah. Josiah reigned over Judah in the fear of the Lord. Read 2 Kings 22:1—23:28. Nahum may have written his book during Josiah's reign.

c) Thebes. Thebes is the Greek name for the Egyptian city of No (Hebrew). (See 3:8.) The capital of Egypt, it was conquered by the Assyrians in 663 B.C. Nahum refers to this conquest in 3:10.

d) Nineveh. The capital of Assyria, it was founded around 2000 B.C. During Nahum's ministry it was at a peak of wealth, power, and fame (read 3:16-17). The city walls were considered to be impregnable, yet Nahum prophesied their fall (e.g., 2:5-6). In 612 B.C. Nineveh was conquered and demolished by the Babylonians, Medes, and Scythians. The city has remained through all the centuries as a heap of desolate ruin.

Recall your earlier studies of the prophet Jonah (see Chart 98). Jonah was a prophet of Israel, whom God sent to preach to Nineveh. Nahum was a prophet of Judah, but his ministry also involved Nineveh. (Read Jonah 1:1-2 and 3:1-10.) What was Jonah's message; the people's reaction; and God's response? Was a specific destruction of Nineveh foretold? Jonah 3:5 says, "Then the people of Nineveh believed in God." Do you think this generation of believers had been replaced by the time Nahum came on the scene?

B. THE BOOK OF NAHUM

1. Date. Nahum wrote his book some time after 663 and before 612 B.C. This dating is based on his *reporting* of the fall of Thebes (3:10), which had already taken place (663 B.C.), and on his *foretelling* the fall of Nineveh (e.g., 2:8-10), which was still future (612 B.C.). Chart 108 shows Nahum's public ministry extending from about 650 to 620 B.C.

2. Theme and purpose. The theme of Nahum may be stated thus: The Lord, in His sovereign holiness and goodness, will bring judgment upon sinful Nineveh, and spare righteous Judah. The book is mostly about Nineveh, the subject which the opening sentence (1:1) introduces. It is also addressed mainly to Nineveh. It is the sequel to the book of Jonah.

Nahum also wrote for the benefit of the people of Judah. He clearly answered questions raised by his brethren, such as:

Why does cruel Nineveh prosper?

Has God abandoned Judah?

Where is justice?

Do these questions have their counterparts in the world today?

II. Survey

1. Read Nahum 1:1. What does this introductory verse suggest as to what Nahum's message is about? Scan the remainder of the book to get the feel of the prophet's burden.

2. Follow the progression of Nahum's thought by using the following outline:

I. God the Sovereign Judge (1:2-8)

(What are the different things said about God here?)

II. Nineveh to Fall, and Judah to Be Protected (1:9—2:2)

Here Nahum alternates back and forth between the two subjects of judgment and deliverance. Observe what is said about Judah or Nineveh in each case:

1:9-12a Nineveh   2:1 Nineveh[16]

1:12b-13[15] Judah   2:2 Judah

1:14 Nineveh

1:15 Judah

III. The Fall (2:3-13)

IV. The Causes (3:1-19)

3. Study the survey Chart 109, and try to determine what each outline or entry is based on, in the Bible text.

4. Note the following on the chart:

a) There is a natural progression in the book. (See bottom of the chart. Also note the progression in the three sections, beginning with Nineveh to fall.)

b) How is the first paragraph (1:1-8) set off from the rest of the book?

c) Study the four outlines which divide the book into two main sections.

d) How is Judah brought into the book?

e) Add to the list of key words.

f) Read the key verses in the Bible text. How do they represent the main theme of the book?

---

15. The verse 1:12b begins with the phrase, "Though I have afflicted you."

16. *The Living Bible* paraphrases the opening lines of 2:1 in this way: "Nineveh, you are finished! You are already surrounded by enemy armies!"

CHART 109

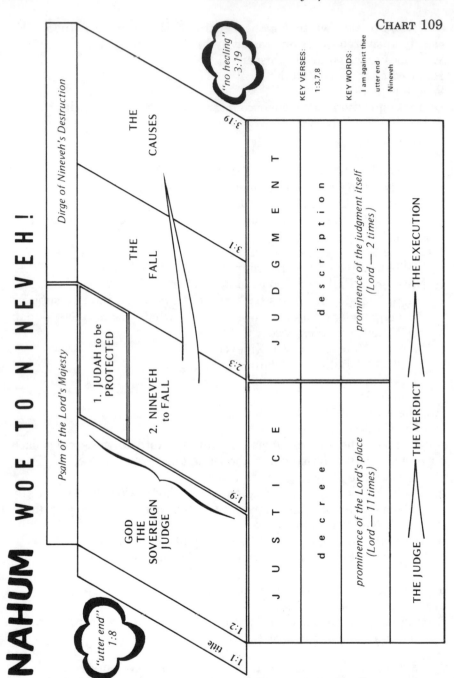

NAHUM WOE TO NINEVEH!

"utter end" 1:8

"no healing" 3:19

KEY VERSES:
1:3,7,8

KEY WORDS:
I am against thee
utter end
Nineveh

Psalm of the Lord's Majesty	Dirge of Nineveh's Destruction
GOD THE SOVEREIGN JUDGE	THE FALL	THE CAUSES
1. JUDAH to be PROTECTED		
2. NINEVEH to FALL		

1:1 title — 1:2 — 1:9 — 2:3 — 3:1 — 3:19

J U S T I C E	J U D G M E N T
decree	description
prominence of the Lord's place (Lord — 11 times)	prominence of the judgment itself (Lord — 2 times)
THE JUDGE	THE VERDICT	THE EXECUTION

III. Applications

1. What does the book of Nahum teach about God?

2. What place does righteous wrath have in the life of a Christian? What are your reactions to these comments:

> Surely there is a place for a book like Nahum even in the revelation of Grace. Instead of taking the Book of Nahum out of the Bible, we had better leave it there. We need it. It reminds us that love degenerates into a vague diffusion of kindly feeling unless it is balanced by the capacity of a righteous indignation. A man who is deeply and truly religious is always a man of wrath. Because he loves God and his fellow men, he hates and despises inhumanity, cruelty and wickedness. Every good man sometimes prophesies like Nahum.[17]

3. How may the Gospel be likened to news about the downfall of one's enemy? (Cf. Nah 1:15 and Rom 10:15.)

IV. Selected Reading

GENERAL INTRODUCTION

Eiselen, F. C. "Nahum." In *The International Standard Bible Encyclopedia,* 4:2109-11.

Ellison, H. L. *The Old Testament Prophets,* pp. 70-72.

Freeman, Hobart E. *An Introduction to the Old Testament Prophets,* pp. 225-31.

Smith, George Adam. *The Book of the Twelve Prophets,* 2:77-113.

COMMENTARIES

Ellicott, Charles J., ed. *Commentary on the Whole Bible,* vol. 5.

Feinberg, Charles L. "Nahum." In *The Wycliffe Bible Commentary.*

Fraser, A. "Nahum." In *The New Bible Commentary.*

Maier, Walter A. *The Book of Nahum, a Commentary.*

ZEPHANIAH: DAY OF DESOLATION AND DELIVERANCE

Zephaniah was one of the last prophets of Judah before the nation fell to the Babylonian invaders. Josiah, who reigned over Judah during Zephaniah's ministry, was the last of the righteous kings of this Southern Kingdom. So the Jews had the offer of much spiritual guidance and help in those years. Their sin in rejecting this light from God is a dark chapter of their history.

I. Background

Before going any further in your study, scan the three chapters of

---

17. Raymond Calkins, *The Modern Message of the Minor Prophets,* p.86.

CHART 110

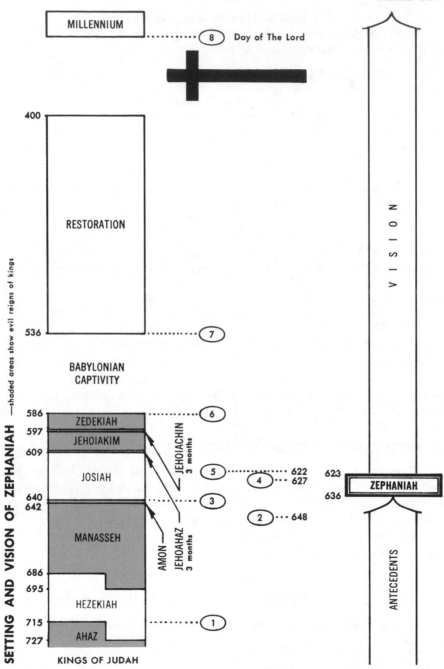

SETTING AND VISION OF ZEPHANIAH — shaded areas show evil reigns of kings

MILLENNIUM

⑧ Day of The Lord

400

RESTORATION

536

⑦

BABYLONIAN CAPTIVITY

586   ZEDEKIAH

597   JEHOIAKIM

609

JOSIAH

640

642

MANASSEH

686

695

HEZEKIAH

715

727   AHAZ

KINGS OF JUDAH

JEHOIACHIN 3 months

AMON

JEHOAHAZ 3 months

⑥

⑤   622

④ ⋯ 627

② ⋯ 648

③

①

VISION

ZEPHANIAH

623

636

ANTECEDENTS

Zephaniah. This will take the book out of the "stranger" category for the survey that follows.

First, refer to Chart 3 to see Zephaniah's place among all the Old Testament prophets. Then look at the setting of Zephaniah's writing by following its antecedents in a chronological order. Chart 110 shows this historical background as well as Zephaniah's vision into the future.

Note on the chart the eight significant points, numbered consecutively. Refer to the chart as you study carefully each of the following eight descriptions.

1. King Hezekiah. He was one of Judah's righteous kings. He may have been the Hizkiah of Zephaniah 1:1(KJV). If so, he was the great-great-grandfather of Zephaniah, the only prophet with royal blood.

2. Birth of Zephaniah. If the prophet was about Josiah's age, he was born around 648 B.C. (cf. 2 Kings 22:1). This was during the wicked reign of Manasseh. The name Zephaniah means "hidden, or protected, by Jehovah." Could it be that his parents gave him this name in gratitude for his life being spared during the atrocities of King Manasseh (2 Kings 21:6; cf. Heb 11:37)? It is interesting to note that an important part of Zephaniah's message concerned the protection of Judah from harm in the day of God's judgment (see 2:3).

Zephaniah's home may have been in Jerusalem. Suggested dates for the term of his public ministry are 636 to 623 B.C.

3. King Josiah. Josiah was a great-grandson of Hezekiah (2 Chron 32:33; 33:20, 25). How then was Zephaniah possibly related to Josiah? Josiah was only eight years old when he began to reign over Judah (2 Chron 34:1). At age sixteen he "began to seek the God of his father David" (2 Chron 34:3). It may very well be that Zephaniah's access to the royal court gave the prophet ample opportunities of witness to the king. In fact, he may have been the key spiritual influence in Josiah's early life.

4. The book of Zephaniah is written (c. 627 B.C.). The prophet probably wrote his book during the early part of Josiah's reign, since there is no reference in the book to Josiah's reform of 622 B.C. (For example, the idolatrous practices condemned in 1:3-6 were dealt with in the reforms.)

5. Josiah's reforms. At age twenty, Josiah began a six-year program of national reform (2 Chron 34:3), which was completed in 622 B.C. (2 Chron 34:8). Read 2 Chronicles 34-35 or 2 Kings 22-23. The sins which Zephaniah condemns in his book were the sins over which Josiah lamented.

6. Fall of Jerusalem (586 B.C.). Zephaniah prophesied judgments for Jerusalem, the first destruction coming about a half century later. His prophecies also referred to judgments of succeeding centuries up to the last days. (This is an example of multiple prophecy, commonly found in the Old Testament.)

7. Restoration (536 B.C. and later). Zephaniah also prophesied restoration of the chosen nation of God's people. This was fulfilled, at least in token measure, when God led His people back to the land at the end of the Babylonian Captivity. But the full measure of restoration is yet to be. (This is another example of multiple prophecy.)

8. Final "day of the LORD." The end-time judgments of the Day of the Lord will usher in the Messianic Kingdom (Millennium), when Zephaniah's prophecies of restoration will be fulfilled on a grand and total scale. Recall that the "day of the LORD" was a prominent subject of Joel's prophecy.

Be sure you are well acquainted with the previous eight points before moving on to the survey of the Bible text.

II. SURVEY

1. First, mark the following paragraph divisions in your Bible: 1:1,2,7,14; 2:1,4,8,12; 3:1,8,14.

2. Earlier in your study you scanned the three chapters of Zephaniah. Now, with pencil in hand, read the book once or twice more, underlining key words and phrases as you read. What repeated phrases strike you as very prominent in this book?

3. What is Zephaniah's message mainly about? Compare the opening verses (1:2-6) with the closing ones (3:14-20).

4. Refer to the survey Chart 111 as you follow the study suggestions given below. Read all the Bible references in your Bible. Try to justify the chart's outlines by the text of the Bible.

5. What is the function of the opening verse (1:1)?

6. How many main divisions in the book does the chart show? Mark your Bible to show the new divisions beginning at 2:4 and 3:8.

7. The title of the chart reflects the keynote of Zephaniah. Read the two key verses cited on the chart. What two outlines develop the subject of the Day of the Lord? What does this tell you about the day? (The word "day" in the phrase "day of the LORD" does not refer to a twenty-four-hour solar day. Rather, it is an extended period of time, whether weeks, months, or even years.)

8. How much of the prophecy deals with Judah? How much deals with Gentile nations?

9. What makes possible a day of deliverance in Zephaniah's prophecy? Observe the function of 2:1-3 as shown on the chart.

10. Compare your answer for question 9 with the conditions a sinner today must fulfill to appropriate the blessings of the Gospel.

11. Read the Bible text to account for the two short sections beginning at 3:1 and 3:6.

12. Note the chart's contrasting phrases taken from the opening and close of the book. Also, read in your Bible contrasting messages of the text:

Judgment: 1:14-18

Restoration: 3:14-17

13. Note the key words listed on the chart. Add to this list as you continue your study in the book.

III. APPLICATIONS

1. Why is it necessary, when studying a book of the Bible, to believe that the book was infallibly inspired? Do you believe Zephaniah's prophecies are wholly accurate?

2. What are some applications of 1:1—3:7 to today? What does this section of Zephaniah teach about God and man?

3. What is your definition of sin? Compare the phrase "against the LORD" (1:17) with 1 John 3:4.

4. Is sin a justifiable cause of the severe judgments described in Zephaniah (e g , 1:17)?

5. What various kinds of sins are exposed in 3:1-5? Are such sins common today?

6. Can a sinner become so hardened in his rebellion against God that any possibility of salvation is cancelled? Is there such a thing as "a point of no return" in this life, spiritually speaking?

7. How do you apply such prophecies as 1:2-6 and 2:1-3 to the end times?

8. The Day of the Lord will be a day of judgment for some and a day of deliverance for others. Relate this to Psalm 76:9.

9. Read 2 Peter 3:10-18. Note the appearance of the phrase "day of the Lord." What spiritual lessons can a Christian learn here in connection with the prophesied Day of the Lord?

10. What does it mean to you that the Lord is "in the midst" of His people (3:5,15,17)? How does a believer sense the presence of the Lord? Why is His presence so vital?

11. The first words of God to the elect people, the Jews, are recorded in Genesis 12:1-3. Read these verses. What prophecies of

CHART 111

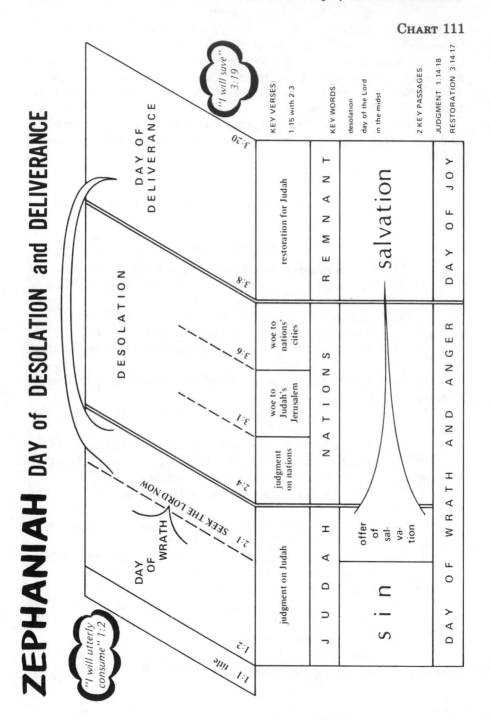

Zephaniah 3:8-20 perfectly fulfill the promises given in the Genesis passage?

12. Relate 3:8-20 to Paul's prophecy of Romans 11:25-28 about what will happen to believing Israel in end times.

13. Reflect on the great truth of 3:15b(KJV): "Thou shalt not see evil any more." When will this be? Compare this prophecy with the descriptions of New Jerusalem in Revelation 21:1—22:5.

14. The Old Testament prophets spoke more about the Messianic Kingdom of the end times than about the earthly life of Jesus. Can you think of reasons why this was so?

15. Do you think it is possible that God can raise up a modern "prophet" today to influence the course of a nation even as He used Zephaniah to influence Josiah and Judah?

IV. Selected Reading

GENERAL INTRODUCTION

Archer, Gleason L. *A Survey of Old Testament Introduction,* pp. 342-43.

Ellison, H. L. *The Old Testament Prophets,* pp. 67-69.

Freeman, Hobart E. *An Introduction to the Old Testament Prophets,* pp. 232-36.

Smith, George Adam. *The Book of the Twelve Prophets,* 2:35-76.

COMMENTARIES

Carson, John T. "Zephaniah." In *The New Bible Commentary.*

Hanke, H. A. "Zephaniah." In *The Wycliffe Bible Commentary.*

Jamieson, Robert; Fausset, A. R.; and Brown, David. *A Commentary, Critical and Explanatory on the Old and New Testaments.*

Laetsch, Theodore. "Zephaniah." In *Bible Commentary, The Minor Prophets.*

HABAKKUK: THE RIGHTEOUS LIVE BY FAITH

Habakkuk was the last of the minor prophets of Judah, called by some "a major minor prophet." J. Sidlow Baxter writes that "the last two or three decades had set in for Judah when Habakkuk took up his pen to write; and it was perhaps to Habakkuk that God first revealed *how near* the end was."[18]

I. Background

A. THE MAN HABAKKUK

The little we know about the man Habakkuk is inferred from his short book. The name Habakkuk means literally "embracer."[19] Of this, Luther wrote:

---

18. J. Sidlow Baxter, *Explore the Book,* 4: 208.

19. Read these verses where the same Hebrew word (translated "embrace") appears: 2 Kings 4:16; Job 24:8(KJV); Ecclesiastes 3:5; Song of Solomon 2:6.

> Habakkuk has a right name for his office. For Habakkuk means a
> heartener, or one who takes another to his heart and his arms, as one
> soothes a poor, weeping child, telling it to be quiet.[20]

The text of 1:1 identifies Habakkuk as a prophet, which in itself
reveals much about his ministry. Some think his call to be a prophet
came while he was serving as a Levitical chorister in the Temple.[21]
This is suggested by the musical notations at 3:1 and at the end of the
book: "For the choir director, on my stringed instruments."[22] The
prophecy of 1:6 points to the fact that Israel, the Northern Kingdom,
had already gone into Assyrian Captivity, for now the Chaldeans
(Babylonians) were threatening Judah. Thus, Habakkuk was a
prophet of Judah.

B. TIMES IN WHICH HABAKKUK MINISTERED

Refer back to Chart 108, which shows Habakkuk to be a contemporary of Jeremiah. There are various views as to exactly when
Habakkuk ministered as a prophet and wrote his book, because the
Bible text does not give direct information on this. The historical
setting of Chart 112 suggests various possibilities of the book's date.
The three strong options for the date of Habakkuk are ⓐ, ⓑ, and
ⓒ, shown on the chart.

ⓐ —after Josiah's reform program (622 B.C.) but *before* Babylon
   (Chaldea) emerged as the threatening world power (612 B.C.).

ⓑ or ⓒ —*after* Babylon emerged as the threatening world power
   (612) and 605). Of the two, ⓑ is the preferred view.

The spiritual condition of Judah when Habakkuk was ministering was one of dark apostasy (1:2-4). The fruits of Josiah's reform
program must have been very temporary, if a prophet of God would
complain about national corruption only a decade later. Observe on
Chart 108 that the last three kings of Judah were evil rulers. Read 2
Chronicles 36:14-16 for a description of the people's heart just before
the Babylonians conquered Judah. Also read Jeremiah 10, which
reveals Judah's sin of idolatry at this time. (Jeremiah, a contemporary of Habakkuk, was Judah's last prophet before Babylonian captivity.)

C. THE BOOK OF HABAKKUK

1. Message. Among the prominent teachings of the book are
these:

---

20. Quoted in Frank E. Gaebelein, *Four Minor Prophets,* p. 142.
21. Cf. 1 Chronicles 25:1. If this is so, his home was in Jerusalem.
22. Compare this reading with the paraphrase of *The Living Bible.*

CHART 112

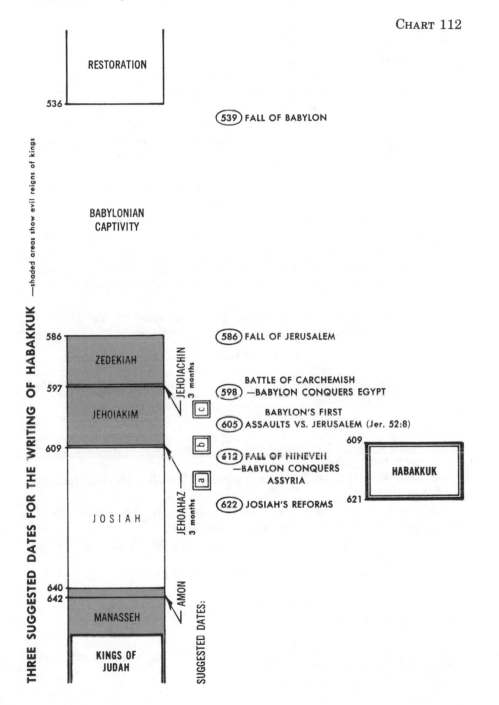

THREE SUGGESTED DATES FOR THE WRITING OF HABAKKUK —shaded areas show evil reigns of kings

RESTORATION

536

(539) FALL OF BABYLON

BABYLONIAN CAPTIVITY

586 — ZEDEKIAH — (586) FALL OF JERUSALEM

JEHOIACHIN 3 months

597 — JEHOIAKIM

BATTLE OF CARCHEMISH
(598) —BABYLON CONQUERS EGYPT

c

BABYLON'S FIRST
(605) ASSAULTS VS. JERUSALEM (Jer. 52:8)

609

b

609

(612) FALL OF NINEVEH
—BABYLON CONQUERS
ASSYRIA

HABAKKUK

JOSIAH

a

JEHOAHAZ 3 months

(622) JOSIAH'S REFORMS

621

640
642 — AMON

MANASSEH

KINGS OF JUDAH

SUGGESTED DATES:

a) Iniquity does *not* triumph.

b) God does not overlook sin.

c) The righteous man lives by his faith.

d) The Lord is God of the universe. Happy is the believer who waits patiently for the manifestations of His will.

e) God wants His children to talk with Him.

2. *Features.* Some interesting features of Habakkuk include:

a) The book is similar to Jonah in that each book opens with the prophet plagued by a problem, and closes with the prophet having experienced God's solution.

b) A large proportion of Habakkuk (about two-thirds) is devoted to conversation between the writer and God.

c) A key verse of the book, 2:4, is quoted in three important New Testament passages. Read Romans 1:17; Galatians 3:11; Hebrews 10:38. The truth of these verses was a keynote of the sixteenth-century Church Reformation, and it is for this reason that Habakkuk has been called the grandfather of the Reformation.

d) the literary quality of Habakkuk is unsurpassed in the Hebrew Scriptures. Concerning chapter 3, Unger writes:

> The magnificent lyric ode of ch. 3 contains one of the greatest descriptions of the theophany in relation to the coming of the Lord which has been given by the Holy Spirit, awaiting fulfillment in the day of the Lord (cf. 2 Thess 1:7-10).[23]

II. Survey

1. Read through the book twice. What words and phrases stand out as prominent ones?

2. Compare 1:1 with 3:1. Also compare 1:2 with 3:18-19. What are your observations?

3. Study the survey Chart 113 very carefully. The questions or suggestions given below are based on the chart.

4. Read each paragraph of the Bible text and assign a title to each paragraph.

5. How much of the book records Habakkuk's words? God's words?

6. Note the three-part outline showing a progression of the prophet's mental attitudes.

---

23. Merrill F. Unger, *Unger's Bible Handbook,* p. 425. "Theophany" is an appearance or manifestation of God to man.

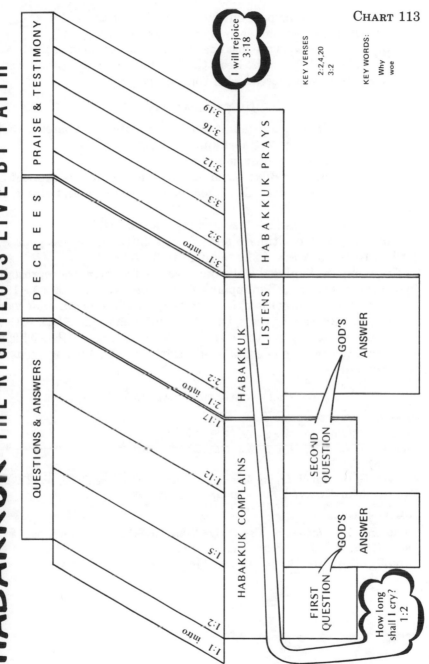

CHART 113

HABAKKUK THE RIGHTEOUS LIVE BY FAITH

QUESTIONS & ANSWERS | DECREES | PRAISE & TESTIMONY

HABAKKUK COMPLAINS | HABAKKUK LISTENS | HABAKKUK PRAYS

1:1 intro | 1:2 | 1:5 | 1:12 | 1:17 | 2:1 intro | 2:2 | 3:1 intro | 3:2 | 3:3 | 3:12 | 3:16 | 3:19

FIRST QUESTION

GOD'S ANSWER

SECOND QUESTION

GOD'S ANSWER

How long shall I cry? 1:2

I will rejoice 3:18

KEY VERSES
2:2,4,20
3:2

KEY WORDS:
Why
woe

7. Note the three-part outline at the top of the chart. Compare the introductory verses of each of those parts.

8. In what sense is the last chapter the highest peak of the book?

9. Note the key words. Read the key verses in the Bible. Add to the two lists as you proceed with your study.

III. APPLICATIONS

1. Does God have a listening ear to complaint, of whatever sort it is? How did God react to Habakkuk's complaining?

2. What other sins does doubt lead to?

3. What does the Bible teach about patience and endurance? See Romans 5:3-5. Why does God often move slowly in performing His work?

4. Compare Galatians 2:20 and Habakkuk 2:4.

5. What is the ultimate test of one's faith? Compare your own faith with Habakkuk's, as he testified in 3:17-19.

6. Compare Paul and Habakkuk, as the two men are represented by their testimonies of Philippians 4:11-13 and Habakkuk 3:17-19.

7. The word "salvation" is an important Bible word. How would you define salvation in the spiritual realm? Read Habakkuk 3:13,18, where the word appears three times. The Hebrew is *yesha,* which is the origin of the name Jesus. Read Matthew 1:21. Why is Jesus the true Saviour?

IV. SELECTED READING

GENERAL INTRODUCTION

Baxter, J. Sidlow. *Explore the Book,* 4: 206-13.

Freeman, Hobart E. *An Introduction to the Old Testament Prophets,* pp. 251-60.

Morgan, G. Campbell. *Living Messages of the Books of the Bible,* pp. 272-86.

Phillips, John. *Exploring the Scriptures,* pp. 153-55.

COMMENTARIES

Davidson, A. B. *Habakkuk.* Cambridge Bible for Schools and Colleges.

Lloyd-Jones, D. Martin. *From Fear to Faith.*

Kerr, David W. "Habakkuk." In *The Wycliffe Bible Commentary.*

28

The Postexilic Prophets
(Haggai, Zechariah, Malachi)

Haggai, Zechariah, and Malachi were the last writing prophets to minister to Israel in Old Testament times. They are called postexilic prophets because they served after the Jews had returned to Canaan from exile in Babylon. See Chart 96. Who were the preexilic prophets, and who were the exilic prophets? Do you see why the postexilic prophets are also called the restoration prophets?

These first pages of the chapter are devoted to a study of the historical setting of Haggai, Zechariah, and Malachi. The Bible text of the three books will come alive to you if, among other things, you have seen what situations moved God to commission the three prophets to write.[1]

The historical books which have the same setting as the postexilic prophets are Ezra, Nehemiah, and Esther. Therefore, it will be helpful to review the backgrounds of those books, studied in chapter 15. Most of that material is not repeated in this chapter.

I. Two Kingdoms and Two Captivities

Before you begin your study of the postexilic prophets, review the historical setting *before* restoration. Recall that when we speak of "restoration" we are referring to the conditions accompanying the *return* of God's people to Canaan *from captivity*. The captivity itself took place in two stages, known as the Assyrian and Babylonian captivities. Refer back to chapter 15 and study again the descriptions of these two captivities. Israel, the Northern Kingdom, was taken captive by the Assyrians in 722 B.C. Judah, the Southern Kingdom, was conquered by the Babylonians, one hundred twenty-six years later, in 586 B.C.

---

1. The prophets also preached many, if not all, of the messages they were divinely inspired to write.

II. Duration of the Babylonian Captivity

The exile began with Nebuchadnezzar's first invasion of Judah in 605 B.C. (2 Chron 36:2-7), and ended with the first return of the Jews to Canaan in 536 B.C.[2] (Ezra 1). See Chart 57.[3]

III. Contemporary Rulers

Review this subject as it is discussed in chapter 15. Identify these names on Chart 57, and relate them to the times of the postexilic prophets: Cyrus, Darius, and Artaxerxes. The name Darius appears three times in each of the books of Haggai and Zechariah.

IV. Jewish Leaders of the Restoration

Review this subject also as it first appeared in chapter 15. Note these names on Chart 57: Zerubbabel, Ezra, Nehemiah, Haggai, Zechariah, and Malachi. Observe on the chart that most of Malachi's ministry took place during Nehemiah's return visit to Babylon. Those were years of backsliding on the part of the Jews in Canaan, when the first spiritual zeal had subsided. Hence, the message of Malachi was mainly about sin and its judgment.

V. Importance of the Restoration for the Jews and the World

The restoration was important for various reasons. For Israel, it showed that God had not forgotten His promise to Abraham concerning the land of Canaan. (Read Gen 13:15 and note the strength of the word "forever".) Hence, the *relocation* of a returning remnant. Hope for a missionary outreach to Gentiles was stirred up in *revival* of true worship, for a key mission of Israel was to show heathen nations what true worship of the true God was. And then, the restoration was directly related to the life and ministry of the coming Messiah, in the *renewal* of the Messianic promises. For example, Bethlehem, Nazareth, and Zion were some of the geographical places woven into the promises concerning Jesus' coming. In about four hundred years Jesus would be born of the seed of David in *Bethlehem,* not in Babylon. The Holy Land of *promise,* not a land of captivity, was where His people would be dwelling when He would come unto them, "his own" (John 1:11).

---

2. If Jeremiah's prophecy (Jer 25:11-12; 29:10) is interpreted from an ecclesiastical standpoint, with the Temple as the key object, then the seventy-year period extended from the destruction of the Temple in 586 B.C. to the year of completion of its reconstruction, which was 516 B.C.

3. Most of the dates of Chart 57 are those of John C. Whitcomb's chart, *Old Testament Kings and Prophets.*

VI. RESTORATION OF END TIMES

Israel's restoration in the sixth and fifth centuries B.C. was but a mere shadow of the final restoration in the Messianic Kingdom of the end times. This is the principle of multiple fulfillment studied earlier. Be ready to apply the principle to the messages of the postexilic prophets. For clear revelation that Israel will play a prominent role in world history of the end times, read Romans 11.

VII. THE MINISTRIES OF THE LAST THREE PROPHETS

See Chart 57 and note that Haggai and Zechariah ministered around the beginning of the restoration period, and Malachi toward the end. In the pages that follow, more will be said about the immediate setting of the writing of each of their books. This may be noted now: the main appeal of Haggai and Zechariah was to inspire the Jews to finish building the Temple which had been discontinued in 534 B.C. (Chart 57), and the burden of Malachi was the tragic apostasy of God's people. Whatever there was of revival and spiritual restoration in Israel's return from exile had, by Malachi's time, degenerated to spiritual coldness with threat of disaster. It is not without significance that the last word of Malachi, and therefore of our Old Testament, is the awful word "curse" (Mal 4:6). What thoughts come to you as you compare this last verse with the Bible's first verse, Genesis 1:1?

HAGGAI: BUILD THE HOUSE, AND I WILL BE GLORIFIED

Haggai is one of the shortest books of the Bible, called by someone "a momentous little fragment." Among its prominent teachings is the necessity of putting first things first. Not long after God led the Jews out of exile back to Jerusalem, the people became self-satisfied and began to neglect the things of the Lord. They were building houses for themselves, but hardly a soul was grieved that the Temple-building project, discontinued fourteen years earlier, was yet at a standstill. To such a stagnant situation, Haggai was sent with God's message.

I. BACKGROUND

(Scan the book of Haggai before proceeding with this study of background.)

A. THE MAN HAGGAI

Very little is known of the prophet Haggai. His name appears in two verses outside of his own book: Ezra 5:1; 6:14. Read these verses.

1. Name. The name Haggai means "festal" or "festive." The root of the word Haggai has the literal meaning of *celebration.* Read 1 Samuel 30:16, where the Hebrew word is translated "dancing." Whatever led Haggai's parents to this name, it was well chosen, for, as one writer has observed, "Haggai was one of the few prophets who had the inexpressible pleasure of seeing the fruits of his message ripen before his very eyes."[4]

2. Home. Haggai was probably born in Babylon during the captivity years. We know nothing about his family. He was among the first contingent of Jews returning to Jerusalem, under the leadership of Zerubbabel, in 536 B.C. (Ezra 2:2).

3. Ministry. The prophet Haggai is often referred to as "The Successful Prophet." No prophet saw a faster response to his message than did Haggai. Also, he has been called "the prophet who said it with bricks." This is because the main subject of his message was the completion of the Temple structure.

Haggai and Zechariah were companions in the prophetic ministry (Ezra 5:1; 6:14). How was the principle of co-working practiced in New Testament times? (Cf. Mark 6:7.) What are the advantages of a dual witness?

B. THE BOOK OF HAGGAI

1. Date. The book of Haggai clearly dates itself: "second year of Darius the king," (1:1), which was 520 B.C. All four messages recorded in the book bear the same date, as to year.

2. Historical setting. As mentioned earlier, the Temple project is the focal issue of the book of Haggai. The story of that project, in the early years, is tragic. To fully appreciate the prophet's burden, the following sequence of events, predating his writing, should be learned. (Read the Bible references, and locate some of the dates on Chart 57.)

586 B.C. Jerusalem and the Temple are destroyed by the Babylonian invaders.

539 B.C. Fall of Babylon. The Persian Empire, ruled by King Cyrus, becomes the world power. The Jews in exile are not subject to Cyrus.

538 B.C. God moves Cyrus to issue a decree permitting and encouraging the Jews to return to their homeland (Ezra 1:1-4).

536 B.C. First return of Jews under Zerubbabel. Read Ezra 1:5—2:70 and Nehemiah 12. The total number of returnees: about fifty thousand (see Ezra 2:64-67).

---

4. J. McIlmoyle, "Haggai," in *The New Bible Commentary,* p. 743.

536-535 B.C. Altar of burnt offerings built at Jerusalem, on the site of the Temple ruins. Feast of Tabernacles kept. Sacrifices observed (Ezra 3:1-6).

Foundations of the Temple laid (Ezra 3:7-13).

535-534 B.C. Opposition to the Temple project by the neighboring Samaritans (Ezra 4:1-5).

534 B.C. Work on the Temple ceases[5] (Ezra 4:24).[6]

536-520 B.C: Israel's ruler is governor Zerubbabel, who represents the king of Persia. Joshua the high priest is their religious leader.

520 B.C. Haggai and Zechariah "prophesied to the Jews who were in Judah and Jerusalem, in the name of the God of Israel" (Ezra 5:1; cf. Hag 1:1). Temple project is resumed (Ezra 5:2; Hag 1:14-15). For how many years had the people neglected the work?

516 B.C. Temple project is finished (Ezra 6:14-15).

Chart 114 shows the ever changing spiritual state of Israel during Old Testament times, and how Haggai's and Zechariah's ministries related to this.

3. *The importance of the Temple.* We may rightly ask why the Temple building was so crucial in the life of the Jews who had returned to Jerusalem. Gleason Archer suggests two basic reasons.

> It should be remembered that much of the Mosaic constitution presupposed the carrying on of worship in such a sanctuary, and the failure to complete a suitable house of worship could lead to a paralyzing of the religious life of the Jewish community. It should also be understood that the second temple was to play a very important role in the history of redemption, for it was in this temple (as remodeled and beautified by Herod the Great) that the Lord Jesus Christ was to carry on His Jerusalem ministry. It was, of course, His advent that fulfilled the promise of Haggai 2:9, "The glory of this latter house shall be greater than of the former."[7]

The Temple building itself, as a symbol, was intended to remind the Israelites that God was a real Person, alive, dwelling in Zion (Joel 3:21), and wanting to enjoy fellowship with man as well as be

---

5. Other factors, besides the Samaritans' harassments, caused the Jews to stop working on the Temple. Among these were: (1) the people's earlier adjustment to worshiping without a temple when they were in Babylon; (2) their disillusionment upon returning, to find mostly desolation, hostility, and hardship; (3) poverty resulting from failure of crops; (4) preoccupation with their own building projects. (See Hobart E. Freeman, *An Introduction to the Old Testament Prophets*, p. 329.)

6. Verses 6-23 of chapter 4 are parenthetical, referring to the Samaritans' later opposition to building Jerusalem's walls, during the reigns of Ahasuerus (486-464) and Artaxerxes (464-423).

7. Gleason L. Archer, *A Survey of Old Testament Introduction*, p. 408.

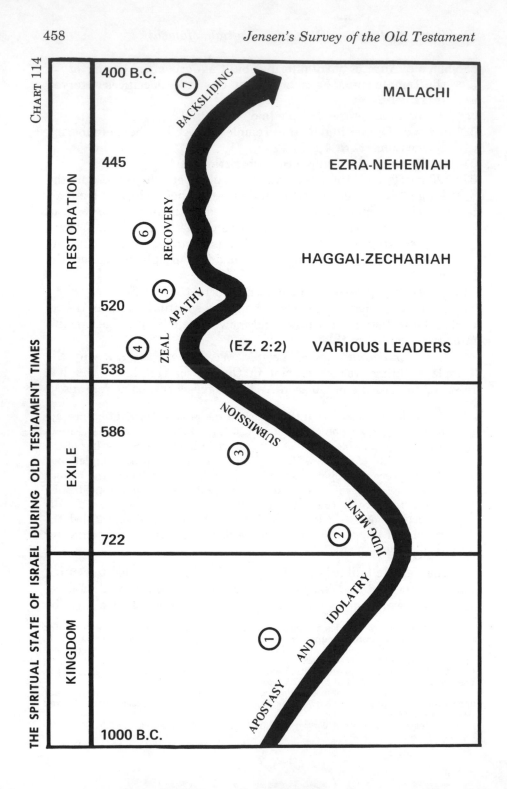

CHART 114

THE SPIRITUAL STATE OF ISRAEL DURING OLD TESTAMENT TIMES

400 B.C. ⑦ BACKSLIDING   MALACHI

445   EZRA-NEHEMIAH

RESTORATION

RECOVERY ⑥

⑤ 520 APATHY   HAGGAI-ZECHARIAH

⑥ 538   ZEAL   (EZ. 2:2) VARIOUS LEADERS

EXILE

586   ③ SUBMISSION

722   ② JUDGMENT

KINGDOM

① APOSTASY AND IDOLATRY

1000 B.C.

worshiped by him. Exodus 25:8, referring to the original tabernacle, gives clear insight into this fellowship aspect: "And let them construct a sanctuary [*miqdash,* "a place set apart"] for Me, that I may dwell among them." There was no higher spiritual experience for a Jew in Haggai's time than by faith to let God as Lord dwell personally in his heart. (Cf. Acts 7:47-48; Isa 66:1-2.) In such an experience the Temple symbol bore its choicest and eternal fruit.

4. Theme of the book. The divine message which Haggai passed on to his Jewish brethren could be summarized thus: "If you want to be restored to a blessed relationship with the Lord, put first things first in your life. For example, resume work on the Lord's Temple."

5. Names in the book. Four important names of the book are mentioned in its opening verses: Haggai the prophet; Darius the king; Zerubbabel the governor; and Joshua the high priest. Observe on Chart 57 the appearances of the first three names. Joshua (also called Jeshua) is listed in Ezra 2:2 as one of the leaders of the first return of exiles.

II. SURVEY

A. FIRST READINGS

1. First, mark paragraph divisions in your Bible, beginning at these verses: 1:1,3,7,12; 2:1,10,20.

2. Scan the book. The purpose of this scanning is to see highlights, feel the tone, and get some general impressions.

3. Scan the book again, with pencil in hand. Underline key repeated words and phrases as you read.

4. Did you notice various date references? Mark these in your Bible: 1:1; 1:15; 2:1; 2:10; 2:20.

5. At what places in the book does this group appear: Zerubbabel, Joshua, remnant? Does Haggai deliver a message to Zerubbabel only, at anyplace in the book?

B. SURVEY CHART

Chart 115 shows, in layout form, how the book of Haggai is organized. Study the chart carefully, then follow the study suggestions given below. Keep referring to the Bible text to justify the observations and outlines that appear on the chart.

1. Note the title given to the book (see 1:8). Did you observe many references to God's house when you scanned the text of Haggai? (An exhaustive concordance will quickly locate all the references.)

2. Compare the book's opening (1:2) and closing (2:23).

3. Study the chronological sequence of the Temple project, begin-

CHART 115

HAGGAI BUILD THE HOUSE, AND I WILL BE GLORIFIED

Book opens with a problem 1:2

Book closes with a promise 2:23

— PUT FIRST THINGS FIRST —

	3 weeks	6/24	2 months	9/24	1 day
6/1					9/24

DIVINE BLESSINGS
messianic — immediate — messianic

	1:7	1:12	1:13	1:15	2:1	7/21	2:10	2:20	2:23

First Sermon	*Response*	*Second Sermon*	*Third Sermon*	*Fourth Sermon*
REPROOF	ASSURANCE	ENCOURAGE-MENT	BLESSING	PROMISE
People are rebuked for discontinuing temple project	People are stirred	Greater glory is promised	Blessing is promised	Zerubbabel is honored

	"in a little while"	"from this day"	"in that day"
	6/24	9/24	9/24

PEOPLE'S WORK PROMINENT · GOD'S WORK PROMINENT

"I called for a drought" 1:11	"I am with you" 1:13	"I will fill" 2:7	"I will bless" 2:19	"I will make thee" 2:23

WORK BEGUN	ENCOURAGEMENT TO FINISH

520 B.C. CHARGE TO RESUME BUILDING

Temple begun 536 B.C.

Temple discontinued 534 B.C.

TEMPLE FINISHED 516 B.C. EZRA 6:15

KEY VERSE: 1:8

KEY WORDS:
consider
word of the Lord
Lord of hosts
house
glory

ning with the date 536 B.C. What three-part outline of Haggai relates to this?

4. How many "sermons" appear in the book? Check your Bible and note that each is dated. Note the dates recorded on the chart. What is the total time span of the book?

5. What is the function of the short paragraph 1:12-15 between the first and second sermons?

6. Study the other outlines shown on the chart.

7. In what parts of the book of Haggai do Messianic prophecies appear?

8. Note the list of key words and phrases.

III. APPLICATIONS

1. Do you learn any practical lessons about procrastination in chapter 1? What are your thoughts about "time" as the word is used in 1:2 and 1:4?

2. Why is a local church building, when truly devoted as the Lord's house, an important *ingredient* of Christianity? Compare this with the Temple of Old Testament times.

3. When God sends or permits financial setback to a believer, what may be His purposes?

4. Why is obedience to God the key to being in His will?

5. What does Haggai 1 teach about how a believer's works are related to his heart?

6. Is unholiness communicable (2:13-14)? How can a Christian guard himself from the defilement of worldly things? Is holiness communicable (2:12)? In what sense can a Christian's good witness influence others?

7. Why was the Temple such an important object in the life of Israel? Relate 1 Peter 2:5 to this, as involving Christians.

8. Apply the following teachings of Haggai about work to the unfinished task of the Church:[8]

a) The Lord's work takes priority over every other obligation of service.

b) Those who obey God and do His work, trusting in His abiding presence and power, are kept from discouragement.

c) The Lord's work demands clean instruments, separated from sin.

d) The Lord's work, believingly carried on, is linked to His sovereign plan for men and nations.

---

8. From Frank E. Gaebelein, *Four Minor Prophets,* p. 244.

IV. SELECTED READING

GENERAL INTRODUCTION

Ellison, H. L. *The Old Testament Prophets,* pp. 117-22.

Freeman, Hobart E. *An Introduction to the Old Testament Prophets,*
    pp. 326-32.

Gaebelein, Frank E. *Four Minor Prophets,* pp. 199-242.

McCurdy, James Frederick. "Haggai." In Lange's *Commentary on the
    Holy Scriptures,* pp. 3-6.

COMMENTARIES

Baldwin, Joyce G. *Haggai, Zechariah, Malachi.*

Earle, Ralph. *Meet the Minor Prophets.*

Jennings, A. C. "Haggai." In *Commentary on the Whole Bible.*

ZECHARIAH: KING OVER ALL THE EARTH

Zechariah, the longest book of the minor prophets, was often
quoted by the New Testament writers. This is because so many of its
prophecies point forward to Christ the Messiah. One Bible scholar has
called Zechariah "the most Messianic, the most truly apocalyptic and
eschatological, of all the writings of the Old Testament."[9]

Visions, symbols, and prophecies of the end times (eschatology)
abound in Zechariah. These are the main ingredients of apocalyptic
literature (Greek *apokalupsis,* meaning "uncovering," "disclosure,"
"revelation"). This is why the book is often referred to as "The Book of
Revelation of the Old Testament." As such, it is very appropriate that
the book appears as the next to the last book of the Christian canon of
the Old Testament.

I. BACKGROUND OF THE BOOK OF ZECHARIAH

A. THE MAN ZECHARIAH

1. Name. The Hebrew name Zechariah means "The Lord remem-
bers." It was a common name in Old Testament times (around thirty
men in the Old Testament are so named). Many parents no doubt
gave the name as an act of gratitude to the Lord for remembering
them with the gift of a baby boy.

2. Family. Zechariah's father was the priest Berechiah; his grandfather, priest Iddo (1:1).[10] Zechariah's family was among the Jewish

---

9. George L. Robinson, "The Book of Zechariah," in *The International Standard
Bible Encyclopedia,* 5: 3136.

10. Ezra 5:1 says Zechariah was a son of Iddo. In Jewish terminology, "son of" often
had the wider designation of "descendant of." It is possible that Berechiah died before
Iddo, causing Ezra to identify Zechariah with the *surviving* ancestor of the priestly line.

exiles who returned from Babylon in 536 B.C. under Zerubbabel (read Neh 12:4, 16). Zechariah was a young child at that time, if he was a young man when he began to prophesy in 520 B.C. (The "young man" of 2:4 may be Zechariah.)

3. Ministry. In 520 B.C., when God began revealing to Haggai the message he should preach and write, Zechariah was ministering to the Jews as a priest, a position passed down from his forefathers (Neh 12:16). Then, two months later, Zechariah was commissioned with a similar prophetic task (cf. Hag 1:1 and Zech 1:1). This made him a prophet-priest, like his predecessors, Jeremiah and Ezekiel. Jewish tradition honors Zechariah (along with Haggai and Malachi) as a priest of the Great Synagogue, responsible for gathering and preserving the sacred writings and traditions of the Jews after the Babylonian Exile.

The main task that Zechariah and Haggai shared was to exhort the Jews to finish rebuilding the Temple. This project had been discontinued in 534 B.C., fourteen years before the prophets began their ministry. Read Ezra 6:14-15 to learn how successful the prophets were. In what year was the Temple completed?

B. THE BOOK OF ZECHARIAH

1. Date. There are datelines in the book of Zechariah: at 1:1; 1:7; and 7:1. The second year of Darius (1:1) was 520 B.C., and the fourth year (7:1) was 518 B.C. The opening words of 8:1 suggest a later revelation to Zechariah, as do the opening words of 9:1. How much later these revelations were given, however, cannot be determined. It is possible that chapters 1-8 were written during the building of the Temple (520-516 B.C.); and chapters 9-14, after the Temple was completed in 516 B.C. (see Chart 116).

2. General contents. Like all biblical prophecy, the book of Zechariah contains both foretelling and forthtelling. The forthtelling is the prophet's appeal to the people concerning their *heart* relationship to God, so that the work of their *hands* (e.g., Temple project) might prosper. The foretelling concerns Israel's fortunes and judgments in the years to come, culminating in the nation's glory when the Messiah comes. Such predictions were intended to make the Jews yearn to see their King.

3. Main purposes. Four purposes of the book may be cited:
a) To bring about spiritual revival. What was the first message of the Lord to the Jews? (See 1:2-3.)
b) To inspire the people to complete the Temple building. See 1:16 and 4:9 for two specific references to the Temple.

c) To comfort and console the people (see 2:13). The Jews were going through severe trials at the time.

d) To register in divine Scripture unmistakable prophecies about the coming Messiah. The fact that the Jews hearing Zechariah's prophecies did not live to see the fulfillments did not detract from the intended inspiration of the prophecies to their souls (cf. 1 John 3:2-3).

There are more prophecies of Christ in Zechariah than in any other prophetic book except Isaiah. Underline these in your Bible now. (The list of verses about fulfillment is a partial list.)

PROPHECY OF CHRIST		FULFILLMENT
Servant	3:8	Mark 10:45
Branch	3:8; 6:12	Luke 1:78, margin (KJV)
King-Priest	6:13	Heb 6:20—7:1
Lowly King	9:9-10	Matt 21:4-5; John 12:14-16
Betrayed	11:12-13	Matt 27:9
Hands pierced	12:10	John 19:37
Cleansing fountain	13:1	Rev 1:5
Humanity and deity	13:7; 6:12	John 8:40; 1:1
Smitten shepherd	13:7-9	Matt 26:31; Mark 14:27
Second coming and coronation	14:5,9	John 10:16; Rev 11:15; 21:27

II. Survey

1. First, mark in your Bible the twenty units shown on Chart 116. That is, draw a line across the page of your Bible at 1:1, at 1:7, at 1:18, and so forth. (Note: The units of chapters 1-8 are paragraphs; those of 9-14 are full chapters.)

2. Now scan the entire book, with pencil in hand. Note especially the opening verse of each of the twenty units. Underline any key words and phrases that strike you.

3. Study Chart 116. Note that the chart divides the book into three main divisions. What are they?

4. How does the paragraph 1:1-6 introduce the book? Is there a formal conclusion to the book?

5. Note where the eight visions are recorded. Read each of these visions in the Bible text, and justify the titles shown on the chart. Note how the words "saw," "looked," or "eyes" introduce the visions.

6. Read 6:9-15. The absence of sight words in 6:9-15 is the reason for not identifying this passage as a vision. How is this

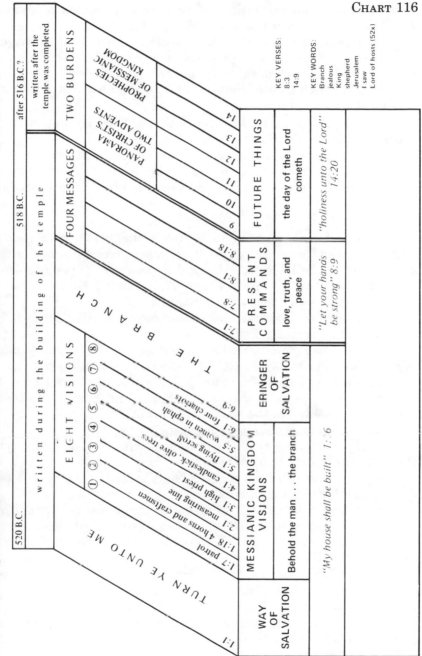

ZECHARIAH KING OVER ALL THE EARTH

	WAY OF SALVATION	MESSIANIC KINGDOM VISIONS	BRINGER OF SALVATION	PRESENT COMMANDS	FUTURE THINGS	
		Behold the man . . . the branch		love, truth, and peace	the day of the Lord cometh	
	"My house shall be built" 1:16		"My house shall be built" 1:6	"Let your hands be strong" 8:9	"holiness unto the Lord" 14:20	

520 B.C. — written during the building of the temple — 518 B.C.

after 516 B.C.? — written after the temple was completed

TURN YE UNTO ME

EIGHT VISIONS
① ② ③ ④ ⑤ ⑥ ⑦ ⑧

1:7 patrol
1:18 4 horns and craftsmen
2:1 measuring line
3:1 high priest
4:1 candlestick, olive trees
5:1 flying scroll
5:5 women in ephah
6:1 four chariots
6:9

THE BRANCH

FOUR MESSAGES

PANORAMA OF CHRIST'S TWO ADVENTS

TWO BURDENS

PROPHECIES OF MESSIANIC KINGDOM

7:1 7:8 8:1 8:18 9 10 11 12 13 14

KEY VERSES:
8:3
14:9

KEY WORDS:
Branch
jealous
King
shepherd
Jerusalem
I saw
Lord of hosts (52x)

paragraph a fitting conclusion to the divine revelation of chapters 1-6?[11] Compare the last words of 6:15 with 1:3.

7. Note on Chart 116 the middle section called "Four Messages." Read from the Bible the four verses cited on the chart. What common phrase introduces each of the messages?

8. Chapters 9-14 are identified as "Two Burdens." Read 9:1 and 12:1 for the origin of this title.

9. Study chapters 9-14 in the Bible text, and try to justify the outlines shown on the chart.

10. Note the title assigned to the book of Zechariah, shown at the top of the chart. Compare this with the key verses. Also, note the key words. You will probably want to add to this list in your later studies.

III. Applications

1. Was Israel intended to be God's channel of revelation to Gentiles in Old Testament days? If so, how successful was the mission? What will be a blessed relationship between the two peoples in the end times (2:11)? Compare Psalm 67; Isaiah 2:3; 60:3.

2. What does 3:1 teach about Satan?

3. Why does God use human instruments to accomplish His crucial work on earth? (Cf. 4:14.)

4. What are your reflections about this truth: "'Not by might nor by power, but by My Spirit,' says the Lord of hosts" (4:6)?

5. What attributes of God are prominent in chapters 1-6?

6. In what sense is the stage being set in Palestine today for events foreshadowed in the book of Zechariah?

7. What is your definition of fasting?

8. Mourning and praying are often associated with fasting in the Bible (Zech 7:5; Acts 13:3). Why?

9. A good measure of a person's heart in fasting is how he acts in days of feasting (Zech 7:6). Why?

10. Is it easy or difficult to visualize the literal fulfillment of a millennial Kingdom on earth? Why? Compare the Lord's words to His people: "This seems unbelievable to you . . . but it is no great thing for me" (Zech 8:6, TLB).

11. The Lord saw the Jews' successful witness to Gentiles as a cause for deep joy (8:19-23). Why is personal witnessing by a Christian such a joyous experience?

12. What have you learned from Zechariah 7-8 which will help you to be a better Christian?

---

11. Recall from 1:1 that all of chapters 1-6 was revealed to Zechariah "in the eighth month of the second year of Darius."

13. The last three chapters of Zechariah are specific prophecies about Israel. But the applications need not be confined to Israel. Go through the three chapters once again and list spiritual truths which may be applied to Christians and non-saved.

IV. Selected Reading

GENERAL INTRODUCTION

Ellison, H. L. *The Old Testament Prophets*, pp. 123-32.

Leupold, H. C. *Exposition of Zechariah*, pp. 1-18.

Robinson, George L. "The Book of Zechariah." In *The International Standard Bible Encyclopedia*, 5:3136-41.

Unger, Merrill F. *Zechariah*, pp. 9-14.

COMMENTARIES

Baldwin, Joyce G. *Haggai, Zechariah, Malachi*.

Baron, David. *The Visions and Prophecies of Zechariah*.

Earle, Ralph. *Meet the Minor Prophets*.

Feinberg, Charles L. *Israel's Comfort and Glory*.

Leupold, H. C. *Exposition of Zechariah*.

Luck, G. Coleman. *Zechariah*. Everyman's Bible Commentary.

Meyer, F. B. *The Prophet of Hope: Studies in Zechariah*.

Unger, Merrill F. *Zechariah*.

MALACHI: WILL A MAN ROB GOD?

The book of Malachi contains the Lord's last recorded words of Old Testament times. In many respects it is a sad book, because it reveals what little progress—if any—Israel had made since the nation was born fifteen hundred years earlier (Gen 12). Dark and distressing as this is, however, the sun of God's grace arises out of its pages; so, when the reader has arrived at the last verses, there is no question but that in the end the day of glory will come for a repentant Israel, as well as for all believers.

I. Background

A. THE MAN MALACHI

The Bible furnishes virtually no biographical information about Malachi. He was a prophet of God (1:1); a contemporary of Nehemiah. His name is an abbreviated form of the Hebrew *Malachiah,* which means "messenger of Jehovah." It is interesting that the word "messenger" appears three times in this short book (read 2:7; 3:1.)

B. THE BOOK OF MALACHI

1. Date. Malachi probably wrote his book around the time of Nehemiah's visit to Babylon, in 433 B.C. (Neh 13:6). See Chart 57. In support of this view are these facts:

a) The Temple project had already been completed, and Mosaic sacrifices were being offered (Mal 1:7-10; 3:1,8). See Chart 57 for the date when the Temple was completed.

b) A Persian governor, not Nehemiah, was ruling the Jews at the time. Read 1:8.[13]

c) The sins denounced by Malachi were the same sins that Nehemiah dealt with during his second term.[14] For example:

laxity and corruption of priests (Mal 1:6—2:9; Neh 13:1-9)

mixed marriages (Mal 2:10-16; Neh 13:23-28)

neglect of tithes (Mal 3:7-12; Neh 13:10-13)

In the words of G. Campbell Morgan, "The failures of the people that angered Nehemiah, inspired the message of Malachi."[15]

(Since Nehemiah and Malachi were contemporaries, it would be very enlightening to study their two books together.)

2. Occasion and message. When Malachi wrote his book, the Jews as a nation had been back in the land of Canaan for about one hundred years. Prophets like Haggai and Zechariah had predicted that God's blessings would be given to the people in days to come, especially in "the day of the LORD." "But several decades had passed and these prophecies of hope were still unfulfilled. The days had become increasingly drab and dreary. It was a period of disappointment, disillusionment, and discouragement, of blasted hopes and broken hearts."[16] The Jews' faith and worship were eroding, and their daily lives showed it. In this backslidden condition they were hypercritical of God's ways. That God would even speak with them is evidence of His long-suffering and mercy.

The main subjects of Malachi's message were the love of God, the sin of the priests and people, judgment for sin, and blessing for righteousness. One cannot help but observe that the Gospel of God has been the same message for sinners of all generations.

3. Features. The most notable feature of this book is its repeated pattern of discourse.[17] Three steps are involved (example is shown): Affirmation (charge or accusation): "You are robbing Me" (3:8).

---

13. The word *pechah,* translated "governor" in 1:8, is a borrowed word, used for the Persian governors in Palestine in postexilic times. See *The Zondervan Pictorial Bible Dictionary,* p. 503.

14. Unfortunately, the revival fires of Nehemiah's earlier ministry (Neh 10:28-39) had by now died out.

15. G. Campbell Morgan, *Voices of Twelve Hebrew Prophets,* p. 151. Another writer has commented, "The Book of Malachi fits the situation amid which Nehemiah worked as snugly as a bone fits its socket" (J. M. P. Smith, quoted in *The International Standard Bible Encyclopedia,* 3:1970.)

16. Ralph Earle, *Meet the Minor Prophets,* p. 105.

17. This pattern has been called didactic-dialectic, or dialogistic.

Interrogation (introduced by "you say"): "But you say, 'How have we robbed Thee?'" (3:8).

Refutation (answer to the question): "In tithes and contributions" (3:8).

The common repeated phrase in these discourses is "you say." It appears eight times: 1:2,6,7; 2:14,17; 3:7,8,13.

Another feature of Malachi's message is his strong emphasis on the Law of God (read 4:4). Also, the book surpasses all other prophetic books in the proportion of verses spoken by the Lord to Israel (forty-seven out of the total of fifty-five).

4. The place of Malachi in the Bible canon. Malachi is both a conclusion and a connecting link. It concludes the story of Israel for the span of 2000-400 B.C., and it is the last prophetic voice of the Old Testament. The book connects the Old Testament with the New Testament by its prophecies of John the Baptist and Christ's first advent. Its "messianic flashes (3:1-6; 4:2) prepare us for the NT revelation and focus our attention on Him who alone is the world's hope."[18] Beyond that, the book reaches into the end times when it prophesies about the final day of the Lord (second advent).

II. SURVEY

Chart 117 is a survey chart showing the general pattern and highlights of Malachi. Study it carefully after you have scanned the entire book and have completed the other usual procedures of survey study. Then follow the study suggestions given below. (Always read the Bible passages which are cited.)

1. The first verse (1:1) is a typical introduction to the book.

2. The last paragraph (4:4-6) is not only a conclusion to the book, but also a fitting conclusion to the whole Old Testament.

3. The first half of the book (1:2—3:15) is mainly about sin. What subjects does Malachi write about after 3:16?

4. What bright prophecy appears at 3:1-6? Why do you think this prophecy is mentioned in the middle of the section about the people's sins?

5. How does the chart compare the beginning and end of Malachi's prophecy?

6. Read the whole book again, following the chart's outline as you read. Try to justify the various outlines on the basis of the Bible text.

7. Note the key words and key verses shown on the chart. Can you add to the list?

---

18. Merrill F. Unger, *Unger's Bible Handbook,* p. 449.

MALACHI WILL A MAN ROB GOD?

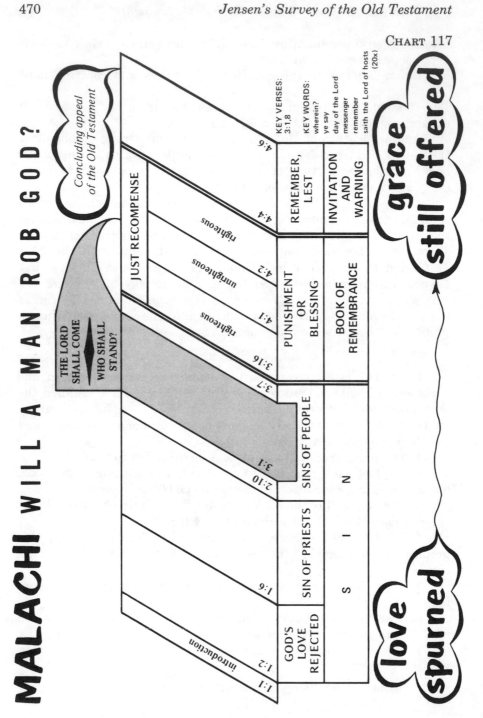

Concluding appeal of the Old Testament

love spurned

grace still offered

	Introduction	GOD'S LOVE REJECTED	SIN OF PRIESTS	SINS OF PEOPLE	PUNISHMENT OR BLESSING	REMEMBER, LEST

THE LORD SHALL COME — WHO SHALL STAND?

JUST RECOMPENSE

righteous / unrighteous / righteous

BOOK OF REMEMBRANCE

INVITATION AND WARNING

S I N S

1:1 1:2 1:6 2:10 3:1 3:7 3:16 4:1 4:2 4:4 4:6

KEY VERSES: 3:1,8

KEY WORDS:
wherein?
ye say
day of the Lord
messenger
remember
saith the Lord of hosts (20x)

III. Applications

1. Are the kinds of sins committed by the priests of Malachi's time being committed by Christian leaders today? How can lay Christians deal with such a problem?

2. Does the·*principle* of tithes and offerings (3:8) apply to today? If so, how? For background of Old Testament origins of the tithe, read Leviticus 27:30-33; Numbers 18:20-32; Deuteronomy 14:22-29. Verses on offerings include Exodus 30:13; Leviticus 7:14; Numbers 15:19-21. A classic New Testament passage on Christian giving is 2 Corinthians 8-9.

3. The last verses of the Old Testament are about obeying God's commandments. What is the Christian's relationship to God's laws, such as the Ten Commandments? Are the commands of the New Testament essentially laws of God?

4. Does God keep "records" of a Christian's daily walk? (See Mal 3:16; 2 Cor 5:9-10.)

5. The commands of Malachi about everyday living are timeless. Ponder the suggestions made by W. Graham Scroggie.

> Malachi's message is eminently necessary and appropriate today, for these abuses have their equivalents in the modern Church. How prevalent is "a form of godliness," the powers being denied; how weak are multitudes of Christians with regard to great moral questions; how frequent is alliance in marriage of saved and unsaved; and how shamefully lax are Christians in the matter of giving of their substance for the maintenance of God's work. To this situation Malachi still speaks.[19]

IV. The Intertestamental Period

The four hundred years between the days of Malachi and the advent of Christ are known as the intertestamental period. They are called the "four hundred silent years" because God did not cause any Scripture to be written during this time. It was a crucial era, for this is when God was preparing the world for the coming of His Son as Saviour and Lord (read Gal 4:4). With the help of outside sources, study the religious, political, social, and secular preparations which were involved.[20] Such a study will enhance your appreciation and

---

19. W. Graham Scroggie, *Know Your Bible*, 1:218.

20. A recommended brief treatment includes Henry E. Dosker, "Between the Testaments," in *The International Standard Bible Encyclopedia*, 1:455-58. For more extensive discussion, consult Charles Pfeiffer, *Between the Testaments;* D. S. Russell, *Between the Testaments;* and F. F. Bruce, *Israel and the Nations*, pp. 120-225. A description of the period, with many excellent maps, is given in *The Macmillan Bible Atlas*, pp. 110-41, by the Jewish authors Johanan Aharon and Michael Avi-Yonah.

understanding of the two Testaments and of the connections between the two.

V. Ten Key Subjects of Old Testament Revealed Truth

Now that you have completed your survey of the books of the Old Testament, it would be very helpful to review the main teachings of this part of God's Scripture. What revealed truths stand out to you? Compare your reflections with the following list of subjects:

1. person and works of God
2. origins of the human race and the universe
3. nature of man
4. sin of man
5. way of salvation; fellowship with God; and worship of God
6. origins and early history of Israel; and prophecies of Israel in the end times
7. philosophy of world history throughout all time
8. prophecies of Christ
9. daily conduct acceptable to God
10. qualities of acceptable service of God, including the mission of the evangel to lost souls

VI. Selected Reading

GENERAL INTRODUCTION

Archer, Gleason L. *A Survey of Old Testament Introduction*, pp. 416-17.
Earle, Ralph. *Meet the Minor Prophets*.
Ellison, H. L. *The Old Testament Prophets*, pp. 133-36.
Freeman, Hobart E. *An Introduction to the Old Testament Prophets*, pp. 347-55.
Rendtorff, Rolf. *God's History*, pp. 65-77.

COMMENTARIES

Baldwin, Joyce G. *Haggai, Zechariah, Malachi*.
Goddard, Burton L. "Malachi." In *The Wycliffe Bible Commentary*.
Keil, Carl Frederick. *The Twelve Minor Prophets*, vol. 2.
Perowne, T. T. *Malachi*. The Cambridge Bible for Schools and Colleges.
Robinson, George. *The Twelve Minor Prophets*.

Appendix

A

Kings of Israel

CHART 118

	KINGS OF ISRAEL	YEARS* OF REIGN	CHARACTER	RELATIONS WITH JUDAH	DETHRONED BY	HISTORY
1	JEROBOAM	22	Bad	War		I Kings 11:26—14:20 II Chronicles 9:29—13:22
2	NADAB	2	Bad	War	Baasha	I Kings 15:25-28
3	BAASHA	24	Bad	War		I Kings 15:27—16:7 II Chronicles 6:1-6
4	ELAH	2	Drunkard	War	Zimri	I Kings 16:8-10
5	ZIMRI	7 days	Murderer	War	Omri	I Kings 16:10-20
6	OMRI	12	Very Bad	War		I Kings 16:16-27
7	AHAB	22	Exceedingly Wicked	Alliance		I Kings 16:28—22:40 II Chronicles 18:1-34
8	AHAZIAH	2	Bad	Peace		I Kings 22:40, 51-53 II Kings 1:1-17 II Chronicles 20:35-37
9	JORAM	12	Bad	Alliance	Jehu	II Kings 3:1-3; 9:14-25 II Chronicles 22:5-7
10	JEHU	28	Bad	War		II Kings 9:1—10:36 II Chronicles 22:7-12
11	JEHOAHAZ	17	Bad	Peace		II Kings 13:1-9
12	JEHOASH	16	Bad	War		II Kings 13:10-25; 14:8-16 II Chronicles 25:17-24
13	JEROBOAM II	41	Bad	Peace		II Kings 14:23-29
14	ZECHARIAH	6 months	Bad	Peace	Shallum	II Kings 15:8-12
15	SHALLUM	1 month	Bad	Peace	Menahem	II Kings 15:13-15
16	MENAHEM	10	Bad	Peace		II Kings 15:16-22
17	PEKAHIAH	2	Bad	Peace	Pekah	II Kings 15:23-26
18	PEKAH	20	Bad	War	Hoshea	II Kings 15:27-31 II Chronicles 28:5-8
19	HOSHEA	9	Bad	Peace		II Kings 17:1-41

APPENDIX B

Kings of Judah   CHART 119

	KINGS OF JUDAH	AGE BEGAN REIGNING	YEARS OF REIGN	CHARACTER	RELATIONS WITH ISRAEL	HISTORY
1	REHOBOAM	41	17	Bad	War	I Kings 12:1—14:31 II Chronicles 10:1—12:16
2	ABIJAM		3	Bad	War	I Kings 15:1-8 II Chronicles 13:1-22
3	ASA		41	Good	War	I Kings 15:9-24 II Chronicles 14:1—16:14
4	JEHOSHAPHAT	35	25	Good	Peace	I Kings 22:41-50 II Chronicles 17:1—20:37
5	JEHORAM	32	8	Bad	Peace	II Kings 8:16-24 II Chronicles 21:1-20
6	AHAZIAH	22	1	Bad	Alliance	II Kings 8:25-29; 9:27-29 II Chronicles 22:1-9
7	ATHALIAH (queen)		6	Bad	Peace	II Kings 8:18, 25-28; 11:1-20 II Chronicles 22:1—23:21; 24:7
8	JOASH	7	40	Good	Peace	II Kings 11:1—12:21 II Chronicles 22:10—24:27
9	AMAZIAH	25	29	Good	War	II Kings 14:1-14 II Chronicles 25:1-28
10	UZZIAH (Azariah)	16	52	Good	Peace	II Kings 15:1-7 II Chronicles 26:1-23
11	JOTHAM	25	16	Good	War	II Kings 15:32-38 II Chronicles 27:1-9
12	AHAZ	20	16	Bad	War	II Kings 16:1-20 II Chronicles 28:1-27
13	HEZEKIAH	25	29	Good		II Kings 18:1—20:21 II Chronicles 29:1—32:33
14	MANASSEH	12	55	Bad		II Kings 21:1-18 II Chronicles 33:1-20
15	AMON	22	2	Bad		II Kings 21:19-23 II Chronicles 33:21-25
16	JOSIAH	8	31	Good		II Kings 22:1—23:30 II Chronicles 34:1—35:27
17	JEHOAHAZ	23	3 months	Bad		II Kings 23:31-33 II Chronicles 36:1-4
18	JEHOIAKIM	25	11	Bad		II Kings 23:34—24:5 II Chronicles 36:5-7
19	JEHOIACHIN	18	3 months	Bad		II Kings 24:6-16 II Chronicles 36:8-10
20	ZEDEKIAH	21	11	Bad		II Kings 24:17—25:7 II Chronicles 36:11-21

Bibliography

Adams, J. McKee. *Biblical Backgrounds.* Rev. ed. Nashville: Broadman, 1965.

Adeney, Walter F. *The Expositor's Bible.* New York: Hodder & Stoughton, n.d.

————. *The Song of Solomon.* The Expositor's Bible. New York: Eaton & Maine, n.d.

Aharoni, Yohanan. *The Land of the Bible.* Philadelphia: Westminster, 1967.

Aharoni, Yohanan, and Avi-Yonah, Michael. *The Macmillan Bible Atlas.* New York: Macmillan, 1968.

Albright, William F. *From the Stone Age to Christianity.* Garden City, N.Y.: Doubleday, 1957.

Alexander, Joseph A. *Commentary on Isaiah.* Reprint. Grand Rapids: n.d.

————. *The Psalms Translated and Explained.* 2 vols. New York: Scribner, Armstrong, 1873.

Allis, Oswald T. *The Five Books of Moses.* Philadelphia: Presbyterian & Reformed, 1943.

————. *God Spake by Moses.* Philadelphia: Presbyterian & Reformed, 1951.

————. *The Old Testament: Its Claims and Its Critics.* Grand Rapids: Baker, 1972.

————. *The Unity of Isaiah.* Philadelphia: Presbyterian & Reformed, 1950.

American Scientific Affiliation Symposium. *Modern Science and Christian Faith.* Wheaton, Ill.: Van Kampen, 1950.

Archer, Gleason. *A Survey of Old Testament Introduction.* Chicago: Moody, 1964.

Armerding, Carl. *Esther.* Chicago: Moody, 1955.

————. *Psalms in A Minor Key.* Chicago: Moody, 1973.

Bailey, Albert Edward. *Daily Life in Bible Times.* New York: Scribner, 1943.

Baldwin, Joyce G. *Haggai, Zechariah, Malachi.* Downers Grove, Ill.: Inter-Varsity, 1972.

Ball, C. J., and Bennett, W. H. *The Book of Jeremiah.* The Expositor's Bible. New York: Doran, n.d.

Baly, Dennis. *The Geography of the Bible.* New York: Harper, 1957.

Barnes, Albert. *Bible Commentary on the Old Testament: Exodus—Ruth.* Grand Rapids: Baker, 1957.

Baron, David. *Rays of Messiah's Glory.* Grand Rapids: Zondervan, n.d.

————. *The Visions and Prophecies of Zechariah.* Reprint. London: Hebrew Christian Testimony to Israel, 1951.

Barton, George A. *Archaeology and the Bible.* Philadelphia: American Sunday-School Union, 1937.

Baughman, Ray E. *Bible History Visualized.* Chicago: Moody, 1963.

Baumann, Hans. *In the Land of Ur.* New York: Random House, 1969.

Baxter, J. Sidlow. *Explore the Book.* 6 vols. Grand Rapids: Zondervan, 1960.

————. *The Strategic Grasp of the Bible.* Grand Rapids: Zondervan, 1968.

Beek, Martin. *Atlas of Mesopotamia.* New York: Nelson, 1962.

Blaikie, William G. Rev. ed. Revised by Charles D. Matthews. *A Manual of Bible History.* New York: Ronald, 1940.

Blair, J. Allen. *Living Patiently.* Neptune, N.J.: Loizeaux, 1966.

Bonar, Andrew A. *A Commentary on the Book of Leviticus.* 5th ed. London: Nisbet, 1875.

Bright, J. *A History of Israel.* Philadelphia: Westminster, 1959.

Bruce, F. F. *The Books and the Parchments.* Rev. ed. Westwood, N.J.: Revell, 1963.

————. *Israel and the Nations.* London: Paternoster, 1963.

Burney, C. F. *The Book of Judges.* 2d ed. London: Rivingtons, 1930.

Burrows, Millar. *What Mean These Stones?* New Haven: Amer. Schools of Oriental Research, 1941.

Carroll, B. H. *Genesis.* New York: Revell, 1913.

Casson, Lionel. *Ancient Egypt.* New York: Time, 1965.

Chadwick, G. A. *Exodus.* Expositor's Bible. New York: Armstrong, 1895.

Chafer, L. S. *Systematic Theology.* Dallas: Seminary Press, 1947.

Chambers, Oswald. *Shade of His Hand.* London: Simpkin Marshall, 1941.

Cheyne, T. K. *The Book of Hosea.* The Cambridge Bible. Cambridge: Cambridge U., 1913.

Chiera, Edward. *They Wrote on Clay.* Chicago: U. Chicago, 1938.

Coates, C. A. *An Outline of the Book of Exodus.* Kingston-on-Thames: Stow Hill Bible & Tract Depot, n.d.

Cook, G. A. *The Book of Judges.* The Cambridge Bible. Cambridge: Cambridge U., 1913.

Cooper, David L. *Messiah: His First Coming Scheduled.* Los Angeles: Biblical Research, 1939.

Corswant, W. A. *A Dictionary of Life in Bible Times.* New York: Oxford, 1960.

Crockett, William Day. *A Harmony of the Books of Samuel, Kings and Chronicles.* Grand Rapids: Baker, 1954.

Culver, Robert D. *Daniel and the Latter Days.* Chicago: Moody, 1954.

————. *The Suffering and the Glory of the Lord's Righteous Servant.* Moline, Ill.: Christian Service, 1958.

Cundall, Arthur E. *Judges and Ruth.* Tyndale Old Testament Commentaries, edited by D. J. Wiseman. Chicago: Inter-Varsity, 1968.

————. *Proverbs to Isaiah 39*. Grand Rapids: Eerdmans, 1968.

Davidson, A. B. *Habakkuk*. The Cambridge Bible. Cambridge: Cambridge U. 1896.

Davis, John J. *The Birth of a Kingdom*. Winona Lake, Ind.: Brethren Missionary Herald, 1970.

————. *Paradise to Prison*. Grand Rapids: Baker, 1975.

Deane, W. J. *Jonah*. Pulpit Commentary, vol. 14. Reprint. Grand Rapids: Eerdmans, 1950.

De Haan, M. R. *Daniel the Prophet*. Grand Rapids: Zondervan, 1947.

————. *Portraits of Christ in Genesis*. Grand Rapids: Zondervan, 1966.

Delitzsch, Franz. *Biblical Commentary on the Psalms*. 3 vols. Reprint. Grand Rapids: Eerdmans, 1949.

————. *Commentary on Isaiah*. 2 vols. Reprint. Grand Rapids: Eerdmans, 1949.

————. *Commentary on the Song of Songs and Ecclesiastes*. Reprint. Grand Rapids: Eerdmans, 1950.

————. *A New Commentary on Genesis*. 2 vols. Edinburgh: T. & T. Clark, 1899.

————. *Proverbs and Solomon*. 2 vols. Reprint. Grand Rapids: Eerdmans, 1950.

De Vaux, Roland. *Ancient Israel: Its Life and Institutions*. London: Darton, Longman & Todd, 1961.

Douglas, J. D., ed. *The New Bible Dictionary*. Grand Rapids: Eerdmans, 1962.

Driver, S. R. *The Book of Genesis*. Westminster Commentary. London: Methuen, 1948.

————. *The Books of Joel and Amos*. The Cambridge Bible. Cambridge: Cambridge U., 1934.

————. *Exodus*. The Cambridge Bible. Cambridge: Cambridge U., 1911.

————. *An Introduction to the Literature of the Old Testament*. Edinburgh: T. & T. Clark, 1950.

Earle, Ralph. *Meet the Minor Prophets*. Kansas City: Beacon Hill, n.d.

Eason, J. Lawrence. *The New Bible Survey*. Grand Rapids: Zondervan, 1963.

Edersheim, Alfred. *The Bible History, Old Testament*. 7 vols. Reprint. Grand Rapids: Eerdmans, 1949.

Ellison, H. L. *Ezekiel: The Man and His Message*. Grand Rapids: Eerdmans, 1956.

————. *The Message of the Old Testament*. Grand Rapids: Eerdmans, 1969.

————. *The Old Testament Prophets*. Grand Rapids: Zondervan, 1966.

————. *The Prophets of Israel*. Grand Rapids: Eerdmans, 1969.

Erdman, Charles R. *The Book of Exodus*. New York: Revell, 1949.

————. *The Book of Genesis*. New York: Revell, 1950.

————. *The Book of Leviticus*. New York: Revell, 1951.

Fairbairn, P. *The Typology of Scripture*. Grand Rapids: Zondervan, n.d.

Feinberg, Charles L. *Israel's Comfort and Glory*. New York: American Board of Missions to the Jews, 1952.

————. *The Prophecy of Ezekiel.* Chicago: Moody, 1969.

Finegan, Jack. *Handbook of Biblical Chronology.* Princeton: Princeton U., 1964.

————. *Light from the Ancient Past.* Princeton: Princeton U., 1959.

Frair, Wayne, and Devis, P. William. *The Case for Creation.* Chicago: Moody, 1967.

Frank, Harry Thomas. *Discovering the Biblical World.* Maplewood, N.J.: Hammond, 1975. Contains very helpful maps.

Free, Joseph P. *Archaeology and Bible History.* Rev. ed. Wheaton, Ill: Scripture Press, 1964.

Freeman, Hobart E. *An Introduction to the Old Testament Prophets.* Chicago: Moody, 1968.

Freeman, James M. *Manners and Customs of the Bible.* Plainfield, N.J.: Logos, 1973.

Gaebelein, A. C. *The Book of Psalms.* New York: Our Hope, 1939.

————. *The Prophet Joel.* New York: Our Hope, 1909.

Gaebelein, Frank E. *Four Minor Prophets.* Chicago: Moody, 1970.

Gaussen, L. *Theopneustia: The Plenary Inspiration of the Holy Scriptures.* Rev. ed. Trans. David Scott. Chicago: Bible Institute Colportage Assn., n.d.

Geisler, Norman L. *Christ: The Theme of the Bible.* Chicago: Moody, 1968.

Geisler, Norman L., and Nix, William E. *A General Introduction to the Bible.* Chicago: Moody, 1968.

Gordon, Cyrus H. "Biblical Customs and the Nuzu Tablets." *Biblical Archaeologist* 3 (February 1940).

————. *The World of the Old Testament.* Garden City, N.Y.: Doubleday, 1958.

Gray, James M. *Synthetic Bible Studies.* New York: Revell, 1923.

Grollenberg, L. H. *Atlas of the Bible.* New York: Nelson, 1956.

Grosvenor, Gilbert, ed. *Everyday Life in Ancient Times.* Washington, D.C.: National Geographic, 1951.

Guthrie, D., and Motyer, J. A., eds. *The New Bible Commentary.* Rev. ed. Grand Rapids: Eerdmans, 1970.

Hahn, H. F. *The Old Testament and Modern Research.* Philadelphia: Muhlenberg, 1954.

Harper, Andrew. *The Song of Solomon.* The Cambridge Bible. Cambridge: Cambridge U., 1907.

Harris, R. Laird. *Man: God's Eternal Creation.* Chicago: Moody, 1971.

Harrison, R. K. *Introduction to the Old Testament.* Grand Rapids: Eerdmans, 1969.

————. *Old Testament Times.* Grand Rapids: Eerdmans, 1970.

Heaton, E. W. *Everyday Life in Old Testament Times.* New York: Scribner, 1956.

————. *The Hebrew Kingdoms.* London: Oxford U., 1968.

Hengstenberg, E. W. *Christology of the Old Testament.* Grand Rapids: Kregel, 1970.

Henry, Carl H., ed. *Revelation and the Bible.* Grand Rapids: Baker, 1958.

Heslop, W. G. *Lessons from Leviticus.* Grand Rapids: Baker, 1945.

Hodge, Charles. *Systematic Theology.* Grand Rapids: Eerdmans, 1871.

Howard, J. K. *Amos Among the Prophets.* Grand Rapids: Baker, 1967.

Hyatt, J. Philip. *Jeremiah, Prophet of Courage and Hope.* New York: Abingdon, 1958.

Ironside, H. A. *Addresses on the Song of Solomon.* New York: Loizeaux, n.d.

———. *Lectures on Daniel the Prophet.* New York: Loizeaux, 1920.

———. *Lectures on the Levitical Offerings.* New York: Loizeaux, 1929.

———. *Notes on the Book of Ezra.* New York: Loizeaux, n.d.

———. *Notes on the Book of Proverbs.* New York: Loizeaux, n.d.

Jamieson, Robert; Fausset, A. R.; and Brown, David. *A Commentary, Critical and Exploratory on the Old and New Testaments.* Vol. 1. Reprint. Grand Rapids: Eerdmans, 1948.

Jennings, F. C. *Studies in Isaiah.* New York: Loizeaux, 1935.

Jensen, Irving L. *Jensen Bible Study Charts,* vol. 2. Chicago: Moody, 1976.

———. *Enjoy Your Bible.* Chicago: Moody, 1969.

———. *Jeremiah and Lamentations.* Everyman's Bible Commentary. Chicago: Moody, 1966.

———. *Joshua: Rest-Land Won.* Everyman's Bible Commentary. Chicago: Moody, 1966.

———. *Numbers: Journey to God's Rest-Land.* Everyman's Bible Commentary. Chicago: Moody, 1964.

———. *Psalms.* Self-Study Guide. Chicago: Moody, 1968.

Johnson, Philip C. *The Book of Daniel.* Grand Rapids: Baker, 1964.

Join - Sambert, Michel. *Jerusalem.* New York: Putnam, 1958.

Keil, C. F. *The Books of the Chronicles.* Grand Rapids: Eerdmans, 1950,

———. "Jonah." In *Biblical Commentary on the Old Testament Minor Prophets,* vol. 1. Reprint. Grand Rapids: Eerdmans, 1951.

———. "Joshua." In *Joshua, Judges, Ruth.* Biblical Commentary on the Old Testament. Reprint. Grand Rapids: Eerdmans, 1950.

———. *The Twelve Minor Prophets.* Vol. 2. Edinburgh: T. & T. Clark, 1900.

Keil, C. F., and Delitzsch, F. *The Books of the Kings.* Biblical Commentary on the Old Testament. Reprint. Grand Rapids: Eerdmans, 1950.

———. *The Books of Samuel.* Reprint. Grand Rapids: Eerdmans, 1950.

———. *The Pentateuch.* 3 vols. Reprint. Grand Rapids: Eerdmans, 1949.

Kellogg, S. H. *The Book of Leviticus.* New York: Hodder & Stoughton, n.d.

Kelso, James L. *Archaeology and the Ancient Testament.* Grand Rapids: Zondervan, 1968.

Kennedy, James H. *Studies in the Book of Jonah.* Nashville: Broadman, 1956.

Kenyon, Kathleen M. *Jerusalem.* New York: McGraw-Hill, 1967.

Kerr, D. W. *Numbers.* The Biblical Expositor. London: Pickering & Inglis, 1960.

Kidner, Derek. *The Proverbs.* Downers Grove, Ill.: Inter-Varsity, 1964.

Kirkpatrick, A. F. *The Book of Psalms.* 3 vols. Cambridge: Cambridge U., 1951.

————. *I, II Samuel.* The Cambridge Bible. Cambridge: Cambridge U., 1930.

Kissane, E. J. *The Book of Isaiah.* Dublin: Browne & Nolan, Richview Press, Vol. 1, 1941; Vol. 2, 1943.

Kitchen, K. A. *Ancient Orient and Old Testament.* Chicago: Inter-Varsity, 1966.

Kraeling, Emil G. *Bible Atlas.* New York: Rand-McNally, 1956.

Krummacher, F. W. *Elijah the Tishbite.* Grand Rapids: Zondervan, n.d.

La Botz, Paul. *The Romance of the Ages.* Grand Rapids: Kregel, 1965.

Laetsch, Theodore. *Jeremiah.* St. Louis: Concordia, 1952.

————. *The Minor Prophets.* St. Louis: Concordia, 1956.

Lammerts, Walter E., ed. *Scientific Studies in Special Creation.* Grand Rapids: Baker, 1971.

Lange, John Peter, ed. *Commentary on the Holy Scriptures.* Translated and edited by Philip Schaff. Grand Rapids: Zondervan, n.d.

LaSor, William Sanford. *Daily Life in Bible Times.* Cincinnati: Standard, 1966.

————. *Great Personalities of the Bible.* Westwood, N.J.: Revell, 1965.

Lee, Robert. *The Outlined Bible.* Westwood, N.J.: Revell, n.d.

Leslie, Elmer A. *Jeremiah.* New York: Abingdon, 1954.

————. *The Psalms.* New York: Abingdon-Cokesbury, 1949.

Leupold, H.C. *Exposition of Daniel.* Columbus, Ohio: Wartburg, 1949.

————. *Exposition of Ecclesiastes.* Columbus, Ohio: Wartburg, 1952.

————. *Exposition of the Psalms.* Columbus, Ohio: Wartburg, 1959.

————. *Exposition of Zechariah.* Reprint. Grand Rapids: Baker, 1971.

Levine, Moshe. *The Tabernacle.* Jerusalem: Soncino, 1969.

Lewis, C. S. *The Problem of Pain.* New York: Macmillan, 1965.

Lindsell, Harold, ed. *Harper Study Bible.* New York: Harper & Row, 1964.

Livingston, G. Herbert. *The Pentateuch in Its Cultural Environment.* Grand Rapids: Baker, 1974.

Lloyd-Jones, D. Martin. *From Fear to Faith.* London: Inter-Varsity, 1953.

Lockyer, Herbert. *All the Doctrines of the Bible.* Grand Rapids: Zondervan, 1964.

Luck, G. Coleman. *Ezra and Nehemiah.* Everyman's Bible Commentary. Chicago: Moody, 1961.

————. *Zechariah.* Everyman's Bible Commentary. Chicago: Moody, 1957.

Mackintosh, C. H. *Notes on the Book of Numbers.* New York: Loizeaux, n.d.

Maclaren, Alexander. *Exposition of Holy Scriptures: Exodus, Leviticus and Numbers.* New York: Hodder & Stoughton, n.d.

————. *The Psalms.* New York: Funk & Wagnalls, 1908.

Maier, Walter A. *The Book of Nahum, A Commentary.* St. Louis: Concordia, 1959.

Manley, G. T. *The Book of the Law.* Grand Rapids: Eerdmans, 1957.

Manley, G. T., ed. *The New Bible Handbook.* Chicago: Inter-Varsity, 1947.

Marsh, Frank Lewis. *Life, Man, and Time*. Escondido, Calif.: Outdoor Pictures, 1967.

——. *Studies in Creationism*. Washington, D.C.: Review & Herald, 1950.

Martin, W. S., and Marshall, A. *Tabernacle Types and Teachings*. London: Pickering & Inglis, n.d.

McClain, Alva J. *Daniel's Prophecy of the Seventy Weeks*. Grand Rapids: Zondervan, 1940.

——. *The Greatness of the Kingdom*. Chicago: Moody, 1959.

McNeile, A. H. *An Introduction to Ecclesiastes*. Cambridge: Cambridge U., 1904.

Mears, Henrietta. *What the Bible Is All About*. Glendale, Calif.: Gospel Light, 1953.

Mendenhall, G. E. "The Census Lists of Numbers 1 and 26." In *Journal of Biblical Literature* 77 (1958).

Merrill, Eugene H. *An Historical Survey of the Old Testament*. Nutley, N.J.: Craig, 1966.

Meyer, F. B. *Exodus*. 2 vols. London: Religious Tract Soc., n.d.

——. *The Prophet of Hope: Studies in Zechariah*. New York: Revell, 1900.

Miller, M.S., and Miller, J. L. *Encyclopedia of Bible Life*. New York: Harper, 1944.

Moore, George Foot. *A Critical and Exegetical Commentary on Judges*. The International Critical Commentary. New York: Scribner, 1901.

Moorehead, W. G. *Outline Studies in the Books of the Old Testament*. New York: Revell, 1893.

Morgan, G. Campbell. *The Analyzed Bible*. New York: Revell, 1944.

——. *The Answers of Jesus to Job*. New York: Revell, 1935.

——. *Hosea*. London: Marshall, Morgan & Scott, 1948.

——. *Living Messages of the Books of the Bible*. New York: Revell, 1912.

——. *Notes on the Psalms*. New York: Revell, 1947.

——. *Studies in the Prophecy of Jeremiah*. London: Oliphants, 1955.

——. *The Ten Commandments*. Westwood, N.J.: Revell, 1901.

Morris, Leon. *Judges and Ruth*. Chicago: Inter-Varsity, 1968.

Naegelsbach, C. W. Edward. *Lamentations*. Lange's Commentary on the Holy Scriptures. Grand Rapids: Zondervan, n.d.

National Geographic Society. *Everyday Life in Bible Times*. Washington, D.C.: National Geographic Soc., 1951.

Newell, Philip R. *Daniel*. Chicago: Moody, 1962.

Newell, William R. *Old Testament Studies*. Vol. 1. Chicago: Moody, 1950.

Oesterley, W. O. E. *The Wisdom of Egypt and the Old Testament*. New York: Macmillan, 1927.

Orni, Efrain, and Efrat, Elisha. *Geography of Israel*. 3rd rev. ed. Philadelphia: Jewish Pubn. Soc. of America, 1973.

Orr, James, ed. *The International Standard Bible Encyclopedia*. 5 vols. Grand Rapids: Eerdmans, 1946.

Pache, René. *Inspiration and Authority*. Chicago: Moody, 1969.

Payne, J. Barton. *Encyclopedia of Biblical Prophecy.* New York: Harper & Row, 1973.

———. *An Outline of Hebrew History.* Grand Rapids: Baker, 1954.

———. *The Theology of the Older Testament.* Grand Rapids: Zondervan, 1962.

Peake, A. S., ed. *Jeremiah and Lamentations.* The New Century Bible. Edinburgh: T. C. and E. C. Jack, 1910.

Pentecost, J. Dwight. *Israel in Prophecy.* Grand Rapids: Zondervan, 1962.

———. *Prophecy for Today.* Grand Rapids: Zondervan, 1961.

———. *Things to Come.* Findlay, Ohio: Dunham, 1958.

Perowne, J. J. Stewart. *The Book of Psalms.* Grand Rapids: Zondervan, 1966.

Pfeiffer, Charles F. *Between the Testaments.* Grand Rapids: Baker, 1959.

———. *The Book of Genesis.* Grand Rapids: Baker, 1958.

———. *The Divided Kingdom.* Grand Rapids: Baker, 1967.

———. *Egypt and the Exodus.* Grand Rapids: Baker, 1964.

———. *Patriarchal Age.* Grand Rapids: Baker, n.d.

Pfeiffer, Charles F., ed. *The Biblical World.* Grand Rapids: Baker, 1966.

Pfeiffer, Charles F., and Harrison, Everett F., eds. *The Wycliffe Bible Commentary.* Chicago: Moody, 1962.

Pfeiffer, Charles F., and Vos, Howard F. *The Wycliffe Historical Geography of Bible Lands.* Chicago: Moody, 1967.

Pfeiffer, R. H. *Introduction to the Old Testament.* New York: Harper, 1941.

Phillips, John. *Exploring the Scriptures.* Chicago: Moody, 1965.

Pieters, Albertus. *Notes on Genesis.* Grand Rapids: Eerdmans, 1943.

Pink, Arthur W. *Gleanings from Elisha.* Chicago: Moody, 1972.

———. *Gleanings in Exodus.* Chicago: Moody, 1962.

———. *Gleanings in Genesis.* Chicago: Moody, 1922.

———. *Gleanings in Joshua.* Chicago: Moody, 1964.

Pinnock, Clark H. *Biblical Revelation.* Chicago: Moody, 1971.

Price, Ira M. *The Dramatic Story of Old Testament History.* 4th ed. New York: Revell, 1945.

Price, Walter K. *The Coming Antichrist.* Chicago: Moody, 1974.

Pritchard, James B. *The Ancient Near East in Pictures.* Princeton: Princeton U., 1969.

Pritchard, James B., ed. *Ancient Near Eastern Texts.* Princeton: Princeton U., 1955.

Purkiser, W. T., ed. *Exploring the Old Testament.* Kansas City, Mo.: Beacon Hill, 1967.

Pusey, E. B. *The Minor Prophets.* Grand Rapids: Baker, 1956.

Ramm, Bernard. *Protestant Biblical Interpretation.* Boston: Wilde, 1956.

Redpath, Alan. *Victorious Christian Service.* New York: Revell, 1958.

Rehwinkel, A. M. *The Flood in the Light of the Bible, Geology and Archaeology.* St. Louis: Concordia, 1951.

Reider, Joseph. *Deuteronomy.* Philadelphia: Jewish Pubn. Soc., 1939.

Rhodes, Arnold B. *The Book of Psalms.* Richmond: John Knox, 1960.

Robinson, George L. *The Bearing of Archeology in the Old Testament.* New York: Amer. Tract Soc., 1944.

―――. *The Twelve Minor Prophets.* New York: Doran, 1926.

Russell, D. S. *Between the Testaments.* London: S. C. M., 1960.

Ryle, H. E. *The Book of Genesis.* Cambridge: Cambridge U., 1914.

The Sacred Land. Atlas of Bible Geography. Philadelphia: Holman, n.d.

Saggs, H. F. *Everyday Life in Babylonia and Assyria.* New York: Putnam, 1965.

―――. *The Greatness That Was Babylon.* New York: Praeger, 1962.

Sampey, John R. *The Heart of the Old Testament.* Rev. ed. New York: Doubleday, 1928.

―――. *Syllabus for Old Testament Study.* New York: Doran, 1922.

Sauer, Erich. *The Dawn of World Redemption.* Grand Rapids: Eerdmans, 1953.

―――. *From Eternity to Eternity.* London: Paternoster, 1954.

Schneider, Bernard N. *Deuteronomy.* Grand Rapids: Baker, 1970.

Schroeder, F. W. J. *Deuteronomy.* Lange's Commentary on the Holy Scriptures. Grand Rapids: Zondervan, n.d.

Schultz, Samuel J. *Deuteronomy.* Everyman's Bible Commentary. Chicago: Moody, 1971.

―――. *Gospel of Moses.* New York: Harper, 1974.

―――. *The Old Testament Speaks.* New York: Harper, 1960.

―――. *The Prophets Speak.* New York: Harper, 1968.

Scroggie, W. Graham. *Know Your Bible.* Vol. 1. London: Pickering & Inglis, 1940.

―――. *The Psalms.* 3 vols. London: Pickering & Inglis, 1953.

Skinner, J. *The Book of the Prophet Isaiah.* The Cambridge Bible. Cambridge: Cambridge U., 1951.

Smith, Arthur E. *The Temple and Its Teaching.* Chicago: Moody, 1956.

Smith, George Adam. *The Book of the Twelve Prophets.* 2 vols. Rev. ed. New York: Harper, 1928.

―――. *The Historical Geography of the Holy Land.* London: Hodder & Stoughton, 1931.

―――. *Jeremiah.* New York: Harper, n.d.

Smith, J.; Ward, W. H.; Bewer, J. *Joel.* The International Critical Commentary. Edinburgh: T. & T. Clark, n.d.

Smith, Wilbur M. *The Incomparable Book.* Minneapolis: Beacon, 1961.

Snaith, Norman H. *The Distinctive Ideas of the Old Testament.* London: Epworth, 1962.

Soltau, Henry W. *The Tabernacle.* Reprint. Fincastle, Va.: Scripture Truth, n.d.

Spence, H.D.M., and Exell, Joseph S., new ed. *The Pulpit Commentary.* 51 vols. New York: Funk & Wagnalls, 1913.

Spink, James F. *Types and Shadows of Christ in the Tabernacle.* New York: Loizeaux, 1946.

Spurgeon, C. H. *The Treasury of David.* 7 vols. New York: Funk & Wagnalls, 1881.

Stevens, Charles H. *The Wilderness Journey.* Chicago: Moody, 1971.

Stonehouse, N. B., and Woolley, Paul, eds. *The Infallible Word.* Grand Rapids: Eerdmans, 1953.

Strong, James. *The Tabernacle of Israel.* Reprint. Grand Rapids: Baker, 1952.

Strong, James, ed. *The Exhaustive Concordance of the Bible.* New York: Abingdon, 1890.

Tan, Paul Lee. *The Interpretation of Prophecy.* Winona Lake: Brethren Missionary Herald, 1974.

Taylor, J. Hudson. *Union and Communion.* London: China Inland Mission, 1914.

Taylor, John B. *A Christian's Guide to the Old Testament.* Chicago: Moody, 1966.

Tenney, Merrill C., ed. *The Zondervan Pictorial Bible Dictionary.* Grand Rapids: Zondervan, 1963.

Thiele, E. R. *The Mysterious Numbers of the Hebrew Kings.* Rev. ed. Grand Rapids: Eerdmans, 1965.

Thomas, D. Winton. *Documents from Old Testament Times.* New York: Harper, 1961.

Thompson, J. A. *The Bible and Archaeology.* Grand Rapids: Eerdmans, 1954.

Unger, Merrill F. *Archaeology and the Old Testament.* Grand Rapids: Zondervan, 1954.

———. *Introductory Guide to the Old Testament.* Grand Rapids: Zondervan, 1952.

———. *Unger's Bible Dictionary.* Chicago: Moody, 1967.

———. *Unger's Bible Handbook.* Chicago: Moody, 1966.

———. *Zechariah.* Grand Rapids: Zondervan, 1963.

Vos, Howard F. *Genesis and Archaeology.* Chicago: Moody, 1963.

Vos, Howard F., ed. *Can I Trust My Bible?* Chicago: Moody, 1963.

Walvoord, John F. *Daniel: Key to Prophetic Revelation.* Chicago: Moody, 1971.

———. *Israel in Prophecy.* Grand Rapids: Zondervan, 1962.

———. *Jesus Christ Our Lord.* Chicago: Moody, 1969.

———. *Millennial Kingdom.* Grand Rapids: Dunham, 1959.

———. *The Nations in Prophecy.* Grand Rapids: Zondervan, 1967.

Walvoord, John F., ed. *Inspiration and Interpretation.* Grand Rapids: Eerdmans, 1957.

Warfield, B. B. *The Inspiration and Authority of the Bible.* Philadelphia: Presbyterian & Reformed, 1948.

Watson, Robert Addison. *Judges and Ruth.* The Expositor's Bible. New York: Armstrong, 1899.

Watson, Thomas. *The Ten Commandments.* Rev. ed. London: Banner of Truth, 1965.

Watts, J. Wash. *Old Testament Teaching.* Nashville: Broadman, 1967.

Watts, John D. W. *Vision and Prophecy in Amos.* Grand Rapids: Eerdmans, 1958.

Whitcomb, John C. *Darius the Mede*. Grand Rapids: Eerdmans, 1959.

———. *The Early Earth*. Grand Rapids: Baker, 1972.

———. *Solomon to the Exile*. Winona Lake, Ind.: Brethren Missionary Herald, 1971.

Whitcomb, John C., and Morris, Henry M. *The Genesis Flood*. Philadelphia: Presbyterian & Reformed, 1962.

Whitley, C. F. *The Exilic Age*. London, Westminster, 1957.

Wight, Fred H. *Manners and Customs of Bible Lands*. Chicago: Moody, 1953.

Williams, A. Lukyn. *Ecclesiastes*. Cambridge: Cambridge U., 1922.

Wilson, Clifford A. *Exploring Bible Backgrounds*. Melbourne, Australia: Word of Truth, 1966.

———. *Exploring the Old Testament*. Rev. ed. Abbotsford, Australia: New Life, 1970.

Wilson, Robert Dick. *A Scientific Investigation of the Old Testament*. Rev. ed. Reprint. Chicago: Moody, 1959.

Wilson, Walter Lewis. *Wilson's Dictionary of Bible Types*. Grand Rapids: Eerdmans, 1957.

Wiseman, Donald J. *Chronicles of Chaldean Kings*. London: Trustees of the British Museum, 1956.

Wolfe, Rolland E. *Meet Amos and Hosea*. New York: Harper, 1945.

Wood, Leon. *A Commentary on Daniel*. Grand Rapids: Zondervan, 1972.

———. *Elijah, Prophet of God*. Des Plaines, Ill.: Regular Baptist, 1968.

———. *A Survey of Israel's History*. Grand Rapids: Zondervan, 1970.

Woods, T. E. P. *Bible History—Old Testament*. Grand Rapids: Eerdmans, 1941.

Young, Edward J. *The Book of Isaiah*. 3 vols. Grand Rapids: Eerdmans, 1965.

———. *An Introduction to the Old Testament*. Grand Rapids: Eerdmans, 1949.

———. *Isaiah Fifty-Three*. Grand Rapids: Eerdmans, 1951.

———. *My Servants the Prophets*. Grand Rapids: Eerdmans, 1955.

———. *Studies in Isaiah*. Grand Rapids: Eerdmans, 1954.

———. *Who Wrote Isaiah?* Grand Rapids: Eerdmans, 1957.

Young, Robert, ed. *Analytical Concordance to the Bible*. Grand Rapids: Eerdmans, n.d.

Zoeckler, Otto. *The Book of Chronicles*. Lange's Commentary on the Holy Scriptures. Grand Rapids: Zondervan, n.d.

———. *Proverbs*. Lange's Commentary on the Holy Scriptures. Grand Rapids: Zondervan, n.d.

———. *The Song of Solomon*. Lange's Commentary on the Holy Scriptures. Grand Rapids: Zondervan, n.d.

Charts

Whitcomb, John C. *Old Testament Patriarchs and Judges*. Rev. ed. Chicago: Moody, 1968.

———. *Old Testament Kings and Prophets*. Rev. ed. Chicago: Moody, 1968.

General Index

This index excludes items in the Table of Contents, charts, maps, and "Key Words and Verses."